The Act of Writing

CANADIAN ESSAYS *for* COMPOSITION

fifth edition

Ronald Conrad

McGraw-Hill Ryerson

Toronto Montreal New York Burr Ridge Bangkok
Bogotá Caracas Lisbon London Madrid
Mexico City Milan New Delhi Seoul
Singapore Sydney Taipei

McGraw-Hill
Ryerson Limited

A Subsidiary of The McGraw·Hill Companies

The Act of Writing
Canadian Essays for Composition
Fifth Edition

ISBN: 0-07-560365-9

1 2 3 4 5 6 7 8 9 10   GTC   8 7 6 5 4 3 2 1 0 9

Printed and bound in Canada.

Care has been taken to trace ownership of copyright material contained in this text. The publishers will gladly take any information that will enable them to rectify any reference or credit in subsequent editions.

Sponsoring Editor: Gord Muschett
Developmental Editor: Marianne Minaker
Supervising Editor: Jennifer Burnell
Copy Editor: Kathy Evans
Production Co-ordinator: Nicla Dattolico
Cover Designer: Liz Harasymczuk
Cover Illustration: Zuboff Square by Wassily Kandinsky, Tretyakov
    Gallery, Moscow/SUPERSTOCK
Typesetter: McGraphics Desktop Publishing Ltd.
Printer: Transcontinental Printing

Canadian Cataloguing in Publication Data

Conrad, Ronald, date
    The act of writing: Canadian essays for composition

5th ed.
ISBN: 0-07-560365-9

1. English language—Rhetoric. 2. Canadian essays (English).* I. Title.

PE1429.C66 1988   808'.0427   C98-931770-6

In memory of my father
Reuben M. Conrad
(1911-1998)
and
my father-in-law
Carl F. Smucker
(1912-1997)

CONTENTS

And then. . .

CHAPTER 1: NARRATION 23

"There were cheers and laughter as Tivadar hit me in the nose
before I got my jacket off. It was not the first time I had tasted my
own blood, but it was the first time a Christian had made it flow."

v

For example. . .

CHAPTER 2: EXAMPLE   67

It's large and purple and. . .

CHAPTER 3: DESCRIPTION 99

wrench my eyes away from the clutch of those empty sockets. The power that I felt was not in the thing itself, but in some tremendous force behind it, that the carver had believed in."

Here's why. . .

It's just the opposite of. . .

CHAPTER 5:
COMPARISON AND CONTRAST   183

In a way, it's like. . .

CHAPTER 6:
ANALOGY AND RELATED DEVICES   219

There are three kinds of them. . .

CHAPTER 7: CLASSIFICATION   243

Here's how it's done. . .

CHAPTER 8: PROCESS ANALYSIS   271

Therefore. . .

CHAPTER 9:
ARGUMENTATION AND PERSUASION 309

"Fourteen of our bright and shining daughters won places in engineering schools, doing things we, their mothers, only dreamed of. That we lost them has broken our hearts; what is worse is that we are not surprised."

Contents by Subject

CHILDHOOD AND OLD AGE

WOMEN IN SOCIETY

OUTSIDERS

THE CITY

THE ENVIRONMENT

WORK

VIOLENCE IN SOCIETY

SCIENCE AND TECHNOLOGY

BUSINESS AND INDUSTRY

THE MEDIA

THE ARTS

LAUGHS

PEOPLES AND PLACES

MAINLY CANADIAN

Acknowledgements

Doris Anderson: "The 51-Per-Cent Minority" from *Maclean's* magazine, January 1980. Reprinted by permission of the author.

Russell Baker: "A Nice Place to Visit" from *The New York Times.* Copyright © 1979 by The New York Times Company. Reprinted by permission.

Dionne Brand: "Job" extracted from *Bread Out of Stone* by Dionne Brand. Copyright © 1984. Reprinted by permission of Knopf Canada.

Collin Brown: "A Game of Tennis" from an interview with Collin Brown by Catherine Dunphy, *The Toronto Star,* p. C8, May 15, 1994. Reprinted with permission of The Toronto Star Syndicate.

Stevie Cameron: "Our Daughters, Ourselves" from *The Globe and Mail,* p. A20, December 6, 1990. Reprinted by permission of the author.

Emily Carr: "D'Sonoqua" from *Klee Wyck,* © 1941, by Emily Carr.

Karen Connelly: "August 4" originally titled "August 4, 1987," from *Touch the Dragon,* copyright Karen Connelly. Turnstone Press, 1987. Reprinted by permission.

Amy Willard Cross: "Safety First, Fun a Distant Second" from *The Globe and Mail,* p. A14, January 8, 1991. Reprinted by permission of the author. .

Paul D'Angelo: "The Step Not Taken" from *The Globe and Mail,* p. A12, April 3, 1995. Reprinted by permission of the author.

Kildare Dobbs: "The Scar" from *Reading the Time* by Kildare Dobbs, 1968. © Kildare Dobbs. Reprinted by permission of the author.

Garry Engkent: "Why My Mother Can't Speak English." Reprinted by permission of the author.

Elinor Florence: "Leaving the Fast Lane for No Lane at All" from *The Globe and Mail,* p. A18, January 7, 1997. Reprinted by permission of the author.

David Foot with Daniel Stoffman: "Boomers and Other Cohorts." Reprinted from *Boom, Bust & Echo: How to Profit from the Coming Demographic Shift* by David K. Foot with Daniel Stoffman. Published by Mcfarlane Walter & Ross, Toronto, 1996.

Sylvia Fraser: "My Other Self" from *My Father's House,* copyright © 1987 by Sylvia Fraser. Reprinted with the permission of Doubleday Canada Ltd.

Josh Freed: "Say Hi or Die" from *Fear of Frying,* 1994. Reprinted by permission of the author.

George Gabori: "Coming of Age in Putnok" from *When Evils Were Most Free,* 1981, by George Gabori. Reprinted by permission of Mrs. Eve Gabori.

Marie Gagnon: "Shelter" from *Bienvenue dans mon cauchemar,* Montréal, VLB Éditeur, 1997. Reprinted by permission of the publisher. Translated by Ronald Conrad.

Biruté Galdikas: "Akmad" from *Reflections of Eden* by Biruté Galdikas. Copyright © 1995 by Biruté M.F. Galdikas. By permission of Little, Brown and Company.

Carol Geddes: "Growing Up Native" from *Homemaker's Magazine,* pp. 37–52, October 1990. Reprinted by permission of the author.

Ray Guy: "Outharbor Menu" from *That Far Greater Bay* by Ray Guy, Breakwater Books Limited, 1976. © Ray Guy. Reprinted by permission of Breakwater Books Limited.

Charles Yale Harrison: "In the Trenches" from *Generals Die in Bed* by Charles Yale Harrison, 1930. Reprinted courtesy of Potlatch Publications Limited.

Martin Hocking: "Capping the Great Cup Debate" from *The Globe and Mail,* p. D10, February 16, 1991. Condensed from papers which appeared in Science *251* (4993), 504–505 (1991), and Environmental Management *15* (6), 731–747 (1991). Reprinted by permission of the author.

Basil Johnston: "Modern Cannibals of the Wilds" from *The Globe and Mail,* p. A13, August 1, 1991. © Basil Johnston; permission of Beverley Slopen Literary Agency/Toronto.

Joy Kogawa: "Grinning and Happy" from *Obasan* by Joy Kogawa, Lester & Orpen Dennys Ltd. c/o Key Porter Books Ltd., Toronto. © 1981 Joy Kogawa. Reprinted by permission of the author.

Bonnie Laing: "An Ode to the User-Friendly Pencil" from *The Globe and Mail,* p. D6, April 29, 1989. © 1989 Bonnie Laing. Reprinted by permission of the author.

David Lam: "Pulling Together" from *Maclean's,* January 30, 1995. Reprinted by permission of *Maclean's.*

Michele Landsberg: "West Must Confront Anonymous Misery of the World's Children" from *The Globe and Mail,* p. A2, November 7, 1987. Reprinted by permission of the author.

Evelyn Lau: "I Sing the Song of My Condo" from *The Globe and Mail,* p. D5, June 17, 1995. Reprinted by permission of the author.

Margaret Laurence: "Where the World Began" from *Heart of a Stranger* by Margaret Laurence, 1980. Used by permission, McClelland & Stewart Inc. *The Canadian Publishers.*

Stephen Leacock: "How to Live to Be 200" from *Literary Lapses* by Stephen Leacock.

Félix Leclerc: "The Family House" excerpted from *Pieds nus dans l'aube,* 1946, pp. 9–14. Collection "Bibliothèque Canadienne-Française," Montréal. Reprinted by permission of Gaetane M. Leclerc. Translated by Philip Stratford. Permission to reprint translation granted by Philip Stratford.

Thierry Mallet: "The Firewood Gatherers" from *Glimpses of the Barren Lands* by Thierry Mallet, 1930. Originally published in *The Atlantic Monthly,* March 1927.

Alberto Manguel: "Reading Ourselves and the World Around Us." Extracted from *A History of Reading* by Alberto Manguel. Copyright © 1996. Reprinted by permission of Knopf Canada.

Brian Maracle: "Out of Touch and Loving It" from *Back on the Rez: Finding the Way Home* by Brian Maracle. Copyright © Maracle Communications, 1996. Reprinted by permission of Penguin Books Canada Limited.

Christie McLaren: "Suitcase Lady" from *The Globe and Mail,* January 24, 1981. Reprinted with permission from The Globe and Mail.

Stuart McLean: "The Shocking Truth About Household Dust" from *The Morningside World of Stuart McLean* by Stuart McLean. Copyright © Stuart McLean, 1989. Reprinted by permission of Penguin Books Canada Ltd.

Anne Michaels: "Hurricane" from *Fugitive Pieces* by Anne Michaels. Used by permission, McClelland & Stewart, Inc. *The Canadian Publishers.*

Susanna Moodie: "Dandelion Coffee" from *Roughing it in the Bush,* 1852.

Naheed Mustafa: "My Body Is My Own Business" from *The Globe and Mail,* p. A26, June 29, 1993. Reprinted by permission of the author.

Michael Ondaatje: "Tabula Asiae" from *Running in the Family* by Michael Ondaatje. Used by permission, McClelland and Stewart, Inc. *The Canadian Publishers.*

Nathalie Petrowski: "The Seven-Minute Life of Marc Lépine" from *Le Devoir,* p. C12, December 16, 1989. Reprinted by permission of Le Devoir. Translated by Ronald Conrad.

Catherine Pigott: "Chicken-Hips" from *The Globe and Mail,* p. A14, March 20, 1990. Reprinted by permission of the author.

Mordecai Richler: "1944: The Year I Learned to Love a German" from the *New York Times Book Review,* February 2, 1986. Copyright © 1986 Mordecai Richler. Reprinted by permission of International Creative Management, Inc.

Erika Ritter: "Bicycles" from *Urban Scrawl* by Erika Ritter, © 1984. Reprinted by permission of Macmillan Canada.

Rita Schindler: "Thanks for Not Killing My Son" from *The Toronto Star,* p. D3, December 30, 1990. Every effort has been made to contact the owner of this copyright material. The publishers will gladly accept any information that will enable them to rectify any reference or credit in subsequent editions.

Carol Shields: "Encounter." First published in *Without a Guide: Contemporary Women's Travel Adventures* (Macfarlane Walter & Ross); reprinted here by arrangement with Bella Pomer Agency Inc.

Judy Stoffman: "The Way of All Flesh" from *Weekend Magazine,* September 15, 1979. Reprinted by permission of the author.

Dan Strickland: "The Last Laugh at Dark-Eyed Susan's Roadside Café" originally published by The Friends of Algonquin Park in *The Raven* (Algonquin Park newsletter) of August 22, 1996, written by Dan Strickland, Chief Park Naturalist, Algonquin Provincial Park. Reprinted by permission of the author.

David Suzuki: "Hidden Lessons" from *The Globe and Mail,* February 7, 1987. Reprinted by permission of the author.

Jan Wong: "Safeguard Your Lives" from *Red China Blues: My Long March From Mao to Now,* copyright © 1996 by Jan Wong. Reprinted with the permission of Doubleday Canada Limited.

To the Student

We hope you like *The Act of Writing*. In our five editions so far, we've put a lot of effort into developing material that is fun to read, that provides issues to debate in class, that inspires you to write about significant matters, and that suggests good books so you can keep on reading after the course is done.

The 50 selections between these covers provide some good reading right now. Notice, though, how the introduction to each author lists more works by that person. And the "Explorations" feature after each selection suggests which of those books are probably most worth reading. Circle the most likely ones to try over the holidays, or next summer, or whenever you have time. (Then keep this book, so you have a record of those choices!) If our selection by Jan Wong or Anne Michaels or Mordecai Richler or Michael Ondaatje or Evelyn Lau especially appeals to you, then treat it like a movie preview: go on to the full-length feature as soon as you can. Remember that in addition to the fun you may have and the insights you may get, the act of opening a book is probably your most direct path to improving your own writing.

Each "Explorations" feature also refers you to at least one Web site. (See "Going Online," p. 18.) As it suggests, if you want to see Michael

Ondaatje's picture, or hear Félix Leclerc sing in French, or see a list of everything David Foot or Dionne Brand has published, go right ahead. Other sites treat issues that come up in our selections. If the subject of gun ownership strikes you as you read the piece by Josh Freed, visit the two Web sites recommended: one by the Violence Policy Center, which lobbies for gun control, and one by the National Rifle Association, which lobbies against it. See their contrasting positions; then ask yourself what your own view is. Or, as "Going Online" also suggests, if you have read Anne Michaels on the effects of the Holocaust in Canada today, visit the suggested Web site: play its interactive game to see whether you, yourself, would have "survived" the Holocaust. Send a letter to a politician, through the David Suzuki Foundation Web site, or check the vast amount of material on First Nations people in the site relating to Brian Maracle's piece on returning to the "rez."

Finally, *The Act of Writing* teaches a philosophy of writing. We hope you consider carefully this book's advice about how good writing is produced in the real world: not just through blueprinting an essay before you write the first word, but through a process of discovery, of "thinking by writing." Do read our overview of the writing process, on pages 1 through 18, with close attention. Free yourself up to try the techniques it suggests, and free yourself from some of the inefficient or even harmful practices of the past. The methods we suggest are based on today's research, but they are also the same ones that most good writers have always used.

R. C.

To the Teacher

The development of any new edition has a double focus: *continuity* and *exploration*. The best of what readers have liked so far is conserved; then new initiatives reach ahead toward renewal. In doing our own fifth edition, we have relied more than ever on reviewers and survey respondents, so that we know what our readers are thinking as we carry out these two tasks. We hope you like the results.

Continuity

Of course the main job of an anthology is to present good selections. In deciding which essays to retain and which to replace, we have stayed close to the wishes of our survey respondents. Of the 17 selections from *The Act of Writing*, fourth edition, that ranked highest in our recent survey, every one has been kept, and of the 32 ranked highest, 28, or 87.5%, have been kept. Through retaining the best — as we have tried to do in every revision so far — we believe that a "core" of well-written and significant favourites has evolved, to give quality and stability as you design your course.

In the core structure of the book, as well, we are not chasing change for the sake of change. In past editions we have dropped and added chapters, in response to readers' wishes. This time the survey and reviews affirmed the book's overall organization, so we have kept it. One area that did raise concern is the chapter "Analogy and Related Devices," which, in the fourth edition, we had expanded because of positive survey results. This time at least two reviewers considered its central device risky to essay writers, since an analogy is a device of imagination more than of logic. So although we did keep the chapter, we reduced it from six essays to four, and added stronger guidelines to the chapter introduction explaining when these devices are and are not appropriate.

Exploration

Of the 50 selections In *The Act of Writing*, fifth edition, you will find 17, or 34%, to be new. This corresponds to the one-third composite recommendation by our survey respondents. But the newness lies even more in the selection of writers than in their number. We have many younger and fresher voices this time, as a new generation of writers continues to take its place in Canada. Substantially more this time are from the West, especially British Columbia, to better balance our contents geographically. There is an increased representation from Quebec and from the First Nations population, and there are many more voices of New Canadians.

As for gender, in the fourth edition we had reached the 50% mark, with 25 selections by women and 25 by men. This time we felt uneasy about that exact split, as if we had been driven by numbers or policy as much as quality. In response, this time we let the balance float to a more natural total of 27 contributors who are women and 23 who are men.

As times continue to change, it is only natural that the focus and emphasis of writers change. We do resolutely maintain *The Act of Writing* as an anthology of Canadian essays, to provide an alternative for teachers who want something of our own in the classroom. Yet at the same time you will find more selections with an international focus, through Canadian eyes — as when Governor General's Award-winner Karen Connelly looks around her at the Thailand she has come to love, and contemplates her approaching return to the "country of cold rocks."

As times change, controversy emerges. You will find many new selections that explore issues: homelessness, democracy vs. totalitarianism in China, the gun culture of California, the isolation of urban life, the pain of racism, and the implications of demographics for the futures of entire generations. To reflect the heightened emphasis on issues, the feature "Ideas for Discussion and Writing," which appears after each selection, is on the average longer, while "Structure" and "Style" are on the average slightly shorter. And since issues are often closely tied to urban life, you will note that the greatest category increase in the Contents by Subject Matter is "The City" — up from four selections to ten.

Finally, a specific feature of the book has changed in this edition: what used to be called "Further Reading," just after each selection, has been retitled "Explorations" and has been given a larger role. We like to think of *The Act of Writing* as an index to independent readings students may wish to do: when they have enjoyed a selection, or its subject, we suggest more related material to read on their own. There are more book titles this time. And since many students are now online, "Explorations" now recommends at least one Web site related to the author and/or theme of each selection. (See "Going Online," p. 18.) And as one site gives links to others, the exploration need never end.

If You Are New to This Book

The Act of Writing, fifth edition, offers flexibility and encourages individualization. The combination of three to eight essays per chapter, with several more identified in cross-references, will yield more selections per unit than you are likely to use. Thus you can individualize, choosing readings that best suit the needs and interests of your particular class. This book also offers a range of difficulty, from essays that are easily accessible to almost all students to others that are, frankly, challenging. (*Note:* The "Table of Contents and Difficulty Ranking" of your instructor's manual ranks all selections by level of difficulty, so if you are new to this book you can more quickly tailor a syllabus to your class.)

The numerous discussion topics after each selection offer a choice of theme and emphasis in classroom debate. "Explorations," as described earlier, suggests books and Web sites for independent investigation. And finally, the "Process in Writing" topic after each essay, the 30 essay topics at the end of each chapter, and the process "Guidelines" tailored for each chapter give a latitude of choice for the individual teacher, the individual class, the individual student.

Note the two tables of contents. The first lists all selections in their chapters arranged by *form of organization* (you can choose from seven essays, for example, that all demonstrate organization through analysis of cause and effect). The second table of contents lists all essays by general *subject*, to help you choose selections of interest to your particular students.

An introductory essay, "The Act of Writing," starts the book off by putting to rest a number of widespread misconceptions about writing that plague students, then attempts to describe what it is that an essayist actually does. It emphasizes the individuality of the writer, the importance of motivation, the role of intuition as well as logic, and a balance of spontaneity and revision in the process of writing. The section "Process and the Computer" then shows how word processing supports these concepts.

The 50 essays are all by Canadians or persons with Canadian experience, but the scope ranges widely: some are about Canada, many are about other countries, and most express such universal themes as childhood, aging, work, technology, war, the city, and the environment. The focus on Canadian essays is not a statement of nationalism. In fact, it is an attempt to provide in Canada the kind of anthology taken for granted in other countries: a collection of works that are mostly universal in theme but that, naturally, draw a good part of their content from the country in which the book will be used. There is no contradiction between this goal and the fact that the fifth edition is our most international so far.

As we have seen, the essays are arranged in chapters that each demonstrate a fundamental pattern of organization. "Narration" starts the book off, because no approach is easier or more motivating for a first assignment than writing a story, in chronological order, about oneself. "Example" and "Description" follow, because these tools of development are used to some degree in almost all writing. "Cause and Effect" and its following chapter, "Comparison and Contrast," are at the centre of the essayist's organizational repertoire. "Analogy and Related Devices" and "Classification" follow "Comparison and Contrast," for they are both varieties of comparison. "Process Analysis," an approach used widely across the curriculum, follows. After all these *forms,* our largest chapter, "Argumentation and Persuasion," explores more fully the writer's most common and basic *purpose:* to make a point. It examines the dualities of deduction and induction, and of argumentation and persuasion, then illustrates their application with eight model essays.

Throughout the book each selection is prefaced with an introduction to the author, designed to interest the student, sometimes to present the author as a role model, and to encourage further reading of the author's works. Then each selection is followed by pedagogical material entitled "Explorations," "Structure," "Style," "Ideas for Discussion and Writing," and in Chapter 9 "Argumentation and Persuasion." Note that in this material different questions serve different purposes. Some are directive, calling attention to major features of the essay. Some are technical, for example focussing on a specific point of language that illustrates a technique. Still others are exploratory, encouraging open-ended response. The instructor's manual offers answers to those questions that are not open-ended and suggests responses to some that are. Read the manual's introduction: it gives more suggestions for using *The Act of Writing*. For each essay, the manual also lists vocabulary that may need attention.

Each of the nine chapters begins with a discussion of how and why to use the form at hand, and ends with a selection of 30 essay topics which complement that form. These topics have been chosen with care, to tap some of the students' deepest concerns and channel them into motivation for writing. The reason for this attention to topics is that no one problem is more destructive to the performance of both student and teacher than dull or superficial subject matter. How can writing be important if its content is not? And how can a teacher enjoy or even tolerate marking without an interest in what the students are saying?

A further "Process in Writing" topic is given after each essay. If class members have had a good discussion about the selection, their motivation and writing performance may be greatest if they explore these topics, which draw upon both the subject and the underlying form of the essay preceding them. And at the end of each chapter are the process guidelines mentioned earlier, individualized for the specific pattern of development in that unit.

Finally, a glossary at the end defines literary terms often used in the discussion questions; when one of these terms is a key part of a passage, it appears in SMALL CAPITALS.

The instructor's manual will be sent gratis upon request.

If You Are Teaching Theme-Based Courses

This anthology is appropriate for interdisciplinary, theme-based courses with teaching goals such as cultural and intercultural understanding, social issues, personal development, or appreciation of the arts. In teaching literature, for example, some teachers draw upon this anthology's introduction to an author such as Margaret Laurence, then her essay, as background for a study of one of her novels. Note also the "Explorations" list which suggests works, either by the same author or thematically related to the author's subject, which students can then pursue in developing an independent study. It also now suggests related Web sites.

To see which of this book's essays will connect with the theme of a course or module you are planning, look over the Contents by Subject. Note also the high proportion of discussion questions that deal with the subject(s) of the readings, and particularly issues.

As a book of Canadian readings, this text can support Canadian Studies courses: note the balance it seeks between content focussed directly on Canada, on content by and about New Canadians who are shaping the Canada of today, and content that expresses our relation to the world. With slightly over half the essays by women, and with several of these focussing directly on women's issues, the text can also play a part in women's studies. Again, check especially the Contents by Subject.

I would like to thank all those who, in one way or another, helped with this project: the many students and colleagues who reacted to essays, and the busy teachers who gave of their time to answer our survey. Thanks also to those teachers who reviewed our previous edition and our new selections, to help us toward the best book possible: Gary Corscadden, New Brunswick Community College; Ingrid Hutchinson, Fanshawe College; George Lyon, Mount Royal College; David O'Rourke, Centennial College; Peter Miller, Seneca College; Sharon Smulders, Mount Royal College; Robert Bright, George S. Henry Academy; Kathryn Lemmon, James Fowler High School; Rob Rankin, Port Moody Secondary School; Maria Rocca Martin, Iona Catholic Secondary School; Diane Slimmon, Cameron Heights Collegiate Institute. Thanks to friends and family who suggested readings to include. I am grateful to several authors who supplied information for their biographical introductions: Paul D'Angelo, Naheed Mustafa, Elinor Florence, Garry Engkent, Catherine Pigott, Judy Stoffman, Dan Strickland and Martin Hocking. Thanks also to Doris Anderson for revising her classic selection for this fifth edition. I appreciate the excellent detective work that Marianne Minaker of McGraw-Hill Ryerson did, in the fine tradition of Norma Christensen, tracking down permissions. (This year we lost Norma, who died after a long illness; she will long be remembered, though, by those who worked with her, and she is honoured each year when McGraw-Hill Ryerson awards the Norma Christensen Prize for Editorial Excellence.) *Un gros merci* to Jocelyne Loranger, who helped with research in Quebec City. My daughter Suzanne helped with contemporary essay topics. And again, the sincerest thanks of all to my wife Mary who, with her good judgement, helped in many ways through every stage of this edition.

R. C.

INTRODUCTION:
THE ACT OF WRITING

Writing is one of the most widely misunderstood of human activities. It is odd that after all the years we have spent in school, after all the hours we have spent reading other people's writing and producing our own, most of us cannot say what really happens when we write. We can describe other complex tasks — driving a car, making pizza, building a radio or searching the Web. But to most people the act of writing is a mystery. Not that we don't have theories, either those told us in school or those we have arrived at ourselves. But many of these theories are misconceptions that actually hinder our efforts to write. Let's look at some of them.

MISCONCEPTION: Writing is like following a blueprint: I figure it all out in advance and then just fill in the details. Of course an outline, used sensibly, will help. But our parents were taught in school that their best thinking should go into a logical and detailed outline — and that the writing itself was secondary. Thus they were reduced to carpenters or plumbers of the written word, who merely sawed, cut and fit pieces in place once the master plan was established. The problem with this reassuringly logical approach is that it views writing as a technology, not

1

as the art that all our practical experience tells us it is. How many of us have given up on a required outline, done our thinking mostly as we wrote the essay itself, then later produced the outline by seeing what we wrote? Or how many of us have painfully constructed a detailed outline in advance, only to find while writing the essay that our real message does not fit the plan?

Writing is exploring! We know which way we are headed and the main landmarks we hope to pass, but not every twist and turn of the path. What a dull trip that would be! Let's leave room for discovery, because our best ideas may occur in the act of writing. The Quebec poet Hector de St.-Denys Garneau actually said, "I cannot think except when writing." Many teachers now reflect the fact of writing as discovery by calling a first draft the *discovery draft*.

But while avoiding the rigor mortis of overplanning, let's not go to the opposite extreme, like Stephen Leacock's famous horseman who "rode madly off in all directions." We do work best with an outline, five or ten or fifteen lines that define the main point and how we intend to support it. But our outline should be a compass on a journey, not the blueprint of a construction project.

MISCONCEPTION: *If I don't hit it right the first time, I've failed*. It's not hard to see where this idea came from: in school we write so many essays and tests within the limits of one class period that writing in a hurry begins to seem normal. But under such conditions, merely producing enough is hard; seriously revising it is even harder. Few people can "hit it right the first time." Professional writers know this; most of them take longer to write than we do. They tinker with words and sentences, they cross out and replace sections, they go through two or three or even five or ten drafts — and sometimes they throw the whole thing out and start over. These writers know by experience that writing is not a hit-or-miss affair with only one try allowed, but a *process*. They know that revision can yield astonishing results.

MISCONCEPTION: *When I write, I am speaking on paper.* If you have heard a tape of yourself speaking, you were no doubt surprised at all the filler words you used. "Uh," "um," "well" and "hmmm" may fill the gaps between your thoughts very well, but hardly help to carry the message. And if you listened closely, you may have been surprised at the number of incomplete statements — fragments that by themselves made little or no sense. Fillers and fragments are tolerated in speech because, after all, we make up our message on the spot. There is no chance to plan, revise, edit or proofread.

But in writing there is, and this fact increases the expectations of your reader far beyond those of your listener. Language in written form can be planned. It is complete. It is precise and concise. It uses standard words. It is punctuated. It follows all the rules. In short, it is a product of the time that its written form allows you to give it, not a spur-of-the-moment, hope-for-the-best effort like the speech that comes so easily from your mouth.

MISCONCEPTION: *The best words are the biggest words.* Variations on this theme are *If my writing looks scholarly it will impress the reader,* and even *If I make my essay so difficult that no one knows what I'm saying, everyone will believe me.* At the roots of these widespread ideas is a notion that writing is a kind of competition between writer and reader. A writer who is obscure enough will make the reader feel like a dummy and will thus win the game. But ask yourself: In real life do you "ambulate" or "walk"? "Expectorate" or "spit"? "Interdigitate" or "hold hands"? "Cogitate" or "think"?

Avoiding this game of writer vs. reader is not easy when so many leaders in business, education and government play it. The first step toward open communication, though, is to think of your reader not as an opponent but as a teammate. You are both moving toward the same goal, which is the reader's clear understanding of your ideas.

Another step is to admit that words small in size can be large in meaning. The best-loved writings in our language (think of the lines from Shakespeare you may have memorized for school) are filled with short words. Writing made of them is more concise, more vivid, and usually more profound than writing made of the elephantine words that some of us ransack the dictionary for. When a long word conveys your meaning best — perhaps like "elephantine" above — by all means use it. But often the writer, like the architect, finds that *less is more.*

MISCONCEPTION: *I don't like to write.* For some unfortunate people this statement is true. But for most who say it, the truth is really "I don't like to *begin* writing." Who does? Staring at that blank page is like staring from a diving board at the cold water below. But a swimmer and a writer both gather the courage to plunge in, and soon they both feel a new sensation: they don't want to come out. Teachers whose students write journals in class see the process at work every day. As class begins, the writers are filled with stress: they chew their pens and frown as they stare at the page to be filled. But in a while they are scribbling furiously, recording in an almost trance-like state their latest experiences, feelings and insights. If the teacher asks them to stop, in order to begin the next activity, they are annoyed: they sigh and *keep on writing* till asked a second or third time to stop.

Let's admit that most writers — and that includes professionals — dread the beginning. Let's also admit that most writers enjoy the rest of it, hard work though it may be.

With some of the most widespread misconceptions behind us now, let's take a fresh look at the act of writing. First, allow for personal differences. *Know yourself!* If you are a person whose desk is piled high with papers and books, whose closet is an avalanche waiting to happen, and whose shoes have not been shined in two years, you may write best by planning little and relying on your spontaneity. If you are a person who plans an August holiday in January, keeps a budget right down to the penny, and washes the car every Wednesday and Saturday whether it needs it or not, you may write best by planning fully.

On the other hand, your natural tendencies may have caused you problems and so may need to be controlled. If your spontaneity has produced writings that don't stay on topic, plan more: make a careful outline. If overorganizing has sucked the life out of your writing, free yourself up: leave more room for discovery as you write. Whatever the case, try to determine and use the approach that works for *you.*

Let's allow also for differences in assignments. If you are dashing off a short personal sketch, your planning may be no more than an idea and a few moments of thought. If you are writing a long research essay, the product of days in the library, you may need an outline two pages long. No single approach works for every person and every assignment. Keep in mind, then, that the process we are about to examine is a *starting point,* a basis, but not a blueprint, for your own writing.

THE BEGINNINGS OF AN ESSAY CAN BE FOUND BY ANSWERING THESE QUESTIONS:

1. *Why am I writing?* This most basic of questions too often goes un-asked. If the answer is "to fill up five pages," "to impress" or "to get an A," you begin with a severe handicap. The immediate reason to write may be a class assignment, but the real reason must be to communicate something of value. Otherwise your motivation is lost and so is your performance. So, from a list of topics, choose the one that means the most to you. If no topic seems significant, devise a way to *make* one significant. Probe the topic through the exercise of freewriting, explained later on. Look at it from a new viewpoint or approach it in some unusual way.

If that fails, and if your teacher is approachable, voice your concern and suggest an alternative topic. One teacher always made students analyze the relative merits of chocolate and vanilla ice cream, on the theory that a dull subject will not distract a writer from the real goals: grammar and style. He was wrong. Research shows motivation to be the single greatest factor in writing performance — and motivation comes from writing about things that matter.

When you write on your own, as in a private journal, you may still need to answer the question *Why am I writing?* Just recording events may not be enough. Add your feelings, your perceptions, and your conclusions about those events. If you have problems, as most people do, confront them on the page. The more you discover yourself and your world through writing, the more important the writing becomes.

2. *How big is my topic?* Classroom essays are shorter than most people realize. A book may contain 100,000 words; a magazine article 2000 or 5000; a classroom essay as few as 500 or even 250. So narrowing the essay topic is more important than most people realize.

One student, who had been a political prisoner, decided to write about economic systems. He knew the subject well and was committed to it. But what he attempted was an analysis of communism, socialism and capitalism — all in two pages! A lack of focus spread his very short essay so thin that it approached the state of saying nothing about everything. It was the barest scratching of the surface, a summary of basic facts most people already know.

If the same person had focussed on his arrest and imprisonment — or even on one day in his cell — he may have said far more about the system he opposed. It is in specifics that we best see generalities. Think of writing as photography. Putting aside the wide-angle lens that includes too much at a distance, look through the telephoto lens that brings you up close to a small part of the subject. Select the part most meaningful to you, the part most characteristic of the whole, then take the picture.

Nearly all the essays in this book are closeups: they explore one situation, one incident, one person or one process. Yet most of them are longer than the essays you will write. So when you choose a topic, judge its size — and if you have to, *change* its size.

3. *What message am I sending?* You may know your topic well. But unless you send a message concerning it, your reader will think *what's the point?* A message is often a value judgement: Are robots dangerous? Will they take away our jobs or someday even rule over us? Or do they help us? Will they free us at last from the dehumanizing tyranny of manual labour? Most of the essays in this book take such a stance, either pro or con, toward their subjects. Some avoid judging their subjects directly, but send other messages: what it's like to be homeless, or how aging is a lifelong process.

If you have chosen a topic because it seems meaningful, you will no doubt have a message to send. What do you most feel like saying about the topic? Once you know, get it down in writing. This THESIS

STATEMENT, as it is often called, normally comes at or near the beginning of an essay. It is an introductory sentence or passage that does more than just tell what the topic is; it clearly states, as well, what you are saying *about* the topic. It lets your reader know what is coming — and, in the process, commits you to a purpose that all the rest of the essay must in one way or another support. It is your guide as you write.

4. *Who is my audience?* Do you talk the same way to a friend and a stranger? To an old person and a child? To a hockey coach and a professor? Probably not. Neither would you write the same way to all readers. In a private journal you can write as freely as you think, for you are your own reader: omissions and excesses of all kinds will be understood and forgiven. In letters to a close friend you are nearly as free, for the reader knows you well enough to supply missing explanations or interpret remarks in the light of your personality. But your freedom shrinks when you write for others: a business person, a public official, a teacher. Now you must fight a misconception shared by many people: *Everyone is like me.*

This idea is seldom articulated but may lurk as a natural assumption in the back of our minds. It is a form of egotism. If you assume everyone is like you, many readers will not accept or even understand your message — because they are *not* like you. They did not grow up in your family, neighbourhood or even country. They are older or younger, or of the opposite sex. They have had different life experiences, so now they have different knowledge and temperaments and values.

Accept these differences as you write. You will never prove your point by quoting Marx to a capitalist, the Bible to an atheist, or Gloria Steinem to a male supremacist. Any argument built on a partisan foundation will collapse if the reader does not accept that foundation. Instead, build from facts or ideas that your reader probably *does* accept: killing is bad, government is necessary, women are human beings, and so on. Is your topic controversial? Then avoid an open display of bias. Calling intellectuals "commies" or abortionists "hired killers" will appeal only to those who shared your view in the first place. (For more on these matters, read the introduction to Chapter 9, "Argumentation and Persuasion.")

Does the reader know what you know? If you write about statistics for a statistics teacher, use any technical terms customary to the field, and avoid the insult of explaining elementary points. But if you write on the same subject for a class exercise in English or a letter to the editor of your hometown newspaper, your reader will be very different: avoid most technical terms, define those you do use, and explain more fully each step of your argument.

The more open you become to the individuality of your reader, the more open your reader becomes to your message. It is a matter of mutual respect.

Prewriting

How do we begin the act of writing, by putting those first words on a page? The philosopher Lao-Tze said, "A journey of a thousand miles begins with the first step." In a way he was right: if we never take that official first step, we will certainly never arrive at our destination. But how much daydreaming and planning do we do beforehand? Do we set out on a journey without consulting the map or the calendar or the tourist brochure or the travel guide — not to mention our bankbook? And do we write an essay without in some way resolving the questions we have just asked:

Why am I writing?
How big is my topic?
What message am I sending?
Who is my audience?

The process of writing, then, begins in thought. But thoughts do not come on command. Like the diver, we look down at the cold water and dread the plunge. Some writers like to "break the ice" by manipulating their environment: finding a quiet spot, going to a favourite chair with good lighting, or slipping a good album into their CD-ROM drive. Others fortify themselves with a good night's sleep, junk food or coffee. Any of these tricks may help, but they all avoid the real issue: How do we begin to *think?*

One direct approach, a variation on the old technique of outlining, is *brainstorming:* once you have roughly identified your subject, just write down words or phrases that relate in any way to it, in a list going down a page. Put down anything that comes, letting one thought lead to another. Some entries will seem off-topic, trivial or even loony, but others may be just what you need: the keys to your essay. Circle them. Put them in order. As crude as this primitive outline may seem, it has served a purpose: your thoughts have begun to arrive. The process is in motion. You have taken that first "step" before even starting the first draft.

A similar but even more powerful "icebreaker" is *freewriting.* Put a blank page on the desk with your watch beside it. Think of your topic.

Now write! Put down anything that comes: sentences, phrases, words —
logical thoughts, hasty impressions, even pure garbage. Do not cease
the physical act of writing, do not even lift the pen from the page, or
your fingers from the keyboard, for at least five minutes. If your next
thought doesn't come, write the last one over and over till the next one
does come. What you produce may surprise you.

Like brainstorming, freewriting is an exercise in free association: the
flow of your thoughts, the sudden leaps of your intuition, will "break
the ice" so you can write. They may do even more: as in brainstorming,
you may end up with a page of scribbling that contains the main points
of your essay. Try to find them. Circle them. Put them in order. See if
your intuition has led the way in answering the questions: *Why am I
writing? How big is my topic? What message am I sending? Who is my audience?* If all goes well, you have already begun your journey.

The First Words

Once your thoughts are flowing comes the next step, the opening passage of your essay. In a very short composition your THESIS STATEMENT
may serve also as the first words. In most longer essays it comes at the
end of an introduction. Only about one-fourth of the selections in this
book start right off with what could be called a thesis statement. What
do the others start with?

Background information: About half the essays in this book lead off by
telling the circumstances in which the topic is set. For examples, see
the beginnings of our selections by Gabori (p. 31), McLean (p. 153),
Richler (p. 172), Foot and Stoffman (p. 255), Lau (p. 274), Hocking
(p. 316), Dobbs (p. 322) and Schindler (p. 342).

Anecdote: A brief story, usually of a humorous or dramatic incident,
can lead into the topic. See Cross (p. 80), Manguel (p. 90), Florence
(p. 159), Pigott (p. 195) and Leacock (p. 281).

Quotation or allusion: The words of a philosopher, of a news report, of
a recognized specialist in the subject, or of anyone with close experience of it can be used to break the ice. See Kogawa (p. 336) and Dobbs
(p. 322).

Sense images: Vivid description can attract a reader's interest to the
topic. See Fraser (p. 38), McLaren (p. 115), Harrison (p. 119) and
Galdikas (p. 190).

A striking comparison or contrast: Showing how things are like or unlike each other is a dramatic way to introduce a topic. See Shields
(p. 26), Cross (p. 80), Suzuki (p. 144), Pigott (p. 195) and Stoffman
(p. 286).

Narrative: Several selections in this book begin by telling a story upon which the essay is based. See Harrison (p. 119), D'Angelo (p. 140), Engkent (p. 164), Pigott (p. 195) and Brand (p. 346).

An unusual or puzzling statement: Such an opening appeals to the reader's curiosity. See Freed (p. 85) and Carr (p. 126).

Figures of speech: A striking METAPHOR, SIMILE or PERSONIFICATION can spark the opening. See Laurence (p. 209), Leclerc (p. 235) and Stoffman (p. 286).

Most of these introductions are short: a couple of sentences or a paragraph or two at the most. And virtually all are designed to *interest* the reader, for a bored reader may not even finish the essay, let alone like or understand it. Writing is fishing. You throw in the line. Your reader tastes the bait (your introduction), bites, is pulled through the waters of your argument, and — if the line of thought doesn't break — lands in your net.

You, the writer, may also be "hooked." Once you have hit upon a strong introduction, one that shows off the drama or importance of your topic, the beginning may carry you along with it. And once you get going, the idea embodied in your thesis statement may pull you through the essay, enabling you to write freely as one page leads to another. You may become less and less aware of your surroundings as you become more and more immersed in your subject. By the time you develop a good beginning, you may experience the act of writing the way one student described it: "At first I couldn't start, but then I couldn't stop."

The Body

An introduction is like a head; it may decide to go somewhere but it needs a body to take it there. The "body" of your essay has the main work to do: following the direction set by your introduction, and especially by your thesis statement, it explains, illustrates, and sometimes attempts to prove your point. But if it ever ignores the direction set by the head, it ceases to do its job. Even the best of explanations, without a purpose, is like one of those unfortunate football players who completes a spectacular run to the wrong goal. On the other hand, we know that writing is discovery. The acts of writing and revising will sometimes take us in a direction better than the old one decided by the introduction. When that happens, correct not the body but the "head" — so the two can move together in the new direction.

The easiest way to keep a direction is to choose a pattern for your essay — and that is what most of this book is about. As you read and discuss the essays that follow, and as you write your own essays, trying out the patterns other writers use, you will explore a range of choices:

Narration: In simple time order, from the first event to the last event, tell a story that illustrates the point.

Example: Give one in-depth example that explains the point, or a number of shorter examples.

Description: Recreate for your reader, through vivid language, your own or someone else's experience with the subject.

Cause and Effect: Explain by showing how one situation or event causes another.

Comparison and Contrast: Explain by showing how two things are like or unlike each other.

Analogy and Related Devices: In comparing two things, use the one to explain the other.

Classification: Make a point by dividing your subject into parts, then explaining each in turn.

Process Analysis: Show how something is done or how something happens.

Argumentation and Persuasion: Using any pattern that works, make your point through logic and/or emotion.

Seldom does one of these methods appear alone. A *process analysis,* for example, is usually told as a *narrative.* Here and there it may use *examples, description* or any of the other patterns to help make its point. But these combinations occur naturally, often without the writer's knowing it. In most cases the only form actually chosen by a writer is the main one that organizes the whole essay.

How do you choose the right form? Let the subject be your guide. In architecture, form follows function. Rather than cram an office into a pre-selected structure, a designer likes to begin with the function of that office. How much space does it need? What shape? What barriers and passageways between one section and another? What front to present to the world?

An essay is much the same: the needs of its subject, if you are open to them, can suggest a form. If the main idea is to explain what something is like, you will tend to choose *examples* and *description.* If the subject is unusual or little known, you may *compare* or *contrast,* or make an *analogy* with something the reader does know. If its parts seem important, you may examine them one by one through *classification.* When some other need is greater, you may use still another form. If you stay open to the subject, whatever it is, this process can be so natural that you *recognize* a form rather than *choose* it.

If the process is natural, then why study these forms at all? Well, architecture students certainly study different kinds of building design, so their future condominiums or shopping centres don't collapse and kill people. Fortunately, readers are not killed by poorly organized essays, but the principle is similar: If the writer has a conscious knowledge of all the possibilities, his or her arguments will be easier to build and will be less likely to collapse.

Consider the longer essay — say, a report or research paper. A jumble of notes sits on your desk. They are in chaos. Even with brainstorming or freewriting, knowing your purpose, having the facts, and completing a thesis statement, you don't know how to coordinate all those facts. First give the natural process its best chance: *sort all your notes into groups of related material*, using a pair of scissors if necessary to divide unrelated points. When everything is in two stacks, or five stacks or ten, let your mind work freely. How do these groups relate to each other? Does one come before another in time? Does one cause another? Does one contradict another? Are they all steps in a process or parts of a whole? Now add your conscious knowledge of the forms: Do you see narration, example, description, cause and effect, comparison and contrast, analogy, classification or process analysis? It is the rare case when one of these forms cannot supply a structure to support your argument.

Right now you are practising them one by one, as the students in architecture school study different structures one by one — so that in all your future writing you will have choices. And for now, you may be using the topics at the end of the readings, or the larger list of topics at the end of each chapter, because they are coordinated to go with the form you have just read and discussed. But in your future writing you will go a step further, making the match yourself between topic and form.

Yet, even when you are looking over 30 choices at the end of a chapter, you are exercising choice: spend a good long time to pick the topic that strikes you as most interesting, most significant — and therefore most motivating. It is writing about things that matter that will most increase your performance — now and always.

Transitions

We have mentioned the passageways inside a building. Without them an office would be useless: no one could move from one room to another to have meetings. Yet some essays are built without passage-ways. One point ends where another begins, without even a "then" or "therefore" or "however" or "finally" to join them. Readers then have to break down walls to follow thoughts from one room to the next.

Help your readers. *You* know why one point follows another, but do *they*? Make sure by supplying transitions: say "although" or "but" or "on the other hand"; say "because" or "as a result" or "since"; say "first" or "next" or "last"; say "for example" or "in conclusion." And when moving readers from one main part of your essay to the next, devote a full sentence or even a paragraph to the job (one good example is para-graph 10 of Doris Anderson's essay).

Your plan may already be the right one, setting your points in their most logical order. Now let that logic show: give your readers a door between every room.

The Closing

We've discussed the beginning, the middle, and transitions between parts. What remains is, of course, the ending. Every essay has one — the point where the words stop. But not all endings are closings. A closing is deliberate. In some clear way it tells the reader that you have not just run out of time, ink or ideas, but that you have chosen to stop here. If you end at just any convenient spot, without engineering an effect to fit your ending, the essay may trail off or even fall flat. But as preachers, composers, playwrights and film directors know, a good clos-ing can be even stronger than a good opening. How do the essays in this book come to a close? They use a variety of devices:

Reference to the opening: Repeating or restating something from the opening gives a sense of culmination, of having come full circle. See the openings and closings by Gagnon (pp. 35 and 36), Maracle (pp. 200 and 202), Lam (pp. 246 and 248), Stoffman (pp. 286 and 293), Kogawa (pp. 336 and 339) and Cameron (pp. 354 and 356).

Contrast or reversal: This ironic device exploits the dramatic potential of the closing. See the openings and closings by Stoffman (pp. 286 and 293) and Cameron (pp. 354 and 356).

Question: A question and its answer, or a question calling for the reader's answer, is a common means of closing. See Landsberg (p. 77), Connelly (p. 108) and Leacock (p. 283).

Quotation: A good quotation, of either prose or poetry, can add au-thority and interest to a closing. See Stoffman (p. 293).

Transition signals: Words, phrases or sentences of transition commonly signal the closing. See Gabori (p. 32), Landsberg (p. 77), Pigott (p. 197) and Johnston (p. 228).

Revealing the significance: Showing the implications or importance of the subject makes for a strong closing. See Shields (p. 28), Gabori (p. 32), Wong (p. 61), Landsberg (p. 77), Michaels (p. 104), Suzuki (p. 146), Johnston (p. 228), Dobbs (p. 328) and Petrowski (p. 351).

Summary: About a fourth of the essays in this book give a summary, either alone or in combination with other closing techniques, but one that is always short. See Mallet (p. 113), McLean (p. 157), Anderson (p. 188), Lau (p. 278) and Hocking (p. 319).

Conclusion: Although "conclusion" is often a label for the closing in general, more accurately it is only one of many closing techniques—the drawing of a conclusion from the discussion in the essay. See Geddes (p. 48), Landsberg (p. 77), Manguel (p. 92), Suzuki (p. 146), Mustafa (p. 151), Richler (p. 178) and Galdikas (p. 193).

Prediction: A short look at the subject's future can very logically close a discussion of that subject's past or present. See Geddes (p. 48), Landsberg (p. 77), Cross (p. 82), Suzuki (p. 146) and Foot (p. 265). Sometimes discussing the future takes the form of a call to action (Landsberg).

You have probably noticed that some authors are named more than once; closings, like openings, can exploit more than one technique. In fact, the more the better. Stay open to techniques that appear while you write, even as you construct a closing using a technique you have deliberately chosen.

Any of these choices will be stronger, though, when used with the most fundamental technique of all: building your whole essay toward a high point or *climax*. Put your points in order from least important to most important, from least useful to most useful, or from least dramatic to most dramatic. (Sometimes you will not know this order till late in the writing. If you are computerized, use your "move" function to rearrange sections without retyping; or if you write by hand, cut drafts apart with scissors to rearrange them.) When everything leads up to that climax, you have set the stage for a closing that applies all the dramatic power of the final position.

When you get there, apply the force of that closing to a real message. Techniques used just for their own sake are cheap tricks. Do not waste them. Instead, use them to underline your basic message, to impress upon your audience one last and most convincing time that what you have to say is significant. Your closing, more than any other part of your essay, can send the reader away disappointed — or moved.

The Process: How Many Drafts?

We have discussed the act of writing as a process in which, rather than trying to "hit it right the first time," we follow a number of steps in the journey toward a good essay. The rest of this book develops that approach. After each selection you will find an assignment called "Process in Writing" that draws on the essay you have just read, suggesting a related topic for an essay of your own. The main steps of the process are given, individualized for the particular topic.

Then at the end of each chapter you will find a whole page of essay topics, designed for practice in the form of organization you have just studied. After them, in each chapter, appear sections called "Process in Writing: Guidelines" which give the steps of a process designed for the organizational form you have just studied. Whether you write from a topic given just after an essay or choose a topic from the end-of-chapter list, remember that these steps are only *guidelines* to the process; use the ones that seem best for each case.

Our "process" of writing is flexible; it is not a blueprint like the elaborate outlines our parents were made to construct. Above all, the process is "recursive" — that is, while you may begin with brainstorming or freewriting, go on to a discovery draft, revise your argument in a further draft or drafts, and finally edit for spelling and punctuation, you may also double back or jump forward at any time. Studies show that professionals writing all kinds of documents in all kinds of fields do this. While generating their "discovery draft" they may stop here and there to improve a word choice or fix punctuation — changes that normally occur later. Or, while they are in the middle of editing or even proofreading, a fine new idea may come thundering out of their mind; so they may back up a few steps, write it out, and add it to their argument, perhaps junking something else they had thought was good. All this is consistent with the reality that *we think while writing.*

Do feel free to transgress the process "guidelines" in these ways, but not so often that you undercut the advantages of the process itself. For example, in writing your discovery draft you may detect some dubious sentence structure. If you must, stop here to edit. But better yet, why not just circle the spot, then come back to fix it later? (Or if you are word processing, insert a signal such as several asterisks in a row.) For now, let the material keep rolling out uninterrupted. Then later on, while you are editing or even proofreading, a whole new idea may come. You could go back even now to fit it in — but this means work, maybe even reorganization. Proceed only if it is a real improvement and if you have the time.

Finally, how many drafts are we talking about? The "guidelines" later on are sometimes vague on this point — because what do we mean by a draft? Is every new copy a draft? If you write by hand, only a good many improvements added between the lines and in the margins qualify the next copy as a new draft. And in word processing, though a new copy can be printed out at any time, it is not a further "draft" until some in-depth editing has been done, and many little changes — or sometimes large! — have been made. In either case, whether writing with a pen or keyboarding, seldom can you write a good essay in only one draft.

On the other hand, a total of four or five or six drafts may be a sign of time wasted just recopying, not revising. You can often reach a point at least close to your best writing performance in two or three real drafts. In practice you might produce a discovery draft, cover it with revisions, then recopy all this into a second draft, cover it with editing, then recopy all this into your good version to hand in (but not until you proofread even it). And if you compose directly on the computer, see the discussion of on-screen editing and drafts in the section that follows, "Process and the Computer."

When do you reach the journey's end? You will know when you get there. It is the point where your response to a significant topic has become so direct, so exact, so forceful, that at last you know exactly what you think. It is clear that you were writing for others, but at this moment it is even clearer that you were writing for yourself.

Process and the Computer

Today only a minority of students write assignments by hand. Why the massive change to electronics? After all, school computer labs are often crowded, and having your own computer and software costs money. Learning word processing from a 600-page manual is daunting. Accidents happen ("My cat jumped on the keyboard and my essay disappeared!"), and hardware can break down. Read "Ode to the User-Friendly Pencil," by Bonnie Laing (p. 331 of this book) for more objections.

However, the growing supremacy of computers as writing tools has a cause so clear it cannot be ignored: as the term implies, word "processing" fits the *process* approach to writing. It is hard to imagine a tool that could better empower us to get our thoughts out in the open, then later to so easily revise and edit them.

This is not the place to discuss details of computer use; these are available in a thousand books, including your own computer manual if you have one. *What the following short summary does, though, is point out strategies: ways the computer can help you apply the process of writing explained and encouraged in the previous pages and throughout the book.* Let's look now at the act of writing by computer, step by step.

1. PREWRITING: We have discussed how freewriting can shake your thoughts loose, get them flowing, get them out in the open — where you can then look them over to find the beginnings of essays. Freewriting by hand, though, is slow; it can resemble those nightmares in which a monster is chasing you but your feet are stuck in mud. Since people think faster than they write, a better way to capture thoughts before they disappear is through the keyboard. (Be sure to master touch typing, either in class or at home using instructional software. If you do not, you may be driving the fastest computer in town, but still producing text at a snail's pace. Remember that with good technique, most people can keyboard three to four times faster than they can write by hand.)

If you do freewrite at top speed on a computer, a rush of thought lasting only a few minutes can result in a page or two of material, which, since it was done so spontaneously, may contain spectacular connections of thought — as in free association exercises. It can be a real search of what's on your mind, what you know about the subject, what you really want to write about, and what your point of view — thus your THESIS STATEMENT — may be. Go for it. At the worst, suppose none of this works out at all. What have you lost? Five or ten minutes of your time.

2. DISCOVERY DRAFT: What is the difference between freewriting and your first draft? Sometimes not much. See what you come up with in step 1; it may be so close to a first draft that you will just begin with it on screen and revise from there.

Other times freewriting just sets a direction, so then it is your discovery draft that begins to establish the text itself. Again, the speed of the computer eases the task. Just as in freewriting, thoughts can come fast. They need to be trapped as they occur, so they are not lost. If you know touch typing, you can do it.

Above all, remember that the task of this first draft is to *generate material.* You are extracting ore from the mine. Sometimes it comes out fairly pure, but usually it needs refining. The time to do that is later: at this stage do not slow down the flow by fixing sentence structure or spelling. That is what later drafts are for. Just keep right on to the end, *extracting the ore.*

Another option: if you are really at home with the speed of touch typing, try this: actually write about three discovery drafts of three different topics or three angles of one topic. Of these, one will surely be better than the others. Keep it to develop, and just discard the others — as a photographer may discard the extra photos taken in the process of getting the good one.

3. FURTHER DRAFTS: Our introductory overview on the previous pages suggests that we do not move from one "draft" to the next until the first one is covered with revisions and corrections. With word processing, though, all this can happen on screen. You go through the discovery draft, using commands to delete words, lines or even pages; move passages around; move a troublesome paragraph off the screen in order to try a new version; and add further examples or explanation at any point, while the surrounding text moves away to make room. Though you can still print out "hard copy" of your first draft on paper, double-spaced, and write on it as you always have before, many people prefer editing right on the screen.

At some point, no one knows exactly when, we might say you have arrived at a second "draft." When you are done for now, save it to your hard drive and to a backup floppy disk, either to the same file (so that the first draft is erased), or to a new file in order to keep both. The next day or so, after your mind has processed things while you thought you were only going about your other tasks, come back to it: "retrieve" the file and continue with the new perspectives of a new day.

How many drafts do you need? Usually two or three, if each is revised in depth. This varies, of course, depending on how much time you have and how important the document is. As the previous part of this book suggests, you are done when "your response to a significant topic has become so direct, so exact, so forceful, that at last you know exactly what you think."

4. SOME TECHNIQUES OF EDITING ELECTRONICALLY: If you've been computerized for a while, you might skip this section. If you're new to word processing, though, see below whether there are tools you have not yet used. Try them out, especially late in the writing as you put the final polish on your essay. Learn the keystroke or mouse commands that tell your system, whichever it is, to do these moves:

- Delete a letter backward or forward, delete a word, delete a line or a page.
- Move the cursor word by word forward or backward, or to either end of a line, to the top or bottom of a page, or to the top or bottom of the document.
- Move a passage, or a whole section, to another place without retyping.
- Search a word (for example, if you overuse "and," as most people do,

have the computer show you each "and," so you can decide which to omit or replace with more exact connections).
- Use the speller. (Remember, though, that it catches only misspellings, not wrong words; continue checking to prevent using words like "to" for "too" or "there" for "their.")
- Use the "count" function of your speller at several points during editing, to track gains in conciseness.
- Use the thesaurus often, since it is so fast, bringing alternative word choices to the screen, to find stronger, clearer, shorter or more exact choices.

5. FINAL FORMATTING: With the computer you could have done this at any stage, but now is the time when most people do it — after the work of generating and shaping their thoughts. Now apply the keystroke or mouse commands that tell your system to do the following: select the margins you wish all around, if they are different from your system's default settings; select the "justification" (whether the right side of the text is even, as the left side is); do any special effects such as italics or boldface for emphasis; number the pages; select line spacing (usually double for essays handed in); and select font and size of type.

Though you may have used "draft" mode, which saves time and ink, to print any hard copy used in editing, for your good copy you will select a high quality of print. It is widely believed that a better looking essay makes a better impression on the reader. While we may object to the psychology behind this concept, we cannot ignore it. With today's ink-jet and laser printers, here is one last fact of computing that operates in our favour.

In summary, then, the computer's speed and flexibility help us explore our thoughts, then its many editing tools help us shape and polish those thoughts. Both these acts of writing are at the heart of the process. In fact, the computer may be your best companion on your writing journey.

Going Online

Now that most students are surfing the Web regularly, this edition offers a new feature: in the "Explorations" section after each reading, one or more World Wide Web sites is given for you to explore. Sometimes they lead to more on the author, including a digital photo or even an audio file. Do you want to see Michael Ondaatje's picture, or hear Félix Leclerc sing a verse of one of his songs in French, or see a bibliography of everything David Foot or Dionne Brand has published? Then go right ahead.

Other recommended sites give more on the subject or subjects of the essay. For example, after reading Josh Freed's selection "Say Hi or Die," about the gun culture of California, you are referred to two opposite sites: one for the Violence Policy Center, which lobbies for gun control, and one for the National Rifle Association, which lobbies against it. These are yours to explore, investigating both sides of the issue as you move toward your own stance. Or after reading Anne Michaels on effects of the Holocaust today in Canada, you are referred to a site that features an interactive game: make your choices and see if you, yourself, could "escape" the Holocaust. Or if you have activism on your mind, after reading David Suzuki on saving the environment, try out the David Suzuki Foundation Web site. It connects you by e-mail to politicians, and encourages you to send them a message.

Of course most sites also have links to other sites, which can send you off on even further explorations. And some are collections of links, such as the site given after Brian Maracle's selection about returning to the "rez": through it you could spend days exploring aspects of aboriginal life in North America.

The Web is being used more and more in research for essays, because of its startling proliferation and because sites are so easy to find, using search terms with a search engine. A serious word of caution, though: you have surely realized that some sites are much better than others. The quality varies from dependable and authoritative (as in many Canadian government sites) to average, shoddy, antisocial or even criminal. The Web is the Wild West of communication: people of every social and political persuasion are on it. So are companies, with their own agendas and products to sell. *When you surf, use your critical sense to separate the worthwhile from the worthless.*

If you have not yet gone online, there are many good manuals and guides available, not to mention the advice of your friends. This is not the place for a how-to-do-it manual, especially when things are changing so fast that what we say could be obsolete by the time this book reaches your hands. Also keep in mind that Web sites come and go. By the time you read this book, some sites we have recommended may be out of operation — but, on the other hand, many good new ones may be operating. For this reason, we would like to close this section with a list of some good search engines. Try them out. If a Web site we suggest has disappeared, do a subject matter search instead. If you really like one of our authors, or have a special interest in his or her subject, do a new search of your own. See what's out there!

Some Good Search Engines

AltaVista	http://www.altavista.digital.com/
Excite!	http://www.excite.com/
Infoseek	http://guide.infoseek.com/
Lycos	http://www.lycos.com/
Open Text	http://www.opentext.com/
WebCrawler	http://www.webcrawler.com/

"Many thought the battle of Bejing was over and the people had won. Most expected the army to go home and stop bothering them. Everyone, myself included, forgot one of Mao's most famous quotations: 'Political power grows out of the barrel of a gun.'"

—*Jan Wong, "Safeguard Your Lives"*

CHAPTER

NARRATION

And then. . .

Telling a story, or *narrating*, is an appealing and natural way to convey information. Every time you tell a joke, trade gossip, invent a ghost story or tell a friend what you did on the weekend, you are narrating. In both speech and writing, telling a story can also be the most direct way to make a point. If your idea or opinion was formed by an experience, a clear account of that experience will help others understand and believe your point.

When the army of China murdered students demonstrating for democracy at Tiananmen Square, you were probably not there. But Jan Wong was. In "Safeguard Your Lives," she *narrates* so we can share her experience and her indignation. She tells of the "heavy gunfire" and the "thick black smoke," she tells how the army "shot directly into the crowds who stampeded screaming and cursing down the Avenue of Eternal Peace," and how "the crowd ran away after each heavy volley, then to my amazement crept back slowly, screaming curses and weeping with rage." She tells how a tank "roared to life and mowed down eleven marchers from behind, killing seven instantly." She tells of "bullets whistling past," and of one that hits the balcony from which she watches the scene below. Could Wong have argued better using the points and logic of a standard essay? Would we as easily have seen what a dictatorship is, or understood how deeply its people desire democracy?

Of course narratives don't have to be violent or even dramatic. When Carol Shields in "Encounter" tells of her walk in the rain, sharing an umbrella with a total stranger in Tokyo, we quickly grasp her underlying point that communication is a universal desire.

Narration is such an all-purpose tool that many authors in other chapters of this book use it too. Charles Yale Harrison *narrates* his own life at war ("In the Trenches," p. 119), although his use of description — an important ingredient of many narratives — is so strong that his selection appears in that chapter instead. Read his passage; see how the blast threw him into the air, how the ground heaved, how he breathed the smoke and tasted his own blood. As readers we tend to identify with him, share his experience, understand his point.

Note that many *examples* used by writers are really bits of *narrative*. As Stuart McLean introduces himself and his playful view of life ("The Shocking Truth About Household Dust," p. 153), he tells of lunching with his journalist friends who discuss their interview with the minister of finance, while he is pushing at his salad and thinking of his own articles about the popsicle or the Yo-Yo.

In some ways narrating is easy. The only research Shields required for "Encounter" was her own experience. And her basic plan of organization was no more complicated than the chronological order in which the events occurred. (A flashback to the past or a glance at the future may intervene, but basically a narrative is the easiest of all writing to organize.) Yet a narrative, like any form of writing, is built on choices.

Choice of scope: Time stretches infinitely toward both the past and future — but where does your narrative most logically begin and end? Include only parts that develop your point. Do you need to dwell on getting dressed, eating breakfast, brushing your teeth and catching the bus, on the day you became a Canadian citizen? Or did the event really begin when you opened the courthouse door? When facts about the past or future are needed, sketch them in briefly so you interrupt the least you can.

Choice of details: Which details count? Reject random or trivial ones and seek those that convey your main impression or idea. When on page 38 Sylvia Fraser tells us that "the ice at Gage Park is best in the morning when it's flint-hard and glass-smooth," that "all is possible" and that "you carve out circles and eights, and nothing exists until you put it there," she is not just making small talk as she begins her narrative. Rather, the cool fresh start of skating on new ice prepares a deadly contrast to the rage that later erupts when her "other self" confronts old problems. Which details are most vivid? Reject weak ones and select those that help the reader *see, hear, feel, smell* or *taste* — in other words those which, by appealing to the senses, help readers live the event.

Choice of connections: Readers love to be "swept along" by narrative. How is this effect achieved? Partly just through a good story. Time signals, though, increase the impact of any story. Like road signs for the driver, terms like "at first," "next," "then," "immediately," "suddenly," "later," "finally" and "at last" show the way and encourage progress. Use these road signs, and others like them, at every curve. Choose carefully, so signals speed your reader in the right direction.

So far we have discussed only the first-person narrative. There are many advantages to writing about yourself. You know your subject well (in fact, is there any subject you know better?), yet in writing about yourself you may better understand your own ideas and actions. Your vital interest in your subject will motivate the writing. And finally, readers appreciate the authenticity of a story told by the very person who lived the event.

But of course it's not always possible or desirable to limit the subject to oneself. A third-person narrative, which tells the actions of others, opens up many more possibilities. Only by writing about others can one discuss past eras, places one has never visited, and events one has never experienced. Kildare Dobbs does this masterfully in his narrative "The Scar," on page 322 of a later chapter. He was not in Hiroshima the day it crumbled beneath an atomic blast, but his research and his imagination almost make it seem so; more importantly, reading his narrative almost makes us feel we were there too.

Note: Many authors in later chapters combine narration with other ways to develop their material. For more examples, see these selections:

Carol Shields

Encounter

Carol Shields is one of the nation's brightest literary stars, as well as chancellor at the University of Winnipeg and professor of writing at the University of Manitoba. Born in Illinois in 1935, she became a Canadian citizen in 1971. After earning an M.A. in English from the University of Ottawa in 1975, Shields embarked on a dual career as teacher and writer — while also living life as a wife and mother, a background that has provided the substance of much of her writing. She has published three volumes of poetry, Others *in 1972,* Intersect *in 1974 and* Coming to Canada *in 1992. What has built her reputation, though, is her fiction. Her early novel* Small Ceremonies *(1976) was both a popular and critical success. Others followed, peopled with characters who, while ordinary, are also portrayed as remarkable (Shields once said in an interview, "It's my life's theme — either we're all ordinary, or none of us are"). In 1988 her novel* Swann *won the Arthur Ellis crime writing award, and was then produced as a feature-length film. It is her most recent fiction, though, that has brought Carol Shields worldwide recognition. Her 1993 novel* The Stone Diaries *stunned the critics with its characterization and style, winning the Pulitzer Prize in America and the Governor General's Literary Award in Canada. Many thousands of readers have followed its main character, Daisy Goodwill, through every stage of her life as a woman in her society. Then in 1997 Shields turned her attention to another "ordinary" character, this time a man, in her bestselling novel* Larry's Party. *Our own selection, published 1994 in Katherine Govier's anthology* Without a Guide: Contemporary Women's Travel Adventures, *is autobiography — yet is, as always, focussed on the ordinary things of life which in the vision of Carol Shields become remarkable.*

1   I was in Tokyo to attend a conference, one of a thousand or so delegates—and that probably was my problem: the plasticized name card and the logo of my organization marked me as someone who desired only to be cheerfully accommodated.

2   The allotted two weeks had passed. A single day in Japan remained, and at last I admitted to myself that I was disappointed. The terrible banality of tourist desire invaded me like a kind of flu. Walking the broad, busy boulevards, I caught myself looking too eagerly, too pre-

ciously, for minor cultural manifestations — the charming way the bank teller bowed when presenting me with my bundle of cash, the colourful plastic food in the windows of restaurants; these were items I was able to record in my travel journal, touching them up in the way of desperate travellers, shaping them into humorous or appreciative annotation on the Japanese people and the exotic city they inhabited.

But Tokyo with its hotels and subways and department stores was a modern industrial complex. Its citizens went to work in the morning, earned money, and travelled home again at night. These homes, to be sure, were impenetrable to me, but the busy working days bore the same rhythms as those found in any large North American city. The traffic noises, the scent of pollution, and the civility of people in the street made me think of — home.

I had hoped for more; what traveller doesn't? Travelling is expensive, exhausting, and often lonely — the cultural confusion, the acres of concrete, the bitter coffee, the unreadable maps, and the rates of exchange that are almost always unfavourable. And then, like a punishment at the end of the traveller's day, there waits a solitary room, and a bed that, however comfortable, is not your bed. What makes all this worth the effort is the shock of otherness that arrives from time to time, rattling loose your bearings and making you suddenly alert to an altered world. But Tokyo was determinedly polite, fulsomely western, a city with a bland, smiling face, ready to welcome me not on its terms but on my own.

I already know that the banquet that was to conclude the conference would be a model of French cuisine. Seven courses, seven different wines. No rice, no noodles, no sushi, no hot radish. It was to be held at the famous Imperial Hotel, which was fifteen or twenty minutes' walk from the somewhat less expensive hotel where I was staying.

I started out in good time. It was a soft spring evening, and the thought of a leisurely stroll was appealing. I would be able to look around one last time, breathe in a final impression that I could perhaps test against my accumulated disappointment, acquiring some fresh point of perception with which to colour and preserve my Japanese sojourn.

At that moment it began to rain. A few drops at first, then it came down in earnest, spotting the silk dinner suit I was wearing and threatening to flatten my carefully arranged hair. I looked about for a taxi or a roof to shelter under, but neither presented itself. The only thing to do, I decided, was to run as quickly as I could the rest of the way.

But a tall man was standing directly in front of me, a man with an umbrella. He was smiling tentatively, and gesturing, and his mouth was moving. But what was he saying? I wasn't sure, since the accent was unfamiliar, but it sounded like "Imperial Hotel?" With a question mark behind it. "Yes," I said, nodding and speaking with great deliberation, "Imperial Hotel," and at that he lifted his umbrella slightly, and invited me under.

9   The umbrella was large and black, resolutely standard, the sort of umbrella found in every city or backwater of the world. "Thank you," I said in Japanese — the only phrase I had mastered — but he only repeated what he had said earlier: "Imperial Hotel?" And tipped his head quizzically in an eastward direction. "Yes," I said again. And we began walking.

10   It seemed only polite to make an effort at conversation. Where was he from? Was he with the conference? Was he a stranger in Japan like myself? He shook his head, uncomprehending, and released a shower of words in an unidentifiable language. Now it was my turn to shake my head. After that, smiling, we continued our walk in a contained silence, as though we had each admitted to the other that language was absurd, that rhetoric was a laughable formality that could be set aside for this brief interval.

11   Suddenly careless of social taboos, and because it's difficult for a short woman to walk with a tall man under an umbrella, I took the stranger's arm. (Thinking about this later, I theorized that he must have gestured minutely with his elbow, inviting my intimacy.) Now, arms linked, we were able to walk together smoothly, stepping over and around the puddles without losing our stride, pausing at traffic lights, stepping down from curbs.

12   We had arrived quickly at our congenial gliding pace, left foot, right foot, left foot again, a forward rhythm with a very slight sideways roll like a kind of swimming. Our mutually constrained tongues, the sound of the pelting rain, and our random possession of a random moment in time, seemed to seal us in a temporary vacuum that had nothing to do with Japan, nor with gender or age or with Hollywood notions about men and women walking in the rain. This was good walking, though, I knew that much — walking that transcended mere movement. Hypnotic walking. Walking toward the unimaginable. And I found myself wanting it to go on and on.

13   But there we suddenly were, at the brilliantly lit entrance of the Imperial Hotel, caught in a throng of people arriving and departing, people who had come from every corner of the globe, and trailing after them their separate languages, their lives, their ribbons of chance connection. The stranger with the umbrella abruptly disappeared. I looked around for him but was unable to recall his face, how he had been dressed. One minute he was there and the next minute he'd vanished, leaving me alone with that primary shiver of mystery that travellers, if they're lucky, hope to hang on to: the shock of the known and the unknown colliding in space.

∆ ∆

Explorations:

Carol Shields,
>*The Stone Diaries*
>*Larry's Party*
>*Swann*
>*Small Ceremonies*

http://www.mwsolutions.com/canlit/authors/shields.asp

Structure:

1. This *narrative* is really two in one: a summary of the author's stay in Tokyo so far, then a real-time narrative of her "encounter" with the stranger. How does the first prepare us for the second? Where does the first end and the second begin? Which of the two phases of *narrative* is more powerful, and why?
2. How does Shields' two-part structure of *narrative* exploit the device of *contrast?*

Style:

1. Carol Shields is one of the nation's best-loved novelists. Does this nonfiction selection seem at all in the vein of fiction? If so, how?
2. Does Shields' STYLE excite admiration, or is it more like a clear window that shows us the events? Which approach do you prefer when you read? When you write? Why?
3. Point out the best FIGURES OF SPEECH in paragraph 12. Also analyze the power of the images that close this selection.

Ideas for Discussion and Writing:

1. "Encounter" narrates a small event — two strangers sharing an umbrella. In what ways, though, may this event be larger than it seems? What truths may it reveal about our lives in general?
2. Writers often seek sensational topics such as disaster, murder, adventure and romance. Were you attracted, though, by Shields' modest tale of "walking toward the unimaginable" (par. 12) with a stranger? If so, what does this show about focus and development in writing?
3. The two strangers of "Encounter" are thrown together by rain. When have you had close communication with strangers through events such as floods or earthquakes; ice, rain or snow storms; accidents; or power blackouts? *Narrate* a story to the class. What does it show about life?
4. Shields discovers "the terrible banality of tourist desire" (par. 2) in a far place which turns out to be "fulsomely western, a city with a

bland, smiling face, ready to welcome me not on its terms but on my own" (par. 4). Why do we become tourists? Why do we seek far places? Are they disappearing? If so, why?

5. Can you communicate, as Shields did, with people who do not speak your language? If your family has immigrated, can your own grandparents speak your language? Suggest techniques to the class.

6. **PROCESS IN WRITING:** *Shields' closing words describe the mystery that travellers seek, "the shock of the known and the unknown colliding in space." Freewrite on this topic for at least five minutes, never stopping the movement of your pen or keyboard, remembering a time when you felt this "shock." Let your words cool off for at least a day, then write the quick discovery draft of a* narrative *based on them. Let it cool off too. Now take stock: Does your introduction prepare us for the story? If not, add. Have you described the persons and the place well enough to help us live the story too? If not, add* SENSE IMAGES. *Do* TRANSITIONS *speed us on? If not, add. And does the action sweep us towards a* CLIMAX? *If not, rearrange. Last of all, check for spelling and punctuation before you print out your best version.*

Note: See also the Topics for Writing at the end of this chapter.

George Gabori

Coming of Age in Putnok

Translated from the Hungarian by Eric Johnson with George Faludy

For much of his life George Gabori (1924–1997) drove taxi and ran a cab company in Toronto. Like many immigrants to this country, though, he had a past he would never forget. Gabori (pronounced Gábori) was born to a Jewish family in the village of Putnok, Hungary. His childhood was happy but short, for when the Germans occupied Hungary and threatened the existence of the Jews, he joined the resistance. He led daring sabotage raids, blowing up German trains, till the Gestapo sent him, still a teenager, to a concentration camp. When later the Russians drove out the Germans, Gabori was as troublesome for the communists as he had been for the Nazis: soon after his release from Dachau, he was breaking rocks in a notorious Soviet labour camp. Always outspoken in favour of democracy, Gabori played a part in the 1956 revolution, then escaped from Hungary to Canada, a "decent land," where years later he wrote his memoirs in Hungarian. With the help of Hungarian poet George Faludy, Eric Johnson condensed and translated the enormous manuscript, and in 1981 it was published. Since then, When Evils Were Most Free *has become a minor Canadian classic and has been translated into a score of other languages. Our selection is its opening passage.*

When I was nine years old my father, victorious after a long argu- 1
ment with my grandfather, took me out of our town's only *cheder* and enrolled me in its only public school. Overnight I was transported from the world of Hebrew letters and monotonously repeated texts to the still stranger world of Hungarian letters, patriotic slogans and walls covered with maps.

Grandfather rolled his eyes and predicted trouble, but it seemed he 2
was wrong. I sat beside a boy my own age named Tivadar, a gentile — everybody was a gentile in that school except me. Tivadar and I got along famously until, after two or three weeks, he approached me in the schoolyard one day and asked me if it was true what the others were saying, that "we" had murdered Jesus.

Strange to tell — for this was 1933 and we were in Hungary — I had 3
never heard about this historical episode, and I left Tivadar amicably

31

enough, promising to ask my father about it. We met again the next morning and I told him what I had learned: that the Romans had killed Jesus, and that anyway Jesus had been a Jew, like me, so what did it matter to the Christians?

4   "That's not true," said Tivadar menacingly.

5   "My father does not lie," I replied.

6   By now a crowd had gathered around us and there was nothing for it but to fight it out. There were cheers and laughter as Tivadar hit me in the nose before I got my jacket off. It was not the first time I had tasted my own blood, but it was the first time a Christian had made it flow. Tivadar was flushed with pleasure and excitement at the applause and not at all expecting it when I lashed out with my fist and sent him sprawling backward on the cobbles. The crowd of boys groaned and shouted to Tivadar to get up and kill the Jew, but poor Tivadar did not move. Frightened, I grabbed my jacket and shoved my way through the crowd stunned into silence by this overturning of the laws of nature.

7   They were silent at home too when I told them what had happened. My father sent for me from his office in the afternoon, and I entered cap in hand. He always wore a braided Slovak jacket at work and looked more like a peasant than a Jewish wine merchant.

8   "Well, who started it?" asked my father, wearing an expression I had never seen on his face before. I was not at all frightened.

9   "He did. I told him what you said about Jesus and he challenged me."

10   My father clamped his teeth on his cigar and nodded, looking right through me.

11   "Jews don't fight," he finally said.

12   "Then why did you put me in a Christian school?" I asked in a loud, outraged whine.

13   "That's why I put you there, my son," he said at last, then swept me up and kissed me on the forehead. "You're learning fast; only next time don't hit him quite so hard."

14   Then he sent me out quickly and I stopped on the landing, startled to hear loud, whooping, solitary laughter coming out of my father's office.

△△△

Explorations:

George Gabori, *When Evils Were Most Free*
George Faludy, *My Happy Days in Hell*
Adam Horvath, "Lives Lived: George Gabori," *The Globe and Mail*, December 7, 1997
Anne Frank, *The Diary of Anne Frank*

Anne Michaels, *Fugitive Pieces*
http://www.holocaustcenter.org/lifechance/lit51.shtml

Structure:

1. What overall pattern organizes this selection?
2. Point out at least ten words or phrases in this *narrative* that signal the flow of time.
3. Scrutinize Gabori's opening paragraph: has he prepared us for the selection? Name every fact revealed about the setting and about the author.

Style:

1. How economical of words is this opening passage of Gabori's life story? How clearly does it reveal the author and his times? Would you predict with any confidence his character or fate as an adult? Do these pages tempt you to read the whole book? Why or why not?
2. *When Evils Were Most Free* is translated and condensed from the Hungarian original. Does this act separate us from Gabori's thoughts? How exact can translations be? If you are bilingual or multilingual, how precisely can you put sayings from one language into another? Can translator Eric Johnson even be seen as a co-author of these pages?
3. In paragraph 6 Gabori states, "It was not the first time I had tasted my own blood. . . ." What makes this image strong?

Ideas for Discussion and Writing:

1. What exactly is the "overturning of the laws of nature" at the end of paragraph 6?
2. Was Gabori's father right to move the boy from a Hebrew *cheder* to a public school? In disproving the STEREOTYPE that "Jews don't fight" (par. 11), has the boy learned a worthy lesson? Or does he merely copy the worst traits of his opponents, thereby becoming like them?
3. Every ethnic group in Canada — including English Canadians — is a minority. Has your minority been persecuted here? If you have been a victim, *narrate* an actual incident, including your own reaction. Like Gabori, give many specifics.
4. What are autobiographies for? What do you think writing your own life story would do for you? For others?
5. **PROCESS IN WRITING:** *Write a chapter of your own autobiography. Select one key incident in your life, then freewrite on it for a few minutes.*

Look over what you have produced, keep the best of it, and from this write your first draft. Have you begun and ended at just the right places, narrating *the event itself but omitting parts that don't matter? Enrich the next draft with more* IMAGES *and examples, following Gabori's lead. Now share your* narrative *with a group of classmates, and adjust whatever does not communicate with this* AUDIENCE. *Finally, read your narrative aloud, with expression, to the whole class.*

Note: See also the Topics for Writing at the end of this chapter.

Marie Gagnon

Shelter*

Translated from the French by Ronald Conrad

Born in 1966 to a middle-class family in a Montreal suburb, Marie Gagnon showed early sensitivity to words and dreams. Then after her studies at l'UQAM (the University of Quebec at Montreal), she lived a time of revolt that took her to the street. There she became a heroin addict, spending several years with the friend who in her memoir she calls "The Prince," and refers to also as "le philosophe des philosophes" — the philosopher of philosophers. As she and her companion experienced hunger, illness, time in hospitals, and the dangers of street life, Gagnon developed her very specialized approach to shoplifting: she learned to steal books, only the best ones, and sometimes even books on commission, to resell and support her heroin habit. Her time in prison followed, during which she wrote the vivid memoir that was published in 1997 as Bienvenue dans mon cauchemar *(Welcome to My Nightmare). It is a collection of poems, journal entries, memories and perceptions as Gagnon attempts to reconcile her previous life with her life behind bars. As the Montreal newspaper* Le Devoir *put it, Gagnon had moved from stealing books to writing them.*

I dreamed about our life on the street. We were cold and hungry. My toes had lost their nails, and the deep snow made walking hard. Sick and broke, we were looking for shelter. The Prince° could no longer stand. Shaken by a dry cough, he advanced bent over, as if hit in the stomach. We had no place to stay, no hope of help, and the police were after us. Just now we had been chased from an apartment building, where for a few minutes under the stairs of the fire escape we had warmed ourselves in each other's arms.

Then suddenly it appeared, imposing and beautiful in the storm. Its steeple was lost in the sky and its portal floated as if suspended. For a moment I saw angels and heard the organ. It warmed me inside. The Prince was at the end of his strength, but, gripping his arm, I made him

---

* Translator's title.
° The Prince: Gagnon's name for her long-time companion, also a heroin addict.

follow me. When he saw where our steps were leading he tried to turn back, but I held fast. Finally he struggled no more, and followed me right to the bottom of the stairs, where he collapsed. I began to run up the stairs. Hope had made me light, airy, serene. I threw myself against the door, but it resisted my push. Today even the temples are closed to misery. Facing the portal, enraged, I howled in the night, betrayed and abandoned. Below, the wasted body of The Prince made a dark spot in the snow, and his moans joined those of the wind.

Back at his side, I put my coat over his shoulders and helped him up. Without looking back, we resumed our search for shelter.

△△

Explorations:

Marie Gagnon, *Bienvenue dans mon cauchemar* (available only in French)
Evelyn Lau, *Diary of a Runaway* (memoir)
George Orwell, *Down and Out in Paris and London* (memoir)
Samuel Beckett, *Waiting for Godot* (theatre)
http://csf.colorado.edu/homeless/index.html

Structure:

1. "Shelter" is one of the shortest pieces in this anthology. Is it long enough to make its point? Does it give enough detail to become more than summary? Does it give a "picture" of Gagnon's life on the street?
2. As a *narrative,* is "Shelter" developed through pure *chronology*? Does it ever stray from straight time order?
3. Point out at least five words or expressions of TRANSITION that speed Gagnon's *narrative.*

Style:

1. In the way it is told, does "Shelter" resemble the dreams you have? How? Or when Gagnon says "I dreamed about our life on the street," do you take "dreamed" in the sense of "thought" or "remembered"? Give reasons for your view.
2. Here is the first paragraph of our selection in the original French:

> **J'ai rêvé à l'époque où nous vivions la rue. Nous avions froid et faim. Mes orteils n'avaient plus d'ongles et je marchais difficilement dans la neige épaisse. Nous étions malades et sans argent, à la recherche d'un refuge. Le Prince ne tenait plus sur ses jambes. Secoué par une toux sèche, il avançait**

plié en deux, comme frappé en plein ventre. Nous n'avions pas de gîte, n'espérions aucun secours et la police était à nos trousses. Peu avant, on nous avait chassés d'un immeuble à logements où, quelques minutes durant, nous avions pu nous réchauffer, enlacés sous l'escalier de secours.

Can you read this? If so, is the translation an exact equivalent, or does the English have to put some things another way? To what extent does the translator have to collaborate, even become a co-author, with the writer?

If you have taken French in school but still can't read the above, give all the reasons why. To really master French, what will you have to do now?

While surfing the Web, have you tried the translation function from a site in another language? How good was the text in English? Describe the results.

Ideas for Discussion and Writing:

1. Does it surprise you that a convict in prison can write a book? That she can write well and poetically?
2. The door of the church is locked. Was Gagnon right to be surprised? Do you know of churches in your town or city that do provide winter shelter for the homeless, or are their doors locked too? Argue for or against their policy.
3. How do you respond to street people where you live? Do you give? Do you buy street weekly newspapers from them? Do you talk? Why or why not?
4. **PROCESS IN WRITING:** *Rewrite Marie Gagnon's narrative, still in first person, but this time with the church door open. From that point on, give your vision of how the event would progress. Like Gagnon, supply many IMAGES to help your reader experience homelessness, and speed the flow of time through TRANSITION SIGNALS. Read your final version aloud, with feeling, to the class.*

Note: See also the Topics for Writing at the end of this chapter.

Sylvia Fraser

My Other Self[*]

*"Writing is healing," says Sylvia Fraser. Born in 1935 in Hamilton, Ontario, Fraser by the 1980s had become an award-winning journalist and the author of five novels (*Pandora, *1972;* The Candy Factory, *1975;* A Casual Affair, *1978;* The Emperor's Virgin, *1980; and* Berlin Solstice, *1984). But signs of trouble had also appeared. Her seemingly happy marriage had fallen apart. Her fiction grew darker in vision and increasingly filled with sexual violence. Then the dam broke. Psychotherapy uncovered what Fraser's "other self" had known for decades: that from her kindergarten year until almost the end of high school, her father had abused her sexually. Now it was clear how her novel* Berlin Solstice *had acquired its intimate and chilling insight into Nazi Germany. As Fraser put it, "Being victimized and essentially tortured by my father, I identified with the Jews. In trying to understand how the Germans could have done what they did, I was trying to understand my father — and I was preparing myself for my own truth" (*The Globe and Mail, *June 4, 1988). The memoir that followed,* My Father's House *(1987), startled both the critics and the public with its honesty, clarity of style and emotional force. The book not only helped to "heal" its author, but ignited public debate on a hidden social problem, encouraging many other incest victims to deal with their past. From this book comes our selection, which dramatizes the victim's "other self" trying to emerge. In 1995* My Father's House *was adopted for theatre and performed in Toronto. Then in 1996 Fraser published two more books,* The Quest for the Fourth Monkey, *an examination of spiritual and paranormal events in her life, and* Ancestral Suitcase, *a novel.*

1   The ice at Gage Park is best in the morning when it's flint-hard and glass-smooth. All is possible. You carve out circles and eights, and nothing exists until you put it there. Sometimes you just race around the rink, your legs sliding like they're on elastic bands, with your breath whistling through your teeth like steam from a locomotive, faster and faster.

2   Soon it's noon. The rink fills with kids in red and blue parkas playing tag or crack the whip.

---

* Editor's title.

"Hi!" It's Joe Baker from school. "Wanna skate?"   3

I prefer to play tag, but I don't want to hurt Joe's feelings and,   4
besides, if I say no to him, maybe Perry Lord won't ask me. Such
delicate weights and balances are the stuff of predating, as I am coming
to know it. Giving my hand to Joe with a bright paste-on smile, I slow
my racing pace to his stodgy rhythm. The sound system squawks out
"Oh, How We Danced on the Night We Were Wed" as we skate around
and around, like the needle on the record. Joe's silence rattles me. I
make chattery conversation. "Did you see The Thing from the Deep?"

By bad luck, the record never ends. The needle hits a crack, repeats   5
"we vowed our true love we vowed our true love we vowed our true
love," then jerks into "Don't Fence Me In." Now Joe links arms, forcing
me to even greater intimacy and an even slower beat, *and making my
other self very, very nervous. She cannot bear to be held or confined.* The game
of tag is breaking up. Joe speaks his only sentence, and it is a lethal one.
"Can I ah take you home if ah you're not doing anything?"

At the word "home" a cold shiver passes through me. I ransack my   6
head for an explanation for the unpleasant way I am feeling and, fail-
ing that, an excuse. "I'll check with Arlene. We came together."

The clubhouse is crowded and noisy and steamy, as always. We jostle   7
for a place on the splintery benches closest to the wood stove. The air
stinks of charred wool — someone's icy mittens left too long on top.
Joe helps me off with my skates, then unlaces his own while I inform
Arlene. "Joe wants to take me home."

"He's cute. You have all the luck."   8

I study Joe through the lens of Arlene's enthusiasm: brown cowlick in   9
wet spikes from his cap, earnest face bent over the task of knotting
skate laces. Cute? Now that I know how I'm supposed to feel, I am
reassured. Well, maybe.

We leave the rink just as the gang takes off in a gossipy pinwheel for   10
the Kozy Korner. I think about suggesting we go too, but I'm afraid Joe
doesn't have any money and I don't want to seem like a gold digger.
Perry Lord tosses a snowball at Cooky Castle but hits Arlene instead.
Tonya Philpott zings one back overhand, the way a boy would. I yearn
to take up the challenge, but being with a boy obliges me to conform to
more ladylike standards. Trapped, I stick my fists in my pockets.

Crunch crunch crunch. Skates knotted over Joe's shoulder, we trudge   11
through the chalky snow. I've already told Joe the plot of The Thing
from the Deep, and since I saw it uptown it wasn't a double feature.
The silence lengthens with the shadows. Joe doesn't seem to mind. I
do.

"Arlene says you got a hundred in arithmetic."   12
"Yeah. So did you."   13
"Yeah. But our test was easier."   14

15 I make the mistake of taking my hand out of my pocket to brush a snowflake. Joe commandeers it. *My other self panics.* How long before I can brush another snowflake and get it back without seeming rude? As I am working out the etiquette of this, two dogs rush the season by attempting to "do it" on the path in front of us. *My other self slips toward hysteria.* I burst into giggles. The blood rises up Joe's protruding ears. He fumbles with his backside: "Are you laughing at the rip in my ski pants?"

16 "No, it isn't that." But I can't stop giggling.

17 "Joker Nash cut it with his skate."

18 "Honest, I didn't even notice." I stifle more giggles in a sneeze. "Ah-choo!"

19 We are approaching my house. The giggles stop. Now my anxiety grows so intense I'm afraid I'll faint. Snatching my hand from Joe's, I pick up a stick and drag it ping ping ping along the fence around St. Cecilia's Home the way I used to as a kid, pretending this is the most important thing in the world. How can I let you hold my hand when I am busy doing this?

20 We turn the corner. Now I see it — a sour-cream frame listing with snow like a milk bottle with the cap frozen off. *Home.* I stop, rooted to the spot. For reasons I can't explain, it's essential that Joe go no farther. I reach for my skates. "I live only a couple of doors away."

21 "I don't mind. I'll carry them to the —"

22 "No!" I yank the skates from Joe's neck, almost beheading him. "I've got to go — by myself."

23 Again Joe blushes from his neck through his ears. "Is it because of the rip in my ski pants? You don't want your parents to see — "

24 "No!" Then more humanely: "Honest. It has nothing to do with you." Pushing past him, I sprint for my father's house, clearing the steps in a single bound. As I open the storm door, the wind catches it.

25 "Don't slam the door!" roars my father from his armchair.

26 *My other self bursts into hysterical weeping.*

27 "What's wrong?" asks my mother.

28 Again, I find myself overcome by an emotion for which I must find a reason. Hurling my skates at her feet, I shout: "Why do I have to wear these old things? They hurt my feet."

29 Wiping her hands on her apron, my mother rallies. "Those skates were new last winter."

30 "Secondhand from Amity. You said I could have new skates for Christmas."

31 "You needed other things." By now I'm racked with weeping I can't control. Not about the skates, though I hear a voice I hardly recognize go on and on about them. "I hate these skates." Rage pours out of me

like lava, devastating everything in its path. It flows around my father, implacable in his asbestos armchair.

It's a relief to be sent upstairs without supper. Flinging myself onto   32
my bed, I pound the pillow till my body is seized with convulsions, *releasing the rage my other self can no longer control.*

△ △

Explorations:

Sylvia Fraser,
>   *My Father's House*
>   *Pandora*
>   *The Ancestral Suitcase*
>   *The Quest for the Fourth Monkey*

Ruth Kempe, *The Common Secret: Sexual Abuse of Children and Adolescents*
Judy Steed, *Our Little Secret: Confronting Child Sexual Abuse in Canada*
http://www.edu.yorku.ca/~wier/sfraser.html

Structure:

1. Does Fraser *narrate* "My Other Self" in straight chronological order?
2. This sequence begins with ice (par. 1) and closes with lava (par. 31). Explain how Fraser's progression of IMAGES parallels her progression of emotion. How do these progressions add force to her narrative?
3. What does Fraser achieve by putting all references to her "other self" in italics?

Style:

1. If the events on these pages occurred when Fraser was young, why does she narrate in the present tense? Would "My Other Self" have been stronger or weaker in the past tense? Why?
2. Where does Fraser use IMAGES that appeal to our senses of sight, touch, hearing and smell? Point out one of each.
3. In paragraph 9 our narrator says, "I study Joe through the lens of Arlene's enthusiasm. . . ." Point out two more METAPHORS in this selection. In paragraph 31 she says, "Rage pours out of me like lava . . . ." Point out two more SIMILES. What do these FIGURES OF SPEECH contribute to the total effect?

Ideas for Discussion and Writing:

1. Fraser stated in an interview, "I think of child abuse as being the AIDS of the emotional world. You cripple that child's emotional system so it can't deal with life" (*The Globe and Mail,* June 4, 1988). Point out all the ways in which our selection dramatizes her comment.

2. Why does Fraser refer to her "other self" in the third person as "she"? What does this usage seem to imply about young Fraser's mental state?

3. Some studies suggest that sexual abuse is an epidemic, with as many as one of every three or four children victimized. The place of these offences has ranged from the family, to the hockey arena, to the orphanage, and to the residential schools to which in past times First Nations children were sent. What could be done to decrease such crimes? To rehabilitate the victims? To rehabilitate the offenders?

4. Fraser traces her fascination with the Holocaust to her feelings about her father (see the introduction to this selection). How fully does our relationship to our parents become a model for our relationship to the world? For example, do children of authoritarian parents grow up to resent authority in the form of employers or government?

5. Have you shared Fraser's experience of writing as healing? Analyze how the process might occur when we write an angry letter to tear up, when we send a letter to the editor, when we write a poem, or when we keep a personal journal.

6. **PROCESS IN WRITING:** *Think of a time when you got carried away by your own emotions. Experience it again by freewriting, never stopping the motion of your pen or keyboard for several minutes. Use the present tense, as Fraser does, to heighten the immediacy of your account. Now narrate a first draft, incorporating the best of your prewriting. In the next draft add more SENSE IMAGES and FIGURES OF SPEECH (remembering the "ice" and "lava" of "My Other Self"). Have you moved the action along with time signals such as "then," "next," "suddenly" or "at last"? Have you trimmed out deadwood? If you report dialogue, have you used quotation marks, and have you begun a new paragraph for each change of speaker? Finally, test your prose aloud before writing the final version.*

Note: See also the Topics for Writing at the end of this chapter.

Carol Geddes

Growing Up Native

Since Carol Geddes tells her own life story in the narrative that follows, there is no need to repeat it all here. Born into the security of her Tlingit First Nations family in the wilds of the Yukon, she was six when she first knew her country's majority culture and began to see the problems it can make for Native people. Since then she has spent her life integrating these two worlds. She celebrates the current "renaissance" of interest in Native culture, yet also values the rest of North American life. "We need our culture," she writes, "but there's no reason why we can't preserve it and have an automatic washing machine and a holiday in Mexico, as well." Hers is a success story. Despite the obstacles, she completed a university degree in English and philosophy, did graduate studies in communications at McGill, and is today a successful filmmaker and spokesperson for her people. In addition to her films Doctor, Lawyer, Indian Chief *and* Place for Our People, *she has produced at least twenty videos on the lives and culture of aboriginal people in Canada. Geddes has been Director of the Yukon Human Rights Commission, and is the first Northerner and first Native person to serve as Director of the Canada Council. In her spare time she does wilderness hiking and fishing in the Yukon where she lives. Our selection, from* Homemaker's *magazine of October 1990, won the National Magazine Awards Foundation Silver Award.*

I remember it was cold. We were walking through a swamp near our home in the Yukon bush. Maybe it was fall and moose-hunting season. I don't know. I think I was about four years old at the time. The muskeg was too springy to walk on, so people were taking turns carrying me — passing me from one set of arms to another. The details about where we were are vague, but the memory of those arms and the feeling of acceptance I had is one of the most vivid memories of my childhood. It didn't matter who was carrying me — there was security in every pair of arms. That response to children is typical of the native community. It's the first thing I think of when I cast my mind back to the Yukon bush, where I was born and lived with my family.

I was six years old when we moved out of the bush, first to Teslin, where I had a hint of the problems native people face, then to Whitehorse, where there was unimaginable racism. Eventually I moved

43

to Ottawa and Montreal, where I further discovered that to grow up native in Canada is to feel the sting of humiliation and the boot of discrimination. But it is also to experience the enviable security of an extended family and to learn to appreciate the richness of the heritage and traditions of a culture most North Americans have never been lucky enough to know. As a film-maker, I have tried to explore these contradictions, and our triumph over them, for the half-million aboriginals who are part of the tide of swelling independence of the First Nations today.

3   But I'm getting ahead of myself. If I'm to tell the story of what it's like to grow up native in northern Canada, I have to go back to the bush where I was born, because there's more to my story than the hurtful stereotyping that depicts Indian people as drunken welfare cases. Our area was known as 12-mile (it was 12 miles from another tiny village). There were about 40 people living there — including 25 kids, eight of them my brothers and sisters — in a sort of family compound. Each family had its own timber plank house for sleeping, and there was one large common kitchen area with gravel on the ground and a tent frame over it. Everybody would go there and cook meals together. In summer, my grandmother always had a smudge fire going to smoke fish and tan moose hides. I can remember the cosy warmth of the fire, the smell of good food, and always having someone to talk to. We kids had built-in playmates and would spend hours running in the bush, picking berries, building rafts on the lake and playing in abandoned mink cages.

4   One of the people in my village tells a story about the day the old lifestyle began to change. He had been away hunting in the bush for about a month. On his way back, he heard a strange sound coming from far away. He ran up to the crest of a hill, looked over the top of it and saw a bulldozer. He had never seen or heard of such a thing before and he couldn't imagine what it was. We didn't have magazines or newspapers in our village, and the people didn't know that the Alaska Highway was being built as a defence against a presumed Japanese invasion during the Second World War. That was the beginning of the end of the Teslin Tlingit people's way of life. From that moment on, nothing turned back to the way it was. Although there were employment opportunities for my father and uncles, who were young men at the time, the speed and force with which the Alaska Highway was rammed through the wilderness caused tremendous upheaval for Yukon native people.

5   It wasn't as though we'd never experienced change before. The Tlingit Nation, which I belong to, arrived in the Yukon from the Alaskan coast around the turn of the century. They were the middlemen and women between the Russian traders and the Yukon inland Indians. The Tlingit

gained power and prestige by trading European products such as metal goods and cloth for the rich and varied furs so much in fashion in Europe. The Tlingit controlled Yukon trading because they controlled the trading routes through the high mountain passes. When trading ceased to be an effective means of survival, my grandparents began raising wild mink in cages. Mink prices were really high before and during the war, but afterwards the prices went plunging down. So, although the mink pens were still there when I was a little girl, my father mainly worked on highway construction and hunted in the bush. The Yukon was then, and still is in some ways, in a transitional period — from living off the land to getting into a European wage-based economy.

As a young child, I didn't see the full extent of the upheaval. I [6] remember a lot of togetherness, a lot of happiness while we lived in the bush. There's a very strong sense of family in the native community, and a fondness for children, especially young children. Even today, it's like a special form of entertainment if someone brings a baby to visit. That sense of family is the one thing that has survived all the incredible difficulties native people have had. Throughout a time of tremendous problems, the extended family system has somehow lasted, providing a strong circle for people to survive in. When parents were struggling with alcoholism or had to go away to find work, when one of the many epidemics swept through the community, or when a marriage broke up and one parent left, aunts, uncles and grandparents would try to fill those roles. It's been very important to me in terms of emotional support to be able to rely on my extended family. There are still times when such support keeps me going.

Life was much simpler when we lived in the bush. Although we were [7] poor and wore the same clothes all year, we were warm enough and had plenty to eat. But even as a youngster, I began to be aware of some of the problems we would face later on. Travelling missionaries would come and impose themselves on us, for example. They'd sit at our campfire and read the Bible to us and lecture us about how we had to live a Christian life. I remember being very frightened by stories we heard about parents sending their kids away to live with white people who didn't have any children. We thought those people were mean and that if we were bad, we'd be sent away, too. Of course, that was when social workers were scooping up native children and adopting them out to white families in the south. The consequences were usually disastrous for the children who were taken away — alienation, alcoholism and suicide, among other things. I knew some of those kids. The survivors are still struggling to recover.

The residential schools were another source of misery for the kids. [8] Although I didn't have to go, my brothers and sisters were there. They told stories about having their hair cut off in case they were carrying head lice, and of being forced to do hard chores without enough food to eat. They were told that the Indian culture was evil, that Indian people were bad, that their only hope was to be Christian. They had to stand up and say things like "I've found the Lord," when a teacher told them to speak. Sexual abuse was rampant in the residential school system.

9   By the time we moved to Whitehorse, I was excited about the idea of living in what I thought of as a big town. I'd had a taste of the outside world from books at school in Teslin (a town of 250 people), and I was tremendously curious about what life was like. I was hungry for experiences such as going to the circus. In fact, for a while, I was obsessed with stories and pictures about the circus, but then when I was 12 and saw my first one, I was put off by the condition and treatment of the animals.

10   Going to school in Whitehorse was a shock. The clash of native and white values was confusing and frightening. Let me tell you a story. The older boys in our community were already accomplished hunters and fishermen, but since they had to trap beaver in the spring and hunt moose in the fall, and go out trapping in the winter as well, they missed a lot of school. We were all in one classroom and some of my very large teenage cousins had to sit squeezed into little desks. These guys couldn't read very well. We girls had been in school all along, so, of course, we were better readers. One day the teacher was trying to get one of the older boys to read. She was typical of the teachers at that time, insensitive and ignorant of cultural complexities. In an increasingly loud voice, she kept commanding him to "Read it, read it." He couldn't. He sat there completely still, but I could see that he was breaking into a sweat. The teacher then said, "Look, she can read it," and she pointed to me, indicating that I should stand up and read. For a young child to try to show up an older boy is wrong and totally contrary to native cultural values, so I refused. She told me to stand up and I did. My hands were trembling as I held my reader. She yelled at me to read and when I didn't she smashed her pointing stick on the desk to frighten me. In terror, I wet my pants. As I stood there fighting my tears of shame, she said I was disgusting and sent me home. I had to walk a long distance through the bush by myself to get home. I remember feeling this tremendous confusion, on top of my humiliation. We were always told the white teachers knew best, and so we had to do whatever they said at school. And yet I had a really strong sense of receiving mixed messages about what I was supposed to do in the community and what I was supposed to do at school.

11   Pretty soon I hated school. Moving to a predominantly white high school was even worse. We weren't allowed to join anything the white

kids started. We were the butt of jokes because of our secondhand clothes and moose meat sandwiches. We were constantly being rejected. The prevailing attitude was that Indians were stupid. When it was time to make course choices in class — between typing and science, for example — they didn't even ask the native kids, they just put us all in typing. You get a really bad image of yourself in a situation like that. I bought into it. I thought we were awful. The whole experience was terribly undermining. Once, my grandmother gave me a pretty little pencil box. I walked into the classroom one day to find the word "squaw" carved on it. That night I burned it in the wood stove. I joined the tough crowd and by the time I was 15 years old, I was more likely to be leaning against the school smoking a cigarette than trying to join in. I was burned out from trying to join the system. The principal told my father there was no point in sending me back to school so, with a Grade 9 education, I started to work at a series of menial jobs.

Seven years later something happened to me that would change my 12 life forever. I had moved to Ottawa with a man and was working as a waitress in a restaurant. One day, a friend invited me to her place for coffee. While I was there, she told me she was going to university in the fall and showed me her reading list. I'll never forget the minutes that followed. I was feeling vaguely envious of her and, once again, inferior. I remember taking the paper in my hand, seeing the books on it and realizing, Oh, my God, I've read these books! It hit me like a thunder-clap. I was stunned that books I had read were being read in university. University was for white kids, not native kids. We were too stupid, we didn't have the kind of mind it took to do those things. My eyes moved down the list, and my heart started beating faster and faster as I suddenly realized I could go to university, too!

My partner at the time was a loving supportive man who helped me 13 in every way. I applied to the university immediately as a mature student but when I had to write Grade 9 on the application, I was sure they'd turn me down. They didn't. I graduated five years later, earning a bachelor of arts in English and philosophy (with distinction).

It was while I was studying for a master's degree in communications 14 at McGill a few years later that I was approached to direct my second film (the first was a student film). *Doctor, Lawyer, Indian Chief* (a National Film Board production) depicts the struggle of a number of native women — one who began her adult life on welfare, a government minister, a chief, a fisherwoman and Canada's first native woman lawyer. The film is about overcoming obstacles and surviving. It's the story of most native people.

Today, there's a glimmer of hope that more of us native people will 15 overcome the obstacles that have tripped us up ever since we began sharing this land. Some say our cultures are going through a renaissance. Maybe that's true. Certainly there's a renewed interest in native dancing, acting and singing, and in other cultural traditions. Even indigenous forms of government are becoming strong again. But we can't forget that the majority of native people live in urban areas and continue to suffer from alcohol and drug abuse and the plagues of a people who have lost their culture and have become lost themselves. And the welfare system is the insidious glue that holds together the machine of oppression of native people.

16   Too many non-native people have refused to try to understand the issues behind our land claims. They make complacent pronouncements such as "Go back to your bows and arrows and fish with spears if you want aboriginal rights. If not, give it up and assimilate into white Canadian culture." I don't agree with that. We need our culture, but there's no reason why we can't preserve it and have an automatic washing machine and a holiday in Mexico, as well.

17   The time has come for native people to make our own decisions. We need to have self-government. I have no illusions that it will be smooth sailing — there will be trial and error and further struggle. And if that means crawling before we can stand up and walk, so be it. We'll have to learn through experience.

18   While we're learning, we have a lot to teach and give to the world — a holistic philosophy, a way of living with the earth, not disposing of it. It is critical that we all learn from the elders that an individual is not more important than a forest; we know that we're here to live on and with the earth, not to subdue it.

19   The wheels are in motion for a revival, for change in the way native people are taking their place in Canada. I can see that we're equipped, we have the tools to do the work. We have an enormous number of smart, talented, moral Indian people. It's thrilling to be a part of this movement.

20   Someday, when I'm an elder, I'll tell the children the stories: about the bush, about the hard times, about the renaissance, and especially about the importance of knowing your place in your nation.

△ △

Explorations:

Carol Geddes, *Doctor, Lawyer, Indian Chief* (NFB film)
Daniel David Moses and Terry Goldie, eds., *An Anthology of Canadian Native Writers in English*
Penny Petrone, ed., *First People, First Voices* (anthology of writings by First Nations people in Canada)
Julie Cruikshank, *Life Lived Like a Story* (interviews with Native Canadian women)

Basil Johnston, *Indian School Days* (memoir)
Hugh Brody, *Maps and Dreams* (anthropology)
http://dickshovel.netgate.net/firstnations.html
http://ayn-0.ayn.ca/

Structure:

1. "I remember it was cold. . . ." says Geddes in her opening sentence, and "Someday, when I'm an elder. . . ." she says in her closing sentence. Most *narratives* in this chapter relate one incident, but "Growing Up Native" tells the highs and lows of a whole life. Has Geddes attempted too much? Or has she got her message across by focussing on the right moments of her life? Cite examples to defend your answer.
2. Did you have the impression of being *told* a story, rather than reading it on the page? Cite passages where "Growing Up Native" comes across as oral history, as a tale told in person. Why does Geddes take this approach?
3. Does Geddes *narrate* in straight chronological order? Point out any flashbacks or other departures from the pattern.
4. Read paragraph 12 aloud. Analyze its power as a TRANSITION between Geddes' past and present.

Style:

1. Geddes' paragraphs are well organized: most begin with a topic sentence, then clearly develop it with examples. Identify five paragraphs that follow this pattern.
2. Why are paragraph 10 and several others so long? Why is paragraph 20 so short?
3. In paragraph 2 Geddes tells of "the sting of humiliation and the boot of discrimination." Find other good FIGURES OF SPEECH in paragraphs 9, 12 and 15.

Ideas for Discussion and Writing:

1. Despite the hardships of living in the bush, does Geddes' childhood sound like a good one? If so, why? Give *examples.*
2. Geddes exposes various ways in which First Nations People have been STEREOTYPED. Point out the worst of these.
3. The white high school of paragraph 11 routinely put Native students in typing instead of science. How do the high schools of your province advise minority students as to course selection and career? Is a minority or working class student shut out from opportunity, or encouraged to try? Give *examples* from your own observation.

4. Geddes envisions First Nations people keeping their culture, yet also having washing machines and holidays in Mexico (par. 16). Discuss techniques for achieving such goals in the urban setting where most Native people now live.

5. **PROCESS IN WRITING:** *Interview someone who either grew up long ago, or who is from a culture very different from yours, to hear her or his life story. Tape the interview, then at home play it back, taking notes. Now choose either one main event of this* narrative *(such as the scene in which Geddes realizes she too can go to university), OR choose to give the overall sweep of the story. Also choose whether to just assemble the best excerpts from the tape to put in writing, OR to summarize the key events in your own words. Load your first draft with the best examples you have. Stay mainly in time order, but do use a flashback or flashforward if they enhance the story. Finally, edit your version for things like spelling and punctuation. Read it aloud to the class. If there is time, also play the interview so the class can see how you chose and arranged the material of your* narrative.

Note: See also the Topics for Writing at the end of this chapter.

Jan Wong

"Safeguard Your Lives"

Jan Wong's life has been the stuff of fiction. Born in 1952 as a third-generation Chinese in Montreal, she was a gifted and popular high school student enjoying the middle-class lifestyle of a prosperous family. But once at McGill, Wong entered radical politics, a path that led her in 1972 to Chairman Mao's China, as the only Canadian university student in the country. There she mastered the language of her ancestors, studied Marxism, and became an ardent revolutionary during the greatest excesses of the Cultural Revolution. As formerly respected leaders, academics and writers were exiled to the countryside and humiliated through such tasks as shovelling manure, "Bright Precious Wong," as she was now called, volunteered for labour in collective farms, married the only American draft resister to go to China during the Vietnam War, and even denounced individuals who seemed open to the West. After six years of gradually realizing abuses of power in the "workers' paradise," Wong returned to Canada, disillusioned. She finished her degree at McGill, did a Master's in journalism at Columbia, then entered the world of capitalism, as business reporter for The Gazette *(Montreal),* The Boston Globe, *and from 1985–87 the* Wall Street Journal *itself. It was not till 1988 that she returned to China, now with her husband and two sons, as China correspondent for* The Globe and Mail *(Toronto). The next year in Beijing she witnessed a key event of the twentieth century — and the subject of our selection — the brutal Tiananmen Square massacre of students protesting against the totalitarian government of the People's Republic. Her vivid reportage of the action, and her inside perspective on its context, took millions of North American readers to the heart of the event. Wong stayed in China till 1994, and today is in Toronto, where she writes direct and ironic feature interviews for* The Globe and Mail. *Our selection is from Wong's runaway bestseller of 1996,* Red China Blues: My Long March From Mao to Now.

On Friday night, June 2, I stayed up all night to chronicle a ridiculous invasion of six thousand unarmed foot soldiers. Some thought the government was trying to position troops near the square. Others believed it was a last attempt to retake the square without violence. Still others thought the soldiers were under orders to topple the Goddess of

51

Democracy.° In any case, the mission failed miserably. I watched as irate citizens upbraided the soldiers, who cowered in bushes across from the Beijing Hotel while radioing frantically for instructions.

2   After sleeping three hours, I gulped down some yogurt and ran out to see what was happening on Saturday. At noon, soldiers fired tear gas on demonstrators who had waylaid an ammunition truck. That afternoon five thousand troops confronted even more demonstrators outside the Great Hall of the People. But except for a beating or two, the showdown was uneventful. At one point, the two sides — soldiers and protestors — even competed to see who best sang "Without the Communist Party There Would Be No New China."

3   The government had lost all credibility. It had buzzed the square with military helicopters — and people laughed. It had tried to send in armored personnel carriers — and old ladies lay down in their path. The night before, it had dispatched foot soldiers — and civilians trapped them in the bushes. Many thought the battle of Beijing was over and the people had won. Most expected the army to go home and stop bothering them. Everyone, myself included, forgot one of Mao's most famous quotations: "Political power grows out of the barrel of a gun."

4   That night around six, on the northeast edge of the city, I spied another military convoy stopped on a road littered with broken glass. The *Globe* didn't publish on Sunday, but by force of habit, I got out of my car and counted eighteen truckloads of soldiers toting AK-47 assault rifles. I noticed their faces. They weren't green recruits but grim-faced, seasoned troops. I also noticed they were no longer wearing canvas running shoes.

5   "They're wearing boots," I told Jim Abrams, the AP° bureau chief, when I called to swap information.

6   "I know," he said. "The army is coming in from every direction."

7   It was clear something would happen tonight. Had the government any finesse, it would have aired a trio of James Bond movies, and everyone would have stayed glued to their television sets. Instead, it broadcast this warning: "Do not come into the streets. Do not go to Tiananmen Square. Stay at home to safeguard your lives." The government might as well have issued engraved invitations.

8   "History will be made tonight," I said melodramatically to Norman. He was tired of all-nighters.

9   "That's what you said last time," he reminded me. I had said the same thing a week earlier when the AP's John Pomfret put out an urgent bulletin, which turned out to be false, that troops were march-

---

° The Goddess of Democracy: a plaster version of the Statue of Liberty erected by students in Tiananmen Square, in defiance of the government.
° AP: Associated Press, an international press agency.

ing down the Avenue of Eternal Peace clubbing anyone in their path. But Norman grudgingly came along for the second time. On the way, we stopped by the Reuters° office, where they were frantically trying to confirm the first death, reportedly at Muxidi, a neighborhood on the far west side of the city. I volunteered to call the Fuxing Hospital in the area. The phone rang and rang, but no one answered, an ominous sign.

I did not know that the massacre had already begun. That Saturday evening, Deng Xiaoping had ordered the army to take the square by using "all necessary measures." At Muxidi, the troops found their way completely blocked by enormous crowds. As they tried to press forward, some in the crowd began stoning the soldiers in the front lines, People's Armed Police troops armed only with truncheons. The People's Armed Police, a huge paramilitary force that Deng had split off from the PLA° in the 1980s, specialized in quelling domestic dissent. Yet their fiberglass helmets cracked under the torrent of stones. Some soldiers were injured. Behind them, their officers, armed with pistols, panicked and began shooting. Behind the People's Armed Police was the 38th Army, toting AK-47s. As all hell broke loose, they also began firing into the dense crowds. Soon soldiers were chasing civilians down alleyways and killing them in cold blood.

Residents screamed curses and hurled dishes and tea cups from their windows. The army units, from the provinces, probably had no idea those buildings housed the Communist Party elite, and raked the apartments with gunfire. Several people died in their homes that night. The nephew of the chief justice of the Supreme Court of China was shot in his own kitchen.

In the confusion, the army even shot some of its own soldiers. Behind the 38th Army was an armored personnel carrier unit belonging to the 27th Army. Driving in the darkness with their hatches down in an unfamiliar city, they inadvertently crushed to death soldiers from the 38th Army.

Norman and I got to the Beijing Hotel around 11 p.m., just as several armored personnel carriers whizzed by. So as not to advertise my presence, I parked the *Globe*'s car on Wangfujing, a busy shopping street adjacent to the hotel. Catherine Sampson, a reporter for the *Times* of London, offered to share her fourteenth-floor room. Simon Long, a BBC reporter, was also there filing a story. I needed quotes, and persuaded Norman to go with me to the square. Before I went out, I ditched my notebook so I wouldn't attract the attention of plainclothes police and, as a precaution against tear gas, stuffed a hankie in my pocket.

10

11

12

13

° Reuters: an international press agency.
° PLA: the People's Liberation Army.

14   The square felt like a cross between a New York street festival and a British soccer riot. All the floodlights had been switched on, presumably for the benefit of the videocameras. Several hundred thousand people milled around, students in T-shirts, women in flowered dresses, roughly dressed peasants with unkempt hair. Parents snapped photos for the memory book of their children posing in front of the Goddess of Democracy. Western tourists in pedicabs filmed the raucous scene with videocameras. Since mid-April, Tiananmen Square had been a bigger tourist draw than the Great Wall.

15   The night before, the invasion of the foot soldiers had been harmless fun. With the radio and television warnings on Saturday evening, people were quivering like excited rabbits waiting to see what would happen next. Every ten minutes or so, a panic rippled through the crowd, sparking a mass stampede. After regrouping, another wave of hysteria hit the crowd, and they fled in a different direction. You had to run with them or risk being trampled to death. Once, I tried to take refuge behind a skinny lamppost, but a dozen others had the same idea.

16   No one had any idea how bad the situation was. Some had heard that the troops had begun to shoot, but the true magnitude of casualties wasn't yet known. People were indignant, not afraid. "It's unspeakable," said one young woman, her hands on her hips. "Worse than fascists." A young man stood on a traffic kiosk with a bullhorn, a small supply of bricks at his feet, shouting, "Down with fascists!" Others like me clutched their hankies. A couple of young men readied Molotov cocktails.

17   Norman and I walked toward the north end of the square, where an armored personnel carrier was burning. "Are there any soldiers inside?" I asked a student in a red headband. "We pulled them out first," he said. In the distance, I saw another armored personnel carrier in flames just in front of the Communist Party headquarters at Zhongnanhai. I had to pinch myself to make sure I wasn't dreaming. I looked at my watch. It was just past midnight on Sunday, June 4, 1989.

18   Some people claimed to hear gunfire. I strained to listen, but the din of stampeding humans was too loud. Someone whispered that the soldiers were holed up inside the Great Hall of the People. An Italian journalist grabbed my arm and told me the troops were inside the Forbidden City and would come pouring out any minute. By 12:50 a.m., I was frightened and tired. I had my quotes. "I'm not a cameraman," I said to Norman. "I've got what I need. Let's go."

19   We made our way back to the Beijing Hotel. Someone had fastened the wrought-iron gates shut with steel wire. We clambered over them and scurried across the parking lot. Plainclothes agents were frisking foreign reporters on the main steps. I walked around them and into the lobby, where a reporter for *USA Today* was filing a story on a pay phone. An agent armed with a pair of heavy shears cut the cord in mid-sen-

tence. The reporter was so astonished his jaw dropped. Without a word, the policeman methodically chopped the wires on the rest of the lobby phones. Norman and I took the elevator up, still unnoticed.

That night, many reporters like myself used the Beijing Hotel as a base of operations. This was not the proverbial wartime-reporting-from-the-hotel-bar-stool-by-jaded-hacks syndrome. The Beijing Hotel had direct-dial telephones, bathrooms and an unparalleled view of the north end of Tiananmen Square. It was so close, in fact, that we were within range of the guns. A small number of reporters, like Andrew Higgins of the *Independent*, stayed among the crowds on the street. And an even smaller number, including UPI's° Dave Schweisberg, remained in the center of the square all night with the students. Still other reporters never left their offices in the diplomatic compounds, relying on reports from their news assistants and wire service copy to write their first stories.

Back in Cathy Sampson's fourteenth-floor room, I moved a chair onto the balcony and began taking notes. Norman and I had left the square in the nick of time. Ten minutes later, the troops rolled in from the west side, the armored personnel carriers roaring easily over make-shift barricades. Protesters hurled stones. A cyclist gave impotent chase. I could hear the crackle of gunfire clearly now. I watched in horror as the army shot directly into the crowds, who stampeded screaming and cursing down the Avenue of Eternal Peace. At first, some protesters held blankets and jackets in front of them, apparently believing the army was using rubber bullets. Only after the first people fell, with gaping wounds, did people comprehend that the soldiers were using live ammunition.

I could not believe what was happening. I swore and cursed in Chinese and English, every epithet I knew. Then I realized I was ruining Simon's tape of the gunfire for his BBC broadcasts. I decided the only useful thing I could do was to stay calm and take the best notes of my life. A crowd below frantically tried to rip down a metal fence to erect another barricade. When it wouldn't budge, they smashed a window of a parked bus, put the gears in neutral and rolled it onto the street. They did that with a second and then a third bus. The rest of the crowd shouted, *"Hao!"* ("Good!").

The troops and tanks began closing in from all directions. At 1:20, I heard bursts of gunfire from the south, then another burst five minutes later. At 2:10, several thousand troops marched across the north side of the square. At 2:15, they raised their guns and fired into the dense crowd. I timed the murderous volley on my watch. It lasted more than a minute. Although the square was brightly lit, the streets surrounding it

° UPI: United Press International, an international press agency.

were dark. I couldn't see clearly if anyone had been hit. I assumed they must have been because of the angle of the guns, the length of the volley and the density of the crowds. A few minutes later I knew I was right as five ambulances raced by the hotel through the crowds. Cyclists and pedicab drivers helped evacuate the wounded and dying. I hadn't even noticed that a man had been shot in the back below my balcony until an ambulance stopped to pick him up.

24   At 2:23, tanks from the east fired their mounted machine guns at the crowds. At 2:28, I counted five more ambulances racing back to the square as people frantically cheered them on. In the distance, I saw red dots trace perfect arcs through the sky. "Fireworks?" I asked, turning to Cathy. Neither of us knew they were tracer bullets, and even if I did, I had no idea they were real bullets, coated with phosphorus to glow in the dark. In my first story, I called them "flares."

25   Cathy heard a bullet hit our balcony and pointed it out to me at the time. I have no memory of it. I should have realized the lead was flying, but I was so completely absorbed in taking notes. Nor did it occur to me that, as soldiers advanced across the north side of the square, pushing back protesters toward the hotel and beyond, our balcony was in the line of fire. The next day, when I examined the bullet hole, I felt nothing. It was insignificant compared to all the death and destruction going on around me. Besides, the hotel felt so normal, with its twin beds, blond-wood furniture and lace curtains. I learned only later that a tourist in the hotel had been grazed in the neck and the neon sign on the roof had been blasted to smithereens.

26   As the soldiers massacred people, the loudspeakers broadcast the earlier government message warning everyone to stay home. I leaned over the balcony to watch some people cowering in the parking lot. The crowd ran away after each heavy volley, then to my amazement crept back slowly, screaming curses and weeping with rage. Perhaps like me, they couldn't believe that the People's Liberation Army was shooting them. Or perhaps the decades of propaganda had warped their minds. Perhaps they were insane with anger. Or maybe after stopping an army in its tracks for days, armed only with moral certitude, they believed they were invincible. By now, I was recording heavy gunfire every six or seven minutes. It occurred to me that was about as much time as it took for people to run two blocks, calm down, regroup and creep back.

27   In the darkness I could make out a double row of soldiers, approximately one hundred and twenty men across. At 2:35, they began firing into the crowds as they marched across the square. With each volley, tens of thousands of people fled toward the hotel. Someone commandeered a bus, drove it toward the soldiers and was killed in a hail of gunfire. The crowd began to scream. "Go back! Go back!" The soldiers responded with another hail of bullets.

By 2:48, the soldiers had cleared a wide swath at the north end of the square. The crowd had thinned a bit. At 3:12, there was a tremendous round of gunfire, lasting several minutes. People stampeded down the Avenue of Eternal Peace. Some hopped the hotel's iron fence. I saw someone hit in the parking lot. Three minutes later, thousands of people were still running and bicycling and screaming hysterically past the hotel. 28

The soldiers strafed ambulances and shot medical workers trying to rescue the wounded. Some cyclists flung bodies across the back of their bicycles. Others just carried the wounded on their backs. Beijing's doughty pedicab drivers pitched in. Between 3:15 and 3:23, I counted eighteen pedicabs pass by me carrying the dead and wounded to the nearby Beijing Hospital, diagonally across from the hotel, or to the nearby Beijing Union Medical Hospital. I realized that I had seen the same driver in a red undershirt several times. The straw matting on his cart was soaked with blood. 29

At the Beijing Union Medical Hospital, someone had the presence of mind to photograph each corpse. The hospital put out an emergency call for all staff to return to work. In the next six hours, they treated more than two hundred victims, cleaning the wounds and stanching the bleeding. The staff sent home every victim who could possibly leave. Every bed was needed, and doctors feared the soldiers might come to the hospital to finish off the wounded. "It was terrible," said one surgeon, who operated without a break for twelve hours. "We are used to handling industrial accidents. We had never seen gunshot wounds before." 30

A Western military attaché told me the army used Type 56 semi-automatic rifles, a Chinese copy of the Soviet AK-47, which fires copper-clad steel-core bullets. The bullets cause terrible wounds because their soft copper jacket often flowers on impact, tearing through the first victim like a jagged knife. At close range, the steel-core bullets are powerful enough to rip through one or two more victims. The Chinese army also fired anti-aircraft machine guns that night, apparently loaded with armor-piercing bullets as thick as a man's thumb. Designed for use against light armored vehicles, their high-tensile carbon-steel bullets have a range of three miles and can easily pass through ten victims at close range. 31

Across Beijing, supplies of blood, plasma and bandages ran out that night. Red Cross workers stood on the sidewalk outside the Children's Hospital and appealed for blood. Chinese, who normally are afraid to give blood even when offered large cash incentives, streamed in to donate. "As soon as we went on the street at 3 a.m., we got a hundred volunteers," Xing Lixiang, director of Beijing's Blood Donation Squad, told me later. 32

I sat on Cathy's balcony and wrote in my notebook: "The people are all unarmed. The army has been firing on them for two hours." Over 33 the loudspeakers, a cultured voice repeated: "The People's Liberation Army has a duty to protect the great socialist motherland and the safety of the capital." Soldiers were now shooting their way into Tiananmen Square from every direction. The barriers people had spent so long making did not stop the tanks at all. I looked at the wounded and dying below, at the pavement chewed up by tank treads, at the smashed barricades and the smoke rising from the square. Amidst the carnage, the traffic lights kept working perfectly; switching from green to yellow to red, and back to green.

34   Beijing was burning. I later learned that enraged protestors killed a number of soldiers with savage ferocity. After an army officer named Liu Guogeng shot four people, he was pulled from his jeep and beaten to death in front of the Telegraph Building, near the Central Committee headquarters. The crowd doused his corpse with gasoline, set it on fire and strung his charred remains, clad only in his socks, from a bus window. So everyone would know he was a soldier, someone stuck an army cap on his head and, in a chilling attempt at levity, put his glasses back on his nose. The furious mob still wasn't satisfied. Someone yanked him down and disembowled him.

35   A twenty-year-old soldier, Cui Guozheng, met a similar fate just across from Pierre Cardin's swank Maxim de Pekin restaurant. Eyewitnesses said that he and another soldier got out after their truck got stuck on a piece of pavement. When the mob attacked the other soldier, Cui jumped back in the truck and fired his machine gun into the crowd, hitting an old woman, a man and possibly a child. The mob stormed the truck. Cui tried to flee and made it as far as the sidewalk before he was tackled. His charred corpse swung from a pedestrian flyover for several days. The government later said that Cui never fired, "in order not to wound the masses by accident."

36   Outside on the hotel balcony, I continued taking notes as bullets flew. At 3:45 a.m. there was another mass panic. This time, the crowd raced all the way down the street, until I was sitting in the middle, between them and the soldiers. Some young men wanted to toss Molotov cocktails. I saw others restrain them. At 3:56, the soldiers let loose another thunderous volley that lasted twenty seconds. I wondered how many other massacres had occurred where a journalist could sit on a balcony with a notebook and record the event down to the minute and the second.

37   At exactly 4 a.m., the lamps in the square snapped off. My heart froze. I could still see the students' tents near the edge of the square. Inside the Great Hall of the People, the lights blazed. I wrote in my notes: "This is it. They're going to kill all the students. Are China's leaders watching from inside the GHOP?" I concentrated on counting a convoy of more than five hundred trucks as it rumbled into the square

from the west. I could hear the thunder of distant gunfire to the south. By now, I was too tired to sit in the chair, so I slumped on the cement floor of the balcony, wrapped in a hotel blanket. By 4:30 a.m., the soldiers had sealed off the northeast corner of the square. Below me, a few thousand die-hards lingered. I couldn't believe my ears when they began singing revolutionary songs and chanting slogans. Some cyclists biked back and forth in the killing zone in front of the hotel.

I learned later that about five thousand students, many from the provinces, huddled that night around the Monument to the People's Heroes. Chai Ling led them in singing the "Internationale." Many had joined the hunger strike as a springtime lark. Now they were sure they were going to die on a cool night in June. When the lights went out, many students started weeping.

At precisely 4:40, the lights snapped back on. A new broadcast tape started. "Classmates," said a metallic male voice. "Please immediately clear the square." The message was repeated. I heard shots ring out in the square. Were they killing the students in cold blood? I later found out the soldiers were blasting away the students' sound system.

The students took a hasty vote and decided to leave. At 4:50, I recorded more heavy gunfire and thick black smoke in the south. At 5:17, the soldiers allowed the frightened students to file out through the south side of the square, making them run a gauntlet of truncheons and fists. The students straggled past the Kentucky Fried Chicken outlet and then north. As they turned west onto the Avenue of Eternal Peace, they saw a row of tanks lined up between them and the square. A retreating student hurled a curse. Suddenly, one of the tanks roared to life and mowed down eleven marchers from behind, killing seven instantly.

Afterwards, the government denied that tanks had crushed students at Tiananmen Square. But there were too many eyewitnesses, including an AP reporter. Eventually I tracked down two of the four survivors. One was a Beijing Sports Institute student whose legs were crushed when he pushed a classmate out of the tank's path. Another was a young factory technician whose right ear was torn off and right arm crushed. When I found him six months later, he was still afraid to leave his home because he knew he was a living contradiction of the government's Big Lie.

Dawn broke cold and gray on Sunday, June 4. As convoys of trucks and tanks rumbled in from the east, people frantically tried to push a bus into their path. One young man ran out and tossed a rock at the tanks. At 5:30, another convoy of a jeep and nine trucks went by, firing at random. People cowered in the bushes. At 5:36, a convoy of thirty trucks entered the square, followed by twenty armored personnel carriers and three tanks. At 5:47, two soldiers dismounted and started shooting their AK-47s into the crowd. I saw many fall to the ground, but I couldn't tell who had been hit and who was simply trying to take cover.

43   As Beijing awoke, ordinary people streamed toward the square, even as the pedicabs brought out more casualties. I saw a little girl and her parents take refuge behind a gray pick-up truck in the Beijing Hotel parking lot. The thick smoke from a burning bus gave some protective cover. By now, I was aware of the bullets whistling past. Still, it seemed unthinkable to stay inside. Over the next hour, I counted dozens of armored personnel carriers and tanks. It was overkill. Whom were they fighting now? Some of the tank drivers seemed lost. I saw three make U-turns, change their minds, then turn around again.

44   With daylight, I could see better. At 6:40, a tank plowed into the Goddess of Democracy, sending her plaster torso smashing to the ground. I saw flames and lots of smoke. Chai Ling, in a dramatic video released in Hong Kong, later testified: "Tanks began running over students who were sleeping in tents. Then the troops poured gasoline on tents and bodies and torched them." (This turned out to be false. The tents *were* set on fire, but apparently no one was in them.) By 6:47, dozens of tanks had lined up in formation at the north end of Tiananmen Square. From a distance, the square looked solid green. The army had finally retaken the square. The broadcast stopped.

45   Cathy switched on the early-morning newscast. Through the open balcony door, we could still hear gunfire. "A small minority of hoodlums created chaos in Beijing," the government announcer said. "The army came in, but not to suppress the students and the masses." I left Cathy, an insomniac, to take notes of the broadcast while I fell into an exhausted stupor on the bed. I had been working day and night without a break for more than seven weeks, and had had almost no sleep in the past seventy-two hours. I awoke with a start a short while later as three military helicopters roared by our window on their way to the square to pick up wounded soldiers, casualties of friendly fire. More ambulances whizzed by. From the balcony, I recorded a lull as a crowd massed outside the hotel. Fifteen minutes later, the soldiers charged forward, firing directly into the crowd. Bodies littered the ground. I saw a couple of people use their own blood to smear slogans on a sheet of plywood propped against a barricade at the intersection. "Kill Li Peng!" said one slogan. "Blood debts will be repaid with blood," read another.

46   By then, I was numb. It seems strange in hindsight — perhaps it was my Chinese starvation genes — but I felt I had to eat. I could tell it was going to be a long, bloody Sunday, and without some food, I knew I would not last the day. When I suggested we try to get breakfast downstairs in the hotel dining room, neither Cathy nor Norman objected. We left Simon Long behind to take notes.

Downstairs, I discovered that many other journalists had spent the   47
night on their balconies and seemed to have the same surreal craving
for scrambled eggs. Mitch Farkas, a husky soundman for CNN, told us
that we had just missed a fight. When the Chinese waitresses announced
there was only coffee, no food, because the chef was too upset to cook,
a couple of reporters became unhinged and started yelling that they
would cook their own breakfast. Suddenly the chef appeared in the
dining room. He was crying. "I've seen too many people killed last
night," he said, his shaking hand resting on a doorknob. Everyone
stared at the ground, ashamed of the boorish behavior of their colleagues. A waitress broke the silence. "We are all Chinese," she said.
"We love our country." Everyone began apologizing to everyone else,
Mitch said, and the cook pulled himself together and announced that
he would feed the reporters because "you are telling the world what
happened."

As he recounted this, Mitch himself started crying. Like us, he was   48
physically and mentally drained. When he broke down, Cathy and I did,
too. I — who cried at the drop of a hat, when Beijing University was
going to expel me, when I couldn't hack the labor at Big Joy Farm —
realized that I hadn't shed a single tear all night. The enormity of the
massacre hit home. So many people had been killed. Although it had
been years since I was a Maoist, I still had harbored some small hope
for China. Now even that was gone. I sat there weeping as the waitresses
passed out plates of toast and fried eggs. None of us could eat.

△ △

Explorations:

Jan Wong, *Red China Blues: My Long March From Mao to Now*
Ha Jin, *Between Silences: A Voice from China* (poems)
http://www.nb.sympatico.ca/Features/Books/china.html
http://www.bookwire.com/boldtype/bkofbook/read.article$2882

Structure:

1. What makes a title good? Do you like this one? What IRONIES lie
   behind the words "Safeguard Your Lives"? (See their source in paragraph 7.)
2. In Wong's *narrative* of an historic event, how conspicuous is the flow
   of time? Is it interrupted by flashbacks? Reread paragraphs 23 and
   24: How do the many references to clock time build momentum and
   feeling?
3. What makes a good closing? Do you like this one? Explain all the
   IRONIES of Wong's final words, "None of us could eat."

Style:

1. Critics say that Nobel Prize winning novelist Ernest Hemingway learned his lean and concrete prose STYLE as a reporter for *The Toronto Star.* Jan Wong writes for *The Globe and Mail.* Do you see qualities of her style that might help your own essays? Is she CONCISE? Are you? Is her writing filled with images and *examples*? Is yours? Does she speed her readers on with TRANSITIONS? Do you?

2. In paragraph 21 Wong tells how ". . . the army shot directly into the crowds, who stampeded screaming and cursing down the Avenue of Eternal Peace." Why does she repeat this street name throughout? What does she imply about the government? And what central device of *persuasion* is she using?

3. Read paragraph 33 aloud to the class. Why does Wong give all these little details? Why does she choose to tell us of the traffic lights still working as Tiananmen Square is in ruins?

Ideas for Discussion and Writing:

1. As a former Maoist ("Bright Precious Wong") during China's Cultural Revolution, and as a Canadian journalist later stationed in the same country, our author sees China from both inside and out. Has your own background (immigration, for example) enabled you to see from more than one point of view? Or what else have you done to broaden your vision? Travel? Language study? A student exchange? Tell the effects.

2. In *Red China Blues* Jan Wong openly shows emotion: she "watched in horror" (par. 21) as troops opened fire on civilians, then "swore and cursed in Chinese and English" (par. 22), and later cried (par. 48). Should she have kept an objective manner, as newspaper reporters are supposed to, or are these subjective parts justified by events? What would you have done?

3. Are the gruesome details of paragraphs 31, 34, 35, 40 and 41 too much? What purposes do they serve?

4. Wong quotes Mao, the "Great Helmsman," who said "Political power grows out of the barrel of a gun" (par. 3). Does it? If so, how has Latin America been able to rid itself of almost all its dictators, who not long ago ruled almost every country?

5. A government announcer says, "A small minority of hoodlums created chaos in Beijing. The army came in, but not to suppress the students and the masses" (par. 45). How does propaganda work? Explain the technique of the "Big Lie" mentioned in paragraph 41.

6. Despite China's 1989 massacre of students at Tiananmen Square and many other violations of human rights, the Canadian federal govern-

ment is pressing for more trade with this giant economic power. Is this right? Should politics and trade be separate or linked?

7. **PROCESS IN WRITING:** *You probably were not at Tiananmen Square in 1989, but have you seen or taken part in another student demonstration, a political protest, a strike, or a mob scene of any kind? Relive the event for a while in your mind, with your eyes shut, then get it down on paper in a fast discovery draft. The next day look it over. Does the action start and end at the right places, leaving unimportant parts out? Do SENSE IMAGES help your reader "see" and "hear" the event? Do time signals and other TRANSITIONS speed the* narrative *on? Does the action rise to a CLIMAX? Edit for these things, using Jan Wong's* narrative *as an example, then check spelling and punctuation before you print out your best version.*

Note: See also the Topics for Writing at the end of this chapter.

Topics for Writing

Chapter 1: Narration

WRITING ABOUT MYSELF

Choose one of these topics as the basis of a narrative about yourself. Tell a good story: give colourful details and all the facts needed to help your reader understand and appreciate the event. (See also the guidelines that follow.)

1. My Brush With the Law
2. The Day I Got Lost
3. The Day I Was Right and My Friends Were Wrong
4. My Encounter With Bureaucracy
5. My Worst Airplane Flight
6. My Moment of Glory in Sports
7. My Most Dangerous Encounter With the Forces of Nature
8. My Encounter With Gambling
9. The Time a Friend Betrayed Me
10. My First Time at a Tanning Salon
11. My Worst (or Best) Restaurant Experience
12. A White Lie That Got Me in Trouble
13. The Day Jealousy Got the Better of Me
14. My Worst (or Best) Encounter With Technology
15. My Luckiest Day

WRITING ABOUT OTHERS

From this list of events, choose one that you witnessed in person. Narrate it, giving colourful details and all the facts needed to help your reader understand and appreciate the event. (See also the guidelines that follow.)

16. An Incident on Public Transit
17. A Transaction in the Underground Economy
18. A Demonstration or Riot
19. The Death of a Family Member or Friend
20. An Important Event in the Life of a Child
21. An Important Event in the Life of an Old Person
22. The Day My Parents First Met (interview one or both before writing)
23. A Prank That Backfired
24. An Accident
25. An Example of Courage in Action
26. A Concert
27. A Violent Incident at a Sporting Event
28. An Unusual Wedding

29. An Incident of Sexism or Racism
30. A Wild Party

Note also the Process in Writing topic after each selection in this chapter.

Process in Writing: Guidelines

Follow at least some of these steps in the act of writing your narrative (your teacher may suggest which ones).

1. *Search your memory, or search any diary or journal that you keep, for an incident that could develop one of our topics.*

2. *When you have chosen an incident, test it by freewriting nonstop for at least five minutes. If the results are good, use the best parts in your first draft. If the results are weak, try another topic.*

3. *Write your first draft rapidly, letting the story just flow out onto the paper or the computer screen. Double-space, leaving room for revision. Do not stop now to fix things like spelling and punctuation, for you will lose momentum. Consider narrating in the* present tense, *making the action seem to happen* now.

4. *Look this draft over: Does it begin and end at just the right places, narrating the event itself but omitting parts that don't matter? If you see deadwood, chop it out.*

5. *In your second draft, add more SENSE IMAGES to heighten realism. Add more time signals, such as "first," "next," "then," "suddenly" and "at last," to speed the action.*

6. *Read a draft to friends, family members or classmates. Does it sound good? Revise awkward passages. Does it communicate with your AUDIENCE? Revise any part that does not.*

7. *Finally, edit for spelling, punctuation and other aspects of "correctness" before printing off your best version. (Save it on disk in case your teacher suggests further revision.)*

Corel Photos

"What feeds we used to have. Not way back in the pod auger days, mind you. That was before my time. I mean not long ago, just before the tinned stuff and the packages and the baker's bread started to trickle into the outports."

—*Ray Guy, "Outharbor Menu"*

CHAPTER

2

EXAMPLE

For example. . .

Many an audience, after struggling to grasp a speaker's message, has been saved from boredom or even sleep by the powerful words *"for example. . . ."* Heads lift up, eyes return to the front, bodies shift in their chairs, and suddenly the message is clear to all.

Writers, like speakers, use examples. Do you enjoy reading pages of abstract reasoning, generalizations, theory without application? You have heard the Chinese proverb "A picture is worth a thousand words." When the writer's words never form "pictures," how can you "see the point"? Of course generalizations have their place. For example, your thesis statement is one, and so are subpoints, summaries and conclusions. These and others are needed, but cannot do the job alone. If you do not "show" as well as "tell," your reader will be like the people in the audience sinking into their seats — until you, like the speaker, say "for example. . . ."

Why not try for at least 50% example content in every essay, to avoid the hot-air approach to writing? The only trouble with using more examples is that you have to know the subject. Two suggestions:

- If you cannot think of examples, then you have probably chosen the wrong topic. Try another. The best essays are like icebergs: only a tenth of what you know shows above the surface, but it is supported by the other nine-tenths.

■ If you cannot think of examples, *find* them. Read. Go to the library. Use the on-line catalogue and periodical indexes. Consult reference works such as the almanac or the encyclopedia. Turn on your computer and search the Net. In other words, do some *work*.

Examples take many forms:

Personal experience: To illustrate your point, narrate an incident you have experienced. Did an earthquake or tornado or ice storm or flood show you the power of nature? Did your accident illustrate the danger of drinking and driving, or did your fire show the danger of smoking in bed? Did a major success or failure demonstrate the importance of your work or planning or persistence?

The experience of others: To illustrate the point, narrate an incident you saw in person or heard about from others. Did your neighbour's unloved child run away from home or rob a milk store or get married at age 16? Did your cousin lose her job because of automation or downsizing or a corporate merger? Did a famous person succeed despite a physical handicap or a deprived childhood?

Hypothetical examples: In a future-oriented society like ours, many arguments speculate about what might happen *if. . . .* Since the event or situation has not yet come to pass, use your best judgement to imagine the results. What would happen if street drugs were legalized? If the forests were all cut? If Quebec separated? If the national debt were paid off? If the polar ice cap melted? If all cars ran on natural gas or electricity? If a world government were adopted?

Quotations: If the words of a poet, politician, scientist or other prominent person illustrate your point clearly and authoritatively, quote them (using quotation marks) and of course state who said them. What did Aristotle, Shakespeare, Machiavelli, Freud, Marx, Einstein, Jane Jacobs, Lester Pearson, Lucien Bouchard or Margaret Atwood say about love or power or sex or money or old age or war? Start with the index of *Colombo's Canadian Quotations* or *Bartlett's Familiar Quotations* to find an apt statement on almost any important topic. Or go online to check out *Bartlett* at **http://www.mit.edu/people/map/bartlett-hack.html**, entering key words for a search.

Statistics: These numerical examples lend a scientific, objective quality to your argument. Tell what percentage of marriages will end in divorce or how many minutes each cigarette takes off your life or how much energy a person consumes travelling by car as opposed to train, bus or airplane. Five good sources of statistics are *Information Please*

EXAMPLE   **69**

Almanac, The World Almanac and Book of Facts, The Corpus Almanac of Canada, Canada Year Book and any good atlas. Be scrupulously honest, because everyone knows how statistics can lie (remember the statistician who drowned in the river that averaged two feet deep!).

Other devices: Later chapters in this book discuss cause and effect, comparison and contrast, and analogy. These devices may be used not only to plan the structure of an entire essay, but also to construct short and vivid examples within the essay.

Almost all good writing has examples, but some writing has so many that they become a means of organizing as well as illustrating. Ray Guy's essay "Outharbor Menu" has a brief introduction, a one-sentence closing, and a body made of nothing but examples. Such a collection could be a mere list of trivia, but Ray Guy — like anyone who writes well — has chosen his examples well for their colour and for the support they give his point.

Like Ray Guy, all the other authors in this chapter — Michele Landsberg, Amy Willard Cross, Josh Freed and Alberto Manguel — have gone far beyond the suggested 50% example content for good essays. Though we could still disagree with their views, it would be astonishing if we did not at least *understand* them after "seeing" them so clearly in action.

Another way to use examples is to let one long one make the point. On page 349 of our final chapter, Nathalie Petrowski develops one extended example of one young man who became a mass murderer. Yet through the single case of Marc Lépine she helps us "see" the situation of many other Canadian youths who may also explode into violence if we do not reduce the pressures our society puts them under. Of course one example — or a hundred — will prove nothing. Statistics come close to proof, especially when based on a large and carefully designed study. But in general an example is not proof; it is a device of illustration and therefore an aid to both understanding and enjoyment.

Note: Authors in other chapters also use many examples, as well as other ways to develop their point. See especially these selections:

Ray Guy

Outharbor Menu

Ray Guy's authentic and direct voice of the Newfoundland outports is witness that, despite globalization and standardization, today's Canada still includes peoples rooted in other ways, other views. Guy was born in 1939 at Arnold's Cove, an isolated fishing village on Placentia Bay. As a child he learned the self-reliance of a life little changed in centuries. Then after attending Memorial University for two years he went to Toronto, where in 1963 he earned a diploma in journalism at Ryerson. Back in Newfoundland he began reporting for the St. John's Evening Telegram, *but found that reporting was not enough. His distaste for the Liberal government of Joey Smallwood, and especially its policy of closing down the outports where for centuries Newfoundlanders had lived by fishing, led Guy to become a political columnist. His satirical attacks on Smallwood were so devastating that many credit him with the Liberals' defeat in the provincial election of 1971. Leaving the* Telegram *when the Thomson chain bought it, Guy went freelance, continuing to pour satire on his targets. More recently Guy has written plays, whose salty humour is much like that of his columns. Some of his best writings are collected in* You May Know Them as Sea Urchins, Ma'am *(1975);* That Far Greater Bay *(1976), which won the Leacock Medal for Humour; and* Ray Guy's Best *(1987). Our selection comes from* That Far Greater Bay.

1　What feeds we used to have. Not way back in the pod auger days,° mind you. That was before my time. I mean not long ago, just before the tinned stuff and the packages and the baker's bread started to trickle into the outports.

2　Out where I come from the trickle started when I was about six or seven years old. One day I went next door to Aunt Winnie's (that's Uncle John's Aunt Winnie) and she had a package of puffed rice someone sent down from Canada.°

° the pod auger days: a common Newfoundland expression meaning "the old days." A pod auger is an auger with a lengthwise groove.
° from Canada: Newfoundland did not join Confederation until 1949, after the time Ray Guy describes.

She gave us youngsters a small handful each. We spent a long time admiring this new exotic stuff and remarking on how much it looked like emmets' eggs. We ate it one grain at a time as if it were candy, and because of the novelty didn't notice the remarkable lack of taste. 3

"Now here's a five cent piece and don't spend it all in sweets, mind." You never got a nickel without this caution attached. 4

Peppermint knobs. White capsules ringed around with flannelette pink stripes. Strong! You'd think you were breathing icewater. They're not near as strong today. 5

Chocolate mice shaped like a crouching rat, chocolate on the outside and tough pink sponge inside. Goodbye teeth. Bullseyes made from molasses. And union squares — pastel blocks of marshmallow. 6

Those mysterious black balls that were harder than forged steel, had about 2,537 different layers of color and a funny tasting seed at the centre of the mini-universe. 7

Soft drinks came packed in barrels of straw in bottles of different sizes and shapes and no labels. Birch beer, root beer, chocolate, lemonade, and orange. 8

Spruce beer, which I could never stomach, but the twigs boiling on the stove smelled good. Home brew made from "Blue Ribbon" malt and which always exploded like hand grenades in the bottles behind the stove. 9

Rum puncheons. Empty barrels purchased from the liquor control in St. John's. You poured in a few gallons of water, rolled the barrel around, and the result was a stronger product than you put down $7.50 a bottle for today. 10

Ice cream made in a hand-cranked freezer, the milk and sugar and vanilla in the can in the middle surrounded by ice and coarse salt. I won't say it was better than the store-bought stuff today but it tasted different and I like the difference. 11

Rounders (dried tom cods) for Sunday breakfast without fail. Cods heads, boiled sometimes, but mostly stewed with onions and bits of salt pork. 12

Fried cod tongues with pork scruncheons.° Outport soul food. Salt codfish, fish cakes, boiled codfish and drawn butter, baked cod with savoury stuffing, stewed cod, fried cod. 13

Lobsters. We always got the bodies and the thumbs from the canning factories. When eating lobster bodies you must be careful to stay away from the "old woman," a lump of bitter black stuff up near the head which is said to be poisonous. 14

I was always partial to that bit of red stuff in lobster bodies but never went much on the pea green stuff although some did. 15

° pork scruncheons: crisp slices of fried pork fat.

16   We ate turrs° (impaled on a sharpened broomstick and held over the damper hole to singe off the fuzz), some people ate tickleaces° and gulls but I never saw it done.

17   We ate "a meal of trouts," seal, rabbits that were skinned out like a sock, puffin' pig (a sort of porpoise that had black meat), mussels and cocks and hens, otherwise known as clams, that squirt at you through air holes in the mud flats.

18   Potatoes and turnips were the most commonly grown vegetables although there was some cabbage and carrot. The potatoes were kept in cellars made of mounds of earth lined with sawdust or goosegrass. With the hay growing on them they looked like hairy green igloos.

19   A lot was got from a cow. Milk, certainly, and cream and butter made into pats and stamped with a wooden print of a cow or a clover leaf, and buttermilk, cream cheese. And I seem to remember a sort of jellied sour milk. I forget the name but perhaps the stuff was equivalent to yogurt.

20   There was no fresh meat in summer because it wouldn't keep. If you asked for a piece of meat at the store you got salt beef. If you wanted fresh beef you had to ask for "fresh meat."

21   Biscuits came packed in three-foot long wooden boxes and were weighed out by the pound in paper bags. Sultanas, Dad's cookies, jam jams, lemon creams with caraway seeds, and soda biscuits.

22   Molasses was a big thing. It was used to sweeten tea, in gingerbread, on rolled oats porridge, with sulphur in the spring to clean the blood (eeeccchhhh), in bread, in baked beans, in 'lassie bread.

23   It came in barrels and when the molasses was gone, there was a layer of molasses sugar at the bottom.

24   Glasses of lemon crystals or strawberry syrup or limejuice. Rolled oats, farina, Indian meal. Home-made bread, pork buns, figgy duff,° partridgeberry tarts, blanc mange, ginger wine, damper cakes.°

25   Cold mutton, salt beef, peas pudding, boiled cabbage, tinned bully beef for lunch on Sunday, tinned peaches, brown eggs, corned caplin.°

26   And thank God I was twelve years old before ever a slice of baker's bread passed my lips.

△ △

° turr: the murre, an edible seabird.
° tickleace: the kittiwake, a kind of gull.
° figgy duff: boiled raisin pudding.
° damper cakes: a kind of bannock made on the damper (upper surface) of a cookstove.
° caplin: a small and edible ocean fish often used by cod fishermen as bait.

Explorations:

Ray Guy,
>   *That Far Greater Bay*
>   *Ray Guy's Best*

Farley Mowat, *This Rock Within the Sea: A Heritage Lost*
Al Pittman, *Once When I was Drowning: Poems*
E. Annie Proulx, *The Shipping News*
http://www.wordplay.com/tourism/folklore.html

Structure:

1. How informative is Ray Guy's beginning? Identify every fact which the opening sentence states or implies about the essay that will follow.
2. At the end Ray Guy exclaims, "And thank God I was twelve years old before ever a slice of baker's bread passed my lips." What does this final sentence do that qualifies it to close the essay?
3. Roughly what percentage of this essay consists of *examples*? Are there enough to make the point? Are there too many?
4. Why does Guy tell the incident of the puffed rice (pars. 2 and 3)? How does it prepare us for the rest of the argument?

Style:

1. Do you find Ray Guy's vocabulary difficult? For what audience is he writing? If he had known people outside Newfoundland would read this essay, what might he have done differently?
2. Does Guy waste words or save them? Give *examples.*
3. Find five sentence fragments. Are they errors? Why does Guy use them?
4. Point out expressions that make the essay folksy and COLLOQUIAL. Does Guy's TONE fit his topic?
5. In paragraph 18 Guy describes root cellars: "With the hay growing on them they looked like hairy green igloos." Where else does he use SIMILES?

Ideas for Discussion and Writing:

1. Through newspaper columns Guy fought the Newfoundland government's policy of forcing people from outports — such as the one described in this essay — to central locations where they would do factory work instead of fish. Should traditional cultures be preserved? Are governments ever right in forcing them to change? Defend your answer with *examples.*

2. Fast-food chains have been Americanizing the eating habits not only of Canada but also of many other countries. In this process what have we gained? What have we lost?

3. **PROCESS IN WRITING:** *Guy refers to "outport soul food" (par. 13). In an essay, describe the "soul food" of your own childhood. Take notes over several days, letting one memory lead to the next. Then fill a draft with large numbers of examples. In further drafts add more SENSE IMAGES and FIGURES OF SPEECH, to bring this cuisine alive for readers who grew up elsewhere. Finally, read aloud to detect repetition or other weak style, before writing the final version.*

Note: See also the Topics for Writing at the end of this chapter.

Michele Landsberg

West Must Confront Anonymous Misery of the World's Children

Michele Landsberg is one of the nation's most liked and trusted journalists, a voice of compassion and common sense. Her career could be summed up in the words Women & Children First, *the title of her 1982 book. In it she collected some of her best earlier newspaper columns on abuses such as rape and domestic violence, but also on the joys of family life such as birth, holiday rituals, graduation and marriage. This split focus illustrates Landsberg's position as feminist: though she fights inequalities suffered by women, she strongly believes in marriage and family life. Her attempts to reconcile these sometimes opposing values lend an often dramatic power to her essays. Landsberg was born in 1939 in Toronto, and studied at the University of Toronto. Since then she has written for* The Globe and Mail, Chatelaine *and* The Toronto Star, *winning National Newspaper Awards for both her columns and feature articles. In 1986 her family interests led to* Michele Landsberg's Guide to Children's Books. *Then living in New York City as wife of Canada's ambassador to the United Nations, Stephen Lewis, Landsberg produced a series of columns for* The Globe and Mail *about New York and about international issues at the UN, which has its headquarters there. One of these articles is our selection, from November 7, 1987. (Its point was in fact realized when in September 1990, 20 countries ratified the United Nations Convention on the Rights of the Child.) To round off her American experiences, two years later Landsberg published* This is New York, Honey! A Homage to Manhattan With Love & Rage.

I nternational Declarations come in for a lot of derision. Any hostile observer at the United Nations Commission on Human Rights in Geneva, for example, might well snicker as delegates lengthily debate each parenthesis, comma, word, in the draft Convention on the Rights of the Child.

The process has gone on for years, and will not come to fruition for several more. Can the verbiage really make that much difference to the millions of the world's children who suffer and die in anonymous misery?

3   Yes. Ten years ago, the mere phrase "children's rights" was, to most people, a joke, a ludicrous extension of the "rights" frenzy of the '70s. Today it has entered our consciousness as a legitimate and forceful claim. The Declaration process itself (now pressing forward more rapidly under the leadership of Poland and Canada), involving hundreds of volunteer organizations and government officials, has turned many governments' attention, some for the first time, to the agony of their children.

4   An essential part of social change is the forcing of this attention. What newspaper, a decade ago, wrote about child labor in the Third World? Now, in recent weeks and months, well-researched documents — from the Christian Science Monitor, the Cox Newspaper Service, the International Defence and Aid Fund, the United Nations sub-commission on the prevention of discrimination against minorities — have heaped up on my desk.

5   They catalogue a horror that has been invisible to most of us.

6   They tell of Gypsy children who are kidnapped or sold from Yugoslavia to criminal gangs in Italy, where they are beaten into performing as thieves and beggars.

7   Thirteen- and 14-year-old girls work 17-hour days at their sewing machines in Manila sweatshops. The pay: 13 cents an hour.

8   That's better than the one cent a day earned by 5-year-olds who weed the tea plantations in Sri Lanka.

9   In the Ashanti Goldfields (jointly owned by the Government of Ghana and a company called Lonrho International), 11-year-old boys labor naked in pools of cyanide to extract gold from rock.

10   Girls as young as 4 are virtual slaves in Moroccan carpet factories, crouched on their benches for 12-hour days, sleeping on the floor next to their looms at night, breathing air thick with fluff and fibre.

11   They compete with Indian carpet-makers for the North American market. In New York department stores like Bloomingdale's, the luscious glowing colors of the carpets fetch prices in the thousands. But the small Indian and Moroccan weavers themselves earn a pittance of pennies an hour.

12   World Health Organization officials are researching the trauma of children as young as 7, in countries like Kenya, who drudge through 15-hour days as household servants. They weep at night, refuse to speak, wet their beds. They mind the babies, scrub dishes, floors and laundry, live like little household animals.

13   Brazil has 30 million street children; many more are actually sold for forced labor. On rice plantations, children of 6 or 7 are primed with alcohol in the pre-dawn to get ready for work. Their beds are the bare ground, their wages a plate of rice; little girls are used as prostitutes by

their overseers. On Brazil's tea plantations, 10,000 children ages 5 to 13 wade through pesticide muck. They get 15 cents for every 52-pound sack of tea they pick and carry.

You'll switch to cocoa? Thousands of Nigerian children are kidnapped — some as young as 5 or 6 — to slave in cocoa plantations.   14

In Mozambique and Angola, 375 of every 1,000 infants die — the   15
highest infant mortality rate in the world — because of devastation caused by South African armed aggression.

Thailand has at least 30,000 child prostitutes. In one Bangkok house,   16
owned by a prominent man active in charity, the little girls crawl through a hole in the wall at the sound of the madame's whistle, and sit on benches wearing numbered shirts, to be picked by customers. Their faces, in Cox News photographs, are ravishingly lovely, shatteringly sad.

In most of these countries, governments are struggling to overcome   17
the kind of poverty that makes child labor a condition of life. Much of the poverty is caused by debt. Third World countries are economically strangled by the high interest rates on the money they owe to us First Worlders.

In some countries, however, it is the government that orchestrates   18
the horror. South African news censorship means that we no longer see the sudden, irrational descent of gun-wielding police from their armored cars to shoot at random as black children scatter, terrified, in the dusty township streets. But volunteer organizations doggedly collect the evidence. They tell us that last year, 59,000 children were detained by South African police.

Children as young as 7 and 8 are cross-questioned for hours in court,   19
denied lawyers or visits from parents. They are so small that all we can see of them over the edge of the dock are their troubled, panicky eyes.

Fathers tell of finding their broken, tortured children lying on con-   20
crete floors of police stations, trembling and speechless and sometimes dying. Children in jail are routinely beaten and whipped; many have been tear-gassed, scarred with boiling water, hosed, electric-shocked, raped, beaten into permanent brain damage or death.

Can a United Nations Convention on children's rights make a differ-   21
ence? The people at work in the field say yes. When enough people absorb the idea that all children have fundamental rights, we lucky ones in the West will begin to accept responsibility. We buy the carpets, the cocoa, the rice, the cheap shirts, the pornography, the South African gold. One day we'll buy the idea that we can, through our foreign policy, help the children.

∆ ∆

Explorations:

Michele Landsberg, *Women & Children First*
Alison Acker, *Children of the Volcano*
Rigoberta Menchu, *I, Rigoberta Menchu: an Indian Woman in Guatemala*
David Parker, *Stolen Dreams: Portraits of Working Children*
Mohammad Qadeer, "Why the Third World Needs Child Labour," *The Globe and Mail*, February 25, 1997, p. A15.
Craig Kielburger, "No Place in the World Needs Child Labour," *The Globe and Mail*, March 7, 1997, p. A19.
http://www.cfc-efc.ca/ccrc/index.htm
http://www.freethechildren.org/index.html

Structure:

1. Landsberg opens her argument with a question (in par. 2) and closes it with another (in par. 21). Both have the same answer. Analyze the effects of these parallels.
2. What share of this essay is *examples*? Are there enough? Too many? Compare "Outharbor Menu" in this chapter. Do you prefer Ray Guy's almost exclusive use of examples, or Landsberg's more mixed use of examples and generalizations? Why?
3. In what ways do Landsberg's many statistics function as *examples*? How important are they to her argument?
4. Explore the parallelism of the words "we buy" in Landsberg's final two sentences: How does it help engineer her closing?
5. What rhetorical principle has Landsberg used in placing "children" as the very last word of her argument?

Style:

1. Analyze how Landsberg uses IRONY in each of these *examples*: the wages of carpet makers compared to the price of their carpets (par. 10–11), our use of tea vs. our use of cocoa (par. 13–14), and the case of the man active in charity who owns a house of child prostitution (par. 16).
2. Has Landsberg achieved a good ratio of content to length? Has her proliferation of *examples* just led to wordiness, or has it fostered CON-CISENESS? Explain.

Ideas for Discussion and Writing:

1. In his article, listed above in "Explorations," Mohammad Qadeer states that in the Third World, "children's work often makes the

difference between starvation and survival when death, displacement or disease strike family." On November 24, 1997 a CBC News documentary argued that when well-meaning North Americans shun products made by child labour in the Third World, many of the children merely change to even worse jobs — such as brick making or metal work, at even lower wages. Yet the young Canadian activist Craig Kielburger, in his article, listed in "Explorations," states that "on average countries that use child labour spend 30 times more on the military than they do on primary education. The biggest barrier to ending child labour is political will." Where is the truth? Look up these articles on microfilm in your school library. Read both sides of the issue, then try to decide who is right. Explain your view to the class, giving *examples* to support it.

2. Why does Landsberg not include *examples* from our own country? Are developed countries free of the problems she cites in developing countries?

3. In closing, Landsberg links our shopping habits to the fate of children in developing countries. Add to her suggestions: What more could we do in Canada, besides selective shopping, to reduce misery among the world's young? In particular, how might we apply Landsberg's idea of using our foreign policy to help the children?

4. **PROCESS IN WRITING:** *For one week read the international section of a daily newspaper, collecting, as Landsberg did, reports with implications for Third-World children. Highlight key* examples, *then choose an event or situation that makes you react. Freewrite to focus your argument. Now draft a letter to the editor of the same newspaper, stating your* THESIS *clearly, then, like Landsberg, letting* examples *from your reading do most of the arguing. Keep in mind that now you have a real* AUDIENCE; *are your vocabulary and whole approach suitable to the kind of person who reads this newspaper? If not, revise. Also cut every scrap of deadwood, because editors like letters short. Finally, show your teacher a draft before writing and mailing the final version. Continue reading the newspaper for a week or two; if you see your letter, bring it to class to share.*

Note: See also the Topics for Writing at the end of this chapter.

Amy Willard Cross

Safety First, Fun a Distant Second

"Write about things that impassion you," advises Amy Willard Cross. She also advises not to write for a living as she does; only rarely, she says, does the freelance writer get to work on topics of personal interest. Cross holds a B.A. in French literature from Wellesley, and has studied in Paris. Since then she has worked as a magazine editor in Los Angeles and Toronto, has broadcast radio essays on the CBC, and has contributed many articles to The Globe and Mail, The Toronto Star, Toronto Life Fashion, Ms, Glamour, Self *and* Working Woman. *Cross is now Special Projects Editor for* Chatelaine. *Several of her writings have been anthologized. She has also published books of her own, such as* The Summer House: A Tradition of Leisure *(1992) and* Summer in America *(1995). Our selection appeared on January 8, 1991 in* The Globe and Mail. *Though Cross does not consider herself a humorist, this essay deftly reduces to absurdity a growing trend in Canada.*

1   **M**y sister used to be fearless. She lived by herself in neighbourhoods where people held riots on their days off. She hitch-hiked. Snorkled in shark-infested waters. Dared.

2   Then she had a child. Her first Christmas as a mother, she met me at the airport in a new car: a big, silver car of European extraction with heavy metal exterior, buttery leather interior.

3   "Nice car, eh?" she said, "We got it for the baby. It's got great crash stats. If I collide with a small import, my hood might crunch, but I could probably hop out and play tennis."

4   "Would you really feel like tennis after trash-compacting somebody — even if he did drive a Japanese car?"

5   "Buckle your seat belt," she said. Despite the one-in-a-something chance of having an accident within a five-mile radius from her house, we arrived unscathed.

6   Once home, it was clear she had redecorated: the look was late 20th-Century Safety. Knee-high plastic gates closed off areas unsupervised by adults. Smoke alarms stood guard in every room, shrieking warnings at exuberant smokers or burnt toast. What really stood out was the TV. It had been moved some 15 feet away from the sofa, so you would need binoculars to see the weather map. I moved closer, turned it on.

"Get back," my sister cried, "you're in the electromagnetic field." 7
Apparently, those friendly watts and volts that had once powered our
nightlight when we were kids and chilled our Jell-O had mutated into
agents of danger that threatened cancer and other bad luck. To contain this malevolent force, plastic covers blocked each plug — staving
off electrocution and keeping electromagnetic fields where they belonged.

Like others who have managed to reproduce themselves genetically, 8
my sister sees potential danger in any situation — call it Dangervision.
As the gift of prophecy yields glimpses of the future, Dangervision
reveals a parallel reality of worst-case scenarios: freak accidents, falls,
fires, or drowning in bath water.

Dangervision probably has an evolutionary role. But even those with- 9
out this second sight get help protecting themselves against themselves.
Well-meaning safety campaigns warn against things most of us avoid
instinctively, slowly undoing the undemocratic notion that only the
fittest survive. Nowadays, anybody can survive — just follow the safety
tips inside every package. In fact, during the past decade accidental
deaths have plummeted. Fewer and fewer people go with a bang,
splat or gurgle; most of us die slowly, remaining eligible for an
open casket. The Heimlich manoeuvre, pool covers, home fire extin-
guishers, child-proof caps, guard rails, seat belts, smoke-free dining rooms
and life vests certainly played a part. Finally, we know that plastic
dry-cleaning bags are *not* toys. And lots of guardian angels are out of
work.

Sure we're living longer, but it seems longer, too. It's hard to have 10
fun when you're being careful. You can't drink champagne on afternoon canoe rides any more — it's the law. Heaven knows, you could
pass out, fall into the lake and drown. You can't feel crispness of wind
in your hair while galloping through the meadows, or racing country
roads on a 10-speed, because helmets trap a steamy, sweaty halo of dead
air around your head. God forbid, the horse could shy, your tire could
blow, and your brains could split open.

Children suffer from safety even more. Their fearlessness is very quickly 11
beaten out of them by adoring parents. Following the advice of kid
safety handbooks, new moms and dads crawl around the floor to experience coffee-table-level perils as their toddler would. They bug their
kid's room with baby intercoms. Parents won't let kids play in the park
without a grown-up around to stop them from climbing trees or swinging upside down. Like Irish crystal, kids get dusted off on important
occasions and handled ever so carefully — after all, there's usually only
one to the set. You wonder, will children raised in padded environ-
ments languish like domesticated animals released into the wild, unable to fend off normal predators?

12   Besides editing all risk from our lives, Dangervision has robbed us of the pleasure of surviving. Those few sweet moments after a close call felt great: nearly fell off the observation deck, nearly drowned, nearly went over the median!

13   Now people take safe, accident-free lives for granted. If the average life span is 73 years, they figure they've got it coming to them. Fate or God's will or bad luck better not get in the way. And if it does, watch out. Accidents don't just happen, they're someone else's fault. And faults get sued. For a lot of money. Disclaimers are posted everywhere in a vain effort to prevent product liability suits: not responsible for accidental dismemberment with the Brush 'Em automatic tooth-cleaning system.

14   Europeans don't share this need to protect their fellow citizens from themselves. They don't ruin architecture with unsightly metal guard rails, but let any stupid tourist climb up fortifications or Roman amphitheatres. The attitude is probably a form of population control for a very crowded continent.

15   Now that cleaners hide behind childproof cabinets, now that railings protect balconies, now that no one smokes in bed after tousling the sheets, we're finally safe. Strangely, people flirt with danger recreationally. The same people with air bags, life vests and smoke alarms spend their weekends heli-skiing, hang-gliding, parachuting and racing cars. So bridled in normal life, people travel miles to dare the latest craze: bungy-jumping. They pay piles of money to jump off bridges attached to nothing but a giant rubber band from which they bounce — narrowly escaping the water's surface. Apparently, it's an exhilarating nearly.

16   By the time the nephew makes it to adulthood accident-free, he'll probably fly straight to Australia and jump some bungies.

△△

Explorations:

Jack Dowie and Paul Lefrere, eds., *Risk and Chance: Selected Readings*
Peter Bernstein, *Against the Gods: The Remarkable Story of Risk*
Aldous Huxley, *Brave New World*
George Orwell, *1984*
http://www.mcleodregional.org/youth/y_safety_check.html

Structure:

1. Rate the opening ANECDOTE: Does it draw our interest? Does it lead into Cross's subject?
2. Show how the device of *contrast* powers both the opening and closing *examples*.

3. Cross's THESIS STATEMENT does not appear in the opening. Where is it?
4. How much room in this essay does Cross give to *examples*? Take out your own latest essay and estimate its example content. Do you need to go higher? How much higher?

Style:

1. Analyze Cross's TONE: does she just amuse us with scenes of ridiculous behaviour, or behind the laughs is there a serious message? Identify one *example* that seems exaggerated or even made up; identify another that seems serious.
2. Cross states that "fewer and fewer people go with a bang, splat or gurgle" (par. 9). What kind of demise does each of these SENSE IMAGES imply? Without the images, how many more words might Cross have needed here?
3. Paragraph 1 ends with sentence fragments. Why? How does the essayist distinguish between fragments as errors and as devices of style?
4. What device powers Cross's observation that "the same people with air bags, life vests and smoke alarms spend their weekends heli-skiing, hang-gliding, parachuting and racing cars" (par. 15)?

Ideas for Discussion and Writing:

1. Has "Dangervision," either your own or other people's, reduced your fun? Give *examples*.
2. Cross states that children's fearlessness "is quickly beaten out of them by adoring parents" (par. 11). Do you agree? If you have children, will you favour their physical safety or their learning to manage risk? In today's society is the latter skill still important?
3. If our society shuns danger, then why do we flock to rides at midways and amusement parks, watch horror and disaster films, and read tabloids that glory in axe murders?
4. If we are "finally safe" from the old dangers Cross describes, have new ones in the world taken their place? Give *examples*. Is there any way to be safe from these as well?
5. **PROCESS IN WRITING:** *Do you believe that taking risks is an essential and desirable part of living, or do you prefer safety? Take a side in your THESIS STATEMENT. Now brainstorm a page full of* examples, *either of dangers that need to be contained, or of legitimate activities that have been unjustly limited (for example, is it good that diving boards are being removed from public pools?). Arrange your examples so the best come last, then write them into a fast discovery draft. When this has "cooled off," look it over. Have you reached an* example *content of 70% to 80%? If not, cross out any*

generalizing that is vague or repetitious, and in its place add more good examples. Do SENSE IMAGES spark your examples? If not, add. Do TRANSITIONS link your examples? If not, add. Finally, read aloud as you fine-tune the argument into a final version.

Note: See also the Topics for Writing at the end of this chapter.

Josh Freed

Say Hi or Die

An anglophone living in Montreal, Josh Freed is a prolific filmmaker, TV personality and director, author of books, and newspaper columnist. He has hosted and directed over 50 documentaries for the CBC's current events feature The Journal; *has produced many shows on Quebec and its relationship with Canada; was interviewer in* Voices of the Holocaust, *a one-hour CBC special; wrote* A Song For Quebec, *a documentary for PBS and the National Film Board about the Quebec independence movement; and was writer and director of* The Last Train *(1990), a portrayal of Canada by train, for PBS and England's Channel 4. In 1980 Freed's book* Moonwebs: Journey Into the Mind of a Cult, *appeared, and was then produced as the feature film* Ticket to Heaven, *winning the Genie Award for best Canadian film of 1984. That same year appeared Freed's bestselling* Anglo Guide to Survival in Quebec, *a lighthearted look at his own minority situation, which went on to play for two years in Montreal as a musical comedy. Freed has further carved out a role for himself as humorist, through weekly newspaper columns in the* Montreal Gazette. *In 1990 appeared an anthology of his pieces,* Sign Language and Other Tales of Montreal Wildlife, *and in 1994 another collection,* Fear of Frying and Other Fax of Life. *From this last comes our selection, based on Freed's stay in California.*

L OS ANGELES — I awoke at 2 a.m. yesterday in truly L.A. style, with a 1 helicopter circling my street and a spotlight scouring the bushes. A megaphone voice was shouting:

"Don't move! We know you're there. Don't move!" 2

So I went back to sleep. I'm getting used to life in L.A. Lawless — the 3 Dodge City of the '90s. As I write, I can hear the ever-present wail of sirens racing off toward muggings, murder and mayhem. The sky here is always sunny but to enjoy the weather it's wise to stay off the streets.

There were 1,100 homicides last year in L.A. proper — a city of 3.5 4 million people. Multiple murders that would be screaming headlines in Canada are buried on Page B6.

In the last month, a fired employee slaughtered three co-workers, a 5 berserk professor shot his whole family, and a judge's son gunned down two policemen. A teenager put on Jim Morrison's song, "The End," and killed his father with an AR-15 assault rifle. Then he killed a police-woman, and himself.

6   The L.A. police union has just launched a pressure campaign, sending out letters to travel agents and tour groups. "Do not come to Los Angeles . . . it is not safe," they warn tourists, though L.A. citizens have known that for years.

7   The city is an armed and alarmed camp.

8   "Car jackings! Muggings! Thieves! These are the facts of L.A. life!" screamed a full-page newspaper ad this week for a sale on car alarms, with features like an "emergency panic button."

9   I wandered into a shop called Gun Heaven (telephone: 938-GUNS) and there weren't many hunting rifles to be seen, only weapons for hunting people. The shelves were stocked with handguns, "hellfire triggers" and "hide-a-holsters." The walls were covered in T-shirts that showed a smoking gun and the words:

10   "I DON'T dial 911."

11   "How do I get a gun?" I asked a short young man with a big gun on his hip, who said his name was V.J.

12   "Have you used one before?" he asked cheerily.

13   "No?, Well, that's no problem, as long as you've got a valid driver's license."

14   He handed me a small registration form, in triplicate, with some boxes to check off attesting I wasn't a felon, drug addict or psychotic mass murderer. And if I was, would I tell him?

15   Then he showed me a choice of gleaming handguns from the *Bounty Hunter* at $350, to a "$99.99 special" that sounded like a disposable coffee filter.

16   "You use it once then throw it away," said V.J.

17   For home protection, V.J. advised a 12-gauge shotgun. "A revolver is easier to get at, but a 12-gauge scares guys off faster, especially when you pump a couple of rounds into the rack.

18   "It packs a lot of visual impact."

19   When I said I was from Canada, V.J. was more impressed than if I'd pulled out an Uzi. "You moved from Montreal to L.A.!? Man, you're crazy! That's like going from heaven to hell."

20   He's right. American cities like L.A. have become eerie combat zones, where you are always instinctively on guard. Like most people here I now think twice before parking on a side street.

21   I gauge how far I must walk, how many doorwells I must pass, and what kind of people. I never walk outside at night, and why would I want to? The only people on the streets carry bedrolls.

22   Restaurants and bars usually provide someone to take the risk of parking your car. It's called "valet parking" — a polite way of saying: PARKING YOURSELF MAY REDUCE LIFE EXPECTANCY.

After a while you don't even think about walking any more. You forget 23
you ever did, along with other simple pleasures we take for granted in
Canada. You don't go to see interesting sights like the Watts tower,
because it is in Watts. You don't look at other drivers, because they may
be looking at you.

You become suspicious of the homeless, of panhandlers, of anyone 24
who looks weird, or different than you. And you understand why many
Americans are now obsessed with Law and Order, instead of justice.

California has recently passed a tough "three strikes and you're out" 25
law, that will automatically throw people in jail for 25 years after their
third felony, even if they've only stolen an orange.

Many police and politicians here admit the new law is unfair and may 26
double the number of jails. But Californians strongly support it and
other states are soon expected to follow. It's a snappy solution with a
snappy American name; if baseball only had two strikes, the law might
be worse.

Americans want revenge and it's easier to throw people in jail after 27
they shoot you than to figure out ways to stop them from shooting you;
easier to arm the entire country than to disarm it.

After all, a city full of guns does have some advantages. Motorists in 28
L.A. are more polite than those back home in Montreal, partly because
they are terrified of offending other drivers.

"Don't honk," said a friend to me recently, when a car swerved in 29
front of us. "They may be armed!"

I suspect guns also contribute to the city's fervor for friendliness, 30
which I've mentioned in other stories. In a land where anyone may
have a gun, you chat with strangers partly to be friendly, but partly to
make sure they are "normal" like you.

Like other big American cities, L.A.'s friendliness has a slightly defen- 31
sive edge. The city's motto could be: "Say hi or die."

△ △

Explorations:

Josh Freed,
> *Fear of Frying and Other Fax of Life*
> *Sign Language and Other Tales of Montreal Wildlife*
Gary Kleck, *Point Blank: Guns and Violence in America*
http://www.vpc.org/index.htm
http://www.pavisnet.com/ncn/nra/index.html

Structure:

1. What standard attention-getting device does Freed use to open his essay? Does it work?
2. Roughly what percentage of Freed's argument consists of *examples?* What is the effect? Have you ever seen *too many* examples in an essay? And is your own writing more likely to have too many or too few?
3. In "Say Hi or Die" Freed *contrasts* the United States to Canada. Point out all these passages. What do they contribute to his argument?

Style:

1. Hold your book at arm's length to see the paragraphs better. Why are there so many, and why are they so short? For what AUDIENCE was Freed writing?
2. Why is Freed the humorist writing about guns and killing? Point out examples of IRONY and humour. Are these appropriate to a life and death topic? Why or why not?

Ideas for Discussion and Writing:

1. Los Angeles and Toronto are cities of similar size, yet the former has about 20 times more homicides per year. Propose at least five things Toronto and other Canadian cities can do to keep from going the way of Los Angeles.
2. On March 24, 1998, two schoolboys, 11 and 13, fired with rifles onto the playground of a Jonesboro, Arkansas, school, killing one female teacher and four girls, and wounding 11 others. Professional trauma counsellor Scott Poland said that week, "The single greatest thing we could do to reduce the murder and suicide of young people is to reduce gun availability." Another specialist, author of books on "killology," Dave Grossman, cited the "sharp increase in violence in every country that is subject to virtually unrestricted television violence" ("Guns R US," *The Globe and Mail,* March 28, 1998, p. A16). What do *you* see as the *cause* or *causes* of homicide? What has Canada done about it? What remains to be done?
3. Do you own a gun? Do your family or friends? Explain to the class why or why not.
4. Visit the two American Web sites listed in "Explorations." (The first is for the Violence Policy Center, which aims to "reduce firearms violence in America," and the second is for the National Rifle Association, which lobbies to prevent gun control.) Select an issue they both address, such as hunting, shooting contests, or current or planned gun legislation. Learn the positions of both organizations,

and report the *contrast* to the class, also telling your own position on the issue and why you have taken it.

5. In paragraphs 28 and 29 Freed describes what newspapers now call "road rage." Do you see it where you live? What are its *causes*?

6. *Contrast* "Law and Order" with "justice" (par. 24).

7. See this book's essays by Petrowski and Cameron, on Canadian mass murderer Marc Lépine. Is his case related or unrelated to the themes of Freed's argument about homicides in America? Tell how.

8. **PROCESS IN WRITING:** *Is your own neighbourhood safe or unsafe? Walk through it to help you remember* examples. *Now fill a page with brainstorming, highlight the best of your notes, and from these write a* THESIS STATEMENT. *Next write a quick discovery draft of your essay, packing it with many vivid* examples *(as Josh Freed does). Later look it over. Will the opening tempt readers, perhaps with an* ANECDOTE? *Does every* example *support the point? (If some do not, consider changing your thesis statement, in the face of the evidence.) Do* TRANSITIONS *speed the reader on? Does some dramatic effect power the closing? Finally, edit for punctuation and spelling before printing out your best version.*

Note: See also the Topics for Writing at the end of this chapter.

Alberto Manguel

Reading Ourselves and the World Around Us[*]

No Canadian writer is more cosmopolitan than Alberto Manguel. Born in 1948 in Buenos Aires, he spent his early childhood in Israel, where his father was Argentinian ambassador. Later, back in Argentina, he was working in a bookstore when he met the legendary and eccentric writer Jorge Luis Borges, who, after a lifetime of reading, was going blind. Soon the young Manguel was employed reading books to him, and in the process began to share Borges' passion for good writing style and for the fantastic in literature. Then, bored with university, Manguel dropped out to live in Italy, France, Tahiti and England, where, in several languages, he began his life's work as editor, translator, critic and writer. His first book was in Spanish: Antología de literatura fantástica argentina *(1973). Then in 1980 a Canadian publisher brought out his first book in English,* The Dictionary of Imaginary Places, *and two years later Manguel moved from England to Canada. Many more books followed:* Black Water: The Anthology of Fantastic Literature *(1983) and* Black Water II *(1990);* Other Fires: Short Fiction by Latin American Women *(1986);* The Oxford Book of Canadian Ghost Stories *(1990);* Canadian Mystery Stories *(1991);* News from a Foreign Country Came *(his first novel, 1991);* The Gates of Paradise: The Anthology of Erotic Short Fiction *(1993);* Meanwhile, in Another Part of the Forest *(1994, with Craig Stephenson);* Fathers & Sons *(1998); and* Mothers & Daughters *(1998). Our present selection comes from the book he spent seven years researching and writing,* A History of Reading *(1996).*

1   I first discovered that I could read at the age of four. I had seen, over and over again, the letters that I knew (because I had been told) were the names of the pictures under which they sat. The boy drawn in thick black lines, dressed in red shorts and a green shirt (that same red and green cloth from which all the other images in the book were cut, dogs and cats and trees and thin tall mothers), was also somehow, I realized, the stern black shapes beneath him, as if the boy's body had been dismembered into three clean-cut figures: one arm and the torso, **b**; the severed head so perfectly round, **o**; and the limp, low-hanging

---

* Editor's title.

legs, **y**. I drew eyes in the round face, and a smile, and filled in the hollow circle of the torso. But there was more: I knew that not only did these shapes mirror the boy above them, but they also could tell me precisely what the boy was doing, arms stretched out and legs apart. **The boy runs**, said the shapes. He wasn't jumping, as I might have thought, or pretending to be frozen into place, or playing a game whose rules and purpose were unknown to me. **The boy runs**.

And yet these realizations were common acts of conjuring, less interesting because someone else had performed them for me. Another reader — my nurse, probably — had explained the shapes and now, every time the pages opened to the image of this exuberant boy, I knew what the shapes beneath him meant. There was pleasure in this, but it wore thin. There was no surprise.

Then one day, from the window of a car (the destination of that journey is now forgotten), I saw a billboard by the side of the road. The sight could not have lasted very long; perhaps the car stopped for a moment, perhaps it just slowed down long enough for me to see, large and looming, shapes similar to those in my book, but shapes that I had never seen before. And yet, all of a sudden, I knew what they were; I heard them in my head, they metamorphosed from black lines and white spaces into a solid, sonorous, meaningful reality. I had done this all by myself. No one had performed the magic for me. I and the shapes were alone together, revealing ourselves in a silently respectful dialogue. Since I could turn bare lines into living reality, I was all-powerful. I could read.

What that word was on the long-past billboard I no longer know (vaguely I seem to remember a word with several *A*s in it), but the impression of suddenly being able to comprehend what before I could only gaze at is as vivid today as it must have been then. It was like acquiring an entirely new sense, so that now certain things no longer consisted merely of what my eyes could see, my ears could hear, my tongue could taste, my nose could smell, my fingers could feel, but of what my whole body could decipher, translate, give voice to, read.

The readers of books, into whose family I was unknowingly entering (we always think that we are alone in each discovery, and that every experience, from death to birth, is terrifyingly unique), extend or concentrate a function common to us all. Reading letters on a page is only one of its many guises. The astronomer reading a map of stars that no longer exist; the Japanese architect reading the land on which a house is to be built so as to guard it from evil forces; the zoologist reading the spoor of animals in the forest; the card-player reading her partner's gestures before playing the winning card; the dancer reading the choreographer's notations, and the public reading the dancer's movements on the stage; the weaver reading the intricate design of a carpet being woven; the organ-player reading various simultaneous strands of music orchestrated on the page; the parent reading the baby's face for signs of joy or fright, or wonder; the Chinese fortune-teller reading the ancient marks on the shell of a tortoise; the lover blindly reading the loved one's body at night, under the sheets; the psychiatrist helping patients read their own bewildering dreams; the Hawaiian fisherman reading the ocean currents by plunging a hand into the water; the farmer reading the weather in the sky — all these share with book-readers the craft of deciphering and translating signs. Some of these readings are coloured by the knowledge that the thing read was created for this specific purpose by other human beings — music notation or road signs, for instance — or by the gods — the tortoise shell, the sky at night. Others belong to chance.

6   And yet, in every case, it is the reader who reads the sense; it is the reader who grants or recognizes in an object, place or event a certain possible readability; it is the reader who must attribute meaning to a system of signs, and then decipher it. We all read ourselves and the world around us in order to glimpse what and where we are. We read to understand, or to begin to understand. We cannot do but read. Reading, almost as much as breathing, is our essential function.

△ △

Explorations:

Alberto Manguel,
   A History of Reading
   The Dictionary of Imaginary Places
   News from a Foreign Country Came
http://www.nald.ca

Structure:

1. Manguel's opening *example* is an ANECDOTE. Does it draw your attention? Does it tempt you to read on?
2. What proportion of this selection consists of *examples*? Has Manguel reached the 50% level? Why does he start with a personal *example* (learning to read) then move on to *examples* of other people "reading"?
3. Read aloud in class the mass of *examples* crowded one after the other into paragraph 5. What is their effect?
4. At age four Manguel sees the drawing of the boy as made of letters, but the letters also spell "boy." Is this a METAPHOR or is it developed fully enough to become an analogy? (See the introduction to Chapter 6: "Analogy and Related Devices.") Then in paragraph 5 when an

architect "reads" the land or a parent "reads" a baby's face, do we have metaphors or has this extended passage become an analogy?

Style:

1. Read paragraph 6 aloud in class, while your classmates put up their hands each time they detect repetition. In a book that took seven years to write, is all this repeating accidental? What is its effect?
2. Examine the third sentence of paragraph 5. How many words does it have? Would you write a sentence this long? Why does Manguel? And why does he wait till the end to give us the key sentence elements, the subject and verb?
3. Placing a key word at the end of paragraphs is a favourite trick of polished writers. Point out each place where Manguel has done this. What are the effects?

Ideas for Discussion and Writing:

1. *Narrate* the first moment when you knew you could read. Or narrate the moment of first reading a second language.
2. About one in six Canadian adults is said to be functionally illiterate. How would your own life be changed if you could not read? Give at least 5 *examples*.
3. Do you know a language that uses not letters but characters? Thinking of Manguel's story of the boy made of letters, show an *example* of a character in your other language that looks like what it means.
4. In paragraph 5 Manguel tells of "the farmer reading the weather in the sky." Can you "read" that language? What weather would you expect from these signs?
   - Wind from the south or east
   - Fluffy cumulus clouds
   - Robins flocking together, agitated
   - A red sky in the morning. In the evening
5. What was the first book you ever read? What is the latest? Your all-time favourite? Your preferred magazine or newspaper? Why?
6. Alberto Manguel reads not only English but also Spanish, French, Italian and several more languages. What language would you like to learn next, and why? Or if you're already multilingual, like many Canadians, give *examples* of how this has affected your life.
7. The average Canadian reads less than one book a year, apart from school texts. By the end of high school he or she has also spent more hours in front of the TV than in the classroom. What are your reactions? How could you, personally, free up more time to read and think?

8. **PROCESS IN WRITING:** *Reviewing question 4, think of a situation (a moment in sports; a social encounter; heavy traffic; the white water in front of your canoe, kayak or raft; etc.), in which you must "read" your surroundings. Freewrite for a few minutes on this, never stopping the motion of your pen or keyboard. Now highlight the best* examples, *and add any more that come. Write these into a quick discovery draft. Read it to a friend or family member for reactions. Is there a tempting introduction? A dramatic closing? Are there* strong *examples? Do they clearly show the act of "reading" your chosen situation? Now edit: Are there empty words to cut? Paragraphs to end with a key word, for emphasis? TRANSITIONS to add? Finally, spelling and punctuation to fix? Now read your best version to the class for reactions.*

Note: See also the Topics for Writing at the end of this chapter.

EXAMPLE **95**

Topics for Writing

Chapter 2: Example

Each topic below is a generalization that needs examples to bring it alive. Choose one that strikes your interest. Freewrite or brainstorm to see if the examples come (either many short ones or one or more long ones). If they don't, try another. If you disagree with what the topic says, reverse it and write from your own viewpoint.

1. First Impressions Can Mislead
2. Canadians Are Becoming More Like Americans
3. Fast Food Is a Menace
4. Canada's Climate Is Changing
5. Parents of Young Children Never Have Enough Time
6. Television Commercials Are Better Made Than the Programs
7. Quebec Is Truly a "Distinct Society"
8. It Is Dangerous to Forget the Power of Nature
9. Sports Imitate Life
10. Most Children Could Teach Their Parents About Computers
11. Honesty Is Still the Best Policy
12. Working to Live Is Better Than Living to Work
13. Technology Is a Person's Best Friend
14. Not Everyone Needs College or University to Be Successful
15. You Are What You Eat
16. Peoples' Choice of Vehicle Can Reveal Their Personality
17. Children Learn Best From Their Parents' Example
18. Prison Is a School for Criminals
19. Superstition is Widespread Even Today
20. Even Children's Television Is Violent
21. We Learn Best from Our Mistakes
22. Our Healthcare System Is Breaking Down
23. The Typical Hollywood Movie Conveys False Values
24. The Cost of Living In the City Is Very High
25. Hockey Is More Violent Than It Used to Be
26. Experience Is the Best Teacher
27. Working at a Job Reduces Performance in School
28. Love Is Blind
29. Maintenance Is More Important Than Some Car Owners Think
30. People and Their Pets Tend to Act Alike

Note also the Process in Writing topic after each selection in this chapter.

Process in Writing: Guidelines

Follow at least some of these steps in developing your essay through examples (your teacher may suggest which ones).

1. *Take time choosing your topic, then try it out through brainstorming or freewriting. Do you have something to say? Can you supply examples? If not, try another topic.*

2. *Visualize your AUDIENCE: What level of language, what TONE, what examples, will communicate with this person or persons? (Remember the kinds of examples listed in our chapter introduction.)*

3. *Do a rapid "discovery draft," double-spaced. Do not stop now to fix things like spelling and punctuation; just get the material safely out on paper.*

4. *The next day, look this draft over. Do your examples make up at least 50% of the content? Or if you give one long example, do you explain it in enough depth? If not, add. Does every example support your main point? If not, revise. Are your examples in order of increasing importance? If not, consider rearranging to build a climax.*

5. *Check your second draft for TRANSITIONS, and if necessary add. Test your prose by reading aloud, then revise awkward or unclear passages. Now use the dictionary and style guide if you need them.*

6. *Proofread your final copy slowly, word by word (if your eyes move too fast, they will "see" what should be there, not necessarily what is there).*

Jacques Boissinot/Canadian Press

"As if released from the grasp of searchlights from the shore, when our house plunged into darkness, it was swept, like every other on the street, fast downstream."

—*Anne Michaels, "Hurricane"*

CHAPTER

3

DESCRIPTION

It's large and purple and. . .

Consider the writer's tools: words in rows on a page. The writer cannot use gestures, facial expression, or voice, as the public speaker does. The writer cannot use colour, shape, motion or sound, as the filmmaker does. Yet words on a page can be powerful. We have all seen readers so involved in the words of a book that they fail to hear their own name called for dinner, or pass their own stop on the bus. These people have entered another world, living at second hand what a writer has lived or at least imagined at first hand.

How does writing do this to us? How does it make experience come alive? There are many ways, and one of them is description. In simulating real life, description makes frequent appeals to our senses:

sight
hearing
touch
smell
taste

In "Hurricane," Anne Michaels makes us see and feel and smell and taste the storm: "The rain hit; needles into my face. I couldn't breathe

99

for the rain, gulping water in mid-air. Strange lights pierced the wind. Icy tar, my river was unrecognizable; black, endlessly wide, a torrent of flying objects."

In "D'Sonoqua," Emily Carr appeals to our senses of smell and sight together when she writes, "Smell and blurred light oozed thickly out of the engine room, and except for one lantern on the wharf everything else was dark." Then in the next paragraph she moves on to hearing and touch: "Every gasp of the engine shook us like a great sob."

Throughout his selection "In the Trenches," Charles Yale Harrison masterfully conveys how a shelling attack looked, sounded, felt, smelled and even tasted (a piece of mud flies into the narrator's mouth. "It is cool and refreshing. It tastes earthy.") We readers were not in the front lines of World War I as Harrison was, but when we read his description we have all too good an idea what it was like. Of course that's his purpose; in showing us the horrors he witnessed, he is saying between the lines that war is a tragedy.

Similarly, behind every descriptive choice you make, behind every image you supply to your reader, should be your own overall purpose. In a warmup exercise such as freewriting, or even as you begin a "discovery draft," you may not yet know that purpose. But the act of writing should soon make it clear: Is your subject scary, inspiring, pitiful, exasperating, ugly, beautiful, calm or violent? Once you know, help your audience to know as well.

Sometimes a piece of descriptive writing has no thesis, because it is presented as a sketch or narrative, not as an essay. Even then, it usually has an underlying purpose, like the value judgement Harrison implies about war. As you produce description, whether in an essay or not, keep that purpose in mind while you choose each detail, each image, each word. Apply it again as you revise. By the time you finish, your description, whether or not it has a thesis, will convey a message.

Figures of speech — such as the similes and metaphors discussed in Chapter 6 — are powerful tools of description. When Emily Carr writes that a person's face is "greeny-brown and wrinkled like a baked apple," or when Thierry Mallet writes that a woman's throat, "thin and bare as a vulture's neck, showed the muscles like cords," the idea of old age is swiftly and powerfully conveyed. Onomatopoetic language — words like "scuttled," "slithered," "grated" and "ooze" — describes by sounding like what it means. Emily Carr enriches her writing with these and many others. (See FIGURES OF SPEECH in the glossary of this book.)

In a description not all words are equal. Use short and strong ones from everyday life, not the long and flabby ones that some amateur writers consider eloquent. Do we really "perspire" or do we "sweat"? "Ambulate" or "walk"? "Altercate" or "argue"? "Ponder" or "think"? "Masticate" or "chew"? "Expectorate" or "spit"? It is obvious that the second term in each case is stronger, more vivid, more descriptive. So why would we use the first?

Choose words that convey the right *feeling* as well as the right dictionary meaning. One student closed a pretty description of the ocean by saying "the water was as still as a pan full of oil." The image of water as oil may imply stillness, but this water is not exactly something we would want to dive into or even watch at sunset — we'd be too busy thinking of pollution! Another person described forest trees in autumn as being the colour of a fire engine. The colour may be right, but will the image of a large truck perched in the tree branches really give us that autumn feeling?

Spend the time, then, to "feel" as well as "think" your words. Search drafts for weak or inexact or inappropriate terms, and replace them. If the right word doesn't come, find it in a dictionary or thesaurus. And realize that your electronic thesaurus is so fast that now you can afford to check out dozens of words, making sure your overall idea or feeling, whatever it is, comes through clearly.

Note: Many authors in other chapters use description to help make their point. See especially these examples:

Sylvia Fraser, "My Other Self," p. 38
Ray Guy, "Outharbor Menu," p. 70
Biruté Galdikas, "Akmad," p. 190
Catherine Pigott, "Chicken-Hips," p. 195
Félix Leclerc, "The Family House," p. 235
Joy Kogawa, "Grinning and Happy," p. 336

Anne Michaels

Hurricane

One of the most dramatic events in publishing is the release of a first novel that so stirs the public and critics that its author moves right to the first rank of novelists. Such is the case with Anne Michaels. Born in 1958 in Toronto, she completed an honours B.A. at the University of Toronto, then began to build a reputation as a poet. Her 1986 volume The Weight of Oranges *was well received, and her 1991 book* Miner's Pond *won several prizes. Meanwhile, though, while teaching creative writing at the University of Toronto, Michaels spent almost a decade researching and writing a novel about the Holocaust and its survivors. When in 1996* Fugitive Pieces *saw light, it became a runaway bestseller in Canada, gathered extraordinary praise from critics internationally, and attracted offers from publishers in over 25 countries. Like many novels by poets,* Fugitive Pieces *is larger than it seems; as it examines the lives of several people damaged by the persecution of the Jews in World War II, it takes on layer after layer of meaning, clothing its portrayals in a language so dense and evocative that a reader must go slowly to feel its truths. Our selection is a characteristic passage, well researched and based on a real event. Four years before Michaels was born, in 1954 Hurricane Hazel had killed 1000 people in Haiti before blasting the Eastern coast of the United States, then dropping over 18 cm of water on Toronto in 24 hours. In the ensuing chaos 81 people died, whole blocks of houses, like that of our narrator Ben, were swept away, and 4000 families, like his, were left homeless. Yet in Anne Michaels' poetic vision, the literal storm only echoes and magnifies another storm once lived by Ben's mother and father, when the violence of the Holocaust caught them up and changed them forever.*

1   One fall day, it would not stop raining. By two in the afternoon it was already dark. I'd spent the day playing inside; my favourite place in the house was the realm under the kitchen table, because from there I had a comforting view of my mother's bottom half as she went about her domestic duties. This enclosed space was most frequently transformed into a high-velocity vehicle, rocket-powered, though when my father wasn't home I also set the piano stool on its side and swivelled the wooden seat as a sailing ship's wheel. My adventures were always

ingenious schemes to save my parents from enemies; spacemen who were soldiers.

That evening, just after supper — we were still at the table — a neighbour pounded at the door. He came to tell us that the river was rising and that if we knew what was good for us we'd get out soon. My father slammed the door in his face. He paced, washing his hands in the air with rage.

The banging that awakened me was the piano bobbing against the ceiling beneath my bedroom. I woke to see my parents standing by my bed. Branches smacked against the roof. It wasn't until the water had sloshed against the second-storey windows that my father agreed to abandon the house.

My mother tied me in a sheet to the chimney. The rain hit; needles into my face. I couldn't breathe for the rain, gulping water in mid-air. Strange lights pierced the wind. Icy tar, my river was unrecognizable; black, endlessly wide, a torrent of flying objects. A night planet of water.

With ropes, a ladder, and brute strength, we were hauled in. As if released from the grasp of searchlights from the shore, when our house plunged into darkness, it was swept, like every other on the street, fast downstream.

We were fortunate. Our house was not one of the ones that floated away with its inhabitants still trapped inside. From high ground I saw erratic beams of light bouncing inside upper floors as neighbours tried to climb to their roofs. One by one the flashlights went dark.

Shouts flared distantly across the river, though nothing could be seen in the pelting blackness.

Hurricane Hazel moved northeast, breaking dams, bridges, and roads, the wind tearing up power lines easily as a hand plucking a stray thread from a sleeve. In other parts of the city, people opened their front doors to waist-high water, just in time to see an invisible driver backing their floating car out of the driveway. Others suffered no more than a flooded basement and months of eating surprise food because the paper labels had been soaked off the tins in their pantries. In still other parts of the city, people slept undisturbed through the night and read about the hurricane of October 15, 1954, in the morning paper.

Our entire street disappeared. Within days, the river, again calm, carried on peacefully as if nothing had happened. Along the edges of the floodplain, dogs and cats were tangled in the trees. Alien bonfires burned away debris. Where once neighbours strolled in the evenings, they now wandered the new banks looking for remnants of personal possessions. Again, one might say my parents were fortunate, for they didn't lose the family silverware or important letters or heirlooms however humble. They had already lost those things.

10 The government distributed restitution payments to those whose houses had been washed away. It was only after my parents died that I discovered they hadn't touched the money. They must have been afraid that someday the authorities would ask for it back. My parents didn't want to leave me with a debt.

11 My father took on as many pupils as he could find. We vanished into a cubbyhole of an apartment nearer to the music conservatory. My father preferred living in an apartment building, because "all the front doors look alike." My mother was frightened whenever it rained, but she was happy to be living high up and also that there were no trees too close to the building to threaten our safety.

12 When I was a teenager I asked my mother why we hadn't left the house sooner.

13 "They banged at the door and shouted at us to leave. For your father, that was the worst."

14 She peered from the kitchen into the hallway to see where my father was, and then, with her hands cupped around my ear, whispered: "Who dares to believe he will be saved twice?"

△ △

Explorations:

Anne Michaels,
> *Fugitive Pieces*
> *The Weight of Oranges* (poems)

Betty Kennedy, *Hurricane Hazel*
John Bentley Mays, *Emerald City*
Anne Frank, *The Diary of Anne Frank*
http://www.holocaustcenter.org/lifechance/lit51.shtml

Structure:

1. Like the novel from which it comes, this passage is a *narrative*. Does everything happen in strict time order, or are there also flashbacks or flashforwards?
2. Does the father's intense reaction to the hurricane and flood have *causes* other than the natural disaster itself? If so, what exactly has *caused* this *effect*?
3. Why does Anne Michaels leave larger spaces between paragraphs 8 and 9, and between 9 and 10?

Style:

1. In her *description* of a natural disaster, Michaels exploits SENSE IMAGES. Identify at least one example each of appeals to sight, hearing, touch and taste.

2. Some of this country's best novels have been written by poets — for example *Obasan*, by Joy Kogawa, and *The English Patient*, by Michael Ondaatje. Anne Michaels is also a poet. Can you tell? What qualities of STYLE does this example of her FICTION share with poetry?

3. Does an exalted or poetic STYLE require unusual, large or learned words? Does Michaels use such a vocabulary, or are her words plain and accessible? Give examples. If you are religious, does the language of your holiest scriptures use an exalted vocabulary, or a plain and direct one? Why?

Ideas for Discussion and Writing:

1. Hurricane Hazel was a weather event that in 1954 devastated parts of Toronto. But to Anne Michaels the novelist, is it more? Does the flood that washes away the family's house echo an earlier storm or flood in their lives? An earlier flood in our collective traditions? Describe the *effect* of these references on our view of the family.

2. Ben's father panics at a knock on the door, and later chooses an apartment building because "all the front doors look alike" (par. 11). Do you know immigrants who fled war or another disaster, and who now in the new country are haunted by the old? Should they try to forget? Or is it better to remain conscious of the past? Give reasons.

3. Ben's parents lived through the infamous Holocaust of World War II, in which the Nazis killed some six million Jews. What were some *causes* of this tragedy? What, if anything, did we learn from it? When and where have other "holocausts" taken place?

4. Visit the Web site listed under "Explorations." Play its interactive Life Chance game, in which you try to survive the Holocaust. Then tell each other in class how you either won or lost.

5. "Our entire street disappeared," says Ben in paragraph 9. Are natural disasters on the rise? Do you hear of more tornadoes, hurricanes, rainstorms, blizzards, floods? If so, name some likely *causes*, and suggest likely solutions.

6. **PROCESS IN WRITING:** *Anne Michaels has painted a word picture of a hurricane and flood. Now with your eyes closed, remember a snowstorm, hurricane, tornado, ice storm, wind storm, flood, forest fire, volcanic eruption or earthquake that you have experienced. Next "paint" a page with SENSE*

IMAGES (appealing to some or all of sight, hearing, touch, smell *and* taste*) so your* AUDIENCE *can live the event through your words. Now put your* description *together in a rapid discovery draft, probably in time order. The next day take stock: are there enough sense images? Have you chosen the best ones? Are your words long and flabby, or short and strong? Have you swept your reader along with* TRANSITIONS*? Finally, edit for things like spelling and punctuation before printing out your best version.*

Note: See also the Topics for Writing at the end of this chapter.

Karen Connelly

August 4*

At age 16 Karen Connelly had become, as she later wrote, "painfully bored with high school and hungry for living knowledge of the world." So she applied to an exchange program and the next year left her home of Calgary, Alberta, for Denchai, a village in northern Thailand. There she lived a year of strong emotion: culture shock, wonder at the sights and smells and sounds of the tropics, pleasure at making new friends, and fulfillment in learning a language and culture and landscape so different from her own. So strong was her desire to live life that she later wrote, "I regret having needed to sleep in Thailand. I should have been awake constantly, I should have learned more." Though it took time from her new life, she wrote regularly in a journal, then for years afterward, living in several more countries, polished these observations till they became Touch the Dragon: A Thai Journal. *When the intensely lyrical work was published in 1992, Connelly became the youngest person ever to win the Governor General's Award for Nonfiction. From this book comes our selection, "August 4." Connelly's list of publications continues to grow: In 1990 she had published a book of poetry,* The Small Words in My Body, *which won the Pat Lowther Memorial Award. In 1993 appeared* This Brighter Prison: A Book of Journeys; *in 1995 another travel memoir,* One Room in a Castle: Letters From Spain, France & Greece; *and in 1997 another book of poetry,* The Disorder of Love. *Connelly now divides her time between Canada and an island in Greece.*

E very day something happens and I don't have time to write it down. When an event goes unwritten, I think, I will not forget this day, that moment, the words from that laughing mouth. There is so much I haven't written down, and even more that I haven't touched. The days tear away so quickly now. I fear I'll wake one morning and discover I'm old. I will look backwards into the past and know that all the years I lived were only a few long moments, and that I never knew enough. I've called the airline in Bangkok to confirm my flight date, August 19, two days short of a full year. I don't want to go back.

1

---

* Editor's title.

2   Every roadside, every wild morning journey to Prae, to the market, even pedalling over the bridge in the morning — again and again, I meet stories and pass them by because there is not enough time to spin out the sensations and web them into words. I am too alive and the days are never still.

3   I ride into the fields and find two women. While they bathe at the well, a blade of grass comes to life and glides onto the stones. The women shriek, the wind blows down from the sky and six sand-coloured dogs lope across the field. In movements from a dance, the women flay the pearled green snake with sticks. It is five feet long, thick as a sailing line, still and bloody on the stones. The women's long hair slides over their shoulders and into their eyes. The *pasins* they wear blossom vermilion, blue, yellow; the sky behind them bruises purple-grey with rain. When one of the women spears the snake with a stick and swings it over her head, the dogs leap barking into the air, underbellies creamy white. As the snake whips beyond them, they rush after it, growling and snapping their jaws.

4   All this splendid horror in seconds, in the rice field behind the monastery. The women bend down again to the water. Was the twisting snake real? Did I see it?

5   Will I remember this sky and the people beneath it? Ajahn Champa° was right when she said a year ago (a year! why so fast?) that Thailand would become a dream to me. It already is, but one I live daily. "Canada will soon be real again," she said the other day. Canada. Canada. I push the word over on my tongue. The country of cold rocks. Was I born there?

6   I believe everything now, take it literally when new market women ask me where I've come from. Without thinking, I answer "the river" or "the school" or "the old temple." I don't even consider another country. This one is enough.

7   Canada? The word itself is a question now.

△ △

Explorations:

Karen Connelly,
   Touch the Dragon: A Thai Journal
   One Room in a Castle: Letters From Spain, France & Greece
Peter Mayle, *A Year in Provence*
Barbara Hodgson, *The Tattooed Map*
Rosa Jordan, *Dangerous Places: Travels on the Edge*

° Ajahn Champa: Connelly's teacher.

Ronald Wright, *Time Among the Maya: Travels in Belize, Guatemala, and Mexico*

Isabella Tree, *Islands in the Clouds: Travels in the Highlands of New Guinea*

http://www.swifty.com/lc/linktext/direct/connelly.htm

http://expedia.msn.com/wg/places/Thailand/BGPEFS.htm

Structure:

1. How do the opening (par. 1) and the closing (pars. 5–7) of this selection reflect each other? What is the effect?
2. Point out the THESIS STATEMENT of this selection.

Style:

1. Why does Connelly write "August 4" in the present tense? Is this choice apt for a *description*?
2. When in paragraph 2 the author tells us "there is not enough time to spin out the sensations and web them into words"; when in paragraph 3 the "blade of grass comes to life"; when the women's garments, their *pasins*, "blossom vermilion, blue, yellow"; and when "the sky behind them bruises purple-grey with rain"; what FIGURE OF SPEECH is the author exploiting? How does it strengthen her *description*?
3. Analyze how ONOMATOPOEIA contributes to the view of Canada expressed in "Canada. Canada. I push the word over on my tongue. The country of cold rocks" (par. 5).

Ideas for Discussion and Writing:

1. Connelly was only 17 when she kept the journal that became *Touch the Dragon*. Yet in paragraph 1 she writes, "I fear I'll wake one morning and discover I'm old. I will look backwards into the past and know that all the years I lived were only a few long moments, and that I never knew enough." Do you find these words chilling? Have you ever thought them? How does Connelly try to fight this fear? How would you?
2. "Every day something happens and I don't have time to write it down," says Connelly in her first words. Is writing the way to retain experience? To interpret and understand it? Or is direct experience the way? Do you keep a diary? A journal? What are the benefits? What are the limits?
3. Connelly sums up the episode of the women, the snake and the dogs as "all this splendid horror. . ." (par. 4). Why "splendid"? Why "horror"?

4. In paragraphs 4 and 5 the author keeps wondering if the things she sees are "real," if she will "remember" them, and if returning from the "dream" of Thailand will make Canada "real" again. Do your own major experiences ever seem unreal? Give an example.

5. In the preface to *Touch the Dragon* Connelly describes her boredom at age 16 in Calgary, and how she hoped "to escape from Canada and go very far away." Have you gone on a student exchange, or had another long experience far away? Was it good or bad? *Describe* one event that gives the flavour of it. Or do you hope to stay right where you are? Tell why. Or have you already come here from another country? If so, have you begun to forget your first home, as Connelly in Thailand began to forget hers? Will you go back to visit? Why or why not?

6. **PROCESS IN WRITING**: *Developing question 5 just above, freewrite on your stay in a faraway place (for an AUDIENCE in Canada), or, if you have immigrated to Canada, on your first months here (for an AUDIENCE in your first country). Do you see an overall point, like Connelly's observation that "I don't want to go back"? If so, put it into a THESIS STATEMENT and incorporate it into your first draft. Now think of your readers in the other country: to help them "live" your experience, do what Connelly did: pack your account with* examples, *with images, with appeals to the senses (sight, hearing, touch, smell, taste). Add these elements of* description *wherever you can. Finally, check for things like spelling and punctuation before you print out your best version.*

Note: See also the Topics for Writing at the end of this chapter.

Thierry Mallet

The Firewood Gatherers[*]

Thierry Mallet joined the French fur company Revillon Frères as an apprentice trader, and went on to establish and oversee a large group of trading posts in the Barrens of the Canadian Arctic. Through each of the 20 years before our selection was published, Mallet had travelled through the region, sometimes at great risk, inspecting those posts. When in 1920 Revillon Frères commissioned Robert Flaherty to make a film on the lives of the Inuit hunters who supplied the furs, it was Mallet who accompanied him and the hunter Nanook in journeys marked by terrible storms and near starvation. The film Nanook of the North *(1922) became a documentary classic, but two years later Nanook, himself, starved to death. As for Mallet, his growing knowledge of the land and its people led him to write a small book,* Plain Tales of the North. *Then in 1930 appeared his second modest volume,* Glimpses of the Barren Lands. *Both were published in New York by Revillon Frères. In them Mallet's style is spare but powerful, a reflection of the Arctic itself. Our selection comes from* Glimpses of the Barren Lands.

O ur camp had been pitched at the foot of a great, bleak, ragged hill, a few feet from the swirling waters of the Kazan River. The two small green tents, pegged down tight with heavy rocks, shivered and rippled under the faint touch of the northern breeze. A thin wisp of smoke rose from the embers of the fire.

Eleven o'clock, and the sun had just set under a threatening bank of clouds far away to the northwest. It was the last day of June and daylight still. But the whole country seemed bathed in gray, boulders, moss, sand, even the few willow shrubs scattered far apart in the hollows of the hills. Half a mile away, upstream, the caribou-skin topeks of an Eskimo settlement, fading away amid the background, were hardly visible to the eye.

Three small gray specks could be seen moving slowly above our camp. Human shapes, but so puny, so insignificant-looking against the wild rocky side of that immense hill! Bending down, then straightening up,

---

[*] Editor's title.

111

they seemed to totter aimlessly through the chaos of stone, searching for some hidden treasure.

4   Curiosity, or perhaps a touch of loneliness, suddenly moved me to leave camp and join those three forlorn figures so far away above me near the sky line.

5   Slowly I made my way along the steep incline, following at first the bed of a dried-up stream. Little by little the river sank beneath me, while the breeze, increasing in strength, whistled past, lashing and stinging my face and hands. I had lost sight momentarily of the three diminutive figures which had lured me on to these heights. After a while a reindeer trail enabled me to leave the coulee and led me again in the right direction, through a gigantic mass of granite which the frost of thousands of years had plucked from the summit of the hill and hurled hundreds of feet below.

6   At last I was able to reach the other side of the avalanche of rocks and suddenly emerged comparatively in the open, on the brim of a slight depression at the bottom of which a few dead willow bushes showed their bleached branches above the stones and the gray moss. There I found the three silent figures huddled close together, gathering, one by one, the twigs of the precious wood. Two little girls, nine or ten years old, so small, so helpless, and an aged woman, so old, so frail, that my first thought was to marvel at the idea of their being able to climb so far from their camp to that lonely spot.

7   An Eskimo great-grandmother and her two great-granddaughters, all three contributing their share to the support of the tribe. Intent on their work, or most probably too shy to look up at the strange white man whom, until then, they had only seen at a distance, they gave me full opportunity to watch them.

8   All were dressed alike, in boots, trousers, and coats of caribou skin. The children wore little round leather caps reaching far over their ears, the crown decorated with beadwork designs. One of them carried on the wrist, as a bracelet, a narrow strip of bright red flannel. Their faces were round and healthy, the skin sunburned to a dark copper color, but their cheeks showed a tinge of blood which gave them, under the tan, a peculiar complexion like the color of a ripe plum. Their little hands were bare and black, the scratches caused by the dead twigs showing plainly in white, while their fingers seemed cramped with the cold.

9   The old woman was bareheaded, quite bald at the top of the head, with long wisps of gray hair waving in the wind. The skin of her neck and face had turned black, dried up like an old piece of parchment. Her cheeks were sunken and her cheek bones protruded horribly. Her open mouth showed bare gums, for her teeth were all gone, and her throat, thin and bare as a vulture's neck, showed the muscles like cords.

Her hands were as thin as the hands of a skeleton, the tip of each finger curved in like a claw. Her eyes, once black, now light grey, remained half closed, deep down in their sockets.

She was stone blind. 10

Squatting on her heels, she held, spread in front of her, a small 11 reindeer skin. As soon as the children dropped a branch beside her, she felt for it gropingly; then, her hands closing on it greedily, like talons, she would break it into small pieces, a few inches long, which she carefully placed on the mat at her feet.

Both little girls, while searching diligently through the clumps of 12 dead willows for what they could break off and carry away, kept absolutely silent. Not only did they never call to one another when one of them needed help, but they seemed to watch each other intently whenever they could. Now and then, one of them would hit the ground two or three times with the flat of her hand. If the other had her head turned away at the time, she appeared to be startled and always wheeled round to look. Then both children would make funny little motions with their hands at one another.

The little girls were deaf and dumb. 13

After a while they had gathered all the wood the reindeer skin could 14 contain. Then the children went up to the old woman and conveyed to her the idea that it was time to go home. One of them took her hands in hers and guided them to two corners of the mat, while the other tapped her gently on the shoulder.

The old, old woman understood. Slowly and carefully she tied up the 15 four corners of the caribou skin over the twigs, silently watched by the little girls. Groaning, she rose to her feet, tottering with weakness and old age, and with a great effort swung the small bundle over her back. Then one little girl took her by the hand, while the other, standing behind, grasped the tail of her caribou coat. Slowly, very slowly, step by step they went their way, following a reindeer trail around rocks, over stones, down, down the hill, straight toward their camp, the old woman carrying painfully for the young, the deaf and dumb leading and steering safely the blind.

△ △

Explorations:

Maurice Metayer, ed. and trans., *I, Nuligak* (autobiography)
Dorothy Eber, ed., *Pitseolak: Pictures out of My Life*
Penny Petrone, ed., *Northern Voices: Inuit Writing in English*
Farley Mowat, *People of the Deer*
http://spirit.lib.uconn.edu/ArcticCircle/CulturalViability/Inupiat/
    1800s.html

Structure:

1. "The Firewood Gatherers" is *narrated* in chronological order. Find at least 15 words or phrases that signal the flow of time.
2. Which paragraphs suspend the narration to *describe?*
3. To what extent is "The Firewood Gatherers" based on *comparison and contrast?*
4. What gives the final sentence its power?

Style:

1. How CONCRETE or ABSTRACT is the language of this selection? Point out passages that illustrate your answer.
2. How economical or wasteful is Mallet's writing? Does all the *description* make this passage wordy? Why or why not?
3. Mallet's description of the old woman, in paragraph 9, is clothed in SIMILES (her throat is "thin and bare as a vulture's neck"). Point out others in this paragraph.
4. In paragraph 5 Mallet tells of "a gigantic mass of granite which the frost of thousands of years had plucked from the summit of the hill and hurled hundreds of feet below." Where else does he use PERSONIFICATION?

Ideas for Discussion and Writing:

1. How do this traditional society and our own differ in their views of the old and the disadvantaged? What would the blind great-grand-mother and her disabled descendants be doing today in your town or city?
2. If you live with your parents and grandparents, analyze the benefits and drawbacks for all three generations. Now imagine yourself re-tired. Would you rather live alone, or with your descendants, or in an institution for others your age? Why? And what things could you now do to feel useful?
3. If you have read "Suitcase Lady" by Christie McLaren, compare the two women. If you had to choose, would you be the Inuit great-grandmother of the Barrens or the homeless "suitcase lady" of Toronto? Why?
4. **PROCESS IN WRITING:** *Go to see the oldest or youngest person you know. Take notes. At home or in class, draft a vivid description. Then in further drafts sharpen word choice, IMAGES and FIGURES OF SPEECH, to present your subject strongly. Test the prose aloud before doing your final version.*

Note: See also the Topics for Writing at the end of this chapter.

Christie McLaren

Suitcase Lady*

When Christie McLaren wrote "Suitcase Lady" she was a student at the University of Waterloo, reporting for The Globe and Mail *as a part of her English co-op work experience. After graduation she spent a year and a half at the* Winnipeg Free Press, *then returned to the* Globe, *where she continued to report on a variety of issues. An avid hiker, skier and canoeist, McLaren channelled her love of the outdoors into several years of reporting on forestry, energy and other environmental issues. Another of McLaren's interests is photography. Though a professional journalist, she has said that "writing is nothing but pain while you're doing it and nothing but relief when it's done. Any joy or satisfaction, I think, is a bit of fleeting luck." McLaren spent several nights with "the Vicomtesse" before hearing the story she reports in this selection. The article first appeared in 1981 in the* Globe.

N ight after night, the woman with the red hair and the purple dress sits in the harsh light of a 24-hour doughnut shop on Queen Street West.

Somewhere in her bleary eyes and in the deep lines of her face is a story that probably no one will ever really know. She is taking pains to write something on a notepad and crying steadily.

She calls herself Vicomtesse Antonia The Linds'ays. She's the suitcase lady of Queen Street.

No one knows how many women there are like her in Toronto. They carry their belongings in shopping bags and spend their days and nights scrounging for food. They have no one and nowhere to go.

This night, in a warm corner with a pot of tea and a pack of Player's, the Vicomtesse is in a mood to talk.

Out of her past come a few scraps: a mother named Savaria; the child of a poor family in Montreal; a brief marriage when she was 20; a son in Toronto who is now 40. "We never got along well because I didn't bring him up. I was too poor. He never call me mama."

She looks out the window. She's 60 years old.

With her words she spins herself a cocoon. She talks about drapes and carpets, castles and kings. She often lapses into French. She lets

1

2

3

4

5

6

7

8

* Editor's title.

115

her tea get cold. Her hands are big, rough, farmer's hands. How she ended up in the doughnut shop remains a mystery, maybe even to her.

9   "Before, I had a kitchen and a room and my own furniture. I had to leave everything and go."

10   It's two years that she's been on the go, since the rooming houses stopped taking her. "I don't have no place to stay."

11   So she walks. A sturdy coat covers her dress and worn leather boots are on her feet. But her big legs are bare and chapped and she has a ragged cough.

12   Yes, she says, her legs get tired. She has swollen ankles and, with no socks in her boots, she has blisters. She says she has socks — in the suitcase — but they make her feet itch.

13   As for money, "I bum on the street. I don't like it, but I have to. I have to survive. The only pleasure I got is my cigaret." She lights another one. "It's not a life."

14   She recalls the Saturday, a long time ago, when she made $27, and laughs when she tells about how she had to make the money last through Sunday, too. Now she gets "maybe $7 or $8," and eats "very poor."

15   When she is asked how people treat her, the answer is very matter-of-fact: "Some give money. Some are very polite and some are rude."

16   In warm weather, she passes her time at the big square in front of City Hall. When it's cold she takes her suitcase west to the doughnut shop.

17   The waitresses who bring food to the woman look upon her with compassion. They persuaded their boss that her sitting does no harm.

18   Where does she sleep? "Any place I can find a place to sleep. In the park, in stores — like here I stay and sit, on Yonge Street." She shrugs. Sometimes she goes into an underground parking garage.

19   She doesn't look like she knows what sleep is. "This week I sleep three hours in four days. I feel tired but I wash my face with cold water and I feel okay." Some questions make her eyes turn from the window and stare hard. Then they well over with tears. Like the one about loneliness. "I don't talk much to people," she answers. "Just the elderly, sometimes, in the park."

20   Her suitcase is full of dreams.

21   Carefully, she unzips it and pulls out a sheaf of papers — "my concertos."

22   Each page is crammed with neatly written musical notes — the careful writing she does on the doughnut shop table — but the bar lines are missing. Questions about missing bar lines she tosses aside. Each "concerto" has a French name — Tresor, La Tempete, Le Retour — and each one bears the signature of the Vicomtesse. She smiles and points to one. "A very lovely piece of music. I like it."

She digs in her suitcase again, almost shyly, and produces a round plastic box. Out of it emerges a tiara. Like a little girl, she smooths back her dirty hair and proudly puts it on. No one in the doughnut shop seems to notice.   23

She cares passionately about the young, the old and the ones who suffer. So who takes care of the suitcase lady?   24

"God takes care of me, that's for sure," she says, nodding thoughtfully. "But I'm not what you call crazy about religion. I believe always try to do the best to help people — the elderly, and kids, and my country, and my city of Toronto, Ontario."   25

△ △

Explorations:

Marlene Webber, *Street Kids: The Tragedy of Canada's Runaways*
George Orwell, *Down and Out in Paris and London*
Rohinton Mistry, *A Fine Balance*
http://csf.colorado.edu/homeless/index.html

Structure:

1. "Suitcase Lady" was a feature article in *The Globe and Mail*. As newspaper journalism, how does it differ from a typical ESSAY?
2. What does the opening *description* achieve?
3. How do the many quotations help the *description*?
4. Explain the IRONY of the closing.

Style:

1. Why is the vocabulary of "Suitcase Lady" so easy?
2. "With her words she spins herself a cocoon," states McLaren in paragraph 8. How appropriate is this METAPHOR?
3. Point out at least five concrete details that help you picture this homeless woman's life. Now think about your own writing: do you also give details, or do you hide behind GENERALIZATIONS?

Ideas for Discussion and Writing:

1. If you have read "The Firewood Gatherers," by Thierry Mallet, compare the worlds of the aboriginal great-grandmother in the Arctic and of the suitcase lady in the big city. In what ways is each person better off? In what ways is each worse off? If you had to choose, which person would you be, and why?
2. "It's not a life," says "the Vicomtesse" in paragraph 13. Is your province currently making life easier or harder for homeless people? Give *examples*.

3. How do you react to people who, like the suitcase lady, "bum on the street"? How often do you give? What makes you give to one person but not another?

4. In paragraph 6 the suitcase lady speaks of her son in Toronto: "We never got along well because I didn't bring him up. I was too poor. He never call me mama." In the area where you live, how much money does a family need to stay together? To avoid quarrels over money? To feel hopeful about the future?

5. **PROCESS IN WRITING:** *Tape an interview with someone who in economic status, age, values or some other respect is your opposite. Then write a profile. Like McLaren, portray your subject through his or her best comments. Now add many IMAGES of physical appearance. Edit for conciseness and finally correctness. Then read your final draft, with feeling, to the class.*

Note: See also the Topics for Writing at the end of this chapter.

Charles Yale Harrison

In the Trenches

Charles Yale Harrison (1898–1954) was born in Philadelphia and grew up in Montreal. His independent spirit revealed itself early: in grade four he condemned Shakespeare's The Merchant of Venice *as anti-Semitic, and when his teacher beat him he quit school. At 16 he went to work for the* Montreal Star *and at 18 joined the Canadian army. As a machine gunner in France and Belgium during 1917 and 1918, Harrison witnessed the gruesome front-line scenes he was later to describe in fiction. He was wounded at Amiens and decorated for bravery in action. After the war Harrison returned to Montreal but soon left for New York, where he began a career in public relations for the labour movement and for numerous humanitarian causes. He also wrote several books, both nonfiction and fiction. By far the best is* Generals Die in Bed, *an account of trench warfare that shocked the public and became the best seller of 1930. Spare in style, biting and vivid, this autobiographical novel was described by the* New York Evening Post *as "the best of the war books." From it comes our selection.*

We leave the piles of rubble that was once a little Flemish peasant town and wind our way, in Indian file, up through the muddy communication trench. In the dark we stumble against the sides of the trench and tear our hands and clothing on the bits of embedded barbed wire that runs through the earth here as though it were a geological deposit. 1

Fry, who is suffering with his feet, keeps slipping into holes and crawling out, all the way up. I can hear him coughing and panting behind me. 2

I hear him slither into a water-filled hole. It has a green scum on it. Brown and I fish him out. 3

"I can't go any farther," he wheezes. "Let me lie here, I'll come on later." 4

We block the narrow trench and the oncoming men stumble on us, banging their equipment and mess tins on the sides of the ditch. Some trip over us. They curse under their breaths. 5

Our captain, Clark, pushes his way through the mess. He is an Imperial, an Englishman, and glories in his authority. 6

119

7   "So it's you again," he shouts. "Come on, get up. Cold feet, eh, getting near the line?"

8   Fry mumbles something indistinctly. I, too, offer an explanation. Clark ignores me.

9   "Get up, you're holding up the line," he says to Fry.

10   Fry does not move.

11   "No wonder we're losing the bloody war," Clark says loudly. The men standing near-by laugh. Encouraged by his success, the captain continues:

12   "Here, sergeant, stick a bayonet up his behind — that'll make him move." A few of us help Fry to his feet, and somehow we manage to keep him going.

13   We proceed cautiously, heeding the warnings of those ahead of us. At last we reach our positions.

Δ Δ Δ

14   It is midnight when we arrive at our positions. The men we are relieving give us a few instructions and leave quickly, glad to get out.

15   It is September and the night is warm. Not a sound disturbs the quiet. Somewhere away far to our right we hear the faint sound of continuous thunder. The exertion of the trip up the line has made us sweaty and tired. We slip most of our accouterments off and lean against the parados. We have been warned that the enemy is but a few hundred yards off, so we speak in whispers. It is perfectly still. I remember nights like this in the Laurentians. The harvest moon rides overhead.

16   Our sergeant, Johnson, appears around the corner of the bay, stealthily like a ghost. He gives us instructions:

17   "One man up on sentry duty! Keep your gun covered with the rubber sheet! No smoking!"

18   He hurries on to the next bay. Fry mounts the step and peers into No Man's Land. He is rested now and says that if he can only get a good pair of boots he will be happy. He has taken his boots off and stands in his stockinged feet. He shows us where his heel is cut. His boots do not fit. The sock is wet with blood. He wants to take his turn at sentry duty first so that he can rest later on. We agree.

19   Cleary and I sit on the firing-step and talk quietly.

20   "So this is war."

21   "Quiet."

22   "Yes, just like the country back home, eh?"

23   We talk of the trench; how we can make it more comfortable.

24   We light cigarettes against orders and cup our hands around them to hide the glow. We sit thinking. Fry stands motionless with his steel helmet shoved down almost over his eyes. He leans against the parapet

motionless. There is a quiet dignity about his posture. I remember what we were told at the base about falling asleep on sentry duty. I nudge his leg. He grunts.

"Asleep?" I whisper. 25

"No," he answers, "I'm all right." 26

"What do you see?" 27

"Nothing. Wire and posts." 28

"Tired?" 29

"I'm all right." 30

The sergeant reappears after a while. We squinch our cigarettes. 31

"Everything O.K. here?" 32

I nod. 33

"Look out over there. They got the range on us. Watch out." 34

We light another cigarette. We continue our aimless talk. 35

"I wonder what St. Catherine Street looks like —" 36

"Same old thing, I suppose — stores, whores, theaters —" 37

"Like to be there just the same —" 38

"Me too." 39

We sit and puff our fags for half a minute or so. 40

I try to imagine what Montreal looks like. The images are murky. All 41
that is unreality. The trench, Cleary, Fry, the moon overhead — this is real.

In his corner of the bay Fry is beginning to move from one foot to 42
another. It is time to relieve him. He steps down and I take his place. I look into the wilderness of posts and wire in front of me.

After a while my eyes begin to water. I see the whole army of wire 43
posts begin to move like a silent host towards me.

I blink my eyes and they halt. 44

I doze a little and come to with a jerk. 45

So this is war, I say to myself again for the hundredth time. Down on 46
the firing-step the boys are sitting like dead men. The thunder to the right has died down. There is absolutely no sound.

I try to imagine how an action would start. I try to fancy the prelimi- 47
nary bombardment. I remember all the precautions one has to take to protect one's life. Fall flat on your belly, we had been told time and time again. The shriek of the shell, the instructor in trench warfare said, was no warning because the shell traveled faster than its sound. First, he had said, came the explosion of the shell — then came the shriek and then you hear the firing of the gun . . . .

From the stories I heard from veterans and from newspaper reports I 48
conjure up a picture of an imaginary action. I see myself getting the Lewis gun in position. I see it spurting darts of flame into the night. I hear the roar of battle. I feel elated. Then I try to fancy the horrors of the battle. I see Cleary, Fry and Brown stretched out on the firing-step.

They are stiff and their faces are white and set in the stillness of death. Only I remain alive.

49   An inaudible movement in front of me pulls me out of the dream. I look down and see Fry massaging his feet. All is still. The moon sets slowly and everything becomes dark.

50   The sergeant comes into the bay again and whispers to me:

51   "Keep your eyes open now — they might come over on a raid now that it's dark. The wire's cut over there — " He points a little to my right.

52   I stand staring into the darkness. Everything moves rapidly again as I stare. I look away for a moment and the illusion ceases.

53   Something leaps towards my face.

54   I jerk back, afraid.

55   Instinctively I feel for my rifle in the corner of the bay.

56   It is a rat.

57   It is as large as a tom-cat. It is three feet away from my face and it looks steadily at me with its two staring, beady eyes. It is fat. Its long tapering tail curves away from its padded hindquarters. There is still a little light from the stars and this light shines faintly on its sleek skin. With a darting movement it disappears. I remember with a cold feeling that it was fat, and why.

58   Cleary taps my shoulder. It is time to be relieved.

Δ Δ Δ

59   Over in the German lines I hear quick, sharp reports. Then the red-tailed comets of the *minenwerfer*° sail high in the air, making parabolas of red light as they come towards us. They look pretty, like the fireworks when we left Montreal. The sergeant rushes into the bay of the trench, breathless. "Minnies," he shouts, and dashes on.

60   In that instant there is a terrific roar directly behind us.

61   The night whistles and flashes red.

62   The trench rocks and sways.

63   Mud and earth leap into the air, come down upon us in heaps.

64   We throw ourselves upon our faces, clawing our nails into the soft earth in the bottom of the trench.

65   Another!

66   This one crashes to splinters about twenty feet in front of the bay.

67   Part of the parapet caves in.

68   We try to burrow into the ground like frightened rats.

69   The shattering explosions splinter the air in a million fragments. I taste salty liquid on my lips. My nose is bleeding from the force of the detonations.

° *minenwerfer:* mine throwing trench mortars.

SOS flares go up along our front calling for help from our artillery. 70
The signals sail into the air and explode, giving forth showers of red,
white and blue lights held aloft by a silken parachute.

The sky is lit by hundreds of fancy fireworks like a night carnival. 71

The air shrieks and cat-calls. 72

Still they come. 73

I am terrified. I hug the earth, digging my fingers into every crevice, 74
every hole.

A blinding flash and an exploding howl a few feet in front of the 75
trench.

My bowels liquefy. 76

Acrid smoke bites the throat, parches the mouth. I am beyond mere 77
fright. I am frozen with an insane fear that keeps me cowering in the
bottom of the trench. I lie flat on my belly, waiting . . . .

Suddenly it stops. 78

The fire lifts and passes over us to the trenches in the rear. 79

We lie still, unable to move. Fear has robbed us of the power to act. I 80
hear Fry whimpering near me. I crawl over to him with great effort. He
is half covered with earth and débris. We begin to dig him out.

To our right they have started to shell the front lines. It is about half 81
a mile away. We do not care. We are safe.

Without warning it starts again. 82

The air screams and howls like an insane woman. 83

We are getting it in earnest now. Again we throw ourselves face down- 84
ward on the bottom of the trench and grovel like savages before this
demoniac frenzy.

The concussion of the explosions batters against us. 85

I am knocked breathless. 86

I recover and hear the roar of the bombardment. 87

It screams and rages and boils like an angry sea. I feel a prickly 88
sensation behind my eyeballs.

A shell lands with a monster shriek in the next bay. The concussion 89
rolls me over on my back. I see the stars shining serenely above us.
Another lands in the same place. Suddenly the stars revolve. I land on
my shoulder. I have been tossed into the air.

I begin to pray. 90

"God — God — please . . ." 91

I remember that I do not believe in God. Insane thoughts race through 92
my brain. I want to catch hold of something, something that will explain this mad fury, this maniacal congealed hatred that pours down on
our heads. I can find nothing to console me, nothing to appease my
terror. I know that hundreds of men are standing a mile or two from
me pulling gun-lanyards, blowing us to smithereens. I know that and
nothing else.

93   I begin to cough. The smoke is thick. It rolls in heavy clouds over the trench, blurring the stabbing lights of the explosions.

94   A shell bursts near the parapet.

95   Fragments smack the sandbags like a merciless shower of steel hail.

96   A piece of mud flies into my mouth. It is cool and refreshing. It tastes earthy.

97   Suddenly it stops again.

98   I bury my face in the cool, damp earth. I want to weep. But I am too weak and shaken for tears.

99   We lie still, waiting . . . .

△ △

Explorations:

Charles Yale Harrison, *Generals Die in Bed*
Erich Maria Remarque, *All Quiet on the Western Front* (novel)
Ernest Hemingway, *A Farewell to Arms* (novel)
Timothy Findley, *The Wars* (novel)
Heather Robertson, ed., *A Terrible Beauty: The Art of Canada at War*
<http://www.rootsweb.com/~ww1can/index.html>
<http://www.schoolnet.ca/collections/audio/welcome.htm>

Structure:

1. In *narrating* his description of trench warfare, does Harrison ever deviate from straight chronological order? If so, where and how?
2. Harrison uses SENSE IMAGES so often that throughout this passage *description* carries the main weight of development. Find one example each of a strong appeal to our senses of sight, hearing, touch, taste and smell.
3. Many of the paragraphs are small, some only a word or two long. Examine paragraphs 25–30, 53–56, and 60–68, determining in each passage why the paragraphs are so short.
4. This account of an artillery attack ends with the words "We lie still, waiting . . . ." Is the ending effective, and if so, how?

Style:

1. What degree of CONCISENESS has Harrison achieved in this selection?
2. Harrison tells of the rat: "I remember with a cold feeling that it was fat, and why" (par. 57). How does he convey so much horror in so few words?
3. Analyze the power of the deceptively simple events of paragraph 89: "A shell lands with a monster shriek in the next bay. The concussion rolls me over on my back. I see the stars shining serenely above us.

Another lands in the same place. Suddenly the stars revolve. I land on my shoulder. I have been tossed into the air."

4. In describing, Harrison exploits FIGURES OF SPEECH. Point out at least one good SIMILE and one good METAPHOR.

5. Why is "In the Trenches" told in the present tense, even though the book in which it appeared was published years after the war?

Ideas for Discussion and Writing:

1. Our narrator relates his first experience of war. What has it taught him?

2. Have you read books or seen films that show war in a positive light? Name them. In what ways does "In the Trenches" differ from those accounts?

3. "In the Trenches" is part of a book entitled *Generals Die in Bed*. Discuss the implications of this title.

4. If you have read "Coming of Age in Putnok," compare the conflict described by George Gabori with that described by Harrison. Does hostility between individuals contribute to hostility between nations?

5. **PROCESS IN WRITING**: *Have you lived through a violent or even life-threatening experience, as Harrison did? Close your eyes and remember it. Then in a rapid first draft,* describe *to your audience what it was really like. How did things look, sound, feel, smell or even taste? Use SENSE IMAGES, as Harrison does, to help your reader know too. The next day look your* description *over. Does it begin and end at the right spots, to emphasize the important things? If not, chop or add. Are there unimportant details? If so, chop. Are some parts "thin"? If so, add. Are paragraphs longer in the slower parts and shorter in the tenser parts, like Harrison's? If not, adjust them. Finally, edit for correctness and style before producing your final version.*

Note: See also the Topics for Writing at the end of this chapter.

Emily Carr

D'Sonoqua

Although Emily Carr (1871–1945) was born to a conservative family in the restrictive atmosphere of 19th-century Victoria, British Columbia, she emerged as one of the nation's most original painters and writers. Strong-willed and independent, she turned down several offers of marriage because she believed men "demanded worship" and would only hold her back. Instead she pursued her goal to San Francisco, London and Paris, where she studied art. Home again, with a new way of seeing inspired by post-impressionist artists in France, she embarked alone on expeditions to remote Native villages along the mainland coast and in the Queen Charlotte Islands, where she expressed on canvas the power she felt in the ruins of ancient cultures. Our selection describes three such trips. The public laughed at her bold and free art, but she kept on. Around 1929 Carr shifted focus to the paintings for which she is now best known, her looming, energetic and explosive visions of the coastal rain forest itself. Emily Carr spent most of her life in poverty, for recognition was late in coming. She managed a rooming house for many years, and would sometimes paint on cardboard because canvas cost too much. In her last years, plagued by ill health, she abandoned painting for writing. Our selection comes from her first and probably best book, published in 1941, Klee Wyck *(the title is her name, "Laughing One," given her by the Nootkas).* Klee Wyck *is an extension of her painting: a collection of word sketches in which language is at once rich and suggestive, yet pared down to the bone. During her lifetime she published two more books,* The Book of Small *(1942) and* The House of All Sorts *(1944). Others appeared after her death:* Growing Pains *(autobiography, 1946);* The Heart of a Peacock *(1953);* Pause: A Sketch Book *(1953); and finally her journals, published as* Hundreds and Thousands *(1966).*

1   I was sketching in a remote Indian village when I first saw her. The village was one of those that the Indians use only for a few months in each year; the rest of the time it stands empty and desolate. I went there in one of its empty times, in a drizzling dusk.

2   When the Indian agent dumped me on the beach in front of the village, he said "There is not a soul here. I will come back for you in two days." Then he went away.

I had a small Griffon dog with me, and also a little Indian girl, who, when she saw the boat go away, clung to my sleeve and wailed, "I'm 'fraid." 3

We went up to the old deserted Mission House. At the sound of the key in the rusty lock, rats scuttled away. The stove was broken, the wood wet. I had forgotten to bring candles. We spread our blankets on the floor, and spent a poor night. Perhaps my lack of sleep played its part in the shock that I got, when I saw her for the first time. 4

Water was in the air, half mist, half rain. The stinging nettles, higher than my head, left their nervy smart on my ears and forehead, as I beat my way through them, trying all the while to keep my feet on the plank walk which they hid. Big yellow slugs crawled on the walk and slimed it. My feet slipped, and I shot headlong to her very base, for she had no feet. The nettles that were above my head reached only to her knee. 5

It was not the fall alone that jerked the "Oh's" out of me, for the great wooden image towering above me was indeed terrifying. 6

The nettle-bed ended a few yards beyond her, and then a rocky bluff jutted out, with waves battering it below. I scrambled up and went out on the bluff, so that I could see the creature above the nettles. The forest was behind her, the sea in front. 7

Her head and trunk were carved out of, or rather into, the bole of a great red cedar. She seemed to be part of the tree itself, as if she had grown there at its heart, and the carver had only chipped away the outer wood so that you could see her. Her arms were spliced and socketed to the trunk, and were flung wide in a circling, compelling movement. Her breasts were two eagle heads, fiercely carved. That much, and the column of her great neck, and her strong chin, I had seen when I slithered to the ground beneath her. Now I saw her face. 8

The eyes were two rounds of black, set in wider rounds of white, and placed in deep sockets under wide, black eyebrows. Their fixed stare bored into me as if the very life of the old cedar looked out, and it seemed that the voice of the tree itself might have burst from that great round cavity, with projecting lips, that was her mouth. Her ears were round, and stuck out to catch all sounds. The salt air had not dimmed the heavy red of her trunk and arms and thighs. Her hands were black, with blunt finger-tips painted a dazzling white. I stood looking at her for a long, long time. 9

The rain stopped, and white mist came up from the sea, gradually paling her back into the forest. It was as if she belonged there, and the mist were carrying her home. Presently the mist took the forest too, and, wrapping them both together, hid them away. 10

"Who is that image?" I asked the little Indian girl, when I got back to the house. 11

12   She knew which one I meant, but to gain time, she said, "What image?"

13   "The terrible one, out there on the bluff." The girl had been to Mission School, and fear of the old, fear of the new, struggled in her eyes. "I dunno," she lied.

14   I never went to that village again, but the fierce wooden image often came to me, both in my waking and in my sleeping.

15   Several years passed, and I was once more sketching in an Indian village. There were Indians in this village, and in a mild backward way it was "going modern." That is, the Indians had pushed the forest back a little to let the sun touch the new buildings that were replacing the old community houses. Small houses, primitive enough to a white man's thinking, pushed here and there between the old. Where some of the big community houses had been torn down, for the sake of the lumber, the great corner posts and massive roof-beams of the old structure were often left, standing naked against the sky, and the new little house was built inside, on the spot where the old one had been.

16   It was in one of these empty skeletons that I found her again. She had once been a supporting post for the great centre beam. Her pole-mate, representing the Raven, stood opposite her, but the beam that had rested on their heads was gone. The two poles faced in, and one judged the great size of the house by the distance between them. The corner posts were still in place, and the earth floor, once beaten to the hardness of rock by naked feet, was carpeted now with rich lush grass.

17   I knew her by the stuck-out ears, shouting mouth, and deep eye-sockets. These sockets had no eye-balls, but were empty holes, filled with stare. The stare, though not so fierce as that of the former image, was more intense. The whole figure expressed power, weight, domina-tion, rather than ferocity. Her feet were planted heavily on the head of the squatting bear, carved beneath them. A man could have sat on either huge shoulder. She was unpainted, weather-worn, sun-cracked, and the arms and hands seemed to hang loosely. The fingers were thrust into the carven mouths of two human heads, held crowns down. From behind, the sun made unfathomable shadows in eye, cheek and mouth. Horror tumbled out of them.

18   I saw Indian Tom on the beach, and went to him.

19   "Who is she?"

20   The Indian's eyes, coming slowly from across the sea, followed my pointing finger. Resentment showed in his face, greeny-brown and wrinkled like a baked apple, — resentment that white folks should pry into matters wholly Indian.

21   "Who is that big carved woman?" I repeated.

"D'Sonoqua." No white tongue could have fondled the name as he did.

"Who is D'Sonoqua?"

"She is the wild woman of the woods."

"What does she do?"

"She steals children."

"To eat them?"

"No, she carries them to her caves; that," pointing to a purple scar on the mountain across the bay, "is one of her caves. When she cries 'OO-oo-oo-oeo', Indian mothers are too frightened to move. They stand like trees, and the children go with D'Sonoqua."

"Then she is bad?"

"Sometimes bad . . . sometimes good," Tom replied, glancing furtively at those stuck-out ears. Then he got up and walked away.

I went back, and, sitting in front of the image, gave stare for stare. But her stare so over-powered mine, that I could scarcely wrench my eyes away from the clutch of those empty sockets. The power that I felt was not in the thing itself, but in some tremendous force behind it, that the carver had believed in.

A shadow passed across her hands and their gruesome holdings. A little bird, with its beak full of nesting material, flew into the cavity of her mouth, right in the pathway of that terrible OO-oo-oo-oeo. Then my eye caught something that I had missed — a tabby cat asleep between her feet.

This was D'Sonoqua, and she was a supernatural being, who belonged to these Indians.

"Of course," I said to myself, "I do not believe in supernatural beings. Still — who understands the mysteries behind the forest? What would one do if one did meet a supernatural being?" Half of me wished that I could meet her, and half of me hoped I would not.

Chug — chug — the little boat had come into the bay to take me to another village, more lonely and deserted than this. Who knew what I should see there? But soon supernatural beings went clean out of my mind, because I was wholly absorbed in being naturally seasick.

When you have been tossed and wracked and chilled, any wharf looks good, even a rickety one, with its crooked legs stockinged in barnacles. Our boat nosed under its clammy darkness, and I crawled up the straight slimy ladder, wondering which was worse, natural seasickness, or supernatural "creeps". The trees crowded to the very edge of the water, and the outer ones, hanging over it, shadowed the shoreline into a velvet smudge. D'Sonoqua might walk in places like this. I sat for a long time on the damp, dusky beach, waiting for the stage. One by one dots of light popped from the scattered cabins, and made the dark seem darker. Finally the stage came.

37   We drove through the forest over a long straight road, with black pine trees marching on both sides. When we came to the wharf the little gas mail-boat was waiting for us. Smell and blurred light oozed thickly out of the engine room, and except for one lantern on the wharf everything else was dark. Clutching my little dog, I sat on the mail sacks which had been tossed on to the deck.

38   The ropes were loosed, and we slid out into the oily black water. The moon that had gone with us through the forest was away now. Black pine-covered mountains jagged up on both sides of the inlet like teeth. Every gasp of the engine shook us like a great sob. There was no rail round the deck, and the edge of the boat lay level with the black slithering horror below. It was like being swallowed again and again by some terrible monster, but never going down. As we slid through the water, hour after hour, I found myself listening for the OO-oo-oo-oeo.

39   Midnight brought us to a knob of land, lapped by the water on three sides, with the forest threatening to gobble it up on the fourth. There was a rude landing, a rooming-house, an eating-place, and a store, all for the convenience of fishermen and loggers. I was given a room, but after I had blown out my candle, the stillness and the darkness would not let me sleep.

40   In the brilliant sparkle of the morning when everything that was not superlatively blue was superlatively green, I dickered with a man who was taking a party up the inlet that he should drop me off at the village I was headed for.

41   "But," he protested, "there is nobody there."

42   To myself I said, "There is D'Sonoqua."

43   From the shore, as we rowed to it, came a thin feminine cry — the mewing of a cat. The keel of the boat had barely grated in the pebbles, when the cat sprang aboard, passed the man shipping his oars, and crouched for a spring into my lap. Leaning forward, the man seized the creature roughly, and with a cry of "Dirty Indian vermin!" flung her out into the sea.

44   I jumped ashore, refusing his help, and with a curt "Call for me at sundown," strode up the beach; the cat followed me.

45   When we had crossed the beach and come to a steep bank, the cat ran ahead. Then I saw that she was no lean, ill-favoured Indian cat, but a sleek aristocratic Persian. My snobbish little Griffon dog, who usually refused to let an Indian cat come near me, surprised me by trudging beside her in comradely fashion.

46   The village was typical of the villages of these Indians. It had only one street, and that had only one side, because all the houses faced the

beach. The two community houses were very old, dilapidated and bleached, and the handful of other shanties seemed never to have been young; they had grown so old before they were finished, that it was then not worth while finishing them.

Rusty padlocks carefully protected the gaping walls. There was the usual broad plank in front of the houses, the general sitting and sunning place for Indians. Little streams ran under it, and weeds poked up through every crack, half hiding the companies of tins, kettles, and rags, which patiently waited for the next gale and their next move. 47

In front of the Chief's house was a high, carved totem pole, surmounted by a large wooden eagle. Storms had robbed him of both wings, and his head had a resentful twist, as if he blamed somebody. The heavy wooden heads of two squatting bears peered over the nettle-tops. The windows were too high for peeping in or out. "But, save D'Sonoqua, who is there to peep?" I said aloud, just to break the silence. A fierce sun burned down as if it wanted to expose every ugliness and forlornness. It drew the noxious smell out of the skunk cabbages, growing in the rich black ooze of the stream, scummed the water-barrels with green slime, and branded the desolation into my very soul. 48

The cat kept very close, rubbing and bumping itself and purring ecstatically; and although I had not seen them come, two more cats had joined us. When I sat down they curled into my lap, and then the strangeness of the place did not bite into me so deeply. I got up, determined to look behind the houses. 49

Nettles grew in the narrow spaces between the houses. I beat them down, and made my way over the bruised dank-smelling mass into a space of low jungle. 50

Long ago the trees had been felled and left lying. Young forest had burst through the slash, making an impregnable barrier, and sealing up the secrets which lay behind it. An eagle flew out of the forest, circled the village, and flew back again. 51

Once again I broke silence, calling after him, "Tell D'Sonoqua —" and turning, saw her close, towering above me in the jungle. 52

Like the D'Sonoqua of the other villages she was carved into the bole of a red cedar tree. Sun and storm had bleached the wood, moss here and there softened the crudeness of the modelling; sincerity underlay every stroke. 53

She appeared to be neither wooden nor stationary, but a singing spirit, young and fresh, passing through the jungle. No violence coarsened her; no power domineered to wither her. She was graciously feminine. Across her forehead her creator had fashioned the Sistheutl, or mythical two-headed sea-serpent. One of its heads fell to either shoul- 54 der, hiding the stuck-out ears, and framing her face from a central parting on her forehead which seemed to increase its womanliness.

55   She caught your breath, this D'Sonoqua, alive in the dead bole of the cedar. She summed up the depth and charm of the whole forest, driving away its menace.

56   I sat down to sketch. What was this noise of purring and rubbing going on about my feet? Cats. I rubbed my eyes to make sure I was seeing right, and counted a dozen of them. They jumped into my lap and sprang to my shoulders. They were real — and very feminine.

57   There we were — D'Sonoqua, the cats and I — the woman who only a few moments ago had forced herself to come behind the houses in trembling fear of the "wild woman of the woods" — wild in the sense that forest-creatures are wild — shy, untouchable.

△ △

Explorations:

Emily Carr,
   Klee Wyck
   The Book of Small   ·
Maria Tippett, *Emily Carr: A Biography*
Doris Shadbolt, *The Art of Emily Carr*
Germaine Greer, *The Obstacle Race*
http://www.tbc.gov.bc.ca/culture/schoolnet/carr/index.htm

Structure:

1. Carr's opening words are, "I was sketching in a remote Indian village when I first saw her." Why are we not shown "her" identity till paragraph 6?
2. Where do the three parts of this selection each begin and end? How do the three images of D'Sonoqua form a progression?
3. A voyage by water precedes Carr's visit to each image. Beyond its structural function, does it have a symbolic role? Consider this passage from paragraph 38:

   There was no rail round the deck, and the edge of the boat lay level with the black slithering horror below. It was like being swallowed again and again by some terrible monster, but never going down. As we slid through the water, hour after hour, I found myself listening for the OO-oo-oo-oeo.

Style:

1. Although Carr is esteemed as a writer, she is better known as a painter. What aspects of her prose remind you of the visual arts? Point out passages that illustrate your answers.
2. What does Carr gain by using words such as "scuttled" (par. 4), "slithered" (par. 8), "grated" (par. 43) and "ooze" (par. 48)?
3. Carr plays with words. Rather than describe the walk as "slimy," she writes that slugs "slimed" the walk. Find other words she uses in fresh ways.
4. What FIGURE OF SPEECH depicts the wharf's "crooked legs stockinged in barnacles" (par. 36)? Where else does it occur? How does it further the *description*?
5. The term "Indian," current when Carr published *Klee Wyck* in 1941, is going out of use. Why? Name all the reasons why many original Canadians now prefer the term "First Nations People."

Ideas for Discussion and Writing:

1. In paragraph 31 Carr states of the second D'Sonoqua, "The power that I felt was not in the thing itself, but in some tremendous force behind it, that the carver had believed in." Is skill itself enough to create art, or must the artist believe in some "tremendous force"?
2. What is art for? Think of these:
   – Monumental architecture, as in banks, cathedrals and airports
   – Pretty paintings and photographs on living room walls
   – Statues of generals on horseback or politicians orating
   – Nonrepresentational art in its many forms: impressionism, cubism, surrealism, expressionism, etc.
   – The images of D'Sonoqua carved in cedar
3. The narrator and others fear D'Sonoqua. Why have humans always imagined monsters such as the Minotaur, Grendel, Dracula, Frankenstein, King Kong and Godzilla, not to mention the traditional witches and ghosts? Do we in some way need them?
4. In what ways might "D'Sonoqua" be considered a feminist essay?
5. **PROCESS IN WRITING:** *Visit the Emily Carr Web site listed in "Explorations," and choose your favourite among the paintings that it shows. Take notes on the appearance of your favourite (colour, texture, form, etc.), and on your reaction to it. Now in a rapid first draft, write your own* description *of this painting. Use frequent sense images, as Carr does in "D'Sonoqua." Later when you edit, remember Carr's advice from her book* Growing Pains: *"...get to the point as directly as you can; never use a big word if a little one will do."*

Note: See also the Topics for Writing at the end of this chapter.

Topics for Writing

Chapter 3: Description

Applying techniques from our chapter introduction, describe one of the following as vividly as you can. (See also the guidelines that follow.)

1. A Concert Crowd
2. A Factory Assembly Line
3. A Food Store of a Culture Not My Own
4. A Thunderstorm, Blizzard, Ice Storm, Tornado, Hurricane, Flood or Earthquake
5. A Retirement Home or Nursing Home
6. A Junkyard or a Dump
7. The Entertainment District of My City on a Saturday Night
8. The Waiting Room of a Doctor's Office or the Emergency Room of a Hospital
9. The Kitchen of a Fast-Food Restaurant
10. My Attic or Basement
11. A Garage or Body Shop In Operation
12. A Cathedral, Palace or Castle That I Have Seen
13. Rush Hour on the Expressway, Subway, Streetcar, Bus or Sidewalk
14. My Mother, Father, Grandmother or Grandfather
15. My Favourite Club on a Saturday Night
16. My Dream House, or Dream Kitchen, or Dream Car, etc.
17. A Piece of Public Art in My Town or City
18. The Interior of a Police Station or Courtroom
19. My School Cafeteria
20. The Hottest or Coldest Day I Have Experienced
21. My Fitness Club or Gym at a Busy Hour
22. A Polluted River or Lake
23. My Room
24. A Laundromat
25. A Market I Have Seen in Another Country
26. A Popular Beach on a Hot Weekend
27. My City or Town Seen From Its Highest Building
28. A Construction Site
29. A Swamp, a Meadow, the Deep Woods or the Seashore
30. A Pool Hall or Video Arcade

Note also the Process in Writing topic after each selection in this chapter.

Process in Writing: Guidelines

Follow at least some of these steps in the act of writing your description (your teacher may suggest which ones).

1. *If you can, take eyewitness notes for your description. If you cannot, choose a topic you know well enough to make good notes from memory.*

2. *Look these notes over. What is your main impression, feeling or idea of the subject? Put it into a sentence (this will be your THESIS, whether or not you will actually state it in the description).*

3. *With your notes and thesis before you, write a rapid first draft, getting your subject safely out on paper or on the computer screen, not stopping now to revise.*

4. *When your first draft has "cooled off," look it over. Does every line of your description contribute to the main overall effect? If not, revise. Does each word "feel" right? When one does not, consult your thesaurus for another.*

5. *In the next draft add more SENSE IMAGES — appeals to sight, hearing, touch, smell and maybe even taste. Add more TRANSITIONS. Read aloud to hear flaws you did not see. Then revise.*

6. *Finally, look over the spelling and punctuation before printing off your good copy. Save the essay on disk in case your teacher suggests further revision.*

Michelle Eissler

"I should have thrown caution to the winds and done the right thing. Not the big-city thing. The right thing. The human thing."

—*Paul D'Angelo, "The Step Not Taken"*

CHAPTER

<4>

CAUSE AND EFFECT

Here's why. . .

Have you heard the true story — and aren't they all supposed to be true? — of the philosophy professor who walked into class to give the final exam? He went to the blackboard and wrote on it one word: *Why?*

He knew that one of our most human traits is a desire to make sense of things by asking *why?* If something good happens, we naturally want to know *why* so we can repeat it. If something bad happens, we want to know *why* so in future we can avoid it. On news reports of earthquakes, hurricanes, fires, floods, accidents and crimes, victims are always shaking their heads and asking "*why?*"

In the financial world investors bite their nails guessing what makes stocks go up or down. Will a growing economy push stocks up? Or will it cause inflation, which will cause us to stop buying things we can't afford, which in turn will reduce the profits of companies and cause stocks to fall? Will a controversial election send stocks crashing? Or will it just clear the air of uncertainty, making stocks soar? Will a devastating earthquake harm the economy and the stock market? Or will the cleanup just create employment, sending stocks up? Using the same data, hundreds of experts reason that stocks will rise, while hundreds of others reason that they will fall. Do these experts, or do we, think cause and effect logic is easy?

Yet it is important. We use it in everyday life, and many of our essays are based on it. So when you investigate causes and effects, think hard to get them right.

Some time ago a church in Florida began a campaign to burn records by Elton John and other rock stars. A survey had reported that 984 out of 1000 teenagers who had become pregnant had "committed fornication while rock music was played." The assumption was automatic: rock music causes pregnancy. Before they lit the first match, though, the church members might have asked what *other* causes contributed to the effect. How many of the music lovers had also taken alcohol or drugs? How many had not thought of birth control? Was the music played because such encounters often take place inside a building, where sound systems also happen to be? The church might also have investigated causes further in the past: What life circumstances or influences of society encouraged these teens to enter the situation in the first place? Finally, the church might have asked how often people this age have listened to Elton John and other musicians while *not* fornicating. Rock music may still be a factor — but who knows without a more objective and thorough search of *causes*? When you trace causes and effects, consider these principles:

Just because one event follows another, don't assume the first causes the second. If a black cat crosses the road just before your car blows up, put the blame where it belongs: not on the cat but on the mechanic who forgot to replace your crankcase oil.

Control your prejudices. If the bank manager refuses to give you a loan, is it because bankers are capitalist exploiters who like to keep the rest of us down? Or is it because this one had to call the collection agency the last time you took out a loan?

Explore causes behind causes. Your employer fired you because you didn't work hard enough. But *why* didn't you work hard enough? Because the job was a bore and the employer was a jerk? Or because you have two other jobs as well, and sleep only three hours a night? And if so, do you work these hours because the car you bought consumes every cent you earn? Finally, the real question may be *why did you buy the car?*

Many events have multiple causes and multiple effects:

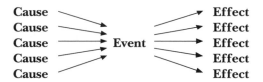

Cause		Effect
Cause		Effect
Cause	Event	Effect
Cause		Effect
Cause		Effect

In addition, each cause may have one or more causes behind it, and each effect may produce further effects, leading to an infinite chain of causality receding into the past and reaching into the future.

Where, then, do you draw the boundaries as you plan an essay of cause and effect? The answer lies in your own common sense: include enough to make the point clearly and fairly, then stop. If your parents are workaholics, a description of *their* behaviour may help a reader understand your own. But do we need to hear about your grandparents as well? If we do, would a quick summary be enough, since we've already heard the details in your parents' case?

All the essays in this chapter show at least one clear-cut cause and at least one clear-cut effect. But while some pay equal attention to both, others focus down to emphasize *mostly* cause or *mostly* effect. And while some show only one major cause or one major effect, others show a great number of causes or a great number of effects. As you choose your own approach to the organization of a cause-and-effect essay, remember above all your purpose: What arrangement will most strongly explain and support your main point? Once you know, use it.

Note: Many essays in other chapters use cause and effect to help make their point. See especially these:

Paul D'Angelo

The Step Not Taken

Paul D'Angelo's usual idea of writing is to tell fish stories, and he admits that his, like most, will stretch the truth. But one day the humour columnist for Canadian Sport Fishing *stepped into a Toronto elevator, and lived the true and sobering story that follows. When it appeared in* The Globe and Mail *of April 3, 1995, it struck a deep chord: dozens of readers sent replies, one of them 5000 words long. Several recounted tragic experiences they had just had themselves, and told how D'Angelo's confession had helped them face their own trials. The author of this thought-provoking essay has an unusual background for a writer. Born in Toronto, Paul D'Angelo never went to university but always read a lot, an activity that gave him a way with words. After high school he left for Europe and Africa, where he spent seven years travelling, working here and there, and just living life. In the meantime, on a visit home he launched a seasonal greeting card business, which still left him seven months a year to roam. For some years now, he and his family have lived in Toronto, where he thinks of himself mostly as an entrepreneur, but goes north to fish pike and bass for fun, and then writes about it in several columns a year. "Write what you live!" he says. Though D'Angelo finds most writing slow and tough, he felt our selection so strongly that he just wrote it right off, to "get it off his chest," and the* Globe *changed only one word. Though he "felt better," his hope that the young man in the elevator would see the article and respond never came true. Perhaps it still could, if that young man should happen to see the pages that follow.*

1 A few weeks ago I was followed into an office-building elevator by a well-dressed young man carrying a briefcase. He looked very sharp. Very buttoned-down. Wearing gold wire-frame glasses, he was of medium height and build with neatly trimmed brown hair and, I would guess, in his mid-20s. Typical junior executive material. There was nothing about him that seemed unusual. Nothing at all to indicate what was about to take place.

2 The elevator had only one control panel, and I excused myself as I leaned over to his side of the car and pushed the button for the 10th floor. He pushed the button for the 15th. The doors of the elevator closed and we began to ascend. Employing typical Toronto elevator etiquette, I stood staring up at the row of floor numbers above the

doors while purposely ignoring my fellow passenger. Then it happened. A sudden strained gasp. Turning toward the noise, I was astonished to see the young man drop his briefcase and burst into tears. Our eyes met for a split second and, as if slapped, he averted his face from me, leaned his head against the wood-panelled wall of the elevator and continued to weep.

And what I did next still shames me. 3

The elevator stopped at the 10th floor and, without looking back, I 4 stepped out. I stood in the hallway, a bundle of mixed emotions, wondering what to do. A combination of guilt and uncertainty washed over me. Should I go up to the 15th floor and make sure he's okay? Should I search him out from office to office? Should I risk the embarrassment it might cause him? Is he mentally disturbed? A manic depressive, perhaps? Is he a suicide just waiting to happen?

I didn't know what to do. So I did nothing. 5

And now he haunts me. Not with fear, of course, but with a sense of 6 regret. I see his face crumbling before he turns to the wall. I see his shoulders heave as he sobs in a combination of sorrow and shame. I wonder now what brought him to that moment in time. How long had he been holding his pain inside before he could no longer contain it? What could possibly have overwhelmed him to such an extent that he was unable to keep from crying out?

Had he just visited the doctor and been told that he had an incurable 7 disease? Was he having marital problems? Was his wife ill? His child? Had someone dear recently died? Was he being laid off? Was he looking for a job and meeting with no success? Was he having financial woes? Was he without friends in the city and crushed by loneliness?

The sorrows of this world are endless. 8

The few people I have told about the incident all say I did the proper 9 thing, the best thing, by leaving the young man alone.

But they are wrong. 10

Like so many things in life, I know now what I should have done 11 then. I should have thrown caution to the winds and done the right thing. Not the big-city thing. The right thing. The human thing. The thing I would want someone to do if they ever found my son crying in an elevator. I should have given him the opportunity to unload his sadness onto my shoulders. I should have reached out a hand and patted him on the back. I should have said something like, "Why don't you let me buy you a cup of coffee and you can tell me all your problems. There's no reason to feel self-conscious. I'll listen for as long as you want to talk."

What would his reaction have been to that? Would he have turned 12 even further to the wall? Or would he have turned on me? Cursing me? Telling me to mind my own damned business? Would he have lashed out at me? Sorrow and insecurity turning to rage? Would he have physically attacked me? Or would he have gone with me for that cup of coffee?

13   I don't know. I'll never know. All I can be certain of is that I left him in that elevator with tears streaming down his face. And that he was alone. All alone.

14   I hope that somehow he gets to read these words, because I want him to know that I'm pulling for him. That I hope things are looking up for him. That I hope his sorrow is in the past. That I hope he is never again burdened with such awful despair. That I am thinking of him. That I said a prayer for him. That I was wrong, dreadfully wrong, not to step forward in his time of need.

15   That I'm sorry.

△ △

Explorations:

Joseph Hartog *et al.*, eds., *The Anatomy of Loneliness*
John Glassco, trans., *Complete Poems of Saint-Denys-Garneau*
http://www.depression.com/

Structure:

1. D'Angelo begins with an ANECDOTE. Is this a good technique? Do you see it often? How well does this one work as an introduction?
2. In paragraph 1 D'Angelo refers to "what was about to take place"; in paragraph 2 he says "Then it happened"; and in paragraph 3 he says "And what I did next still shames me." Why does he keep building suspense? What does this do for his AUDIENCE?
3. Identify D'Angelo's THESIS STATEMENT.
4. Tell how paragraph 10 works as a TRANSITION between parts. Why is it only one sentence long?
5. Where does D'Angelo ask himself *why?* Where does he ask *what if?* What *causes* does he imagine? What *effects?* And how important are these to the essay?

Style:

1. How CONCISE is this selection? Can you find any wasted words at all?
2. Read paragraphs 14 and 15 aloud in class. Why has D'Angelo given us a series of partial sentences? Why do most begin with "That..."? Is this repetition accidental or deliberate? What effect does it achieve?
3. Why does D'Angelo's last paragraph contain only three words?

Ideas for Discussion and Writing:

1. If you were Paul D'Angelo, what would you have done when the young man on the elevator began to cry? Why do you think he was crying? Do you, like our author, live in the big city? Describe a time when the actions of a stranger made you wonder how to react. Did you take the risk of involvement? Or did you do the "big-city thing"? Why? And now what do you think you should have done?

2. Did this selection bring tears to your own eyes? If so, in which parts? Is it good for an essayist to seek emotion in the reader?

3. Describe the favourite techniques of subway, streetcar, bus and elevator riders to preserve their solitude in rush hour. Arrange chairs as in a public transit vehicle, and role-play the situation in class.

4. Our essay title, "The Step Not Taken," is probably a reference to "The Road Not Taken," a poem by Robert Frost, in which the poet wonders what his journey would have been like had he taken the other fork in the path. Is this a universal theme? Describe a fork in your own path. Imagine to what destination "the road not taken" might have led you.

5. **PROCESS IN WRITING:** *You are the young man — or, if you like, a young woman — in the elevator that day, and you have read Paul D'Angelo's article in* The Globe and Mail. *Now answer him in a letter telling the* causes *of your pain, and responding to his shame at not helping. Look over your first draft: have you found all the main* causes? *Are there also important* causes *behind causes? Have you used* TRANSITION SIGNALS *to highlight the logic (words like "because," "therefore," "as a result of," "so," etc.)? Revise. Now check for punctuation and spelling before printing out your best version.*

Note: See also the Topics for Writing at the end of this chapter.

David Suzuki

Hidden Lessons*

David Suzuki is a scientist who, as host of the CBC's popular and long-lived television series The Nature of Things, *has become one of Canada's best-known public figures. Born in Vancouver in 1936, he earned a Ph.D. at the University of Chicago in 1961, specializing in genetics, then quickly gained an international reputation for his genetic research on fruit flies. In 1969 he won a prize as "outstanding research scientist in Canada," and since then has received many other awards, grants and honorary degrees. He lectures internationally, writes a syndicated newspaper column, and in addition to scholarly publications has written many books for a larger audience, among them* Metamorphosis *(autobiography, 1987),* Inventing the Future: Reflections on Science, Technology and Nature *(1989),* The Japan We Never Knew *(1996), and many books explaining nature to children. In 1990 he created the David Suzuki Foundation (see "Explorations" for its Web site address), a think tank with 15,000 supporters, whose goal is to influence environmental policy. In all these activities Suzuki rejects the narrowness that sometimes underlies the specialized vision of the research scientist, and instead works to educate the larger public about both the promise and dangers of science: the application of little-understood technologies; unchecked economic and industrial expansion; and the consequent devastation of other plant and animal species through our consumption of their habitat. Suzuki is literally trying to save the planet. "If I didn't," he said in a 1998 CBC special about his life, "I couldn't look my children in the eye." The essay that follows, from the February 7, 1987,* Globe and Mail, *pursues this goal in an especially concrete way.*

1   In spite of the vast expanse of wilderness in this country, most Canadian children grow up in urban settings. In other words, they live in a world conceived, shaped and dominated by people. Even the farms located around cities and towns are carefully groomed and landscaped for human convenience. There's nothing wrong with that, of course, but in such an environment, it's very easy to lose any sense of connection with nature.

---

* Editor's title.

In city apartments and dwellings, the presence of cockroaches, fleas, ants, mosquitoes or houseflies is guaranteed to elicit the spraying of insecticides. Mice and rats are poisoned or trapped, while the gardener wages a never-ending struggle with ragweed, dandelions, slugs and root-rot. We have a modern arsenal of chemical weapons to fight off these invaders and we use them lavishly.

We worry when kids roll in the mud or wade through a puddle because they'll get "dirty." Children learn attitudes and values very quickly and the lesson in cities is very clear — nature is an enemy, it's dirty, dangerous or a nuisance. So youngsters learn to distance themselves from nature and to try to control it. I am astonished at the number of adults who loathe or are terrified by snakes, spiders, butterflies, worms, birds — the list seems endless.

If you reflect on the history of humankind, you realize that for 99 per cent of our species' existence on the planet, we were deeply embedded in and dependent on nature. When plants and animals were plentiful, we flourished. When famine and drought struck, our numbers fell accordingly. We remain every bit as dependent upon nature today — we need plants to fix photons of energy into sugar molecules and to cleanse the air and replenish the oxygen. It is folly to forget our dependence on an intact ecosystem. But we do whenever we teach our offspring to fear or detest the natural world. The urban message kids get runs completely counter to what they are born with, a natural interest in other life forms. Just watch a child in a first encounter with a flower or an ant — there is instant interest and fascination. We condition them out of it.

The result is that when my 7-year-old daughter brings home new friends, they invariably recoil in fear or disgust when she tries to show them her favorite pets — three beautiful salamanders that her grandfather got for her in Vancouver. And when my 3-year-old comes wandering in with her treasures — millipedes, spiders, slugs and sowbugs that she catches under rocks lining the front lawn — children and adults alike usually respond by saying "yuk."

I can't overemphasize the tragedy of that attitude. For, inherent in this view is the assumption that human beings are special and different and that we lie outside nature. Yet it is this belief that is creating many of our environmental problems today.

Does it matter whether we sense our place in nature so long as we have cities and technology? Yes, for many reasons, not the least of which is that virtually all scientists were fascinated with nature as children and retained that curiosity throughout their lives. But a far more important reason is that if we retain a spiritual sense of connection with all other life forms, it can't help but profoundly affect the way we act. Whenever my daughter sees a picture of an animal dead or dying, she asks me fearfully, "Daddy, are there any more?" At 7 years, she already knows about extinction and it frightens her.

8   The yodel of a loon at sunset, the vast flocks of migrating waterfowl in the fall, the indomitable salmon returning thousands of kilometres — these images of nature have inspired us to create music, poetry and art. And when we struggle to retain a handful of California condors or whooping cranes, it's clearly not from a fear of ecological collapse, it's because there is something obscene and frightening about the disappearance of another species at our hands.

9   If children grow up understanding that we are animals, they will look at other species with a sense of fellowship and community. If they understand their ecological place — the biosphere — then when children see the great virgin forests of the Queen Charlotte Islands being clearcut, they will feel physical pain, because they will understand that those trees are an extension of themselves.

10   When children who know their place in the ecosystem see factories spewing poison into the air, water and soil, they will feel ill because someone has violated their home. This is not mystical mumbo-jumbo. We have poisoned the life support systems that sustain all organisms because we have lost a sense of ecological place. Those of us who are parents have to realize the unspoken, negative lessons we are conveying to our children. Otherwise, they will continue to desecrate this planet as we have.

11   It's not easy to avoid giving these hidden lessons. I have struggled to cover my dismay and queasiness when Severn and Sarika come running in with a large wolf spider or when we've emerged from a ditch covered with leeches or when they have been stung accidentally by yellowjackets feeding on our leftovers. But that's nature. I believe efforts to teach children to love and respect other life forms are priceless.

△ △

Explorations:

David Suzuki, *Metamorphosis*
Rachel Carson, *Silent Spring*
Annie Dillard, *Pilgrim at Tinker Creek*
Robert Ornstein and Paul Ehrlich: *New World, New Mind*
Henry David Thoreau, *Walden*
http://www.nceet.snre.umich.edu/EndSpp/ES.new.html
http://www.vkool.com/suzuki/exercise.html

Structure:

1. What device of emphasis sparks the opening sentence, and how does it begin to introduce Suzuki's subject?
2. Does Suzuki explore more fully the *causes* or the *effects* of children's attitudes toward nature? Which paragraphs analyze mostly causes and which mostly effects? Is Suzuki right to place the causes first?
3. How long a chain of *cause and effect* does Suzuki show us? Point out each link.
4. Suzuki no doubt hopes his argument will spur us to action. Does his closing promote this goal? When he admits in paragraph 11 that "It's not easy to avoid giving these hidden lessons," are you discouraged or challenged?

Style:

1. Describe Suzuki's prose: Is it full of strategies calculated to affect us, or is it a plain and direct message? Which mode do you prefer when you read? When you write? Why?
2. Why is paragraph 6 the shortest one of the essay?

Ideas for Discussion and Writing:

1. Do you dread insects, worms, snakes, mice or weeds? If so, how did you learn to? How close are your attitudes to those of your parents? What actual dangers, if any, may these life forms pose to you?
2. In paragraph 8 Suzuki writes, "there is something obscene and frightening about the disappearance of another species at our hands." Elsewhere he has stated that two species an hour disappear from the earth, mostly because we "develop" natural habitats for our own profit. How important to you is a new paper mill, a logging project in the rain forest, a highway, dam, subdivision, ski resort, oil well or aluminum smelter — compared to the existence of a species? Defend your view.
3. First we learned to shun *racism,* and then *sexism.* Is *speciesism* next? Argue for or against our present belief that we are far more important than other members of our ecosystem.
4. How desirable is economic growth when it is based on exploiting nature? If we could save the rivers, the lakes and the rain forests by consuming less, how would you react? How large a cut in income would you accept to achieve the goal: 10 percent, 25 percent, 50 percent — or none at all? Defend your view.
5. Choose an endangered Canadian plant or animal species you have heard about in the news, and which raises your concern. Now visit the David Suzuki Web site given in "Explorations." Select the "Exer-

cise Democracy" function. Compose an e-mail message to the prime minister and/or your member of Parliament, telling what you believe should be done to save this species. Send the message. If it is answered, share both the message and the answer with the class.

6. **PROCESS IN WRITING:** *Choose a current newspaper or newsmagazine article about an environmental problem. In response, write a short but hard-hitting letter to the editor exposing the* effects *of this problem. Since editors love conciseness, polish your second draft till every word counts. Cut deadwood. Use your thesaurus, paper or electronic, to replace vague or weak terms with exact and strong ones. "Show" through examples rather than "telling" through generalizations. Now try out a draft on an* AUDIENCE *of three or four classmates; incorporate their best advice before mailing your final copy. Then watch the next issues to see if your message is published. If an editor has cut any part of your letter, analyze why: Was the part wordy? Off topic? General instead of specific?*

Note: See also the Topics for Writing at the end of this chapter.

Naheed Mustafa

My Body Is My Own Business

Born in England, Naheed Mustafa moved as an infant to Canada. In 1992 she completed an honours degree in political science and history at the University of Toronto, specializing in Third-World development. Then she studied journalism at Ryerson Polytechnic University until moving to Pakistan to be with her husband, who was working for the Food and Agricultural Organization of the United Nations. There, Mustafa wrote about development issues such as literacy and the environment, for local newspapers and magazines (her articles were in English because, although she speaks Urdu, she does not read or write it). She believes that, however well intentioned the international aid efforts of developed countries, many donors give only for disasters like earthquakes and famines, while ignoring basic development work such as education. Living again in Toronto, Mustafa now combines freelance editing work with raising her two daughters. "Almost anybody who's willing to work hard enough can learn to write very well," she says. Mustafa also states that wearing the hijab, *as described in her essay (from the July 29, 1993,* Globe and Mail), *is a requirement of her Muslim faith.*

I often wonder whether people see me as a radical, fundamentalist Muslim terrorist packing an AK-47 assault rifle inside my jean jacket. Or maybe they see me as the poster girl for oppressed womanhood everywhere. I'm not sure which it is. 1

I get the whole gamut of strange looks, stares and covert glances. You see, I wear the *hijab,* a scarf that covers my head, neck and throat. I do this because I am a Muslim woman who believes her body is her own private concern. 2

Young Muslim women are reclaiming the *hijab,* reinterpreting it in light of its original purpose — to give back to women ultimate control of their own bodies. 3

The Koran teaches us that men and women are equal, that individuals should not be judged according to gender, beauty, wealth or privilege. The only thing that makes one person better than another is her or his character. 4

5   Nonetheless, people have a difficult time relating to me. After all, I'm young, Canadian born and raised, university-educated — why would I do this to myself, they ask.

6   Strangers speak to me in loud, slow English and often appear to be playing charades. They politely inquire how I like living in Canada and whether or not the cold bothers me. If I'm in the right mood, it can be very amusing.

7   But why would I, a woman with all the advantages of a North American upbringing, suddenly, at 21, want to cover myself so that with the *hijab* and the other clothes I choose to wear, only my face and hands show?

8   Because it gives me freedom.

9   Women are taught from early childhood that their worth is proportional to their attractiveness. We feel compelled to pursue abstract notions of beauty, half realizing that such a pursuit is futile.

10   When women reject this form of oppression, they face ridicule and contempt. Whether it's women who refuse to wear makeup or to shave their legs or to expose their bodies, society, both men and women, have trouble dealing with them.

11   In the Western world, the *hijab* has come to symbolize either forced silence or radical, unconscionable militancy. Actually, it's neither. It is simply a woman's assertion that judgment of her physical person is to play no role whatsoever in social interaction.

12   Wearing the *hijab* has given me freedom from constant attention to my physical self. Because my appearance is not subjected to public scrutiny, my beauty, or perhaps lack of it, has been removed from the realm of what can legitimately be discussed.

13   No one knows whether my hair looks as if I just stepped out of a salon, whether or not I can pinch an inch, or even if I have unsightly stretch marks. And because no one knows, no one cares.

14   Feeling that one has to meet the impossible male standards of beauty is tiring and often humiliating. I should know, I spent my entire teenage years trying to do it. I was a borderline bulimic and spent a lot of money I didn't have on potions and lotions in hopes of becoming the next Cindy Crawford.

15   The definition of beauty is ever-changing; waifish is good, waifish is bad, athletic is good — sorry, athletic is bad. Narrow hips? Great. Narrow hips? Too bad.

16   Women are not going to achieve equality with the right to bare their breasts in public, as some people would like to have you believe. That would only make us party to our own objectification. True equality will be had only when women don't need to display themselves to get atten-

tion and won't need to defend their decision to keep their bodies to themselves.

△ △

Explorations:

Bharati Mukherjee, *Jasmine* (novel)
Salman Rushdie, *Shame* (novel)
Richard Gordon, *Anorexia and Bulimia: Anatomy of a Social Epidemic*
Naomi Wolf, *The Beauty Myth: How Images of Beauty Are Used Against Women*
http://www.al-muslim.org/women/hijab.htm
http://www.smcm.edu/Users/tplasane/EMAXSON/BULIMIA.HTM

Structure:

1. Why does Mustafa open with two STEREOTYPES? Do they draw your attention? Do they go straight to her topic?
2. In her argument does Mustafa give more attention to *causes* or *effects*? Name the main causes. Name the main effects.
3. Why does Mustafa explore effects *first* and causes *after*, reversing the logical order of the two?
4. Identify the TRANSITION in which Mustafa actually asks "why" and answers with "because. . . ," as she moves from *effects* to *causes*.

Style:

1. Ending on a key word is a powerful device of emphasis. Note the final word in each half of Mustafa's argument; what makes "freedom" and "themselves" good choices for these positions?
2. Language can speak through rhythm as much as through words. Read aloud the first sentence of paragraph 6, then analyze how its sound reinforces its meaning.

Ideas for Discussion and Writing:

1. Mustafa says male standards of beauty for women are "impossible" and that feeling the need to meet them is "humiliating" (par. 14). Is she right? Whether you are male or female, give examples of your own to defend or attack her view.
2. Examine the PARADOX of paragraph 8: that the effect of covering oneself with the *hijab* is "freedom." Do non-Muslims have means of shielding themselves, as well, from the unreasonable scrutiny and expectations of others? Name any such techniques you have used.
3. Though part of her background is the culture of another country, Mustafa is Canadian. If you too have origins in another culture, how

fully do you plan to retain the clothes, the foods, the religion and language of that culture, while living in Canada? Predict the *effects* of your decision.

4. Mustafa confesses that as a teen she was a "borderline bulimic" (par. 14). What do you see as the main *causes* of bulimia and anorexia nervosa? What *causes* women, not men, to be the main victims?

5. At the library look through an illustrated history of art, taking notes on how the ideal of beauty in women has changed through the centuries. Then report your findings to the class, showing illustrations as evidence for your conclusions.

6. Watch your favourite television channel for one hour, taking notes on how women are presented both in programs and commercials. Then report to the class on the attitudes, especially any STEREOTYPES, which you detected. What *effects*, in both male and female viewers, do you think these attitudes will *cause*?

7. **PROCESS IN WRITING:** *Do question 6 above, except as an essay. Look over your notes, then choose a THESIS STATEMENT that expresses the main effect(s) on viewers of the examples you observed. Now write a rapid first draft, supporting your thesis statement with large numbers of these examples. When the draft has "cooled off" look it over. Do the causes and effects seem reasonable? Have you tried to be objective, rather than interpret according to your own prejudices? Are there causes behind causes, or effects of effects, which might enrich your analysis? Do transitions such as "since," "because" and "therefore" help the audience follow your logic? If not, add. Finally, edit for things like punctuation and spelling before doing the final version. Read it to the class, and be ready to answer questions from other points of view.*

Note: See also the Topics for Writing at the end of this chapter.

Stuart McLean

The Shocking Truth About Household Dust

Stuart McLean is a broadcaster with a difference. Though he jokes about aiming for the "cutting edge of journalism," it is the odd little details of life — the Yo-Yo, the Popsicle, or our present subject, household dust — that catch his attention and delight his audiences. "He sees what sparkles in the ordinary and he cel-ebrates the common stuff of which most of our lives are made," says The Edmonton Herald. *Born in Montreal in 1948, McLean studied at Sir George Williams. After a time producing CBC Radio's* Sunday Morning, *he began to write a weekly series of quirky and poignant essays for CBC Radio's* Morningside, *where, appearing with host Peter Gzowski, he won a fanatic audience. In 1989 he gathered 30 of the radio essays in a book,* The Morningside World of Stuart McLean. *One of these was our selection, which former* Morningside *producer Catherine Pigott (see her own essay on page 195) calls "legendary." McLean also contributed to* The New Morningside Papers *(1987) and* The Latest Morningside Papers *(1989) edited by Gzowski, and in 1992 published his own second book* Travels in Smalltown Canada. *Then followed* Stories from the Vinyl Café *(1995) and the anthology* When We Were Young: A Collection of Canadian Stories *(1996). McLean has also written documenta-ries and a feature film,* Looking for Miracles. *He now combines writing with education; since 1984 McLean has been Director of Broadcast Journalism at Ryerson Polytechnic University.*

S o. From time to time I joke about being out on the cutting edge of journalism. If pressed, however, I would be the first to admit that the majority of what I seem to end up writing about lies well off the beaten track. I try hard to follow world events. I do. But it is a struggle. I am easily distracted by those bits in my newspaper about the parrot who has been taught to whistle a Chopin sonata by the out-of-work conduc-tor. And once I have read something like that, I just can't help myself.

This can be a problem for somebody like me who counts among his friends a number of this country's distinguished journalists. We go out for lunch together, my friends and I, and they will argue for hours about the implications of their upcoming interview with the minister of finance, while I push at my salad and silently ponder my profile of the

Popsicle, or the history of the Yo-Yo. I leave these lunches determined to do something journalistically credible before I see anyone again.

3   Such was my mood on an otherwise pleasant Tuesday afternoon several years ago. I would, I seethed, storming through the Yonge Street lunch crowd with my elbows just a little too far from my sides, uncover a real story. In this frame of investigative frenzy I returned to my desk and, unfortunately, fell into a telephone conversation with my friend Robert Krulwich of CBS about . . . dust. Common household dust. As usual, Krulwich had some questions that neither of us could answer. Dust questions.

4   Like how come the dust on the top of your refrigerator lies there like a layer of velvet, while the stuff under your bed rolls around like tumbleweeds in the interior of British Columbia? And the little specks in the sunbeam, are they floating or falling? And where does dust come from, anyway? How come you can vacuum your heart out one day and the next morning there'll be a dust bunny in the cupboard?

5   As the afternoon wore on, my need to know the answer to these and other puzzles overtook whatever it was I was supposed to be doing. I should have known better, but I shrugged and reached for the phone. What follows is the weird and shocking truth I discovered that day about household dust. Like all good stories it begins at the beginning.

6   Ever wonder where dust comes from? How about outer space? There is extraterrestrial dust in your living-room. Probably not a lot of it, but it is there, and I offer that up at the beginning as a kind of warning, because this is going to get a lot weirder before we are finished. Space dust comes from meteorites. When meteorites strike the earth's atmosphere they disintegrate and turn to, you guessed it, dust, increasing the bulk of our planet, incidentally, by 10,000 tons a year. I am told by eminent scientists who study dust that if you were to run your finger along a window ledge somewhere, anywhere, you are almost certain to pick up some dust from outer space.

7   I learned about space dust from a Dr John Ferguson, who is a dust scientist for Bristol-Myers. They are the folks who produce, among other things, Endust, so he should know. He did assure me that meteorites are not the major cause of the dust in my house.

We create an awful lot of dust by our daily living inside the house, the most common thing being, of course, through our cooking and our grooming habits, or the clothes that we wear. Also, there's the normal wearing away of the interior of the house — paint chipping off, bits of paper coming from wallpaper, things like that.

8   In fact, the majority of the dust in your house comes from the house itself and everything in it, wearing away. The same thing happens outdoors. There is a lot of concrete dust floating around, for example.

Every time someone drives down the road, tiny bits of road are knocked off, and these microscopic bits float away and become specks of dust on someone's basement window. There is also rubber dust that comes from the tires that are busy wearing away the street, and chances are they will end up on the same basement window.

To these normal, everyday happenings you have to add something 9
called "dust events" — things like volcanic eruptions, forest fires and other natural phenomena that spew ash into the atmosphere.

But that's not all — a significant amount of the dust in your home is, 10
in fact, made up of little bits and pieces of you. In this way, you are no different from the wallpaper in your bathroom. The outermost layer of your skin is known as the stratum corneum. You shed your stratum corneum every three days, just like a snake. That's about fifty thousand skin cells. Or so says Dr Charles McLeod, a pathologist from Washington, D.C., who recently studied dust for *Discover* magazine.

> **If you brush through your hair in the right light, you can see small flecks of dander or dandruff that flake off your scalp, and this process is continuous on all the skin surfaces of your body. People are constantly shedding little flakes of dead skin. It is a normal process.**

Now we come to the good part. Having established where dust comes 11
from, it is time to take a closer look at dust itself. This is the part that upsets people. If you are squeamish about these sorts of things you might consider putting this book away now. There are only a few pages left anyway and you might be better off, happier, more relaxed just not knowing about this next bit.

Don't say I didn't warn you. There are, uh, animals that live in the 12
dust in your house. Millions and millions of animals. They are called dust mites. And they may be tiny, but they are the most horrible little creatures you can imagine. They feed on floating bits of skin. They suck in air through their toes. And they look like monsters from outer space. Don't take my word for it. Dr McLeod has actually looked at dust mites, face to face, through a microscope.

> **They have these very large mouth parts that allow them to chew their food. And depending on the stage at which you look at them, they may have up to eight legs. Have you ever seen a lobster? Have you ever seen a cockroach? Well, imagine breeding those two and looking at their offspring, and you have a good idea of what dust mites look like. They're not insects, now, they're mites. Insects only have six legs. Nobody has ever counted, but you could estimate that there are millions of mites per square yard of space. They don't take up a whole lot of room. They don't make any noise, so you'd never know they're there. If you accumulated enough of them and you bunched them**

together, you could see them with the naked eye. I'd say it would take a couple of dozen to cover the head of a pin, though.

13   Dust mites can walk on their hideous eight legs, but for a mite to travel, say, across the room, would be roughly the equivalent of you setting off from Moose Jaw to walk to Come-by-Chance to pick up the morning paper. So you can understand why mites don't do a lot of walking. What they like to do is ride air currents. Every time you take a deep breath and blow it out, you're helping a bunch of mites get around.

14   The good news about these little beasts is that they won't touch you, and they won't eat you. Dr Edward Baker is an acarologist in Alabama (which means that he studies mites, Alabaman or otherwise). He once took a garbage pail full of mites and taped them, under capsules, to various parts of his arm. He was prepared to let them nosh away to their hearts' delight on his stratum corneum, but when he took off the tape, they were all dead. Apparently, dust mites only go after the bits and pieces that slough off. That's the good news.

15   The bad news about dust mites is that they have normal bodily functions. Twenty times a day each mite produces a mite pellet. When people say they are allergic to dust, they really mean they are allergic to things in the dust. It might be pollen — there is a lot of pollen in dust — but it could be that they are allergic to mite poop.

16   There is no getting around dust mites. As long as you keep sloughing off, as long as there is dust, there are going to be mites. If you have a vacuum cleaner in your closet, there are, right now, in the bag with the dust, millions of mites, grazing happily. Turn on the vacuum and the mites go turtle. They pull their hideous lobster legs into their hideous bodies and wait until you have finished. Then they come out again and graze. Tonight when you climb into bed, you will be sharing it with about two million dust mites. So you might as well start thinking about them as your friends, because there is nothing else you can do about them.

17   Another thing you can do nothing about is the dust that floats in the sunbeam. I used to wonder if I left the house quietly and let the air get real still, whether all that dust would settle, and I could sneak back in and vacuum it up before it started floating again. Dr Ferguson set me straight.

The larger particles are actually falling. But if the particles are small enough, the movement of the air is sufficient to keep them suspended. A layman's way of looking at that is if you toss a tin can into the air and you shoot at it with a bullet, you can keep that can suspended indefinitely so long as you can keep hitting it with a bullet. Essentially, if you have a particle of dust that is light enough, the movement of the air molecules behave just like the bullets from that gun. They will keep bouncing into the dust particle and keep it suspended.

Some dust particles are so light that a simple wave of your hand or even the cat walking across the kitchen will send them swirling up. And there it stays, unless, of course, the dust was to meet its mortal enemy — rain. Dust hates rain. It loves safe places where, through friction or electrostatic energy or, best of all, grease, it can cling to other bits of dust and fulfil its *raison d'être* — become a dust ball. Since grease is dust's best friend, dust's favourite place is, of course, the kitchen. And in the kitchen, says Dr Ferguson, the place where dust reigns supreme is . . .   18

> . . . **usually behind your refrigerator, or in the circulating fan above your stove or range. It accumulates on the fan because it is so close to the stove where the cooking fats and oils are volatilized. The grease sticks to the blades of the fan and the dust sticks to the grease. Your refrigerator works the same way because it's constantly recirculating the air in back of the coils for cooling. That will collect the fats and the oils and serve as a good sticking place for the dust as well.**

And that, more or less, is the story of dust. Some of it might have upset you, but there's not much you can do about it. You could dust more, I guess, or dust better, but it won't do much good. Better just to accept it. Come to terms with the dust in your life. Remember that it is someone's home (ugly they may be, malevolent they are not). It contains matter from outer space. And, after all, you put a lot of yourself into making it.   19

△ △

Explorations:

Stuart McLean,
> *The Morningside World of Stuart McLean*
> *Welcome Home: Travels in Smalltown Canada*
> *Stories from the Vinyl Café*

http://www.neosoft.com/users/s/sreifler/acarosn1.htm

Structure:

1. "What follows is the weird and shocking truth I discovered that day about household dust," writes McLean in paragraph 5. What does a THESIS STATEMENT do? Is this a good one?
2. McLean's introduction fills paragraphs 1-5. Point out everything this material does to prepare us for his argument.
3. Analyze the role of *contrast* in paragraphs 1-3 of McLean's introduction.
4. Does McLean analyze mostly *causes* or mostly *effects*? Does he focus on *multiple causes of one effect*, on *one cause of multiple effects*, or on *multiple causes and effects both*?

5. Point out the major *cause(s)* of dust, and point out the major *effect(s)* of dust, in this cause and effect argument.

Style:

1. "The Shocking Truth About Household Dust" was first read as a script over CBC Radio. Identify 10 words or phrases, such as "mite poop" in paragraph 15, which people would say but normally not write in an essay. Despite its very informal TONE, does this selection work as an essay? Why or why not?
2. How many sentence fragments do you see on these pages? Are fragments acceptable in a personal essay? A more formal essay? A research essay?

Ideas for Discussion and Writing:

1. Would you have imagined a whole essay about a topic as lowly as dust? Yet does it strike your interest? Does McLean's advice to "come to terms with the dust in your life" (par. 19) mean any more than just housecleaning? Can something as small as dust be a SYMBOL of larger things? Explain.
2. How does it strike you, that dust is "made up of little bits and pieces of you" (par. 10)? Analyze the power of this statement.
3. When in paragraph 6 dust on our window sills is said to come from outer space, are you interested? If so why? In which chapter of this book are whole essays powered by this device?
4. Astronomers say that an average galaxy has a hundred billion stars, and the universe has around a hundred billion galaxies. McLean writes that your bed probably contains two million dust mites, yet we know that even a mite dwarfs its own molecules and atoms. Do such *contrasts* of size make you uneasy? Analyze all the reasons why.
5. **PROCESS IN WRITING:** *On a starry night spend a while outside, contemplating the size and age of the universe. Then think of our Earth. Do you know the forces that* caused *it to form? Now go inside to freewrite on this subject, putting on paper what you know. If there are gaps, investigate the next day in the library. Now make a short outline: choose how many links in the chain of* cause and effect *you wish to include, so as to control this very large topic. Now write a draft. Looking it over, see if you have used enough* TRANSITION *signals to highlight causality. Have you helped your* AUDIENCE *by defining any technical terms? Have you, like McLean, used examples to make hard parts clear? Finally, edit for style and correctness as you produce your best version.*

Note: See also the Topics for Writing at the end of this chapter.

Elinor Florence

Leaving the Fast Lane for
No Lane at All*

Born in 1951, Elinor Florence grew up on a farm near Battleford, Saskatchewan, and attended a one-room country school. After studies at the University of Saskatchewan and a Bachelor of Journalism at Carleton University, in Ottawa, she travelled through Europe, freelanced in Los Angeles, and worked as a journalist at weekly and daily newspapers in all four Western provinces. Then divorced with a young daughter, she turned again in 1990 to freelancing. Her life took another turn in 1993 when she married a widower with three young children. While her husband stayed home, she spent two years as an editor for the government of British Columbia. Then when her husband, a mining construction manager, was asked to build a gold mine in Mexico, the whole family spent 18 months in Chihuahua and weekends in an ancient mountain village. On completion of the mine, they moved to Invermere, in southeastern British Columbia, the setting of Florence's essay. She is now a freelance writer again, and dreams of completing her first novel. "Leaving the Fast Lane for No Lane at All" was published under a different title in the The Globe and Mail of January 7, 1997.

T his spring my family moved, with great excitement and trepidation, from a busy Vancouver suburb to a picturesque alpine town on the eastern edge of British Columbia, population 3,000.   1

We had the same reasons for wanting to leave the city as do many of our acquaintances — growing population density, with all its attendant problems such as traffic and pollution; a hope of shielding our children from the "junk culture" that undeniably rears its head everywhere but snarls louder in cities; greater access to outdoor recreation (my husband); and a nostalgic yearning to live in a community that has golden wedding celebrations and fall suppers and store clerks who know your name (me).   2

But it still wasn't easy to get up and go. Long after we had repeatedly crunched the numbers and resolved to live on our nest egg plus my husband's freelance income as a mining consultant, we vacillated.   3

---

* Editor's title.

4   What sparked our final decision was a rainy Vancouver weekend when we made, between the two of us, 23 separate trips driving our four children to soccer, swimming lessons and birthday parties. Monday morning, we put our house on the market.

5   Since the big move we have discovered many unlooked-for benefits from small-town life — among them, that not one of the 200 bicycles parked outside the elementary school carries a lock, and that people here still hand out homemade goodies to trick-or-treaters on Halloween.

6   But the greatest factor that has bettered our lives is being unchained from the steering wheel. In moving here, we left the fast lane — not for the slow lane, but for no lane at all.

7   Entire days pass in which we do not enter a vehicle. I haven't had so many idle hours, rich with potential, since giving birth. Sunrise and sunset seem to have drifted farther apart. Instead of saying: "Oh my gosh, is it three o'clock already?" I find myself saying: "Is it only three o'clock?"

8   We walk one kilometre downtown to do the errands, fetch the mail (there is no delivery in our town), and pick up a copy of The Globe and Mail, which surprisingly arrives at the corner store each day by 9 a.m. The grocery store delivers free of charge.

9   My new freedom struck home a couple of weeks after we arrived, when I had a 10:30 a.m. appointment with the optometrist. Worried about being late, I left the house 15 minutes early to drive downtown. Exactly 90 seconds later I was seated in his waiting room. (To complete this happy experience, at 10:18 a.m. he stuck his head out of his door and said: "I haven't any other patients waiting, so come on in!")

10   Our children, too, have more leisure time. They don't have to beg us for rides, or spend boring hours in the back seat, or listen to us complain about their conflicting schedules. They walk to school, to sports, to music lessons and to visit friends. All three adolescent children were able to find summer jobs — babysitting and mowing lawns — because they no longer require transportation. With a single family rule — "be home before supper" — we're all in a better mood.

11   If we are not driving our life away, neither is anyone else. This single factor might account for the slower pace here. Our fellow townsfolk simply have more hours in a day for pursuing friendships and interests. Last week I overheard the bank teller dictating her bread recipe to a customer who was taking notes on the back of a deposit slip.

12   This attitude is reflected in an unwritten law that we embrace wholeheartedly: no children's activities on weekends. All lessons and sports take place after school. On a Saturday, it is not uncommon to see teenagers actually out in public with their parents, at the single movie theatre or the weekly hockey game, or eating at the Blue Dog Cafe.

(There are no fast-food restaurants here, as there is no market for "fast" food.)

The financial benefits are significant, too. In Vancouver we paid about $300 a month to buy gas for our family van and our commuter car. Now we pay $75 a month to fuel our van only. Insurance on the van in this low-risk driving area has fallen from $1,357 to $907. Since we drive only to the nearest airport (100 kilometres) and to Calgary (300 kilometres) for the occasional shopping trip, we have let the insurance lapse on our rarely used second car, for a further reduction of $1,209. Total annual savings: $4,359.

Most importantly, we sense that our lives here are likely to last longer. We are at a lower risk of death or injury in a traffic accident. We have eliminated the stressful effects of urban driving: the traffic jams, the potential for being rear-ended at any given moment, the desperate search for parking, and concerns about the air-quality index. I'm not even counting the proven benefits of walking. Since moving here I haven't yet had one of my all-too-common colds, and my chronic eczema has disappeared.

Perhaps my attitude will change. Perhaps our teenagers will begin to pine for malls, and my husband will long to take power lunches with his mining colleagues, and I will miss finding the morning newspaper at my front door. But not so far.

CBC Radio is beamed into our living room from Vancouver each afternoon. And when dusk is falling and the announcer describes my former one-hour commute route — which led me from Richmond to North Vancouver, over two bridges and through 49 separate traffic lights — I want to throw back my head and howl with joy.

△ △

Explorations:

Stephen Leacock, *Sunshine Sketches of a Little Town*
Margaret Laurence, *A Bird in the House* (short stories)
E. Annie Proulx, *The Shipping News*
Helen and Scott Nearing, *Living the Good Life*
http://www.city.vancouver.bc.ca/aboutvan.html

Structure:

1. Review the arrow chart on p. 138 of this chapter's introduction. Does Florence follow its pattern of multiple *causes* leading to an *event*, which then has multiple *effects*?
2. As she explains her family's move from Vancouver to Invermere, why does Florence give *causes* first and then *effects*? Which paragraphs

explain mostly causes, and where does the focus then shift to effects? Why are so many more effects given?

3. Would this selection be at home in the following chapter, "Comparison and Contrast"? Point out five strong *contrasts* Florence makes between Vancouver and Invermere.

4. A strong way to interest and convince readers is to fill at least half your essay with *examples*. Has Florence reached this 50% level? Which paragraphs are entirely or almost entirely examples? Check your own latest essay: did you reach the 50% threshold?

Style:

1. Judging by her vocabulary and style, what kind of AUDIENCE do you think Florence is writing for?

2. Analyze the closing words of this essay. What gives them their power?

Ideas for Discussion and Writing:

1. Are you a car owner? If so, tell the class at least five *causes*. Then tell at least five *effects* (social, academic, financial, environmental, etc.). If you do not own a car, give at least five techniques for getting along without one in the city.

2. Do you like city driving? Or do you, like Elinor Florence, dread it? Tell a story to illustrate your view.

3. Florence and her family saved $4,359 in car expenses the first year by moving from Vancouver and cutting back from two vehicles to one. If you have a car, what do you shell out each year for payments? Insurance? Parking? Licence tag? Fuel? Repair and maintenance? Depreciation? Now add up all these economic *effects*, and tell the total to the class.

4. Take the total from question 3 above (how much extra you spend per year to drive a car), and enter it into your scientific calculator. Suppose you got rid of your car, and with the money saved by taking transit instead for one year, bought a stock mutual fund. If you remained invested at a typical average gain of 12% annually, what would your one year of transportation savings grow to in ten years? Twenty? Thirty?

5. An idea found in Buddhism is that one's real wealth is measured not by what one has, but by what one can do without. What do *you* think: is it better to need less money or to make more? *Compare* or *contrast* your strategy to that of Elinor Florence and her family.

6. Florence notes in paragraph 5 that "not one of the 200 bicycles parked outside the elementary school carries a lock," and that, in paragraph 11, she "overheard a bank teller dictating her bread recipe to a customer . . . ." Do you live in a small town? If so, add your own

examples of its advantages. Is small-town life all good, though? Tell at least one thing that makes you long for the city.

7. Since she has been walking more in the small town, Florence has had no more colds, and her "chronic eczema has disappeared" (par. 14). What physical activities do you enjoy: walking? Hiking? Aerobics? Swimming? Canoeing? Skiing? Team sports? Other? Tell the *effects* on your health, both mental and physical.

8. **PROCESS IN WRITING:** *Enlarge on question 1: Think of the effects of car ownership in our society. Fill at least a page with brainstorming or freewriting. Now see how much material you have; do you need to focus down on one area of the topic, such as the financial or the environmental? Do you have a main overall idea? Put it into a THESIS STATEMENT. Now write a rapid first draft, not stopping now to fix things like spelling or punctuation. The next day look it over: does it have at least 50% example content, like Elinor Florence's essay? If not, add. Does it look at causes behind causes, or effects of effects? If necessary, add. Does it have TRANSITIONS between parts? If not, add. Finally, do any extra words get in the way? If so, cut.*

Note: See also the Topics for Writing at the end of this chapter.

Garry Engkent

Why My Mother Can't Speak English

*Born in 1948 in Mon-Lau, a village on the Pearl River of China, Garry
Engkent was a small boy when the Communist Army invaded. His father had
already been two years in Canada by the time the son and wife made their way to
Hong Kong. There a bribe allowed the boy to cross the bridge (a clan cousin was
there to receive him). Six months later the mother, too, was allowed into "the
Fragrant Harbour." After a time as refugees, they were at last reunited with the
father in North Bay, Ontario. As Engkent writes, his mother never did learn
English, but he himself was quickly acculturated. Though his education includes
a Ph.D. in English (1980) from the University of Ottawa, he remembers an
earlier "education" — absorbing American culture from countless hours in movie
theatres. Engkent can still speak Cantonese, but almost no one in Canada knows
his village dialect. He has taught writing and literature at many universities:
Ottawa, Alberta, Guelph, Toronto and Ryerson. To "write about what you
know" is not enough, he tells his students; add the widest reading possible, to
produce writing that "comes out alive." Engkent's own narrative is based mostly
on fact, though fictionalized in some details; since he was away at the time, it
was a cousin who helped the mother who could not speak English become a
citizen of Canada.*

1   **M**y mother is seventy years old. Widowed for five years now, she lives
    alone in her own house except for the occasions when I come
home to tidy her household affairs. She has been in *gum san*, the golden
mountain, for the past thirty years. She clings to the old-country ways so
much so that today she astonishes me with this announcement:

2   "I want to get my citizenship," she says as she slaps down the *Dai Pao*,
"before they come and take away my house."

3   "Nobody's going to do that. This is Canada."

4   "So everyone says," she retorts, "but did you read what the *Dai Pao*
said? Ah, you can't read Chinese. The government is cutting back on
old-age pensions. Anybody who hasn't got citizenship will lose everything. Or worse."

5   "The *Dai Pao* can't even typeset accurately," I tell her. Sometimes I
worry about the information Mother receives from the biweekly com-

munity newspaper. "Don't worry — the Ministry of Immigration won't send you back to China."

"Little you know," she snaps back. "I am old, helpless, and without citizenship. Reasons enough. Now, get me citizenship. Hurry!"   6

"Mother, getting citizenship papers is not like going to the bank to cash in your pension cheque. First, you have to —"   7

"Excuses, my son, excuses. When your father was alive —"   8

"Oh, Mother, not again! You throw that at me every —"   9

"— made excuses, too." Her jaw tightens. "If you can't do this little thing for your own mother, well, I will just have to go and beg your cousin to. . . ."   10

Every time I try to explain about the ways of the *fan gwei*, she thinks I do not want to help her.   11

"I'll do it, I'll do it, okay? Just give me some time."   12

"That's easy for you," Mother snorts. "You're not seventy years old. You're not going to lose your pension. You're not going to lose your house. Now, how much *lai-shi* will this take?"   13

After all these years in *gum san* she cannot understand that you don't give government officials *lai-shi*, the traditional Chinese money gift to persons who do things for you.   14

"That won't be necessary," I tell her. "And you needn't go to my cousin."   15

Mother picks up the *Dai Pao* again and says: "Why should I beg at the door of a village cousin when I have a son who is a university graduate?"   16

I wish my father were alive. Then he would be doing this. But he is not here, and as a dutiful son, I am responsible for the welfare of my widowed mother. So I take her to Citizenship Court.   17

There are several people from the Chinese community waiting there. Mother knows a few of the Chinese women and she chats with them. My cousin is there, too.   18

"I thought your mother already got her citizenship," he says to me. "Didn't your father —"   19

"No, he didn't."   20

He shakes his head sadly. "Still, better now than never. That's why I'm getting these people through."   21

"So they've been reading the *Dai Pao*."   22

He gives me a quizzical look, so I explain to him, and he laughs. 23

"You are the new generation," he says. "You didn't live long enough in *hon san*, the sweet land, to understand the fears of the old. You can't expect the elderly to renounce all attachments to China for the ways of the *fan gwei*. How old is she, seventy now? Much harder."   24

"She woke me up this morning at six, and Citizenship Court doesn't open until ten."   25

26   The doors of the court finally open, and Mother motions me to hurry. We wait in line for a while.

27   The clerk distributes applications and tells me the requirements. Mother wants to know what the clerk is saying, so half the time I translate for her.

28   The clerk suggests that we see one of the liaison officers.

29   "Your mother has been living in Canada for the past thirty years and she still can't speak English?"

30   "It happens," I tell the liaison officer.

31   "I find it hard to believe that — not one word?"

32   "Well, she understands some restaurant English," I tell her. "You know, French fries, pork chops, soup, and so on. And she can say a few words."

33   "But will she be able to understand the judge's questions? The interview with the judge, as you know, is an important part of the citizenship procedure. Can she read the booklet? What does she know about Canada?"

34   "So you don't think my mother has a chance?"

35   "The requirements are that the candidate must be able to speak either French or English, the two official languages of Canada. The candidate must be able to pass an oral interview with the citizenship judge, and then he or she must be able to recite the oath of allegiance —"

36   "My mother needs to speak English," I conclude for her.

37   "Look, I don't mean to be rude, but why didn't your mother learn English when she first came over?"

38   I have not been translating this conversation, and Mother, annoyed and agitated, asks me what is going on. I tell her there is a slight problem.

39   "What problem?" Mother opens her purse, and I see her taking a small red envelope — *lai-shi* — I quickly cover her hand.

40   "What's going on?" the liaison officer demands.

41   "Nothing," I say hurriedly. "Just a cultural misunderstanding, I assure you."

42   My mother rattles off some indignant words, and I snap back in Chinese: "Put that away! The woman won't understand, and we'll be in a lot of trouble."

43   The officer looks confused, and I realize that an explanation is needed.

44   "My mother was about to give you a money gift as a token of appreciation for what you are doing for us. I was afraid you might misconstrue it as a bribe. We have no intention of doing that."

45   "I'm relieved to hear it."

46   We conclude the interview, and I take Mother home. Still clutching the application, Mother scowls at me.

"I didn't get my citizenship papers. Now I will lose my old-age pension. The government will ship me back to China. My old bones will lie there while your father's will be here. What will happen to me?"   47

How can I teach her to speak the language when she is too old to learn, too old to want to learn? She resists anything that is *fan gwei*. She does everything the Chinese way. Mother spends much time staring blankly at the four walls of her house. She does not cry. She sighs and shakes her head. Sometimes she goes about the house touching her favourite things.   48

"This is all your dead father's fault," she says quietly. She turns to the photograph of my father on the mantel. Daily, she burns incense, pours fresh cups of fragrant tea, and spreads dishes of his favourite fruits in front of the framed picture as is the custom. In memory of his passing, she treks two miles to the cemetery to place flowers by his headstone, to burn ceremonial paper money, and to talk to him. Regularly, rain or shine, or even snow, she does these things. Such love, such devotion, now such vehemence. Mother curses my father, her husband, in his grave.   49

When my mother and I emigrated from China, she was forty years old, and I, five. My father was already a well-established restaurant owner. He put me in school and Mother in the restaurant kitchen, washing dishes and cooking strange foods like hot dogs, hamburgers, and French fries. She worked seven days a week from six in the morning until eleven at night. This lasted for twenty-five years, almost to the day of my father's death.   50

The years were hard on her. The black-and-white photographs show a robust woman; now I see a withered, frail, white-haired old woman, angry, frustrated with the years, and scared of losing what little material wealth she has to show for the toil in *gum san*.   51

"I begged him," Mother says. "But he would either ignore my pleas or say: 'What do you need to know English for? You're better off here in the kitchen. Here you can talk to the others in our own tongue. English is far too complicated for you. How old are you now? Too old to learn a new language. Let the young speak *fan gwei*. All you need is to understand the orders from the waitresses. Anyway, if you need to know something, the men will translate for you. I am here; I can do your talking for you.'"   52

As a conscientious boss of the young male immigrants, my father would force them out of the kitchen and into the dining room. "The kitchen is no place for you to learn English. All you do is speak Chinese in here. To survive in *gum san*, you have to speak English, and the only way you can do that is to wait on tables and force yourselves to speak English with the customers. How can you get your families over here if you can't talk to the immigration officers in English?"   53

54   A few of the husbands who had the good fortune to bring their wives over to Canada hired a retired school teacher to teach a bit of English to their wives. Father discouraged Mother from going to those once-a-week sessions.

55   "That old woman will get rich doing nothing. What have these women learned?" *Fan gwei* ways — make-up, lipstick, smelly perfumes, fancy clothes. Once she gets through with them, they won't be Chinese women any more — and they certainly won't be white either."

56   Some of the husbands heeded the words of the boss, for he was older than they, and he had been in the *fan gwei's* land longer. These wives stayed home and tended the children, or they worked in the restaurant kitchen, washing dishes and cooking *fan gwei* foods, and talking in Chinese about the land and the life they had been forced to leave behind.

57   "He was afraid that I would leave him. I depended on him for everything. I could not go anywhere by myself. He drove me to work and he drove me home. He only taught me how to print my name so that I could sign anything he wanted me to, bank cheques, legal documents . . . "

58   Perhaps I am not Chinese enough any more to understand why my mother would want to take in the sorrow, the pain, and the anguish, and then to recount them every so often.

59   Once, I was presumptuous enough to ask her why she would want to remember in such detail. She said that the memories didn't hurt any more. I did not tell her that her reminiscences cut me to the quick. Her only solace now is to be listened to.

60   When my father died five years ago, she cried and cried. "Don't leave me in this world. Let me die with you."

61   Grief-stricken, she would not eat for days. She was so weak from hunger that I feared she wouldn't be able to attend the funeral. At his grave side, she chanted over and over a dirge, commending his spirit to the next world and begging the goddess of mercy to be kind to him. By custom, she set his picture on the mantel and burned incense in front of it daily. And we would go to the cemetery often. There she would arrange fresh flowers and talk to him in the gentlest way.

62   Often she would warn me: "The world of the golden mountain is so strong, *fan gwei* improprieties, and customs. They will have you abandon your own aged mother to some old-age home to rot away and die unmourned. If you are here long enough, they will turn your head until you don't know who you are — Chinese."

63   My mother would convert the months and the days into the Chinese lunar calendar. She would tell me about the seasons and the harvests and festivals in China. We did not celebrate any *fan gwei* holidays.

64   My mother sits here at the table, fingering the booklet from the Citizenship Court. For thirty-some years, my mother did not learn the

English language, not because she was not smart enough, not because she was too old to learn, and not because my father forbade her, but because she feared that learning English would change her Chinese soul. She only learned enough English to survive in the restaurant kitchen.

Now, Mother wants *gum san* citizenship. 65

"Is there no hope that I will be given it?" she asks. 66

"There's always a chance," I tell her. "I'll hand in the application." 67

"I should have given that person the *lai-shi*," Mother says obstinately. 68

"Maybe I should teach you some English," I retort. "You have about six months before the oral interview." 69

"I am seventy years old," she says. "*Lai-shi* is definitely much easier." 70

My brief glimpse into Mother's heart is over, and it has taken so long to come about. I do not know whether I understand my aged mother any better now. Despite my mother's constant instruction, there is too much *fan gwei* in me. 71

The booklet from the Citizenship Court lies, unmoved, on the table, gathering dust for weeks. She has not mentioned citizenship again with the urgency of that particular time. Once in a while, she would say: "They have forgotten me. I told you they don't want old Chinese women as citizens." 72

Finally, her interview date is set. I try to teach her some ready-made phrases, but she forgets them. 73

"You should not sigh so much. It is bad for your health," Mother observes. 74

On the day of her examination, I accompany her into the judge's chamber. I am more nervous than my mother. 75

Staring at the judge, my mother remarks: "*Noi yren.*" The judge shows interest in what my mother says, and I translate it: "She says you're a woman." 76

The judge smiles, "Yes. Is that strange?" 77

"If she is going to examine me," Mother tells me, "I might as well start packing for China. Sell my house. Dig up your father's bones, and I'll take them back with me." 78

Without knowing what my mother said, the judge reassures her. "This is just a formality. Really. We know that you obviously want to be part of our Canadian society. Why else would you go through all this trouble? We want to welcome you as a new citizen, no matter what race, nationality, religion, or age. And we want you to be proud — as a new Canadian." 79

Six weeks have passed since the interview with the judge. Mother receives a registered letter telling her to come in three weeks' time to take part in the oath of allegiance ceremony. 80

With patient help from the same judge, my mother recites the oath and becomes a Canadian citizen after thirty years in *gum san*. 81

82   "How does it feel to be a Canadian?" I ask.

83   "In China, this is the eighth month, the season of harvest." Then she adds: "The *Dai Pao* says that the old-age pension cheques will be increased by nine dollars next month."

84   As we walk home on this bright autumn morning, my mother clutches her piece of paper. Citizenship. She says she will go up to the cemetery and talk to my father this afternoon. She has something to tell him.

ΔΔΔΔΔΔΔΔΔΔΔΔΔΔΔΔΔΔΔΔΔΔΔΔΔΔΔΔΔΔΔΔΔΔΔΔΔΔΔΔΔΔΔΔΔΔ

Explorations:

Bennett Lee and Jim Wong-Chu, eds., *Many-Mouthed Birds: Contemporary Writings by Chinese-Canadians*
Denise Chong, *The Concubine's Children* (memoir)
Wayson Choy, *The Jade Peony* (novel)
Sky Lee, *Disappearing Moon Cafe* (novel)
Amy Tan, *The Joy Luck Club* (novel; also made into an acclaimed feature film now out on video)
Women's Book Committee, *Jin Guo: Voices of Chinese-Canadian Women* (memoirs)
http://cicnet.ci.gc.ca

Structure:

1. The author says this piece is at least partly fiction. How well has its chronological *narrative* mode served to present the *cause and effect* message?
2. In just a few pages there are 84 paragraphs. Why so many? Why are some so short?
3. As he tells why after 30 years his mother does not speak English, the narrator examines several *causes*: the isolation of her work as cook (pars. 51–52), obstruction by her conservative husband (pars. 54–57), and finally her age. While these all play a part, what is the key reason he finally grasps in paragraphs 62–64? Does he deplore or admire this motivation for not learning English?
4. In this piece Engkent explores mostly *causes*, but what *effect* emerges at the end? How strong is it in the life of the mother and son? How well does it serve as a closing?

Style:

1. Why does Engkent sprinkle his account with Chinese terms: *gum san, Dai Pao, fan gwei, lai-shi, hon san* and *noi yren*? Does he define each? Do they confuse, or do they enrich the argument? Give reasons.

2. In what tense has Engkent written? What are the advantages of this tense for narratives?

Ideas for Discussion and Writing:

1. All Canadians, except First Nations people, have a background of immigration. When did it take place in your family? Tell the *causes.* Tell the main *effects.*

2. In Vancouver, Toronto and Montreal, many New Canadians can shop, eat, worship, read, listen to radio or see TV and movies, go out, and work — all in their first language. Why learn English or French?

3. To maintain her identity, the narrator's mother speaks only her first language. If you were born in another country, what are *your* techniques for retaining your identity here?

4. Americans view their society as a "melting pot" where new arrivals assimilate, but Canadians have viewed theirs as a "mosaic" where immigrants are encouraged, even funded, to keep their language and culture. Which METAPHOR do you prefer? Which philosophy works best for the individual? For the nation? Defend your view with reasons.

5. In the past, most Canadians accepted the "Two Nations" concept of our history and culture, and the legal fact that French and English are Canada's official languages. Yet now many English Canadians and many Quebec sovereigntists call bilingualism a waste of money, and many New Canadians ask why French takes precedence over their own language now spoken by many in Canada. What is the solution? What are the implications for Quebeckers? For French Canadians living outside Quebec? For English Canadians living in Quebec? For First Nations people? For New Canadians?

6. **PROCESS IN WRITING:** *Through periodical indexes, CD-ROM data bases of periodicals, or press releases listed in the government Web site given in "Explorations," examine Canada's current immigration policies. Focus on one question — for example, are we accepting fewer or more immigrants? Encouraging or discouraging political refugees? Practising racism or fairness in our selection criteria? Make notes on the* effects *of the policy you have selected and, looking them over, write a* THESIS STATEMENT. *Now do a rapid discovery draft, tracing these* effects. *When it "cools off," look it over. Do linking words such as "since," "because" and "therefore" emphasize the* cause and effect *logic? Do examples help the reader "see" your point? Is all deadwood cut? If not, revise. Finally, check for spelling and punctuation as you produce your good draft. Read it aloud to the class, and be ready to answer questions asked from other points of view.*

Note: See also the Topics for Writing at the end of this chapter.

Mordecai Richler

1944: The Year I Learned
to Love a German

Mordecai Richler is a widely read novelist and the liveliest Canadian essayist of his generation. His well-crafted, ruthlessly satirical prose devastates its targets: hypocrisy, pretension, self-righteousness, prejudice, provincialism and nationalism (he attacks all these in our selection). Born in 1931 to a working-class family in the Jewish quarter of Montreal, Richler left in 1951 for Paris, where he wrote his first novel. He returned to work at the CBC, then from 1954 to 1972 lived and wrote in England, and since 1972 has lived in Quebec. Richler has produced many novels: The Acrobats *(1954),* Son of a Smaller Hero *(1955),* A Choice of Enemies *(1957),* The Apprenticeship of Duddy Kravitz *(1959),* The Incomparable Atuk *(1963),* Cocksure *(1968),* St. Urbain's Horseman *(1971),* Joshua Then and Now *(1980),* Solomon Gursky Was Here *(1989) and* Barney's Version *(1997). Both* Duddy Kravitz *and* Joshua *were made into films, as was his children's book* Jacob Two-Two Meets the Hooded Fang *(1975). Many of Richler's essays and articles have been gathered in collections such as* Shovelling Trouble *(1972),* Home Sweet Home: My Canadian Album *(1984) and* Broadsides: Reviews and Opinions *(1990). His 1992 book* Oh Canada! Oh Quebec! *has been his most controversial: Richler's claims of unfair language laws and of past anti-Semitism in Quebec stirred debate in both the French and English press. Our own selection is from the* New York Times Book Review *of February 2, 1986. It is a revised version of his introduction to the Book-of-the-Month-Club edition of a classic antiwar novel,* All Quiet on the Western Front, *by Erich Maria Remarque.*

1 Reading was not one of my boyhood passions. Girls, or rather the absence of girls, drove me to it. When I was 13 years old, short for my age, more than somewhat pimply, I was terrified of girls. They made me feel sadly inadequate. As far as I could make out, they were attracted only to boys who were tall or played for the school basketball team or at least shaved. Unable to qualify on all three counts, I resorted to subterfuge. I set out to call attention to myself by becoming a character. Retreating into high seriousness, I acquired a pipe, which I chewed on ostentatiously, and made it my business to be seen everywhere, even at school basketball games, absorbed by books of daunting significance. Say, H. G. Wells's "Short History of the World" or Paul de Kruif's

"Microbe Hunters" or John Gunther inside one continent or another. I rented these thought-provoking books for three cents a day from a neighborhood lending library that was across the street from a bowling alley where I used to spot pins four nights a week.

Oh, my God, I would not be 13 again for anything. The sweetly scented girls of my dreams, wearing lipstick and tight sweaters and nylon stockings, would sail into the bowling alley holding hands with the boys from the basketball team. "Hi," they would call out, giggly, nudging one another, even as I bent over the pins, "how goes the reading?"

The two women who ran the lending library, possibly amused by my pretensions, tried to interest me in fiction.

"I want fact. I can't be bothered with *stories*," I protested, waving my pipe at them, affronted. "I just haven't got the time for such nonsense."

I knew what novels were, of course. I had read "Scaramouche," by Rafael Sabatini, at school, as well as "Treasure Island" and some Ellery Queens and a couple of thumpers by G. A. Henty. Before that there had been Action Comics, Captain Marvel, Batman and — for educational reasons — either Bible Comics or Classic Comics. All these treasures I bought under the counter, as it were. They were passed hand to hand on dark street corners. Contraband. Our samizdat. The reason for this being that in 1943 the dolts who prevailed in Ottawa had adjudged American comic books unessential to the war effort, a drain on the Canadian dollar.

Novels, I knew, were mere romantic make-believe, not as bad as poetry, to be fair, but bad enough. Our high school class master, a dedicated Scot, had been foolish enough to try to interest us in poetry. A veteran of World War I, he told us that during the nightly bombardments on the Somme he would fix a candle to his steel helmet so that he could read poetry in the trenches. A scruffy lot, we were not moved. Instead we exchanged knowing winks behind that admirable man's back. Small wonder, we agreed, that he had ended up no better than a high school teacher.

My aunts consumed historical novels like pastries. My father read Black Mask and True Detective. My mother would read anything on a Jewish subject, preferably by I. J. Singer or Sholem Asch, though she would never forgive the latter for having written "The Nazarene," never mind "Mary" and "The Apostle." My older brother kept a novel, "Topper Takes a Trip," secure under his mattress in the bedroom we shared, assuring me that it was placed at just such an angle on the springs that if it were moved so much as a millimeter in his absence he would know and bloody well make me pay for it.

I fell ill with a childhood disease. I no longer remember which, but obviously I meant it as a rebuke to those girls in tight sweaters who continued to ignore me. Never mind, they would mourn at my funeral, burying me with my pipe. Too late, they would say, "Boy, was he ever an intellectual!"

9   The women from the lending library, concerned, dropped off books for me at our house. The real stuff. Fact-filled. Providing me with the inside dope on Theodor Herzl's childhood and "Brazil Yesterday, Today, and Tomorrow." One day they brought me a novel: "All Quiet on the Western Front" by Erich Maria Remarque. The painting on the jacket that was taped to the book showed a soldier wearing what was unmistakably a German Army helmet. *What was this,* I wondered, *some sort of bad joke?*

10   Nineteen forty-four that was, and I devoutly wished every German left on the face of the earth an excruciating death. The Allied invasion of France had not yet begun, but I cheered every Russian counterattack, each German city bombed, and — with the help of a map tacked to my bedroom wall — followed the progress of the Canadian troops fighting their way up the Italian boot. Boys from our street had already been among the fallen. Izzy Draper's uncle, Harvey Kugelmass's older brother. The boy who was supposed to marry Gita Holtzman.

11   "All Quiet on the Western Front" lay unopened on my bed for two days. A time bomb ticking away, though I hardly suspected it. Rather than read a novel, a novel written by a German, I tuned in to radio soap operas in the afternoons: "Ma Perkins," "Pepper Young's Family." I organized a new baseball league for short players who didn't shave yet, appointing myself commissioner, the first Canadian to be so honored. Sifting through a stack of my father's back issues of Popular Mechanics, I was sufficiently inspired to invent a spaceship and fly to Mars, where I was adored by everybody, especially the girls. Finally, I was driven to picking up "All Quiet on the Western Front" out of boredom. I never expected that a mere novel, a stranger's tale, could actually be dangerous, creating such turbulence in my life, obliging me to question so many received ideas. About Germans. About my own monumental ignorance of the world. About what novels were.

12   At the age of 13 in 1944, happily as yet untainted by English 104, I couldn't tell you whether Remarque's novel was

       a. a slice of life
       b. symbolic
       c. psychological
       d. seminal.

13   I couldn't even say if it was well or badly written. In fact, as I recall, it didn't seem to be "written" at all. Instead, it just flowed. Now, of course, I understand that writing that doesn't advertise itself is art of a very

high order. It doesn't come easily. But at the time I wasn't capable of making such distinctions. I also had no notion of how "All Quiet on the Western Front" rated critically as a war novel. I hadn't read Stendhal or Tolstoy or Crane or Hemingway. I hadn't even heard of them. I didn't know that Thomas Mann, whoever he was, had praised the novel highly. Neither did I know that in 1929 the judges at some outfit called the Book-of-the-Month Club had made it their May selection. But what I did know is that, hating Germans with a passion, I had read only 20, maybe 30, pages before the author had seduced me into identifying with my enemy, 19-year-old Paul Baumer, thrust into the bloody trenches of World War I with his schoolmates: Müller, Kemmerich and the reluctant Joseph Behm, one of the first to fall. As if that weren't sufficiently unsettling in itself, the author, having won my love for Paul, my enormous concern for his survival, then betrayed me in the last dreadful paragraphs of his book:

"He fell in October 1918, on a day that was so quiet and still on the whole front, that the army report confined itself to the single sentence: All quiet on the Western Front.   14

"He had fallen forward and lay on the earth as though sleeping. Turning him over one saw that he could not have suffered long; his face had an expression of calm, as though almost glad the end had come."   15

The movies, I knew from experience, never risked letting you down like that. No matter how bloody the battle, how long the odds, Errol Flynn, Robert Taylor, even Humphrey Bogart could be counted on to survive and come home to Ann Sheridan, Lana Turner or — if they were sensitive types — Loretta Young. Only character actors, usually Brooklyn Dodger fans, say George Tobias or William Bendix, were expendable.   16

Obviously, having waded into the pool of serious fiction by accident, I was not sure I liked or trusted the water. It was too deep. Anything could happen.   17

There was something else, a minor incident in "All Quiet on the Western Front" that would not have troubled an adult reader but, I'm embarrassed to say, certainly distressed that 13-year-old boy colliding with his first serious novel.   18

Sent out to guard a village that has been abandoned because it is being shelled too heavily, Katczinsky, the incomparable scrounger, surfaces with suckling pigs and potatoes and carrots for his comrades, a group of eight altogether: 19

"The suckling pigs are slaughtered. Kat sees to them. We want to make potato-cakes to go with the roast. But we cannot find a grater for the potatoes. However, that difficulty is soon got over. With a nail we punch a lot of holes in a pot lid and there we have a grater. Three   20 fellows put on thick gloves to protect their fingers against the grater, two others peel the potatoes, and the business gets going."

21   The business, I realized, alarmed — no, *affronted* — was the making of potato latkes, a favorite of mine as well as Paul Baumer's, a dish I had always taken to be Jewish, certainly not a German concoction.

22   What did I know? Nothing. Or, looked at another way, my real education, my lifelong addiction to fiction, began with the trifling discovery that the potato latke was not of Jewish origin, but something borrowed from the Germans and now a taste that Jew and German shared in spite of everything.

23   I felt easier about my affection for the German soldier Paul Baumer once I was told by the women from the lending library that when Hitler came to power in 1933 he had burned all of Erich Maria Remarque's books and in 1938 he took away his German citizenship. Obviously Hitler had grasped that novels could be dangerous, something I learned when I was only 13 years old. He burned them. I began to devour them. I started to read at the breakfast table and on streetcars, often missing my stop, and in bed with benefit of a flashlight. It got me into trouble. I grasped, for the first time, that I didn't live in the center of the world but had been born into a working-class family in an unimportant country far from the cities of light: London, Paris, New York. Of course this wasn't my fault, it was my inconsiderate parents who were to blame. But there was, I now realized, a larger world out there beyond St. Urbain Street in Montreal; a world that could be available to me, even though — to my mother's despair — I had been born left-handed, ate with my elbows on the table and had failed once more to lead the class at school.

24   Preparing myself for the *Rive Gauche,*° I bought a blue beret, but I didn't dare wear it outside, or even in the house if anybody else was at home. I looked at but lacked the courage to buy a cigarette holder. But the next time I took Goldie Zimmerman to a downtown movie and then out to Dinty Moore's for toasted tomato sandwiches, I suggested that instead of milkshakes we each order a glass of *vin ordinaire.* "Are you crazy?" she asked.

25   As my parents bickered at the supper table, trapped in concerns now far too mundane for the likes of me — what to do if Dworkin raised the rent again, how to manage my brother's college fees — I sat with but actually apart from them in the kitchen, enthralled, reading for the first time, "All happy families are alike but an unhappy family is unhappy after its own fashion."

° *Rive Gauche:* the "Left Bank" of Paris, traditional quarter of students and intellectuals.

Erich Maria Remarque, born in Westphalia in 1897, went off to war, directly from school, at the age of 18. He was wounded five times. He lost all his friends. After the war he worked briefly as a schoolteacher, a stonecutter, a test driver for a tire company and an editor of Sportbild magazine. His first novel, "Im Westen Nichts Neues," was turned down by several publishers before it was brought out by the Ullstein Press in Berlin in 1928. "All Quiet on the Western Front" sold 1,200,000 copies in Germany and was translated into 29 languages, selling some four million copies throughout the world. The novel has been filmed three times; the first time, memorably, by Lewis Milestone in 1930. The Milestone version, with Lew Ayres playing Paul Baumer, won Academy Awards for best picture and best direction.

Since "All Quiet on the Western Front" once meant so much to me, I picked it up again with a certain anxiety. After all this time I find it difficult to be objective about the novel. Its pages still evoke for me a back bedroom with a cracked ceiling and a sizzling radiator on St. Urbain Street, mice scrabbling in the walls, a window looking out on sheets frozen stiff on the laundry line, and all the pain of being too young to shave, an ignorant and bewildered boy of 13.

Over the years the novel has lost something in shock value. The original jacket copy of the 1929 Little, Brown & Company edition of "All Quiet on the Western Front" warns the reader that it is "at times crude" and "will shock the supersensitive by its outspokenness." Contemporary readers, far from being shocked, will be amused by the novel's discretion, the absence of explicit sex scenes, the unbelievably polite dialogue of the men in the trenches.

Δ Δ Δ

The novel also has its poignant moments, both in the trenches and when Paul Baumer goes home on leave, an old man of 19, only to find insufferably pompous schoolmasters still recruiting the young with mindless prattle about the fatherland and the glory of battle. Strong characters are deftly sketched. Himmelstoss, the postman who becomes a crazed drillmaster, Tjaden, the peasant soldier, Kantorek, the schoolmaster. On the front line the enemy is never the Frogs or the Limeys, but the insanity of the war itself. It is the war, in fact, and not even Paul Baumer, that is the novel's true protagonist. In a brief introduction to the novel Remarque wrote: "This book is to be neither an accusation nor a confession, and least of all an adventure, for death is not an adventure to those who stand face to face with it. It will try simply to tell of a generation of men who, even though they may have escaped its shells, were destroyed by the war."

30   Since World War I we have become altogether too familiar with larger horrors. The Holocaust, Hiroshima, the threat of a nuclear winter. Death by numbers, cities obliterated by decree. At peace, as it were, we live with the daily dread of the missiles in their silos, ours pointed at them, theirs pointed at us. None of this, however, diminishes the power of "All Quiet on the Western Front," a novel that will endure because of its humanity, its honor and its refusal to lapse into sentimentality or strike a false note. It is a work that has earned its place on that small shelf of World War I classics alongside "Goodbye to All That," by Robert Graves, and Ernest Hemingway's "A Farewell to Arms."

△ △

Explorations:

Mordecai Richler,
  The Apprenticeship of Duddy Kravitz
  St. Urbain's Horseman
  Barney's Version
Erich Maria Remarque, *All Quiet on the Western Front*
Charles Yale Harrison, *Generals Die in Bed* (novel)
Ernest Hemingway, *A Farewell to Arms* (novel)
http://alvin.lbl.gov/bios/Richler.html/
http://babelfish.altavista.digital.com/cgi-bin/translate?

Structure:

1. How does the long opening prepare us for Richler's argument? What do paragraphs 1 and 2 achieve? Paragraphs 3–6?
2. Why does Richler devote so little of his argument to the original *causes* of his reading, and so much to the *effects*?
3. Point out every *effect* on young Richler of reading novels, as shown especially in paragraphs 11, 13–17, 18–22, and 23.
4. Richler uses spaces to divide the essay in parts. What advantages does this technique have? Do you use it?
5. What technique does Richler exploit when in the closing paragraph he refers to nuclear weapons?

Style:

1. Richler's overall message is serious. Why, then, does he poke fun at adolescence, at his own and others' reading habits, at high school English, at the movies and at other targets? Do his humour and even SATIRE help or hurt the argument? Defend your answer with reasons.
2. A key technique of both novelists and essayists is to clothe abstractions in concrete IMAGES — to "show, don't tell." Point out how Richler does so in paragraphs 11, 24, and 27.

3. Explain the IRONY of calling Paul Baumer "an old man of 19" (par. 29). Using this example, analyze how irony promotes CONCISENESS.
4. Is the METAPHOR of Remarque's novel as a "bomb" (par. 11) well chosen for this topic?

Ideas for Discussion and Writing:

1. Almost every writer, like Richler, has read voraciously. Analyze the apparent *cause-and-effect* relationship: Why does reading other people's writing improve our own? Have you read enough? What are the *causes* of your attitude towards reading? What are the *effects*?
2. Richler admits that, as a Jewish boy growing up during the war, he "devoutly wished every German left on the face of the earth an excruciating death" (par. 10). Why *every* German? Do you see a STEREOTYPE behind this passage? Does it apply to those Germans who hid persecuted Jews? To those who fled Hitler's power, or even tried to assassinate him? Does it apply to Erich Maria Remarque? To Paul Baumer? Are other stereotypes more reliable? Those of women, teenagers, old people, Newfoundlanders, Quebeckers, Jews, Russians?
3. After reading 20 to 30 pages of *All Quiet on the Western Front*, Richler is "seduced" by the author into "identifying" with his "enemy," and even feels "betrayed" when, at the end, Paul Baumer dies. Cite another passage where Richler's reading of fiction dispels STEREOTYPES.
4. "I never expected that a mere novel, a stranger's tale, could actually be dangerous," says Richler in paragraph 11. How can a novel be "dangerous"? Why did Hitler burn this one and strip its author of citizenship (par. 23)? Name other books burned or censored. What may such cases reveal about the role of the writer in society?
5. Extend Richler's analysis to other media. List several films you have recently seen or TV serials you have followed. Which were "dangerous," challenging received attitudes? Which were "safe," propping up received attitudes? Argue with examples.
6. **PROCESS IN WRITING:** *Choose either a "dangerous" or a "safe" film or TV series from the previous question. Now in an essay of cause and effect, show how the chosen work affected you: Did it just reinforce old opinions, or did it change your mind? First brainstorm: jot down scenes in which the work either reassured or disturbed you. Now turn the best of these notes into a draft. Did the act of writing call up forgotten details? Add them. Did it challenge your view of the work's "danger" or "safety"? If so, change your THESIS STATEMENT and adjust the argument. Now strengthen TRANSITIONS to speed your argument and highlight its causality. Cut deadwood. Finally, test your prose aloud before writing the final version.*

Note: See also the Topics for Writing at the end of this chapter.

Topics for Writing

Chapter 4: Cause and Effect

Analyze the cause(s) and/or effect(s) of one of the following. (See also the guide-lines that follow.)

1. Alien Mania
2. The Underground Economy
3. The Use of Video Lottery Terminals
4. Being Adopted
5. The Use of Credit Cards
6. Moving From a House to an Apartment, or Vice Versa
7. Dieting
8. Having a Home Office
9. Moving to a New School
10. Learning More Than One Language
11. Holding a Job While in School
12. Internet Addiction
13. Being the Oldest, Youngest or Middle Child of a Family
14. Downsizing of a Company
15. Marrying as a Teenager
16. Perfectionism
17. Moving to Another Country
18. Being a Twin
19. Pirating of Software
20. Procrastination
21. Drinking and Driving
22. Popularity in High School
23. Homelessness
24. Borrowing Money
25. Pornography
26. TV Addiction
27. Achieving Self-Confidence
28. Moving Out on Your Own
29. Gambling
30. Road Rage

Note also the Process in Writing topic after each selection in this chapter.

Process in Writing: Guidelines

Follow at least some of these steps in writing your essay of cause and effect (your teacher may suggest which ones).

1. *In the middle of a page, write the subject you wish to explore in your essay of* cause and effect. *Now around it write many other words that it brings to mind. Connect related items with lines, then use this cluster outline to focus your argument.*

2. *Write a quick first draft, getting it all out on the computer screen or the paper without stopping now to revise.*

3. *When this version has "cooled off," analyze it, referring to our chapter introduction: Have you begun and ended at the right places in the chain of causality? If not, cut or add. Have you found the* real causes *and the* real effects? *If not, revise. Do you also need* causes of causes, *or* effects of effects? *If so, add.*

4. *In your next draft sharpen the* TRANSITIONS, *using expressions like "since," "although," "because" and "as a result" to signal each step of your logic.*

5. *Share this version with a group of classmates. Revise any places where this* AUDIENCE *does not follow your logic.*

6. *Finally, edit for things like spelling and punctuation before printing out your best version. Save the essay on disk in case your teacher suggests further revision.*

Mike Constable

*"Women workers earn, on an average, only 70 cents for every $1 a man gets —
even though on an average, women are better educated than men."*

—*Doris Anderson, "The 51-Per-Cent Minority"*

CHAPTER 5

COMPARISON AND CONTRAST

It's just the opposite of. . .

Y ou may have heard the old Chinese proverb, "I felt sorry for myself because I had no shoes, until I met a man who had no feet." How much more we suddenly know about both the shoes and the feet, thinking of them together! This is the power of comparison and contrast.

See Mike Constable's cartoon on the opposite page. What is happening? All the runners are in starting position, awaiting the same shot from the same referee, and no doubt aiming for the same finish line. These are the *comparisons* (similarities). Yet at the same time there are *contrasts* (differences). Three of the runners are men, but only one is a woman. The referee holding his gun is also a man, unlike the woman contestant. She will run in skirt and high heels, while the men clearly will not. Worst of all, the men will run straight ahead, while she must race uphill to reach their level. Is there any way the woman can win this race?

Though the cartoon has both comparisons and contrasts, clearly it is the contrasts that send the message — men have advantages in the race of life. In the essay that follows, Doris Anderson uses words to send the same message through the same logic. Though of course there are similarities between the lives of women and men, it is the differences, the *contrasts*, that build Anderson's point that women, though a "majority" in numbers, are a "minority" in power.

When using the logic of comparison and contrast in your own essays, you, too, may find both similarities and differences. Though it is possible to explore both, the need to focus means that using one is often better — and the choice is usually the more dramatic and interesting one: *contrast.*

You have experienced contrast if you have ever known culture shock. As you enter a new country, the look of the buildings and streets, the smells in the air, the sounds, the language and customs, all seem strange — because you are contrasting them to what you just left. And if you stay a long time, the same happens in reverse when you return: home seems strange because you are contrasting it to the place where you've just been. The cars may seem too big, the food too bland, the pace of life too fast. Travel is one of the great educational experiences: through contrast, one place puts another in perspective.

In a comparison and contrast essay, it is essential to choose two subjects *of the same general type:* two countries, two sports, two poems, or two solutions to unemployment. For example, in our chapter Russell Baker focusses on two cities, Toronto and New York, systematically comparing their taxis, noise, garbage, dogs, subway, vandalism and other aspects of urban life. Despite his comic tone, and despite any disagreements we might have as to his verdict, by the time Baker gets done we have the impression of having read a logical argument. After all, Toronto and New York are in the same category: big cities.

But suppose that instead of comparing two cities, Baker had compared a city and an anthill. After all, there are similarities: both are crowded, both are highly organized, both have housing with many rooms located off corridors, etc. But no matter how much fun he might have had or what insights he might have got across, he would prove nothing — for the simple reason that people are not insects. His essay would be an *analogy,* a more imaginative but less logical kind of argument, which we will explore in the next chapter.

Once you have chosen your two subjects of the same general type, you face another choice: how to arrange them. There are two basic ways:

Divide the essay into halves, devoting the first half to Toronto and the second to New York. This system is natural in a very short essay, because your reader remembers everything from the first half while reading the second half. It is also natural when for some reason the items are more clearly discussed as a whole than in parts.

Divide the subjects into separate points. First compare taxis in both cities, then noise in both cities, then garbage in both cities, and so on through your whole list of points. This system is most natural in long essays: putting related material together helps the reader to grasp comparisons or contrasts without the strain of recalling every detail from ten pages back.

Baker organizes by "separate points" even in his brief essay, because the approach fits his way of poking fun at New York: in describing how Toronto controls its garbage, he implies, without even naming his own city, that New York is full of litter. He could not have achieved this degree of conciseness had he isolated the two sides of each topic into their own "halves" of the essay.

Although "halves" are often best for short papers and "separate points" are often best for long papers, be open to the needs of your particular subject, treatment and purpose. As Russell Baker has done, choose the approach that will most strongly deliver your message.

Finally, the very act of comparing or contrasting means you need *examples* — either a large number of short ones or a small number of long ones. If these do not make up at least half the content of your essay, you are losing power. Add more.

To generate your examples and points, why not draw a line down the middle of a blank page and put the name of your subjects at the top of each column? Now brainstorm a list of points under each heading. Connect related items from left to right with lines, and, seeing relationships, decide your thesis. Is cash better than credit? Is income tax fairer than sales tax? Are motorcycles more dangerous than cars? Whatever you believe is the truth, now write your essay, letting the many examples show your reader why.

Note: Many essays in other chapters use comparison and contrast to help make their point. See especially these:

Josh Freed, "Say Hi or Die," p. 85
Thierry Mallet, "The Firewood Gatherers," p. 111
Elinor Florence, "Leaving the Fast Lane for No Lane at All," p. 159
Margaret Laurence, "Where the World Began," p. 209
Judy Stoffman, "The Way of All Flesh," p. 286
Martin Hocking, "Capping the Great Cup Debate," p. 316
Kildare Dobbs, "The Scar," p. 322
Bonnie Laing, "An Ode to the User-Friendly Pencil," p. 331 (a strong example of comparison and contrast developed through "separate points")
Stevie Cameron, "Our Daughters, Ourselves," p. 354

Doris Anderson

The 51-Per-Cent Minority

Doris Anderson is one of Canada's leading advocates of women's rights. After earning her B.A. at the University of Alberta in 1945, she wrote radio scripts, worked in advertising, then in 1951 joined the staff of Chatelaine. *As editor in chief from 1957 to 1977, Anderson added to the magazine's family fare articles on the social and economic status of women. In 1981, while she was serving as president of the Canadian Advisory Council on the Status of Women, her sudden resignation, in protest against the government's reluctance to guarantee equality of men and women in the new constitution, sparked a campaign by women that did achieve a constitutional guarantee of their rights. From 1982 to 1984 Anderson was president of the National Action Committee on the Status of Women, an umbrella group representing millions of women in numerous organizations. Anderson has published novels,* Two Women *in 1978,* Rough Layout *in 1981 and* Affairs of State *in 1988. In addition to her many editorials and articles, she has written two nonfiction books,* The Unfinished Revolution *(on the status of women in 10 European countries as well as Canada and the United States) and an autobiography,* Rebel Daughter *(1996). Our own selection "The 51-Per-Cent Minority" first appeared in 1980 in* Maclean's. *Anderson has revised and updated this classic for our present edition.*

1   In any Canadian election the public will probably be hammered numb with talk of the economy, energy and other current issues. But there will always be some far more startling topics that no one will talk about at all.

2   No one is going to say to all new Canadians: "Look, we're going through some tough times. Three out of four of you had better face the fact that you're always going to be poor. At 65 more than likely you'll be living below the poverty level."

3   And no one is going to tell Quebeckers: "You will have to get along on less money than the rest of the country. For every $1 the rest of us earn, you, because you live in Quebec, will earn 70 cents."

4   I doubt very much that any political party is going to level with the Atlantic provinces and say: "We don't consider people living there serious prime workers. Forget about any special measures to make jobs for

you. In fact in future federal-provincial talks we're not even going to discuss your particular employment problems."

And no politician is going to tell all the left-handed people in the   5
country: "Look, we know it looks like discrimination, but we have to save some money somewhere. So, although you will pay into your company pension plan at the same rate as everyone else, you will collect less when you retire."

And no one is going to say to Canadian doctors: "We know you do   6
one of the most important jobs any citizen can perform, but from now on you're going to have to get along without any support systems. All hospital equipment and help will be drastically reduced. We believe a good doctor should instinctively know what to do — or you're in the wrong job. If you're really dedicated you'll get along."

As for blacks: "Because of the color of your skin, you're going to be   7
paid less than the white person next to you who is doing exactly the same job. It's tough but that's the way it is."

As for Catholics: "You're just going to have to understand that you   8
will be beaten up by people with other religious beliefs quite regularly. Even if your assailant threatens to kill you, you can't do anything about it. After all, we all need some escape valves, don't we?"

Does all of the above sound like some nihilistic nightmare where   9
Orwellian forces have taken over? Well, it's not. It's all happening right now, in Canada.

It's not happening to new Canadians, Quebeckers, residents of the   10
Atlantic provinces, left-handed people, doctors, blacks or Indians. If it were, there would be riots in the streets. Civil libertarians would be howling for justice. But all of these discriminatory practices are being inflicted on women today in Canada as a matter of course.

Most women work at two jobs — one inside the home and one   11
outside. Yet three out of four women who become widowed or divorced or have never married live out their old age in poverty.

Women workers earn, on an average, only 70 cents for every $1 a   12
man gets — even though on an average, women are better educated than men.

And when companies base pension plans on how long people live,   13
women still pay the same rates as men but often collect less.

What politician could possibly tell doctors to train each other and get   14
along without all their high technology and trained help? Yet a more important job than saving lives is surely creating lives. But mothers get no training, no help in the way of a family allowance, inadequate day-care centres, and almost nonexistent after-school programs.

No politician would dream of telling blacks they must automatically   15
earn less than other people. But women sales clerks, waitresses and hospital orderlies often earn less than males doing the same jobs. It

would be called discrimination if a member of a religious group was beaten up, and the assailant would be jailed. But hundreds of wives get beaten by their husbands week in and week out, year after year. Some die, yet society still tolerates the fact that it's happening.

16   Women make up 51 per cent of the population of this country. Think of the kind of clout they could have if they used it at the polls. But to listen to the political parties, the woman voter just doesn't exist. When politicians talk to fishing folk they talk about improved processing plants and new docks. When they talk to wheat farmers they talk of better transportation and higher price supports. When they talk to people in the Atlantic provinces they talk about new federal money for buildings and more incentives for secondary industry. When they talk to ethnic groups they talk about better language training courses. But when they think of women — if they do at all — they assume women will vote exactly as their husbands — so why waste time offering them anything? It's mind-boggling to contemplate, though, how all those discriminatory practices would be swept aside if, instead of women, we were Italian, or black, or lived in Quebec or the Atlantic provinces.

△ △

Explorations:

Doris Anderson,
   The Unfinished Revolution
   Rebel Daughter: An Autobiography
Simone de Beauvoir, *The Second Sex*
Naomi Wolf, *The Beauty Myth: How Images of Beauty Are Used Against Women*
Margaret Atwood, *The Handmaid's Tale* (novel)
http://www.nlc-bnc.ca/digiproj/women/ewomen.htm

Structure:

1. Is this essay mainly a *comparison* or a *contrast?*
2. Does Anderson argue "point by point" or by "halves"?
3. Point out the passage of TRANSITION between Anderson's discussion of minorities and her discussion of women.
4. Why does this feminist essay never mention women until halfway through? How does this tactic help Anderson reach the potentially hostile 49 percent of her AUDIENCE which is male?
5. If you have read *1984* or *Animal Farm*, tell how the reference to George Orwell in paragraph 9 helps make Anderson's point.
6. Why does the closing offer a series of new *examples?* Why are they so short?

Style:

1. How important is the title of an essay? What should it do? How effective is this one, and why?
2. Anderson's essay appeared in *Maclean's*, a magazine for the general reader. Name all the ways in which her essay seems designed for that person.

Ideas for Discussion and Writing:

1. Explain the IRONY of Anderson's claim: in what sense are women, 51 percent of the population, a "minority" in Canada?
2. Anderson states in paragraph 11, "Most women work at two jobs — one inside the home and one outside." Suppose that someday you and your partner both have full-time jobs. If you are a woman, how much of the housework will you expect your partner to do? If you are a man, how much of the housework will you expect your partner to do? Defend your view with reasons.
3. "The 51-Per-Cent Minority" first appeared in 1980. Revising it for this edition 19 years later, Anderson was able to raise from 61 cents to 70 cents the amount that a woman earns for every dollar a man earns. At this rate of change, equal pay will not arrive until 2062 A.D., 82 years after the essay was written. Explain why.
4. In paragraph 16 Anderson writes, "Women make up 51 per cent of the population of this country. Think of the kind of clout they could have if they used it at the polls." Do you agree that women have not yet used their votes to best advantage? If so, why not? How could they begin to?
5. **PROCESS IN WRITING:** *Write an essay that* contrasts *the way society trains girls to be women with the way society trains boys to be men. First divide a page into halves, one for each sex, and fill each half with* examples. *Now from these notes choose contrasting pairs. Decide whether to organize the pairs by* "halves" *or* "point by point," *then write a rapid first draft, double-spaced. In your next draft strengthen the* TRANSITIONS, *especially signals such as* "but," "on the other hand," "however," *and* "yet," *which point out con-trast. Share a draft with classmates in small groups to see if all parts work. Revise any that do not. Finally, read your best version aloud to the whole class, and be ready to answer questions asked from other points of view.*

Note: See also the Topics for Writing at the end of this chapter.

Biruté Galdikas

Akmad

When writers draw on deep experience, their words can assume a startling immediacy. Such is the case with Biruté Galdikas, who has spent a quarter of a century braving the mosquitoes, vipers and leeches of Borneo's rain forest to understand a species that shares all but two percent of its genetic material with humans — the orangutan. Hers has been a long journey. Born in Germany to Lithuanian parents en route to Canada, she grew up in Toronto, studied at the University of British Columbia, and in 1978 earned her Ph.D. in anthropology from UCLA. Her doctoral research was suggested by the famed British anthropologist Louis Leakey, who encouraged her to found a research camp on the Indonesian island of Borneo. In the years that followed, she became Leakey's "third angel," along with his other protégées Jane Goodall, who has spent her life researching chimpanzees, and Dian Fossey, who spent 22 years studying gorillas and was murdered for her efforts to protect them. What Galdikas has achieved has been the longest continuous study ever made of a mammal in the wild, resulting in new understandings of primates and, by extension, of ourselves. Our selection is the opening passage of her book Reflections of Eden: My Years With the Orangutans of Borneo *(1995). The "ex-captives" mentioned in paragraph 5 are individuals returned from captivity in zoos, research labs and private homes, to be trained to live as wild orangutans. Scientific opinion changed on this point, though, around 1992: ex-captives are now thought to endanger the wild population by spreading disease from elsewhere. Galdikas now divides her time between observing the orangutans of the rain forest (aided by her husband Pak Bohap, a tribal president and co-director of the orangutan program there); leading efforts to protect these shy animals through the Orangutan Foundation International; and lecturing part of each year at Simon Fraser University, where she is professor of anthropology.*

1   Akmad and I were alone by the edge of the great forest of Borneo, the second largest continuous stretch of tropical rain forest in the world. Akmad had just given birth, and her gentle, elongated orangutan face with its delicately etched features looked tired. The light of the late afternoon sun shone eerily through Akmad's long auburn hair, silhouetting her form in an incandescent halo.

I wanted to photograph the tiny, wrinkled, nude face of Akmad's newborn infant. I moved forward on my knees and elbows and focused on the baby's elfin face pressed to her mother's bosom. Moving my hand gently, I shifted the little infant. Her bright orange hair, newly dry from the fluids of birth, was soft and fluffy and contrasted with the deep, almost mahogany red of her mother's longer, coarser coat. Despite my touch, the infant rested quietly in her mother's arms. Akmad's liquid brown eyes remained expressionless. She seemed unaware of my hand on her newborn. Her arm brushed carelessly across my leg as she reached for a pineapple, almost as if I didn't exist. The magical soft light, peculiar to dusk in Borneo, etched the scene in gold, a moment transfixed in time.

Other orangutans began to emerge from the trees and descend to the ironwood causeway that runs from Camp Leakey, my research base deep in the forest, to the Sekonyer Kanan River six hundred feet away. Mr. Achyar, the camp feeder, appeared pushing a cart of food. In his forties and very slight, like a shadow, he walked with the slow, deliberate gait typical of older Indonesians. His Green Bay Packers T-shirt, faded from the equatorial sun and countless sudsy beatings in the name of cleanliness, was a reminder that the outside world intruded even here in Borneo.

Mr. Achyar stooped low as he passed by us, twisting sideways politely, his right arm and shoulder bent forward in a pose reminiscent of a figure on an ancient Egyptian mural. His bow reflected the courtesy typical of traditional Dayaks. Paradoxically, these most gentle and courteous of any people were once fierce headhunters, the "wild men of Borneo."

The spell continued as Mr. Achyar began chanting. He called the orangutans in a singsong voice, like a supplicant in an ancient ritual, the names of ex-captive orangutans like the names of spirits. His voice rose over the trees, "Pola, Kusasi, Hani, Kuspati, Siswoyo."

Mr. Achyar had been feeding the mature ex-captive orangutans at Camp Leakey for seven years. Of all my Dayak assistants, he was the one most trusted by the orangutans. Many Indonesians called him a *pawong*, a person who has the power to call wild animals to him. He had no children of his own and had developed a special relationship with the orangutans, referring to them as his children. His devotion to them was obvious as he moved among them in a careful, solicitous way, making certain each received an equal share of rice, bananas, and pineapple. Although Mr. Achyar was slim and slightly stooped, in this particular orangutan hierarchy he was the dominant male. Gigantic wild male orangutans who occasionally came to camp, attracted by orangutan females, deferred to him.

7   Dusk ends suddenly in the tropics, and I felt hurried. I twirled the focusing mechanism on my Nikon, clicking rapidly. I wanted to record this moment, to celebrate this as yet unnamed female infant on the day of her birth.

8   To take a clearer picture, I moved back from Akmad and her baby and crouched nine or ten feet away. A piece of dry fern had caught in the infant's hair, obscuring her face. Mr. Achyar was nearby cutting pineapples into quarters. He was closer to Akmad than I. Speaking in the hushed voice that the moment dictated, I asked him to take the fern from the infant's hair. Nestled on her mother's side, the baby was dozing peacefully, her miniature fingers clenched tightly around strands of her mother's hair.

9   Mr. Achyar gently approached Akmad and slowly reached over to remove the fern. Akmad seemed oblivious to his approach. My fingers closed around the lens, preparing for another shot. The golden light still held.

10   Never, not in a millennium, could Mr. Achyar or I have anticipated Akmad's reaction to his simple gesture. His fingers never touched the infant's head. Without warning, Akmad recoiled. Baring her teeth, she exploded. Her hair went erect, tripling her size, and she lunged at Mr. Achyar, her fangs glistening, the soft expression on her face gone. Not large for an adult female orangutan, Akmad weighed about seventy pounds. Yet leveraged, taut muscles provide even female orangutans with the strength of perhaps five men. An orangutan female's teeth can rip off a person's scalp or arm. Had Mr. Achyar not been so agile, he would have been badly mangled. However, he leaped back in one motion. Akmad did not pursue her attack. Her point made, she simply sat down and picked up the pineapple she had been eating. Her face was once again expressionless.

11   Shocked, Mr. Achyar stared at Akmad as if his own child had turned on him. "Not once, not ever before," he gasped in bewilderment. "I have never been attacked by an orangutan before. They are all my children and my friends." He sighed, "Akmad is the gentlest of them all. I never expected her to attack me."

12   I moved over to Akmad and gazed at the infant nestled against her. Without hesitating, I reached out and pulled the fern from her infant's hair. Akmad did not even blink to acknowledge me. Her eyes were focused elsewhere, somewhere in the distance. She was back in the universe orangutans inhabit.

13   Emboldened, I carefully moved the infant into a better position for a photograph in the fading light. As I gently tugged at her, the infant squealed. Akmad's opaque, inner-directed gaze did not change. I glanced at Mr. Achyar, who was watching me intently. The wonder on his face

was palpable. I, too, was amazed. Up to that moment I had never imagined the degree to which Akmad accepted me.

△ △

Explorations:

Biruté Galdikas, *Reflections of Eden: My Years With the Orangutans of Borneo*
Linda Spalding, *The Follow*
Jane Goodall, *Through a Window: My Thirty Years With the Chimpanzees of Gombe*
Dian Fossey, *Gorillas in the Mist*
http://fas.sfu.ca.lh/css/gcs/scientists/Galdikas/galdikas.html

Structure:

1. This selection is the opening passage of Galdikas' book. What does it do to invite your attention? Does it make you want to read about the rest of her life with the orangutans?
2. Akmad viciously attacks Mr. Achyar, yet peacefully accepts our author. Why? Explore in class all the reasons you can think of to explain this extreme *contrast.*
3. One theme running through *Reflections of Eden* is behavioural similarities between the great apes and humans, the overwhelming percentage of whose genes are shared. Point out every aspect of this *comparison* that you see so far in these first pages of Galdikas' book.

Style:

1. Read paragraph 2 aloud in class, to feel its style. Now read paragraph 10, and feel its style as Akmad attacks Mr. Achyar. Point out all the *contrasts* you can in the language Galdikas uses to describe peace and to describe violence.
2. What technique is Galdikas using when she ends this passage with the word "me"?
3. How FORMAL or INFORMAL is Galdikas' STYLE? Who do you think is her intended AUDIENCE?

Ideas for Discussion and Writing:

1. Why do people love animals? Do you love your pet? If so, tell why. If you have no pet, tell why.
2. How close a kinship should humans feel with wild animals? With the Earth's plants? Would the death of the last orangutan, or clearcutting of the last virgin forest, hurt us? If so, how? Would you take a cut in

pay, or accept higher taxes, to fund conservation? If so, how much? Defend your view with examples.

3. Argue for or against the use of primates such as chimpanzees in laboratory experiments. Give reasons.

4. We have learned to reject sexism, racism, ageism and several other "isms." Is "speciesism" next? Defend your view with reasons.

5. Though she grew up in Canada, Biruté Galdikas has spent most of her adult life in the rain forest of Borneo. Could you adapt to such a *contrast* of environment? Tell about your past encounter with a very new place.

6. **PROCESS IN WRITING:** *Imagine that orangutans could write. You are Akmad, the new mother. Compose a letter to Biruté Galdikas explaining the central* contrast *of this selection: why you viciously attacked your "camp feeder" Mr. Achyar, yet accepted without protest Dr. Galdikas' touching and even moving your newborn. (If possible, first read the whole book* Reflections of Eden *for more insight.) Do a quick first draft. Leave it at least a day, then take stock: does it provide* examples? *Does it involve the reader by describing, as Galdikas does? Read the draft aloud, to detect and change any weakness of style. Is your* STYLE *suitable for an educated* AUDIENCE *such as Dr. Galdikas? Edit for things like punctuation and spelling before printing out your best version. Finally, read aloud in class this letter to a human, and call on a volunteer "Dr. Galdikas" to respond.*

Note: See also the Topics for Writing at the end of this chapter.

Catherine Pigott

Chicken-Hips*

How does a piece of writing begin? Here is an example. Seeing a documentary film about eating disorders, The Famine Within, *and interviewing its director Katherine Gilday for a magazine article, Catherine Pigott recalled her own time in Africa. It was years earlier, in 1983, while teaching English at a teachers' college, that she had shared the home and culture of a Gambian family. Then returning to Canada, she suffered culture shock: through African eyes she saw North American ideas of eating and bodily appearance as cruel and misguided. In response to this mix of new experience and earlier memories, she wrote the essay that follows (*The Globe and Mail, *March 20, 1991), a celebration of the natural life she knew in Africa. Not only is its message cross-cultural but also its form: Pigott says "I was aware of speaking as I wrote," as in the oral tradition of African narrative. Now she applies this philosophy daily in her profession. After her return she worked for a time in print journalism, but then entered the world of radio: first the* CBC Radio News, *then the CBC's celebrated* Morningside, *where, as a producer, she found guests for host Peter Gzowski, and researched and developed a broadcast a day. From there she moved on to* Sunday Morning, *and is now a producer for the CBC's* This Morning. *Pigott thinks of her writing for radio as "not for the eye but the ear." It is direct, simple, natural. She offers similar advice to students writing essays: "Write for the ear as well as the eye."*

T he women of the household clucked disapprovingly when they saw   1
me. It was the first time I had worn African clothes since my arrival in tiny, dusty Gambia, and evidently they were not impressed. They adjusted my head-tie and pulled my *lappa,* the ankle-length fabric I had wrapped around myself, even tighter. "You're too thin," one of them pronounced. "It's no good." They nicknamed me "Chicken-hips."

I marvelled at this accolade, for I had never been called thin in my   2
life. It was something I longed for. I would have been flattered if those ample-bosomed women hadn't looked so distressed. It was obvious I fell far short of their ideal of beauty.

---

* Editor's title.

195

3   I had dressed up for a very special occasion — the baptism of a son. The women heaped rice into tin basins the size of laundry tubs, shaping it into mounds with their hands. Five of us sat around one basin, thrusting our fingers into the scalding food. These women ate with such relish, such joy. They pressed the rice into balls in their fists, squeezing until the bright-red palm oil ran down their forearms and dripped off their elbows.

4   I tried desperately, but I could not eat enough to please them. It was hard for me to explain that I come from a culture in which it is almost unseemly for a woman to eat too heartily. It's considered unattractive. It was even harder to explain that to me thin is beautiful, and in my country we deny ourselves food in our pursuit of perfect slenderness.

5   That night, everyone danced to welcome the baby. Women swivelled their broad hips and used their hands to emphasize the roundness of their bodies. One needed to be round and wide to make the dance beautiful. There was no place for thinness here. It made people sad. It reminded them of things they wanted to forget, such as poverty, drought and starvation. You never knew when the rice was going to run out.

6   I began to believe that Africa's image of the perfect female body was far more realistic than the long-legged leanness I had been conditioned to admire. There, it is beautiful — not shameful — to carry weight on the hips and thighs, to have a round stomach and heavy, swinging breasts. Women do not battle the bulge, they celebrate it. A body is not something to be tamed and moulded.

7   The friends who had christened me Chicken-hips made it their mission to fatten me up. It wasn't long before a diet of rice and rich, oily stew twice a day began to change me. Every month, the women would take a stick and measure my backside, noting with pleasure its gradual expansion. "Oh Catherine, your buttocks are getting nice now!" they would say.

8   What was extraordinary was that I, too, believed I was becoming more beautiful. There was no sense of panic, no shame, no guilt-ridden resolves to go on the miracle grape-and-water diet. One day, I tied my *lappa* tight across my hips and went to the market to buy beer for a wedding. I carried the crate of bottles home on my head, swinging my hips slowly as I walked. I felt transformed.

9   In Gambia, people don't use words such as "cheating," "naughty," or "guilty" when they talk about eating. The language of sin is not applied to food. Fat is desirable. It holds beneficial meanings of abundance, fertility and health.

10   My perception of beauty altered as my body did. The European tourists on the beach began to look strange and skeletal rather than "slim." They had no hips. They seemed devoid of shape and substance. Women

I once would have envied appeared fragile and even ugly. The ideal they represented no longer made sense.

After a year, I came home. I preached my new way of seeing to anyone who would listen. I wanted to cling to the liberating belief that losing weight had nothing to do with self-love.

Family members kindly suggested that I might look and feel better if I slimmed down a little. They encouraged me to join an exercise club. I wandered around the malls in a dislocated daze. I felt uncomfortable trying on clothes that hung so elegantly on the mannequins. I began hearing old voices inside my head: "Plaid makes you look fat. . . . You're too short for that style. . . . Vertical stripes are more slimming. . . . Wear black."

I joined the club. Just a few weeks after I had worn a *lappa* and scooped up rice with my hands, I was climbing into pink leotards and aerobics shoes. The instructor told me that I had to set fitness goals and "weigh in" after my workouts. There were mirrors on the walls and I could see women watching themselves. I sensed that even the loveliest among them felt they were somehow flawed. As the aerobics instructor barked out commands for arm lifts and leg lifts, I pictured Gambian women pounding millet and dancing in a circle with their arms raised high. I do not mean to romanticize their rock-hard lives, but we were hardly to be envied as we ran like fools between two walls to the tiresome beat of synthesized music.

We were a roomful of women striving to reshape ourselves into some kind of pubertal ideal. I reverted to my natural state: one of yearning to be slimmer and more fit than I was. My freedom had been temporary. I was home, where fat is feared and despised. It was time to exert control over my body and my life. I dreaded the thought of people saying, "She's let herself go."

If I return to Africa, I am sure the women will shake their heads in bewildered dismay. Even now, I sometimes catch my reflection in a window and their voices come back to me. "Yo! Chicken-hips!"

△ △

Explorations:

Joetta Schlabach, *Extending the Table: A World Community Cookbook*
Richard Gordon, *Anorexia and Bulimia: Anatomy of a Social Epidemic*
Katherine Gilday, dir., *The Famine Within* (documentary film)
Naomi Wolf, *The Beauty Myth: How Images of Beauty Are Used Against Women*
http:/www.gambia.com/

Structure:

1. "Chicken-Hips" is mainly a *contrast* of ideals of beauty in Gambia and Canada. Point out at least two other things that the essay *compares*.
2. Does Pigott organize her *contrast* mainly "point by point" or by "halves"?
3. How selectively does the author choose details from her year in Africa? In paragraph 1, for example, has she told anything at all that is not vital to her theme?
4. What classic techniques of organization does Pigott exploit in her opening and closing?

Style:

1. The Gambian women nicknamed our author "Chicken-hips" because of her relative thinness. Create five other METAPHORS they could have used to say the same thing.
2. Where do SENSE IMAGES most strongly help us "see" the author's point?
3. Judging by Pigott's vocabulary, what sort of *audience* is she aiming for in her essay?

Ideas for Discussion and Writing:

1. How important to you is the appearance of your body? Is there an ideal of shape or size that you try to reach? Describe it to the class. What sources gave you this ideal?
2. Why, in our society, is it mostly women who go on diets, and mostly women who suffer and die from *anorexia nervosa*?
3. In paragraph 5 thinness reminds Gambians of "things they wanted to forget, such as poverty, drought and starvation." On the other hand, the Duchess of Windsor once remarked, "Never too rich and never too thin." How do *you* see thinness? *Compare* or *contrast* your view to one of the above, and give reasons.
4. Have you, like Pigott, lived in another country? Tell the class one major thing the other culture taught you about life. Now that you are here, are you remembering or forgetting the lesson?
5. Many people from developed countries go abroad, as did Pigott, to "teach" those in developing countries. Imagine her Gambian friends coming to your school to "teach" you. How easy or difficult would it be to learn their lessons? And what might they learn in return?
6. In paragraph 10, watching the "skeletal" Europeans at the beach, Pigott states "My perception of beauty altered. . . ." Examine the illustrations in a book of art history, taking notes on how our current

view of human beauty differs from those of past periods. Report these differences to the class, showing illustrations as examples.

7. **PROCESS IN WRITING:** *Remember a time when you set out to change your body through a diet, athletics, aerobics, bodybuilding or other means. On a blank piece of paper draw a vertical line. Entitle the left column "before" and the right column "after," then brainstorm to develop the* contrast. *Now looking at these notes, decide your thesis: In which version of yourself did you actually feel happier, the before or after? Now write a rapid first draft, proceeding either by "halves" or "point by point." The next day look it over: Do images help your audience "see" you? If not, add. Is your draft at least 50% examples? If not, add. Are any words wasted? If so, cut. Finally, edit for things like grammar and spelling, then produce your good version.*

Note: See also the Topics for Writing at the end of this chapter.

Brian Maracle

Out of Touch and Loving It

Like Carol Geddes, Brian Maracle is a spokesperson for the Native community who has achieved prominence in Canadian public life. He was five when his family left the Six Nations Grand River Territory, near Brantford, Ontario, for New York State. In time he earned two college degrees, lived in Vancouver then in Ottawa, and made a name for himself in journalism as a reporter for The Globe and Mail *and host of the CBC radio program* Our Native Land. *Specializing in aboriginal issues, he also became an activist in the Native self-government movement. But when in 1993 legislative changes to the Indian Act made it possible for Maracle and his wife to move back to their original reserves (unfortunately in two different places, hers in British Columbia and his in Ontario), the two decided to "go home." Maracle moved alone into a 150-year-old log house near where he had lived as a child. Soon he had traded his newspapers, television watching and the Internet for hard physical labour: installing a woodstove, chopping firewood, and repairing his new home. But old habits die hard. In the midst of his new life on the "rez," Maracle was soon drawn again to politics and issues — the complicated matters of how to preserve the traditional Mohawk culture, language and spirituality, and how to govern the band according to Native, not European, models. Then a year after his return, Maracle told of his new life in a well-received book,* Back on the Rez: Finding the Way Home *(1996). From it comes our selection.*

1   Over the past two weeks I have been so busy unpacking and trying to get settled that I have begun to lose touch with the outside world. Just today, for instance, I realized I have not read a newspaper since I moved here.

2   Two weeks without reading a paper! It doesn't seem possible. I have read a newspaper, often two, almost every day for the past thirty years. A small forest must have been cut down to provide the newsprint for all the papers I've read. And now that I've finally broken the daily newspaper habit, I realize I don't miss the petty sensationalism, the staged events, the obsession with celebrities and the filler copy that passes for news.

3   I haven't completely lost touch, though. I listen to CBC Radio so I know something about "the news." I talk long-distance with people

from the outside who presumably still read newspapers every day, and if another World War started, I assume they'd tell me about it. In that way, I'm becoming a lot like the people around me. Most of my neighbours and relatives don't read the paper every day and they don't seem to be suffering. The people in the coffee shops here don't talk about Bosnia or the Bloc Québécois.

The broken newspaper habit, though, is just one measure of the way   4
I have dropped out of one world and entered another. I realized today, for example, that I have not hooked my computer back up to the Internet. Before I moved I was plugged into all the computer newsgroups about my two passions in life — fishing and native affairs. But there was so much information on the system it took me forty-five minutes a day just to skim it. Most of the postings on this electronic bulletin board were, for me, useless and irrelevant. I'm not terribly interested, for example, in an ongoing argument over the derivation of some word in the Dakota language, and I don't care what trout flies are working right now on the upper stretch of some river in Idaho.

And that was just reading the stuff! Heaven forbid if I actually replied   5
to a message and got locked into one of those discussions that go on forever. I fought the urge to reply to some of the more inane and provocative postings because I knew I would end up sparring with some argumentative know-it-all who just has to have the last word (in other words, someone just like me).

So, in spite of all the dire warnings about how people who are not   6
"plugged in" will be left behind in the coming revolution, I will not plug myself back into the Internet. I will continue, instead, to use my computer as a glorified typewriter and I don't care if I ever get back onto the information highway.

And as for getting plugged back into the world of television, I have   7
stopped fiddling with the television antenna and I have given up trying to get CBC-TV. I will content myself therefore with the two-and-a-half channels I do get — and I will plan on doing a lot more reading.

The only problem is that getting something good to read will not be   8
easy around here. Decent newspapers are hard to come by, there is no bookstore on the reserve and the band library, to put it as charitably as I can, needs a lot of work. But at least the corner stores here sell magazines. Boy, do they ever. At the front of the rack you'll find their top-of-the-line reading material — *The National Enquirer, Tattoo World* and *True Confessions*. At the back of the rack you'll find *Penthouse, Swank* and *Hustler*. But you won't find *Maclean's, Chatelaine* or even *People* maga-zine. You have to drive seven miles into Brantford for those. And even in Brantford you won't find *Harper's, Saturday Night* or *The New Yorker*. For those you have to drive thirty miles into Hamilton. I can give up the newspaper, the Internet and CBC-TV, but I can't give up magazines, so

it looks as though I will be visiting Hamilton a lot more often than I thought.

9   After being back on the reserve for two weeks, I have taken stock of my new situation. Yes, I have lost touch with the outside world in some ways, but there are many new things in my life that more than make up for the loss of the old.

10   I am more active, for one thing, because there's a lot of physical work involved in whipping this old house into shape. I don't mind getting sweaty and tired. I don't even mind getting stiff and sore, because I can feel the physical labour strengthening my body, invigorating my mind and soothing my soul.

11   And after forty years of living under streetlights, I am especially thrilled by the nighttime sky. Every night before I go to bed I stand in the darkness and stare in awestruck wonder at a universe of dazzling lights twinkling in the infinite blackness.

12   There are lots of other things I like about being back on the territory.

13   When I call an office in Ohsweken (even some places in Brantford) and they ask me my name, I like being able to say "Brian Maracle." Period. That's because until I moved back here, whenever someone asked me my name I would say, automatically, "Brian Maracle. That's spelled M-A-R-A-C-L-E." But I don't have to do that any more because the people here know the name and know how to spell it. And they don't say, "Gee, what a funny name." If they say anything about my name, it's usually to ask if I am related to someone.

14   Another thing I like about living here is going into a store and bumping into guys I worked with twenty years ago in the States. I like being able to renew old acquaintances with guys like me who have finally moved home. I like being introduced to people at a coffee shop and finding out we're related. I like being able to see my sister, grandmothers, aunts, uncles, cousins, nieces, nephews and in-laws anytime and all the time.

15   What it comes down to, I guess, is that I love the sense of belonging I finally have. I love the warmth and security that comes from the feeling of being wrapped in a sheltering cocoon of family and community.

16   So maybe I am losing touch with the outside world. But I don't miss it at all. Not one little bit.

△ △

Explorations:

Brian Maracle, *Back on the Rez: Finding the Way Home*
Henry David Thoreau, *Walden*
Helen and Scott Nearing, *Living the Good Life*

Julie Cruikshank, *Life Lived Like a Story* (interviews with Native Canadian women)
Linda Jaine and Drew Hayden, eds., *Voices: Being Native in Canada*
http://www.lookup.com/homepages/74329/indian.html

Structure:

1. Identify Maracle's THESIS STATEMENT.
2. How does Maracle's closing (the three short sentences of paragraph 16) relate to his introduction? What effect is achieved?
3. Does Maracle develop the *contrast* of his life off and on the "rez" mainly "point by point" or through "halves"? If the latter, where is the TRANSITION between the two parts?

Style:

1. How FORMAL or INFORMAL is Maracle's STYLE? (Look at his sentence lengths, his vocabulary, and whether he uses COLLOQUIAL language.) Who do you see as his intended AUDIENCE?
2. Analyze all the IRONIES at work in Maracle's list of magazines (par. 8).
3. In paragraph 15 the author is "wrapped in a sheltering cocoon of family and community." Find three more METAPHORS in this selection.

Ideas for Discussion and Writing:

1. In this selection from *Back on the Rez: Finding the Way Home*, Brian Maracle leaves the "outside world" where he had been a journalist and political activist, to gain the "sheltering cocoon of family and community" (par. 15). Argue for or against his move. Could you have done it? Or have your actions been a *contrast* to his, moving from your own community into the "outside world"? Give examples and reasons for your stance.
2. Look over "Growing Up Native," p. 43, by filmmaker Carol Geddes. Has she done the opposite of Maracle, moving from Native community to the larger society? Or does she now live in both worlds?
3. In paragraphs 4-6 Maracle portrays the Internet as a waste of time. Are you hooked? If so, what do you get out of it? And what are you giving up? Give *examples.*
4. "The people in the coffee shops here," Maracle reports, "don't talk about Bosnia or the Bloc Québécois." Do you watch the news? Read a newspaper? Do "news junkies" just have a good excuse for wasting time, or does a grasp of current events help them in their lives?
5. **PROCESS IN WRITING:** *Visit the "Native American Sites" given in "Explorations" (a long menu of links to First Nations sites of all kinds). Spend time exploring, then choose one that portrays life in one aboriginal group.*

Take notes or print. Now go into your word processing program and type the title "My Own Daily Life" at the top of the screen. Brainstorm on this for five to ten minutes, filling the screen with notes. Then take stock: boldface the most important points. Now ask yourself: have I found mostly comparisons *or* mostly contrasts *to the portrayal of Native life in my chosen Web site? Express your overall view in a* THESIS STATEMENT. *Now choose whether to organize "point by point" or by "halves," then write a rapid discovery draft. Later read it aloud, to detect unclear parts or weak style, then revise. Finally, check the punctuation before printing out a good copy.*

Note: See also the Topics for Writing at the end of this chapter.

Russell Baker

A Nice Place to Visit

Russell Baker is probably America's favourite humorist, for many years author of the "Observer" column in The New York Times. *Since 1993 he has also been host of the PBS television broadcast* Masterpiece Theatre. *It was a month's stay in Toronto that gave Baker the material for our selection, a contrast of cities. Those who have read him already will recognize his distinctive approach: the zany and inventive humour, the satire on human foibles, and the mocking imitations of formal, scholarly or scientific language. Basic to all this is his stance as "observer": he has a keen eye for the telling details that breathe life into writing. Baker was born in 1925 in Virginia. After a degree at Johns Hopkins in 1947, and employment from 1947 to 1954 at the* Baltimore Sun, *he did political reporting for* The New York Times. *A columnist since 1962, he now takes the whole of American life for his subject, but especially his own city, "the Big Apple." Hundreds of Baker's columns have been collected in books, among these* No Cause for Panic *(1964),* Poor Russell's Almanac *(1972) and* The Rescue of Miss Yaskell and Other Pipe Dreams *(1983). His autobiography* Growing Up *won a Pulitzer Prize in 1983, and its sequel* The Good Times *appeared in 1989. Then in 1993 was published the anthology* Russell Baker's Book of American Humor. *Our own selection appeared first in* The New York Times, *then in Baker's book* So This Is Depravity *(1980).*

Having heard that Toronto was becoming one of the continent's noblest cities, we flew from New York to investigate. New Yorkers jealous of their city's reputation and concerned about challenges to its stature have little to worry about. 1

After three days in residence, our delegation noted an absence of hysteria that was almost intolerable and took to consuming large portions of black coffee to maintain our normal state of irritability. The local people to whom we complained in hopes of provoking comfortably nasty confrontations declined to become bellicose. They would like to enjoy a gratifying big-city hysteria, they said, but believed it would seem ill-mannered in front of strangers. 2

Extensive field studies — our stay lasted four weeks — persuaded us that this failure reflects the survival in Toronto of an ancient pattern of social conduct called "courtesy." 3

4   "Courtesy" manifests itself in many quaint forms appalling to the New York. Thus, for example, Yankee fans may be astonished to learn that at the Toronto baseball park it is considered bad form to heave rolls of toilet paper and beer cans at players on the field.

5   Official literature inside Toronto taxicabs includes a notification of the proper address to which riders may mail the authorities not only complaints but also compliments about the cabbie's behavior.

6   For a city that aspires to urban greatness, Toronto's entire taxi system has far to go. At present, it seems hopelessly bogged down in civilization. One day a member of our delegation listening to a radio conversation between a short-tempered cabbie and the dispatcher distinctly heard the dispatcher say, "As Shakespeare said, if music be the food of love, play on, give me excess of it."

7   This delegate became so unnerved by hearing Shakespeare quoted by a cab dispatcher that he fled immediately back to New York to have his nerves abraded and his spine rearranged in a real big-city taxi.

8   What was particularly distressing as the stay continued was the absence of shrieking police and fire sirens at 3 A.M. — or any other hour, for that matter. We spoke to the city authorities about this. What kind of city was it, we asked, that expected its citizens to sleep all night and rise refreshed in the morning? Where was the incentive to awaken gummy-eyed and exhausted, ready to scream at the first person one saw in the morning? How could Toronto possibly hope to maintain a robust urban divorce rate?

9   Our criticism went unheeded, such is the torpor with which Toronto pursues true urbanity. The fact appears to be that Toronto has very little grasp of what is required of a great city.

10   Consider the garbage picture. It seems never to have occurred to anybody in Toronto that garbage exists to be heaved into the streets. One can drive for miles without seeing so much as a banana peel in the gutter or a discarded newspaper whirling in the wind.

11   Nor has Toronto learned about dogs. A check with the authorities confirmed that, yes, there are indeed dogs resident in Toronto, but one would never realize it by walking the sidewalks. Our delegation was shocked by the presumption of a town's calling itself a city, much less a great city, when it obviously knows nothing of either garbage or dogs.

12   The subway, on which Toronto prides itself, was a laughable imitation of the real thing. The subway cars were not only spotlessly clean, but also fully illuminated. So were the stations. To New Yorkers, it was embarrassing, and we hadn't the heart to tell the subway authorities that they were light-years away from greatness.

13   We did, however, tell them about spray paints and how effectively a few hundred children equipped with spray-paint cans could at least give their subway the big-city look.

It seems doubtful they are ready to take such hints. There is a dis- 14
turbing distaste for vandalism in Toronto which will make it hard for
the city to enter wholeheartedly into the vigor of the late twentieth
century.

A board fence surrounding a huge excavation for a new high- 15
rise building in the downtown district offers depressing evidence of
Toronto's lack of big-city impulse. Embedded in the fence at intervals
of about fifty feet are loudspeakers that play recorded music for passing pedestrians.

Not a single one of these loudspeakers has been mutilated. What's 16
worse, not a single one has been stolen.

It was good to get back to the Big Apple. My coat pocket was bulging 17
with candy wrappers from Toronto and — such is the lingering power
of Toronto — it took me two or three hours back in New York before it
seemed natural again to toss them into the street.

∆ ∆

Explorations:

Russell Baker,
  Poor Russell's Almanac
  Growing Up
  Good Times
  Ed., *The Norton Book of Light Verse*
Tom Wolfe, *The Bonfire of the Vanities* (novel)
Michele Landsberg, *This Is New York, Honey! A Homage to Manhattan,
  With Love and Rage*
http://www.tourism-toronto.com/abou_mn.html
http://www.citysearchnyc.com/New_York/

Structure:

1. How vital to this selection are its *examples*? What ratio of space do
   they take up? Point out three or four that work especially well, and
   tell why they do.
2. What considerations do you think led Baker to organize his *contrast*
   not by "halves" but rather "point by point"? Argue for or against his
   method.
3. Baker often omits the New York side of a point. Are these gaps accidental or deliberate? Do they hinder or help us as readers? Explain.

Style:

1. Baker's title, "A Nice Place to Visit," is unfinished. What is the rest of
   this saying, and why are we left to complete it ourselves?

2. How soon did you detect Baker's heavy IRONY? Where did you first realize he means the opposite of what he says?
3. In paragraph 9 Baker writes, "Our criticism went unheeded, such is the torpor with which Toronto pursues true urbanity." Why is the language of this humorous essay so FORMAL? What effect is achieved?
4. Explain the IRONY in each of these passages:
   A. "comfortably nasty confrontations" (par. 2)
   B. "a gratifying big-city hysteria" (par. 2)
   C. "bogged down in civilization" (par. 6)
   D. "a robust urban divorce rate" (par. 8)
   E. "the vigor of the late twentieth century" (par. 14)
5. In his closing Baker calls New York "the Big Apple." Explore the CONNOTATIONS of this METAPHOR.

Ideas for Discussion and Writing:

1. Baker confines his *contrast* of Toronto and New York to the relatively minor topics of taxis, noise, garbage, dogs, the subway and vandalism. Either in class discussion or on paper, extend his contrast to more serious urban problems such as pollution, drugs, poverty and violent crime.
2. Statistics regularly reveal more murders in American cities than in Canadian ones of equal size; the difference sometimes reaches proportions as high as ten to one. Give all the reasons you can think of to explain this *contrast*.
3. **PROCESS IN WRITING:** *During spare moments this week, record in a journal your main impressions of the city or town around you. On other pages, record memories of a city or town elsewhere. Now freewrite on this material several minutes to confirm which place you prefer. Next write a discovery draft of an essay that* contrasts *the two, showing through examples why you prefer one of them. Use Baker's* point-by-point *approach. Choose your own TONE, humorous or serious, and maintain it. Finally, show the piece to a group of classmates, then, incorporating their best suggestions, write your final version.*

Note: See also the Topics for Writing at the end of this chapter.

Margaret Laurence

Where the World Began

Margaret Laurence's untimely death in 1987 was mourned across the nation by readers who had seen their own humanity reflected in her novels, and by many writers who had lost a generous friend. Born in 1926 in the prairie town of Neepawa, Manitoba, and educated in Winnipeg, Laurence spent 1950 to 1957 in Somalia and Ghana with her engineer husband. There she began to write some of the best fiction yet produced by a Canadian about a developing country. Laurence later separated from her husband, and in 1962 moved with her children to England. In her writing, though, she returned to western Canada. Renaming her home town "Manawaka" and recasting it in fiction, she completed what is probably our best-loved Canadian novel, The Stone Angel *(1964). It is the story of proud and stubborn Hagar Shipley, one of many strong women who would be central to Laurence's fiction. More novels followed:* A Jest of God *(1966),* The Fire-Dwellers *(1969), and* The Diviners *(1974; adapted as a CBC television special in 1992). These, along with her book of collected short stories* A Bird in the House *(1970), made of "Manawaka" and its people a celebrated microcosm of the larger world. By the early seventies Laurence had returned to Canada, settling in Lakefield, Ontario. But* The Diviners *was to be her last novel. She now turned to activism as a feminist, human rights advocate, and foe of the nuclear arms race. "It is my feeling," she wrote, "that as we grow older we should become not less radical but more so." In her last years she worked tirelessly to save the planet that she had first known "where the world began." Our selection is from Laurence's 1976 book of essays,* Heart of a Stranger.*

A strange place it was, that place where the world began. A place of incredible happenings, splendours and revelations, despairs like multitudinous pits of isolated hells. A place of shadow-spookiness, inhabited by the unknowable dead. A place of jubilation and of mourning, horrible and beautiful.

It was, in fact, a small prairie town.

Because that settlement and that land were my first and for many years my only real knowledge of this planet, in some profound way they remain my world, my way of viewing. My eyes were formed there. Towns like ours, set in a sea of land, have been described thousands of times as dull, bleak, flat, uninteresting. I have had it said to me that the railway trip across Canada is spectacular, except for the prairies, when it would be desirable to go to sleep for several days, until the ordeal is over. I am always unable to argue this point effectively. All I can say is — well, you really have to live there to know that country. The town of my childhood could be called bizarre, agonizingly repressive or cruel at times, and the land in which it grew could be called harsh in the violence of its seasonal changes. But never merely flat or uninteresting. Never dull.

4   In winter, we used to hitch rides on the back of the milk sleigh, our moccasins squeaking and slithering on the hard rutted snow of the roads, our hands in ice-bubbled mitts hanging onto the box edge of the sleigh for dear life, while Bert grinned at us through his great frosted moustache and shouted the horse into speed, daring us to stay put. Those mornings, rising, there would be the perpetual fascination of the frost feathers on windows, the ferns and flowers and eerie faces traced there during the night by unseen artists of the wind. Evenings, coming back from skating, the sky would be black but not dark, for you could see a cold glitter of stars from one side of the earth's rim to the other. And then the sometime astonishment when you saw the Northern Lights flaring across the sky, like the scrawled signature of God. After a blizzard, when the snowploughs hadn't yet got through, school would be closed for the day, the assumption being that the town's young could not possibly flounder through five feet of snow in the pursuit of education. We would then gaily don snowshoes and flounder for miles out into the white dazzling deserts, in pursuit of a different kind of knowing. If you came back too close to night, through the woods at the foot of the town hill, the thin black branches of poplar and chokecherry now meringued with frost, sometimes you heard coyotes. Or maybe the banshee wolf-voices were really only inside your head.

5   Summers were scorching, and when no rain came and the wheat became bleached and dried before it headed, the faces of farmers and townsfolk would not smile much, and you took for granted, because it never seemed to have been any different, the frequent knocking at the back door and the young men standing there, mumbling or thrusting defiantly their requests for a drink of water and a sandwich if you could spare it. They were riding the freights, and you never knew where they had come from, or where they might end up, if anywhere. The Drought and Depression were like evil deities which had been there always. You understood and did not understand.

6   Yet the outside world had its continuing marvels. The poplar bluffs and the small river were filled and surrounded with a zillion different grasses, stones, and weed flowers. The meadowlarks sang undaunted from the twanging telephone wires along the gravel highway. Once we

found an old flat-bottomed scow, and launched her, poling along the shallow brown waters, mending her with wodges of hastily chewed Spearmint, grounding her among the tangles of yellow marsh marigolds that grew succulently along the banks of the shrunken river, while the sun made our skins smell dusty-warm.

My best friend lived in an apartment above some stores on Main Street (its real name was Mountain Avenue, goodness knows why), an elegant apartment with royal-blue velvet curtains. The back roof, scarcely sloping at all, was corrugated tin, of a furnace-like warmth on a July afternoon, and we would sit there drinking lemonade and looking across the back lane at the Fire Hall. Sometimes our vigil would be rewarded. Oh joy! Somebody's house burning down! We had an almost-perfect callousness in some ways. Then the wooden tower's bronze bell would clonk and toll like a thousand speeded funerals in a time of plague, and in a few minutes the team of giant black horses would cannon forth, pulling the fire wagon like some scarlet chariot of the Goths, while the firemen clung with one hand, adjusting their helmets as they went. 7

The oddities of the place were endless. An elderly lady used to serve, as her afternoon tea offering to other ladies, soda biscuits spread with peanut butter and topped with a whole marshmallow. Some considered this slightly eccentric, when compared with chopped egg sandwiches, and admittedly talked about her behind her back, but no one ever refused these delicacies or indicated to her that they thought she had slipped a cog. Another lady dyed her hair a bright and cheery orange, by strangers often mistaken at twenty paces for a feather hat. My own beloved stepmother wore a silver fox neckpiece, a whole pelt, *with the embalmed (?) head still on.* My Ontario Irish grandfather said, "sparrow grass," a more interesting term than asparagus. The town dump was known as "the nuisance grounds," a phrase fraught with weird connotations, as though the effluvia of our lives was beneath contempt but at the same time was subtly threatening to the determined and sometimes hysterical propriety of our ways. 8

Some oddities were, as idiom had it, "funny ha ha"; others were "funny peculiar." Some were not so very funny at all. An old man lived, deranged, in a shack in the valley. Perhaps he wasn't even all that old, but to us he seemed a wild Methuselah figure, shambling among the underbrush and the tall couchgrass, muttering indecipherable curses or blessings, a prophet who had forgotten his prophesies. Everyone in town knew him, but no one knew him. He lived among us as though only occasionally and momentarily visible. The kids called him Andy Gump, and feared him. Some sought to prove their bravery by tormenting him. They were the mediaeval bear baiters, and he the lumbering bewildered bear, half blind, only rarely turning to snarl. Everything 9 is to be found in a town like mine. Belsen,° writ small but with the same ink.

10   All of us cast stones in one shape or another. In grade school, among the vulnerable and violet girls we were, the feared and despised were those few older girls from what was charmingly termed "the wrong side of the tracks." Tough in talk and tougher in muscle, they were said to be whores already. And may have been, that being about the only profession readily available to them.

11   The dead lived in that place, too. Not only the grandparents who had, in local parlance, "passed on" and who gloomed, bearded or bonneted, from the sepia photographs in old albums, but also the uncles, forever eighteen or nineteen, whose names were carved on the granite family stones in the cemetery, but whose bones lay in France. My own young mother lay in that graveyard, beside other dead of our kin, and when I was ten, my father, too, only forty, left the living town for the dead dwelling on the hill.

12   When I was eighteen, I couldn't wait to get out of that town, away from the prairies. I did not know then that I would carry the land and town all my life within my skull, that they would form the mainspring and source of the writing I was to do, wherever and however far away I might live.

13   This was my territory in the time of my youth, and in a sense my life since then has been an attempt to look at it, to come to terms with it. Stultifying to the mind it certainly could be, and sometimes was, but not to the imagination. It was many things, but it was never dull.

14   The same, I now see, could be said for Canada in general. Why on earth did generations of Canadians pretend to believe this country dull? We knew perfectly well it wasn't. Yet for so long we did not proclaim what we knew. If our upsurge of so-called nationalism seems odd or irrelevant to outsiders, and even to some of our own people *(what's all the fuss about?)*, they might try to understand that for many years we valued ourselves insufficiently, living as we did under the huge shadows of those two dominating figures, Uncle Sam and Britannia. We have only just begun to value ourselves, our land, our abilities. We have only just begun to recognize our legends and to give shape to our myths.

15   There are, God knows, enough aspects to deplore about this country. When I see the killing of our lakes and rivers with industrial wastes, I feel rage and despair. When I see our industries and natural resources increasingly taken over by America, I feel an overwhelming discouragement, especially as I cannot simply say "damn Yankees." It should never be forgotten that it is we ourselves who have sold such a large amount

---

° Belsen: a notorious Nazi death camp.

of our birthright for a mess of plastic Progress.° When I saw the War Measures Act being invoked in 1970, I lost forever the vestigial remains of the naive wish-belief that repression could not happen here, or would not. And yet, of course, I had known all along in the deepest and often hidden caves of the heart that anything can happen anywhere, for the seeds of both man's freedom and his captivity are found everywhere, even in the microcosm of a prairie town. But in raging against our injustices, our stupidities, I do so *as family*, as I did, and still do in writing, about those aspects of my town which I hated and which are always in some ways aspects of myself.

The land still draws me more than other lands. I have lived in Africa   16
and in England, but splendid as both can be, they do not have the power to move me in the same way as, for example, that part of southern Ontario where I spent four months last summer in a cedar cabin beside a river. "Scratch a Canadian, and you find a phony pioneer," I used to say to myself in warning. But all the same it is true, I think, that we are not yet totally alienated from physical earth, and let us only pray we do not become so. I once thought that my lifelong fear and mistrust of cities made me a kind of old-fashioned freak; now I see it differently.

The cabin has a long window across its front western wall, and sitting   17
at the oak table there in the mornings, I used to look out at the river and at the tall trees beyond, green-gold in the early light. The river was bronze; the sun caught it strangely, reflecting upon its surface the near-shore sand ripples underneath. Suddenly, the crescenting of a fish, gone before the eye could clearly give image to it. The old man next door said these leaping fish were carp. Himself, he preferred muskie, for he was a real fisherman and the muskie gave him a fight. The wind most often blew from the south, and the river flowed toward the south, so when the water was wind-riffled, and the current was strong, the river seemed to be flowing both ways. I liked this, and interpreted it as an omen, a natural symbol.

A few years ago, when I was back in Winnipeg, I gave a talk at my old   18
college. It was open to the public, and afterward a very old man came up to me and asked me if my maiden name had been Wemyss. I said yes, thinking he might have known my father or my grandfather. But no. "When I was a young lad," he said, "I once worked for your great-grandfather, Robert Wemyss, when he had the sheep ranch at Raeburn." I think that was a moment when I realized all over again something of great importance to me. My long-ago families came from Scotland and Ireland, but in a sense that no longer mattered so much. My true roots were here.

° for a mess of plastic Progress: allusion to Genesis 25, in which the hunter Esau sells his birthright to his brother Jacob for a mess of "pottage."

19   I am not very patriotic, in the usual meaning of that word. I cannot say "My country right or wrong" in any political, social or literary context. But one thing is inalterable, for better or worse, for life.

20   This is where my world began. A world which includes the ancestors — both my own and other people's ancestors who become mine. A world which formed me, and continues to do so, even while I fought it in some of its aspects, and continue to do so. A world which gave me my own lifework to do, because it was here that I learned the sight of my own particular eyes.

△ △

Explorations:

Margaret Laurence,
> *The Stone Angel*
> *The Diviners*
> *A Bird in the House* (short stories)
> *Dance on the Earth* (memoir)

James King, *The Life of Margaret Laurence*
Alice Munro, *Lives of Girls and Women*
Sinclair Ross, *As for Me and My House*
http://www.library.yorku.ca/depts/asc/mlwho.htm
http://alvin.lbl.gov/bios/Laurence.html

Structure:

1. What organizational goals does Laurence achieve by repeating her title phrase in both the opening and closing?
2. Early in the essay, Laurence puts her main point into a THESIS STATEMENT. Identify it.
3. Does Laurence mostly *compare* or *contrast* her prairie town to the nation as a whole?
4. Point out three qualities of her home town that Laurence later sees in her nation — or even in the world as a whole. Cite a passage to illustrate each *comparison.*
5. What key role do paragraphs 12–14 play in organizing the argument?
6. Point out three paragraphs that develop this essay mainly through *description.* Which one seems to convey most strongly the flavour of Laurence's prairie childhood? Point out its best IMAGES and tell what each contributes.
7. Why does Laurence end with the word "eyes"?

Style:

1. Why does Laurence begin with pairs of opposites ("A place of jubilation and of mourning, horrible and beautiful" — par. 1)?

2. Like Emily Carr in "D'Sonoqua," Laurence plays with words. Discuss the effects of these terms: "zillion" (par. 6), "wodges" (par. 6), "clonk" (par. 7), "cannon forth" (par. 7) and "gloomed" (par. 11).

3. To *describe* winter on the prairie, paragraph 4 gives a profusion of SENSE IMAGES. While one person slowly reads this passage aloud, other class members can raise their hand each time they detect an appeal to their sense of sight, hearing or touch. What is the total effect of these images?

4. In paragraph 3 the prairie is "a sea of land," and in paragraph 4 it becomes "white dazzling deserts." Locate at least five other FIGURES OF SPEECH in this essay, and analyze the impact of each.

Ideas for Discussion and Writing:

1. "Why on earth did generations of Canadians pretend to believe this country dull?" Laurence asks in paragraph 14. What is your answer? How dull or exciting do you consider your corner of Canada? Defend your view with examples.

2. "Everything is to be found in a town like mine. Belsen, writ small but with the same ink," Laurence writes in paragraph 9. Give one image of "Belsen, writ small" that you saw in your own childhood neighbourhood. Name one time and place in Canada where "Belsen" has been "writ large."

3. In paragraph 15 Laurence calls her home town a "microcosm" (literally "small world"). As you think of the town or the city neighbourhood of your own childhood (whether in Canada or abroad), does it also seem a microcosm of the world? Does it bear out Laurence's idea that "anything can happen anywhere" (par. 15)? And as you imagine other "microcosms" around the world, do you see mostly *comparisons* with or *contrasts* to the people in your own?

4. **PROCESS IN WRITING:** *Write your own essay of* comparison, *entitled "Where My World Began," showing your childhood town or neighbourhood as a microcosm of the nation — or, if you like, of the world as a whole. First brainstorm to produce a page of notes, in any order. Now choose the best, put them in ascending order of importance (to create a climax), and from them write your first draft. In the next draft add more SENSE IMAGES to convey a sense of place (as Laurence does), and add any examples needed to illustrate your points. Now share your argument with a small group of classmates, and apply the best of their suggestions as you revise toward the final version. Read the result aloud, with expression, to the class.*

Note: See also the Topics for Writing at the end of this chapter.

Topics for Writing
Chapter 5: Comparison and Contrast

Compare and/or contrast one of the following pairs. (See also the guidelines that follow.)

1. A Café and a Restaurant
2. The Stock Market and the Casino
3. To Like Someone and to Love Someone
4. Skiing and Snowboarding
5. A Part-Time Job and a Full-Time Job
6. Canadians and Americans
7. Reading and Skimming
8. A Two-Parent Family and a Single-Parent Family
9. A Wedding and a Divorce
10. My First Language and My Second Language
11. The Saver and the Spender
12. Being Physically Fit and Being Physically Unfit
13. Large Pets and Small Pets
14. Working for a Large Company and Working for a Small Company
15. The Authoritarian Parent and the Permissive Parent
16. Roller Blading and Ice Skating
17. Banking with a Cash Machine and Banking at the Counter
18. City People and Country People
19. Large Families and Small Families
20. Two Current Fads in Clothing
21. The Conformist and the Nonconformist
22. Using Credit and Using Cash
23. The Classical Music Fan and the Rock Music Fan
24. Marriage and Living Common Law
25. The Pessimist and the Optimist
26. Eating at Home and Eating Out
27. Behaving Assertively and Behaving Aggressively
28. The Cuisine of My First Country and the Cuisine of My Second Country
29. Canoeing and Kayaking
30. Letters and E-Mail Messages

Note also the Process in Writing topic after each selection in this chapter.

Process in Writing: Guidelines

Follow at least some of these steps in writing your essay of comparison and contrast (your teacher may suggest which ones).

1. *Spend enough time with the topic list to choose the item that best fits your interest and experience.*

2. *Draw a line down the middle of a blank page. Brainstorm: jot down notes for subject "A" on the left and for subject "B" on the right. Now join related items with lines, then take stock of what you have: Is A better than B? Is it worse? Similar? Opposite? Or what? Express their relationship to each other in a THESIS STATEMENT.*

3. *Now choose either "halves" or "separate points" to organize your argument, depending on the nature and size of your subject, then work your notes into a brief outline.*

4. *Write a rapid first draft, not stopping now to revise or edit.*

5. *Later analyze what you have produced: Does it follow your outline? If not, is the new material off-topic, or is it a worthwhile addition, an example of "thinking in writing"? Revise accordingly.*

6. *Try your prose aloud, to test the style. Cut all deadwood. Sharpen word choice. Add any missing examples. Strengthen TRANSITIONS.*

7. *Now edit for things like spelling and punctuation before printing out your good copy. Save it on disk, in case your teacher suggests further revision.*

Andrew Vaughan/Canadian Press

". . . *chainsaws whined, Caterpillar tractors with huge blades bulled and bat-*
tered their way through the forest, uprooting trees to clear the way for automatic
shearers that topped, limbed and sheared the trunks."

—*Basil Johnston,* "*Modern Cannibals of the Wilds*"

CHAPTER

⟨6⟩

ANALOGY AND RELATED DEVICES

In a way, it's like. . .

One student wrote this memory of a Toronto childhood:

I heard and felt a rumbling from the ground, looked up and saw a huge red metallic monster with a tail on the end approach us. "Run, run," I said, "before it eats us." My mother reassured me that no fear was necessary. The monster slowly rolled up beside us, opened its mouth, and we went in.

As adults, we know that monsters have not roamed the shores of Lake Ontario for millions of years, and that they were not red but probably green! We also know that monsters and streetcars have little in common. Yet who would say this *analogy* does not clearly express the child's first encounter with a streetcar? It may even help us, as adults, to view with new eyes something that we have taken for granted. *(A warning, though: as explained in the following pages, what an analogy will **not** do for us is prove anything at all logically. An essay based on this device is more in the realm of creative writing than of factual argumentation.)*

In this chapter Basil Johnston describes another monster — the weendigo of Native American legend that eats humans who wander outside at night. In its new version the weendigo consumes not humans but pine, spruce, cedar and the wildlife that lives there. Though we know the forest industry is not staffed by monsters but by decent men and women trying to make a living, we cannot help but see, through Johnston's eyes, the "monstrous" destruction of clearcutting.

In the last chapter we discussed how two items from the same category — say, two cities — can be explained logically through comparison and contrast. By seeing how Toronto and New York are alike or unlike, we gain a clearer understanding of both. An *analogy*, though, brings together two apparently *unlike* items from *different* categories (such as a monster and a modern industry). Instead of using the two to explain each other, it more often uses one as a device to explain the other. It is not the monsters we investigate but the monstrous aspects of the streetcar or the forest industry.

In the last chapter we speculated whether, instead of comparing two cities, we could compare a city and an anthill. To those of us who live in chambers along the corridors of apartment buildings or who each day crowd into holes in the ground to take the subway, the similarities may be all too clear. We do see right away that such an argument is hardly logical, for the very good reason that people are not insects. And we would certainly not want to base a factual paper, such as a research essay, on this device. Yet in a very informal or humorous paper, the analogy may be a fresh, thought-provoking way to express aspects of city life.

Topics that are unfamiliar or abstract almost cry out for analogies to explain them. Thus in the eighties, the term "computer virus" swept the world. These electronic "diseases" "infect" computer programs, "spreading" an "epidemic" of "contagion." The "outbreaks" of various "strains" feature names such as AIDS.II, Amoeba B, Anthrax, Cancer.2538, Cholera.A, Infector.1005, Leprosy, Lockjaw.573, Malaria, Measles.212, Parasite.871, Pinworm.2150B, Plague.2647, Ringworm.ow, and Virus-90. These electronic diseases "contaminate" programs, erase memory or even attack hardware. Of course "antiviral" software to "vaccinate" the patient has been developed, with brand names like "Flu Shot +," "Data Physician," "Antidote," "AntiVirus," "Virus RX," "ViruSafe" and "Vaccine 1.0." In addition, "safe computing practices" have been recommended to avoid infection by viruses such as "PC AIDS" (*Time* magazine).

Then in the nineties the world of computers seized on another analogy to depict another emerging subject: the "Information Highway." One issue, alone, of *PC Computing* used the terms "octane," "roadside assistance," "on-ramp," "detour," "rest stop," "tollboth," "dead end," "rut," "U-turn," "fast lane" and "hotrods for the Information Superhighway." The "hotrods," of course, were the computers advertised in the magazine.

Have we already seen the first big analogy of the new millennium? Newspapers are describing the current frenzy of corporate mergers and takeovers as "marriage." Will we soon read of "courtship" between banks, of "romance" between telephone companies, of "honeymoons," and then, sadly, of "divorce," as megacorporations sell off their less profitable operations?

If we do, the power of this analogy — as in all analogies — will come not so much from its originality as from its breadth, especially the heavy borrowing of vocabulary from the one item to portray the other. The further you develop such links between your two items — such as a destructive computer program and a virus — the better the analogy.

Yet even a brief statement, such as "A destructive computer program is like a virus," can have value. As a *simile* it is not much of an argument in itself, but is a concrete statement that can be used in support of another argument. While a *simile* states that one thing is *like* another, a *metaphor* states that one thing *is* another ("A destructive computer program is a virus"). Both devices occur often in poetry and in fiction, and of course in essays. This chapter's last selection, Félix Leclerc's description of his boyhood home, contains a steady stream of similes and metaphors that convey a vividly poetic sense not only of the place but also of the author's feelings about it. Though nothing objective has been proven, a message has certainly been given.

In closing, again a **WARNING***: Do not confuse the pleasures of the analogy with the logic of argumentative devices such as comparison and contrast, or cause and effect. Save the analogy for personal essays, humorous pieces and satires, in which its free-wheeling poetic nature is appropriate.*

Note: For more examples of analogy and related devices, see these essays in other chapters:

Analogy:
Anne Michaels, "Hurricane," p. 102
Erika Ritter, "Bicycles," p. 250
Dan Strickland, "The Last Laugh at Dark-Eyed Susan's Roadside Café," p. 296

Simile, metaphor and other figures of speech:
Karen Connelly, "August 4," p. 107
Charles Yale Harrison, "In the Trenches," p. 119
Emily Carr, "D'Sonoqua," p. 126
Margaret Laurence, "Where the World Began," p. 209
Nathalie Petrowski, "The Seven-Minute Life of Marc Lépine," p. 349

Collin Brown

A Game of Tennis*

Born in Kingston, Jamaica, in 1965, Collin Brown immigrated to Canada with his parents at age seven. He is now president of The Unity Group Corporation, a Toronto firm that specializes in creating business opportunities for minorities. (He also plays tennis, the source of his analogy in this essay.) A busy executive who thinks nothing of working late nights and weekends at the office, Brown and his "hybrid of business professionals" have created enterprises such as a greeting card manufacturer, the National Business Alliance of Canada, and an accounting service. Many more are in the works. "I thrive on people telling me 'you can't do that'," says Brown. After high school he immediately started his own business as an interior decorator, but realized it was not going to be as easy as he thought. So putting the business on hold, he attended Toronto's Centennial College to study business and marketing. Two years after his studies, he was employing over 20 people in his first company. Since then his interests have extended to real estate, finance, publishing and business development. Brown sits on numerous boards and has been involved in many initiatives for youth empowerment. His true passion, though, is motivational speaking, which allows him to help others through what he has learned. "Dare yourself to dream," he says. "If your mind can perceive it you can surely achieve it. Translate that dream into a goal and be sure that every step you take is in line with that objective. Use every obstacle as a stepping stone, look for the good in every situation, be realistic and persistent, don't stray from your goal and you will succeed." Our selection began as an interview by Toronto Star *reporter Catherine Dunphy, published on May 15, 1994. Later Mr. Brown changed the order of paragraphs and added a few more details.*

1   I grew up at Martingrove and Albion Road. It hasn't gained that negative a reputation — yet — not like its sister neighbourhood Jamestown, which is two minutes away.

2   Growing up in North Etobicoke, I had a lot of time to examine the issues of race relationships and crime versus economics. I look at this issue of single parenthood and it is not rampant only in the black communities. It is prevalent in a lot of communities.

---

* Editor's title.

The whole circumstance is not one of race, creed, colour or anything like that. It is economic frustration that you see. The key issue here is the sense of hopelessness prevalent in so many communities today, and that is what we are here to change.

The issue is one of power. Unlike a lot of people out there, I'm not angry at anyone for suppressing anyone else. You know the saying, all is fair in love and war? It's like you and I go out to play a game of tennis and we bet $100 and you win. What do I do? Do I sit and complain that you won, that you took my $100? Or do I do something about it?

If we go back and you beat me again, and you still win, I become frustrated, and you're thinking "why even bother playing a guy I can beat anytime, every time." I'm no challenge to you, so why bother playing? That is what is happening in certain communities, not only the black community. When the power is in one place and there's no sharing, I can't win.

What I have decided to do, though, is practice, practice to be the best. I will learn and understand the rules of the game, then I will call you up and say I can beat you. I'll bet you $1000. I'll go to the table with something tangible. No more monkeying around. We play and I win. I beat you; you respect me. It's not an issue of domination, there's a sense of friendship involved. You don't respect someone you beat all the time. That's the bottom line.

When I was sitting in biology class, I was making plans to buy my own home. Everybody laughed, of course, but a few years later it was a different ball game. I bought my first house at 19 and have bought and sold many more since. I learned to look at the successes of people who had done what I wanted to do, people like Bill Cosby, who have really overcome the odds and exemplified that, hey, being wealthy and respected is not impossible.

I can tell you that I am going to be one of the wealthiest men in this country and mean it because that is my goal. Not only wealth for the sake of wealth but wealth for the sake of having the power to make the changes necessary to create more opportunities for those who need it. That essentially is my goal.

And I dare you to tell me I can't achieve it.

△△

Explorations:

Stephen Covey, *The Seven Habits of Highly Effective People*
Rubin "Hurricane" Carter, *The Sixteenth Round*
Lorris Elliott, ed., *Other Voices* (anthology)
Austin Clarke, *The Origin of Waves* (novel)
Francis Henry, *The Caribbean Diaspora in Toronto*

http://www.tenniscanada.com/
http://www.adworld.on.ca/int/bbpa/index.html

Structure:

1. Printed interviews really have two authors — the speaker and the interviewer who often organizes and rearranges what the speaker says. In the *Star* version Brown's dream of buying a house comes *before* the analogy, but for our version Brown moved it *after*. Which position is better? Why?
2. The *analogy* of success in tennis and life came naturally to Brown, because he plays tennis. What analogy from your own life could develop the same argument?
3. How fully does Brown develop his *analogy* of practising to become "the best" at sport and career? Point out all parallels he makes.
4. Why does Brown close with a paragraph of only 11 words? Is it effective? If so, why?

Style:

1. Brown gave his recipe for success in an interview. Point out all the ways in which, as a result, its STYLE is INFORMAL and conversational. Is this TONE a good match for the subject matter? Give reasons.
2. In paragraphs 4-6 Brown seems almost to challenge you personally to tennis and a bet. To what extent does this approach involve you as you read?

Ideas for Discussion and Writing:

1. Actor Bill Cosby was a role model for Brown's early dreams of success (par. 7). Who are your own role models? Choose one, and describe how she or he inspires you.
2. Brown says he is "not angry at anyone for suppressing anyone else" (par. 4). Are you? If so, give one example to show why. Give one concrete suggestion how your anger could be channelled to improve the situation.
3. It used to be said that the battles of England were won on the playing fields of Eton. To what extent does our society view athletics as training for competition in life, and even in war? Give examples from your own experience or observation.
4. Brown has given his recipe for success; what is yours?
5. INTERVIEW: Prepare good questions in advance, then interview a career person you know and admire (a family member, friend, neighbour, teacher, doctor, etc.) to find her or his recipe for success. Later as you play the tape back, take notes to help you put the

parts in a logical order. Now write out the person's remarks, as Catherine Dunphy of the *Star* wrote those of Collin Brown. Are they in a good order? (Is there an introduction? Do examples illustrate at the right spots? Do points increase in significance towards the end? Is there a conclusion?) Now edit punctuation and spelling. Finally, read your good version to the class.

6. **PROCESS IN WRITING:** *Does success seem to you like a ladder to climb? Or a mountain? A road to follow? A game of chance? A particular sport? Whatever* analogy *comes to you, freewrite on it for a few minutes to get the ideas flowing, then take stock of what you have written. Are there enough parallels between the two items to build a real analogy? If not, try again with a new comparison. If so, now write your first draft, rapidly, not stopping now to edit. When this version has "cooled off," look it over. Have you missed any steps or other areas of comparison? Add them. Have you supplied transition words like "now," "next," "suddenly," "finally," etc. to speed the action? If not, add. Finally, edit spelling and punctuation as you produce your best version.*

Note: See also the Topics for Writing at the end of this chapter.

Basil Johnston

Modern Cannibals of the Wilds

Basil Johnston is well known as a writer, and as a teacher of Ojibway (Anishinabe) language, mythology and history for twenty-five years in the Department of Ethnology of Toronto's Royal Ontario Museum. Born in 1929 on the Parry Island Reserve in Ontario, he went to the Cape Croker public school, then at the Spanish Residential School experienced the cultural dislocations of the residential school system which he would later describe in his book Indian School Days *(1988). He completed his education at Loyola College in Montreal and at the Ontario College of Education. Johnston has become a strong voice of First Nations people in Canada. Though he teaches and lectures extensively on Ojibwa history, culture and language, it is his books that have reached the greatest audience:* Ojibway Heritage *(1976),* How the Birds Got Their Colours *(1978),* Moose Meat and Wild Rice *(1978),* Tales the Elders Told *(1981),* Ojibway Ceremonies *(1982),* By Canoe and Moccasin *(1986),* Tales of the Anishinaubaek *(1993), and* The Manitous: The Spiritual world of the Ojibway *(1995). Our selection is from the August 1, 1991,* Globe and Mail. *In it Johnston goes beyond his usual role of imparting Ojibway culture; in his portrait of the new "weendigo" he cuts right to the heart of modern Canadian values.*

1   Woods and forest once mantled most of this land, this continent. It was the home of the Anishinabek (Ojibway, Ottawa, Potowatomi, Algonquin), their kin and their neighbours. It was also the home of the moose, the deer, the caribou, the bear, their kindred and their neighbours. It was as well the home of the thrushes, the sparrows, the hawks, the tanagers, the ravens, the owls, their cousins and their neighbours. Mosquitoes, butterflies, caterpillars, ants, moths, their kind and their neighbours had a place therein.

2   Not only was it home, but a wellspring from which all drew their sustenance, medicine and knowledge.

3   Also dwelling in the woods and forests were weendigoes, giant cannibals who fed upon human flesh to allay their perpetual hunger. They stalked villages and camps, waiting for, and only for, the improvident, the slothful, the gluttonous, the promiscuous, the injudicious, the insa-

226

tiable, the selfish, the avaricious and the wasteful, to be foolish enough to venture alone beyond the environs of their homes in winter.

But no matter how many victims a single weendigo devoured raw, he could never satisfy his hunger. The more he ate, the larger he grew, and the larger he grew, the greater his hunger. The weendigo's hunger always remained in proportion to his size.   4

Even though a weendigo is a mythical figure, he represents real human cupidity. What the old-time storyteller meant to project in the image of the weendigo was a universal and unchanging human disposition. But more learned people declared that no such monster ever existed, that he was a product of superstitious minds and imaginations.   5

As a result, the weendigo was driven from his place in Anishinabe traditions and culture, ostracized through disbelief and skepticism. It was assumed, and indeed it appeared as if, the weendigo and his brothers and sisters had passed into the Great Beyond, like many North American Indian beliefs and practices and traditions.   6

Actually, the weendigoes did not die out; they have only been assimilated and reincarnated as corporations, conglomerates and multinationals. They have taken on new names, acquired polished manners and renounced their craving for human flesh for more refined viands. But their cupidity is no less insatiable than their ancestors'.   7

One breed subsists entirely on forests. When this breed beheld forests, its collective cupidity was stirred as it looked upon an endless, boundless sea of green — as in greenbacks. They saw beyond, even into the future. Money. Cash. Deposits. Bank accounts. Interest. Reserves. Investments, securities, bonds, shares, dividends, capital gains, assets, funds, deals, revenue, income, prosperity, opulence, profits, riches, wealth, comfort.   8

They recruited woodsmen with axes, crosscut saws and Swede saws, sputters, shovels, cant hooks, grapples, chains, ropes, files and pikes, and sent them into the woods to fell, hue, saw, cut, chop, slash and level. The forests resounded with the clash of axes and the whine of saws as blades bit into the flesh of spruce, pine, cedar, tamarack and poplar to fill the demands of the weendigoes in Toronto, Montreal, Vancouver, New York, Chicago, Boston, wherever they now dwelt. Cries of "Timber!" echoed across the treetops, followed by the rip and tear of splintering trees, and thundering crashes.   9

And as fast as woodsmen felled the trees, teamsters delivered sleighload after sleighload to railway sidings and to the rivers. Train after train, shipload after shipload of logs were delivered to the mills.   10

Yet as fast as the woodsmen cut, as much as they cut, it was never fast enough. The quantity always fell short of the expectations of the weendigoes, their masters.   11

12   "Is that all? Should there not be more? We demand a bigger return for our risks and our investments. Only more will satisfy us. Any amount will do, so long as it's more, and the more the better."

13   The demands were met for more speed and more pulp, more logs and more timber. Axes, saws, woodsmen, horses and teamsters were replaced, and their blows and calls no longer rang in the forest. In their place, chainsaws whined, Caterpillar tractors with huge blades bulled and battered their way through the forest, uprooting trees to clear the way for automatic shearers that topped, limbed and sheared the trunks. These mechanical weendigoes gutted and desolated the forests, leaving death, destruction and ugliness where once there was life, abundance and beauty.

14   Trucks and transports operated day and night delivering cargo with a speed and quantity that the horses and sleighs could never have matched.

15   Yet the weendigoes wanted still more, and it didn't matter if their policies and practices of clear-cutting their harvest of timber and pulp resulted in violations of North American Indian rights or in the further impairment of their lives.

16   Nor does it matter to them that their modus operandi permanently defiles hillside and mountainside by erosion. They are indifferent to the carnage inflicted upon bears, wolves, rabbits, thrushes, sparrows, warblers. Who cares if they are displaced? What possible harm has been done? Nor does it seem as if these modern weendigoes have any regard for the rights of future generations to the yield of Mother Earth.

17   The new, reincarnated weendigoes are little different from their forebears. They are more omnivorous than their ancestors, however, and the modern breed wears elegant clothes and comports itself with an air of cultured and dignified respectability.

18   Profit, wealth, comfort, power are the ends of business. Anything that detracts from or diminishes the anticipated return, be it taking pains not to violate the rights of others, or taking measures to ensure that the land remains fertile and productive for future generations, must, it seems, be circumvented.

19   And what has been the result of this self-serving, self-glutting disposition? In 10 short decades, these modern weendigoes have accomplished what at one time seemed impossible; they have laid waste immense tracts of forest that were seen as beyond limit as well as self-propagating, and ample enough to serve this generation and many more to come.

20   Now, as the forests are in decline, the weendigoes are looking at a future that offers scarcity. Many others are assessing the weendigoes' accomplishments not in terms of dollars but in terms of damage — the damage they have inflicted on the environment and the climate and on botanical and zoological life.

△ △

Explorations:

Basil Johnston,
> *How the Birds Got Their Colours*
> *Indian School Days*

Agnes Grant, ed., *Our Bit of Truth: An Anthology of Canadian Native Literature*

Linda Jaine and Drew Hayden, eds., *Voices: Being Native in Canada*

Limits to Growth: A Report for the Club of Rome's Project on the Predicament of Mankind

Elizabeth May, *At the Cutting Edge: The Crisis in Canada's Forests*

M. T. Kelly, *A Dream Like Mine* (novel)

Margaret Atwood, *Strange Things: The Malevolent North in Canadian Literature*

http://www.for.gov.bc.ca/hfp/pubs/standman/atcc/atcc.htm

http://www.sierraclub.ca/prairie/clearcut.html

Structure:

1. Is "Modern Cannibals of the Wilds" a FABLE? (See glossary.) How are fables supposed to work? How does this one?
2. Why does Johnston open by listing so many animals, birds and insects whose "home" was once most of this continent?
3. Point out the paragraph of TRANSITION where we move from the old weendigo to the new one. Point out the THESIS STATEMENT.
4. Analyze how paragraphs 15 and 16 employ *cause and effect.*
5. Point out all the ways Johnston portrays the Canadian forestry industry as a monster and cannibal. How fully has he developed his *analogy*? Invent another *analogy* for those who agree with the forestry industry's actions, and develop it, verbally, for the class.

Style:

1. Where do we more often see words like "mantled," "kindred," "improvident" and "slothful"? Describe Johnston's TONE. Why do you think he chose it for this subject?
2. Read paragraph 9 aloud to the class, with feeling, so all can experience its ONOMATOPOETIC language. Which words sound like what they mean? What is the overall effect?
3. How CONCISE is Johnston's analogy? What techniques make it so?
4. Why is the METAPHOR "flesh" of paragraph 9 so appropriate to Johnston's portrayal of the weendigoes?

Ideas for Discussion and Writing:

1. If our human forestry industry is a "cannibal," then in what sense is it "eating" us as well as trees?
2. "The more he ate, the larger he grew, and the larger he grew, the greater his hunger" (par. 4). What if one day the monster's "food" runs out? When our forestry industry can no longer "eat" and "grow," will it "survive"? What can we do now to either reduce its appetite or extend its food supply?
3. Defend or attack the clearcutting of forests that continues in British Columbia and most of Canada. Defend or attack the actions of Greenpeace, in convincing many European companies not to buy Canadian paper made through clearcutting.
4. Conservationists often claim that in Canada we do not "harvest" but "mine" the forests. Extend these images into *analogies*, by giving parallels. *Contrast* the philosophies behind both.
5. What particularly qualifies Basil Johnston, a First Nations person, to write on this subject?
6. **PROCESS IN WRITING:** *In paragraph 16 Johnston refers to our "Mother Earth." Expand this widespread metaphor into an essay of analogy. First write the term "Mother Earth" in the centre of a page, then fill the surrounding space with other words it brings to mind. Connect related items with lines. Determine your main point. Now draw upon this cluster outline as you do a rapid first draft. When it has "cooled off," look it over. Do examples always help the reader "see" your point? If not, add. Does your TONE fit this important subject? If not, adjust. Is everything on topic? If not, cut. Finally, revise for things like spelling and punctuation as you produce your best version.*

Note: See also the Topics for Writing at the end of this chapter.

Michael Ondaatje

Tabula Asiae*

In 1992 Michael Ondaatje won the English-speaking world's most prestigious literary award, the Booker Prize, for his novel The English Patient; *then in 1996 the film version on which he had collaborated, starring Juliette Binoche, Naveen Andrews, Willem Dafoe, Kristin Scott Thomas and Ralph Fiennes, won nine Oscars and became an international sensation. Ondaatje's complex and richly intercultural novel had given new force to a growing pattern: writers from the margins of the old British Empire are steadily moving to the centre of English-speaking literature. In more than one way Ondaatje is the least "Canadian" of our major writers. He was born in 1943 in Ceylon (now Sri Lanka) to the family of eccentric aristocrats he later portrayed in his fictionalized autobiography* Running in the Family (1982). *His works are often set outside our borders and, as in* The English Patient, *share a lyrical, often surreal, often cinematic style that suggests other places and other influences. Ondaatje left Sri Lanka for England in 1954, and continued in 1962 to Canada, taking a B.A. at the University of Toronto and an M.A. at Queen's. Since 1971 he has taught at Glendon College, York University, in Toronto, and has also had a full career as editor. As a writer, Ondaatje was first a poet:* The Dainty Monsters *appeared in 1967, then in 1969* The Man with Seven Toes, *in 1973* Rat Jelly, *and in 1979* There's a Trick with a Knife I'm Learning to Do: Poems 1963–1978. *This last won the Governor General's award, as had his 1970 book of poetry and prose,* The Collected Works of Billy the Kid. *In 1976 was published his richly poetic first novel,* Coming through Slaughter, *about a jazz musician in New Orleans, then in 1987 his panoramic novel of Toronto in the 1930s,* In The Skin of a Lion, *which introduced characters later seen in* The English Patient. *From beginnings as a poet, Ondaatje has become a major Canadian and world novelist. Our present selection is from his autobiography* Running in the Family.

O n my brother's wall in Toronto are the false maps. Old portraits of Ceylon. The result of sightings, glances from trading vessels, the theories of sextant. The shapes differ so much they seem to be   1

---

* Editor's title.

* *Tabula Asiae:* Map of Asia (in Latin; apparently the words Ondaatje sees on his brother's old maps of Ceylon.)

translations — by Ptolemy, Mercator, François Valentyn, Mortier, and Heydt — growing from mythic shapes into eventual accuracy. Amoeba, then stout rectangle, and then the island as we know it now, a pendant off the ear of India. Around it, a blue-combed ocean busy with dolphin and sea-horse, cherub and compass. Ceylon floats on the Indian Ocean and holds its naive mountains, drawings of cassowary and boar who leap without perspective across imagined 'desertum'° and plain.

2   At the edge of the maps the scrolled mantling depicts ferocious slipper-footed elephants, a white queen offering a necklace to natives who carry tusks and a conch, a Moorish king who stands amidst the power of books and armour. On the south-west corner of some charts are satyrs, hoof deep in foam, listening to the sound of the island, their tails writhing in the waves.

3   The maps reveal rumours of topography, the routes for invasion and trade, and the dark mad mind of travellers' tales appears throughout Arab and Chinese and medieval records. The island seduced all of Europe. The Portuguese. The Dutch. The English. And so its name changed, as well as its shape, — Serendip, Ratnapida ("island of gems"), Taprobane, Zeloan, Zeilan, Seyllan, Ceilon, and Ceylon — the wife of many marriages, courted by invaders who stepped ashore and claimed everything with the power of their sword or bible or language.

4   This pendant, once its shape stood still, became a mirror. It pretended to reflect each European power till newer ships arrived and spilled their nationalities, some of whom stayed and intermarried — my own ancestor arriving in 1600, a doctor who cured the residing governor's daughter with a strange herb and was rewarded with land, a foreign wife, and a new name which was a Dutch spelling of his own. Ondaatje. A parody of the ruling language. And when his Dutch wife died, marrying a Sinhalese° woman, having nine children, and remaining. Here. At the centre of the rumour. At this point on the map.

△ △

Explorations:

Michael Ondaatje,
   Running in the Family
   The Collected Works of Billy the Kid
   In the Skin of a Lion
   The English Patient (both the novel and the video of the film)
Douglas Barbour, *Michael Ondaatje* (Twayne's World Author Series, 835)

° desertum: empty land.
° Sinhalese (or Singhalese): the largest population group of Sri Lanka.

Ed Jewinski, *Michael Ondaatje: Express Yourself Beautifully* (Canadian Biography Series)

Essays on Canadian Writing, No. 53, Summer 1994 (special issue on Ondaatje)

http://www.cariboo.bc.ca/ae/engml/friedman/ondaatje.htm

http://www.randomhouse.com/releases/9611/0-679-74520-3.html

http://alvin.lbl.gov/bios/Ondaatje.html

Structure and Style:

1. Why is "Tabula Asiae" so short? Because it says less than longer selections? Because it communicates differently? If the latter, what techniques has Ondaatje used that many authors in this book have not?

2. Ondaatje was first a poet. How CONCISE is poetry compared to PROSE? Why? Is there a sharp division between the two, or can they share techniques? Can they ever be so alike that they almost merge? Where is "Tabula Asiae" in this spectrum, and why?

3. In paragraph 1 Ondaatje describes the shape of Ceylon in early "false maps" as an "amoeba" and a "stout rectangle." Are these comparisons METAPHORS or *analogies?* Why?

4. In paragraph 1 Ondaatje goes on to call Ceylon a "pendant off the ear of India." What FIGURE OF SPEECH is this? Does he develop it fully enough to make it an analogy?

5. In paragraph 3 Ceylon is "the wife of many marriages." Explain how, and tell what FIGURE OF SPEECH this is.

6. In paragraph 4 the "pendant" becomes a "mirror." In what sense? And again, is this image a METAPHOR or an *analogy?*

7. In what sense do the "false maps" of Ondaatje's brother in Toronto constitute an *analogy* of Ceylon?

8. "Serendip" is an early name for Sri Lanka, as paragraph 3 says. In a reference dictionary, find the connection between this name and our word "serendipity."

Ideas for Discussion and Writing:

1. The Sri Lanka of "Tabula Asiae" — mysterious, romantic and legendary — is not at all the Sri Lanka of the encyclopedia or TV newscast. Why has Ondaatje chosen a SUBJECTIVE, poetic way to present the land of his childhood?

2. "Tabula Asiae" is a chapter of Ondaatje's autobiography *Running in the Family.* If you wrote your own, how far back in time could you begin? Who are your earliest known ancestors? When and where did they live? Do you think their homeland or their personalities helped make you who you are today?

3. Ondaatje's brother puts old maps of Ceylon on his wall in Toronto. When people change countries, should they cherish and preserve their past, as the Ondaatjes do, or forget the past while making a new life? If your family has immigrated to Canada, which are you doing, and why? If English is your second language, will you retain your first? If so, how? Will you someday teach it to your children? Why or why not?

4. **PROCESS IN WRITING:** *Immigration has occurred at some point in the background of all Canadians, even First Nations people. Choose one of these topics:*

   – *My ancestral homeland*
   – *The arrival of my ancestor(s) in Canada*
   – *My immigration to Canada*

   Select the best one for you. Focus it to fit your circumstances, knowledge and interest. Now take a page of notes, perhaps consulting a parent, grandparent, or family records. Sense the importance, even the heroic, legendary or mythic qualities you may see in this topic — then write your "discovery draft." In the next version heighten these overtones by clothing bare fact in the kinds of poetical devices Ondaatje has used in his account (see FIGURES OF SPEECH, *and especially* METAPHOR, *in the Glossary). Make each image, each word choice, reflect your overall vision of this piece of your past. Finally, test the prose by reading aloud, before printing out the good copy.*

Note: See also the Topics for Writing at the end of this chapter.

Félix Leclerc

The Family House[*]

Translated from the French by Philip Stratford

Though as he got older his own music went out of style, Félix Leclerc (1914–1988), Quebec's original chansonnier, *set the example for a generation of popular singers who during the sixties and seventies were a vital force in Quebec's "Quiet Revolution." As singer Gilles Vigneault put it, Leclerc was "the father of us all." Referred to by the media simply as "Félix," honoured by the annual "Félix" music awards named after him, Leclerc spent his last years as unofficial poet laureate of Quebec, a sage to whom the public turned for words in time of crisis. When Quebec mourned the death of nationalist leader René Lévesque in 1987, it was Leclerc whose words were carved on the tomb: "The first page of Quebec's true and beautiful history has been turned. Now he takes his place among the few liberators of their people." And when Leclerc died soon after, Quebeckers mourned another fallen leader. Leclerc was born in La Tuque. After announcing, acting and writing for Radio-Canada in the thirties and early forties, he acted for several years with a theatre company. Then in 1951 he arrived at Paris, where, singing his own rough-hewn songs in music halls, he won instant acclaim as "Le Canadien." But despite his success as songwriter and singer, Leclerc viewed himself primarily as a writer. He published more than a dozen books, including poetry, plays, fables, stories and novels. Among his most widely read have been* Adagio *(1943) and* Allegro *(1944), two collections of his fables and stories written for radio;* Pieds nus dans l'aube *(1946), the autobiographical novel from which our selection comes; and his novel* Le fou de l'île *(1958), translated by Philip Stratford in 1976 as* The Madman, the Kite and the Island.*

W̲e were all, brothers and sisters alike, born in a long three-storey wooden house, a house as humped and crusty as a loaf of home-made bread, as warm and clean inside as the white of the loaf.

Roofed over with shingles, harbouring robins in its gables, it looked itself like an old nest perched up there in the silence. Taking the north wind over the left shoulder, beautifully adjusted to nature, from the

---

[*] Translator's title.

roadside one might also have mistaken it for an enormous boulder stranded on the beach.

3   In truth it was a stubborn old thing, soaking up storms and twilight, determined not to die of anything less than old age, like the two elms beside it.

4   The house turned its back squarely on the rest of town so as not to see the new subdivision with its shiny little boxes as fragile as mushrooms. Looking out over the valley, highroad for the wild St. Maurice river, it focused as if in ecstasy on the long caravan of blue mountains over there, the ones that flocks of clouds and the oldest seagulls don't seem able to get over.

5   With its rusty sides, its black roof and its white-trimmed windows, our common cradle crouched over a heavy cement foundation sunk solidly in the ground like a ship's anchor to hold us firm, for we were eleven children aboard, a turbulent, strident lot, but as timid as baby chicks.

6   A big, robust, rough fieldstone chimney, held together by trowel-smoothed mortar, began in the cellar near the round-bellied furnace just above that drafty little iron door that sticking a mirror into you could see the stars. Like the hub of a wheel it rose through the floors distributing spokes of heat, then broke through to the outside as stiff as a sentinel with a plumed helmet and smoked there with windswept hair, close to a grey ladder lying along the roof. The grey ladder and the sooty little door, we were told, were not for human use, but for an old man in red who in winter jumped from roof to roof behind reindeer harnessed in white.

7   From top to bottom our home was inhabited: by us in the centre like the core of a fruit; at the edges by parents; in the cellars and attics by superb and silent men, lumberjacks by trade. In the walls, under the floors, between the joists, near the carpets, and in the folds of the lampshades lived goblins, gnomes, fairies, snatches of song, silly jokes and the echoes of games; in the veins of our house ran pure poetry.

8   We had a chair for rocking in, a bench for saying prayers, a sofa to cry on, a two-step staircase for playing trains. Also other fine toys that we didn't dare touch, like the two-wired bird with its long beak and the bell in its forehead that talked to the grown-ups. A flower-patterned linoleum was our garden; a hook in the wall, a bollard to tie up our imaginary boats; the staircases were slides; the pipes running up the walls our masts; and armchairs miniature stages where we learnt with the hats, gloves and overcoats of our elders how to make the same faces that we wear today but without finding them funny.

9   A vast corridor divided the ground floor lengthwise. A few rung-backed chairs made a circle in one corner; above them a row of hooks like question marks disappeared beneath the coats of visitors who came to consult Papa, the biggest timber merchant in the valley. The living

room and a bedroom for visitors stood side by side. The living room, with its black piano, its net curtains, its big blue armchair, its gold-framed pictures, a few old-style chairs upholstered in satin (particularly a spring-rocker dressed up like an old lady out of the past with tassels on the hem of her dress) gave our lives a quality of Sunday celebration. Our parents' bedroom closed its door on impenetrable secrets. In its obscurity slumbered an old dresser full of camphor-scented sheets between which my mother hid mysterious notebooks, repositories of the exact hour of our birth, the names of godfathers and godmothers, and very private family events.

To the left of the hall a smoking room served as my father's study   10
and as library for all of us. A door opened to the dining room — classroom would be more exact, for we only ate there once or twice a year. In the sewing room between the sewing machine and an enormous cupboard stood the sofa, ready to be cried on. At the back of the house, spreading the full width, was our gay and singing kitchen: the cast-iron stove with its built-in mirror, the red kitchen cupboards, the white muslin curtains hanging like fog in the narrow windows, and the patches of sunlight playing on the left of the long family table. There shone the ever-burning lamp, known to all people throughout all time as the soul of the home. There we were told of good news and bad. There Papa signed our school report cards. There in the high rocking chair we would often sit in silence to think of facts of creation discovered that day and ponder on the strange and marvellous world we had fallen into.

The first floor was lined with children's bedrooms. There were eight,   11
I think, divided between girls and boys. In the girls' rooms it was cleaner, rosier, airier than the boys'. On the walls they pinned up tiny frames, graceful silhouettes and sprigs of flowers. On ours we stuck huge vulgar calendars, of hunters waiting for game and old gents smoking rubbed tobacco.

Our room, the most spacious on the floor, looked out on the garden,   12
its black earth full as a cornucopia, and cut through with straight little paths that we walked down every evening, watering under the watching eyes of the cottontails.

We each had our own bed, a little white bed with a real straw mattress   13
and iron bedposts ending in brass knobs where we hung our clothes, our slingshots, and our hands clasped in prayer.

On the second floor a screened veranda jutted out in a bow like a   14
pilot-house. It was a veritable observation post dominating the waves of the valley like those of the sea: waves of snowstorms, waves of loggers in springtime, waves of poor families gathering wild fruit, waves of falling leaves, of showers of sunshine, of the beating of birds' wings, of paths traced by children, hunters and fishermen. On hot nights we slept

there above the waves on that wooden porch which was also the children's playroom. Soldiers, teddy bears, drums, little wooden shoes, dolls seated at table before empty china plates, all keeping good company together. A tin bridge built long ago by my eldest brother served as access to this cardboard world.

15   On the floor above, behind a bull's-eye window, stretched the attic, a long deserted dusty cage, dormitory in winter for several lumberjacks. Between the three-legged chairs and the family portraits, these men on their mattresses, devoured by fatigue, tumbled headlong each night into sleep.

16   And like the crew of a happy ship, thinking neither of arrivals nor of departures, but only of the sea that carries them, we sped through childhood all sails set, thrilled with each morning and every night, envying neither distant ports nor far cities, convinced that our ship was flying the best colours and that we carried on board all necessary potions to ward off pirates and bad luck.

17   The house we lived in was number 168, rue Claire-Fontaine.

△△△

Explorations:

Félix Leclerc,
> *The Madman, the Kite and the Island*
> *Pieds nus dans l'aube* (available only in French)

Philip Stratford, ed., *Chez nous* (anthology of writings from Quebec, translated into English)

Félix-Antoine Savard, *Boss of the River*

Germaine Guèvremont, *The Outlander*

Jacques Ferron, *Tales from an Uncertain Country* (short stories, in translation)

Related Web sites in French:
> http://www.microtec.net/~martrick/leclerc.htm
> http://www.microtec.net/~martrick/chanson.htm

Structure:

1. Leclerc packs this selection with FIGURES OF SPEECH, but develops only one image so fully as to make it an *analogy*. What is it? Which paragraphs develop it?
2. What is the overall point of this selection, and where does Leclerc most openly state it?

Style:

1. Do you see twice as many METAPHORS and SIMILES here as in most of the other selections? Four times as many? Ten times as many? What effect does this concentration of figures of speech give?

2. Point out ten SIMILES, ten METAPHORS and five cases of PERSONIFICATION in this selection. Are these figures of speech well chosen to build a single dominant impression?

3. Do you imagine "The Family House" was easy or hard to translate from French to English? Is an exact translation possible? If you speak two or more languages, how easy or hard is it to translate thoughts from one to another?

Ideas for Discussion and Writing:

1. In paragraph 8 Leclerc tells how the children imitated their elders, learning "how to make the same faces that we wear today but without finding them funny." Do you sense in "The Family House" a regret for lost childhood? Do you regret the loss of your own? Do most of us? If so, give reasons.

2. Almost everything Leclerc wrote expresses the same happiness and security that we find in "The Family House." Do happy children such as he depicts here usually become happy adults? Can troubled children also become happy adults? Give examples.

3. "Coming of Age in Putnok" is the opening of George Gabori's autobiography, while "The Family House" is the opening of Félix Leclerc's autobiographical novel. Compare the two. Which gives more facts? More feeling? More insight into the author's background and personality? Which would more strongly motivate readers to finish the book?

4. **PROCESS IN WRITING:** *Like Leclerc, depict your own childhood home in such a way as to strongly convey your feelings about it and your life there. First generate a page of SIMILES, METAPHORS and SENSE IMAGES that "show" your memories of home. Now search these notes for a common theme such as Leclerc's vision of a house as a ship. Next write a "discovery draft" to develop this analogy, using images from your notes, and new ones that come as you write. In further drafts chop out each word that does not in some way support the overall effect. Read your final version aloud, with feeling, to the class.*

Note: See also the Topics for Writing at the end of this chapter.

Topics for Writing

Chapter 6: Analogy and Related Devices

Choose either a complete topic from items 1–15, or a subject from items 16–30 to complete. Then in an essay, extend your analogy as far as you can. (See also the guidelines that follow.)

1. An Industrial Worker as a Robot
2. A Career as Marriage
3. School as a Factory
4. The Rain Forest as the Lungs of the Planet
5. The Playing Field as a Battlefield
6. Prejudice as a Wall
7. Dancing as Life
8. Music as a Drug
9. White Blood Cells as an Army
10. The Public Debt as a Cancer
11. A Career as War
12. A Person You Know as the Pet He or She Keeps
13. A Corporation as an Octopus
14. The City as a Jungle
15. Novels as Dreams
16. Television as ——————————————————————
17. A Sports Team as ——————————————————————
18. Population Growth as ——————————————————————
19. Dating as ——————————————————————
20. Old Age as ——————————————————————
21. Crime as ——————————————————————
22. Video Games as ——————————————————————
23. Chess as ——————————————————————
24. Marriage as ——————————————————————
25. Parents as ——————————————————————
26. The Internet as ——————————————————————
27. E-mail as ——————————————————————
28. Pollution as ——————————————————————
29. Money as ——————————————————————
30. The Planet Earth as ——————————————————————

Note also the Process in Writing topic after each selection in this chapter.

Process in Writing: Guidelines

Follow at least some of these steps in writing your essay of analogy (your teacher may suggest which ones).

1. *Choose or devise a topic you really like, because motivation is the single greatest factor in writing performance.*

2. *If you complete one of the topics from 16 to 30, be sure to invent an* analogy *(with two items from different categories), not a* comparison and contrast *(with two items from the same category). Know which item is your real subject, and which one exists merely to explain the other.*

3. *Now freewrite on your topic, to achieve the spontaneity and originality that spark a good analogy.*

4. *Incorporate the best of this freewriting into your first draft. Let the ideas flow, not stopping now to revise or edit.*

5. *In your next version add any more points of comparison that come to you (a strong analogy is fully developed). Read your prose aloud to detect awkward passages, and revise. Trim deadwood. Heighten TRANSITIONS.*

6. *Finally, edit for things like spelling and punctuation, before printing out your best version. Save it on disk, in case your teacher suggests further revision.*

"I'm speaking of the era of the high-strung thoroughbred bicycle, whose rider had also made advances, from pedalling peacenik to a hunched and humorless habitué of the velodrome, clad in leather-seated shorts, white crash helmet, and fingerless gloves, whizzing soundlessly. . . ."

—Erika Ritter, "Bicycles"

CHAPTER

7

CLASSIFICATION

There are three kinds of them. . .

Our world is so complex that without classification we are lost. To call a friend we use an alphabetized phone book. To find oranges we head for the fruit section of the supermarket. To buy a used bicycle we go right to the *classified* section of the newspaper. Putting things into categories is one of our most common methods of thought, both for good and for bad. Who would search the whole dictionary when the word in question begins with "T"? What student, *classified* into grade five, would look for the grade six *class*room?

Yet as Hitler and other racists have shown, classifying people can lead to stereotypes and stereotypes can lead to violence. Ethnic jokes may seem innocent *(Why does it take two WASPs to change a light bulb? One makes the gin and tonics while the other calls the electrician)*. But such a characterization makes it hard for others to view a member of that group as an individual. If all WASPs (or all Quebeckers or Calgarians or women or Catholics or unemployed people or environmentalists or police officers) are classified as the same, we have dehumanized them. Dislike and even persecution are now possible. At its extreme, this process has led to genocides such as the bloody conquest of the Americas by Europeans, the extermination of the Jews by Nazi Germany, and the butchery of more recent "ethnic cleansing" in countries as diverse as Rwanda and the former Yugoslavia.

Be careful, then, not to let a classification become a stereotype. For example, our society may have practical reasons to group people by age, but let's always leave room for individuals: not all teenagers drive recklessly, not all 40-year-olds are divorcing, and not all 80-year-olds are in the rocking chair. Many teens don't even have a licence, some 40-year-olds have never married, and a few people in their eighties still run marathons.

Whatever its subject, your essay of classification needs at least three categories, because only two would form a comparison and contrast. And it should have no more than you can adequately develop — seldom more than five or six. (David Foot's essay in this chapter has an unusual nine categories, but since each is one age group, in order, of the Canadian population, his logic is foolproof. Note how many pages it takes, though, to develop this number of categories.) To be logical a classification normally follows these guidelines:

Classify all items by the same principle. A study of major world religions would probably include Islam, Christianity, Judaism, Buddhism and Hinduism — but not atheism, which is the opposite of religious belief.

Do not leave out an obvious category, such as Buddhism, which has many millions of followers. On the other hand, if your neighbour forms a new religious group that attracts a dozen people to its meetings, including it as a world religion would clearly not make sense.

Do not let categories overlap. Though a classification of world religions might include Islam, Christianity, Judaism, Buddhism and Hinduism, it would not include Catholicism — because it is a subgroup of Christianity.

Classifying is not easy; it is a real exercise in logic. Keep applying the guidelines.

Also observe the main principle of any essay: *Know your purpose.* Exactly *why* are you comparing the three kinds of parents or the four kinds of teachers or the five kinds of friends? Is it because you have a vision of what a good parent or teacher or friend is, and want to share it with others? Is it because bad experiences lead you to warn against certain kinds of parents or teachers or friends? Like any argument, an essay of classification makes a point — otherwise it is "pointless." Try freewriting or brainstorming for five or ten minutes to get thoughts flowing and ideas on paper. Look these over. Let them help you decide not only what the content of your classification might be, but also its thesis. Since thinking is not easy, you need all the help you can get —

and some of the best help comes from your own pen: while it is writing, you are thinking.

Note: For another example of classification, see this essay in a later chapter:

Judy Stoffman, "The Way of All Flesh," p. 286

The Hon. David Lam

Pulling Together

The Honourable David See-Chai Lam, born in Hong Kong in 1923, has had a long career in business and public life, culminating in his term from 1988 to 1995 as Lieutenant Governor of British Columbia. With a B.A. from Lingnam University and an M.B.A. from Temple University, he became in 1960 the CEO of Ka Wah Bank Ltd. of Hong Kong. Then, immigrating to the "golden mountain" which he celebrates in his essay, he became in 1968 the president of Canadian International Properties Limited. When Dr. Lam was invited ten years later to be the lieutenant-governor of his new home, British Columbia, he underwent the uncertainties described in his essay below, at first declining because he was "living in a province with a history of discrimination against Chinese," because he was "getting old," and because English was not his first language. Reconsidering, though, he did accept the post, and, with the aid of his much-loved wife Dorothy Lam, found great fulfillment in the job through "building bridges" among the many population groups of British Columbia. Our selection, published in Maclean's *of January 30, 1995, reflects this experience in acceptance, belonging and contribution. Now retired from government, Dr. Lam lives in Vancouver, where he enjoys golf and boating.*

1   Once, Asians came to North America for jobs, albeit somewhat menial ones. Particularly in the West, there was ready work on the railway, in laundries and in chop suey houses. With the gold rush and its opportunity to strike it rich, this continent became known in China as the "golden mountain."

2   Today, Canada continues to attract Asians, although the lure is no longer gold. Instead, they come for things that a lot of us in Canada take for granted: stability, a peaceful life, law and order, education, generally friendly and understanding people.

3   As one of those who chose to settle in Canada over 28 years ago, I would like to offer a brief ABC for others hoping to make a new home here.

4   The A is for acceptance. And that goes two ways. Prospective immigrants must be accepted by the federal immigration department. But even if the government accepts you, your peace of mind and happiness will depend very much upon how you are accepted in your community.

Of course, newcomers could reject the broader Canadian community and choose to live only among their own people. But that choice is self-defeating: one becomes inward-looking, cut away from the mainstream of society. There is really no way to enjoy what Canada has to offer if one lives in either a physical or psychological ghetto. So, it is a duty of sorts to strive for acceptance. 5

There are always difficulties arising from different value systems, a different cultural style. Speaking loudly, getting things done in the quickest manner, bragging about accomplishments and wealth — all might be commonplace in Hong Kong and totally acceptable in many other parts of the world. But they are not so in Canada. 6

Here, we try to minimize friction between people. We downplay displays of wealth. We respect good manners. Such simple courtesies as saying good morning and thank you are daily expressions of respect for others. 7

The B represents belonging. This is a very important feeling. People who do not belong always feel impermanent. As with people who reside in a hotel, no matter how beautiful it may be, they are constantly reminded that they are transients. 8

People who divide their time between Canada and another country become "astronauts" — flying too high and fast to put down real roots or to feel a sense of belonging. They are not found just among Chinese immigrants. Some Canadians who spend half of their time in California or in Florida might also be considered astronauts. When they are asked to become involved in community services, many say: "Ah, but in a couple of months I will return to Canada . . . ," or, ". . . I'll be leaving for the States." 9

If you want to feel that you belong, ask yourself: how much do I care about what happens in my community and related issues such as crime, a clean neighborhood, volunteering to pitch in. 10

The C stands for contribution. And this is the easiest thing of all to achieve. In this new country, in this new community, in this new neighborhood in which we have started to take root, commitment makes a strong statement that you belong. You can give without loving; but you cannot love without giving. 11

When I was initially approached to consider being nominated as lieutenant-governor of British Columbia, I turned it down. My negative side told me: "You are living in a province with a history of discrimination against Chinese. You are getting old. You speak English as a second language. Don't do it." 12

Fortunately, however, my positive side saw an opportunity to build bridges among people of different cultures, different ethnic backgrounds and different races. After 6$\frac{1}{2}$ years, I have experienced tremendous love and respect from the people of Canada as a whole, and particularly 13 from those in British Columbia. I feel proud to be a Canadian, because I truly appreciate the quality of its people.

14   I was brought up in Hong Kong to be so conscious of racial differences that we had derogatory nicknames for everyone. That is no way to go through life. It is like carrying a little bit of poison in the mind. And the world is changing. The day is quickly coming when people with only one culture will find it difficult to compete, let alone to prosper.

15   Don't talk to me about "tolerance." Tolerating someone is like holding your breath: you are telling the world that you can hold your breath longer than anyone else. I say, let us celebrate differences — not tolerate them.

16   I believe in multiculturalism because it adds to our strength. The Asia-Pacific region is the fastest-growing region in the world. And it is just across the ocean from British Columbia. Let us turn the people of all the races living in Canada into partners. Let us build a "golden mountain" for all of us.

△ △

Explorations:

Bennett Lee and Jim Wong-Chu, eds., *Many-Mouthed Birds: Contemporary Writings by Chinese-Canadians*
Wayson Choy, *The Jade Peony* (novel)
Sky Lee, *Disappearing Moon Cafe* (novel)
Amy Tan, *The Joy Luck Club* (novel; also made into an acclaimed feature film now out on video)
http://cicnet.ci.gc.ca

Structure:

1. Why does David Lam both open and close his essay with the same expression, "golden mountain"? What effect does this repetition achieve?
2. How do you rate Lam's "brief ABC" as a *classification*? Are its three categories enough? Is any obvious category left out? Do any overlap? Are all *classified* by the same principle? Do you think the organizational device of the "ABC" has distorted Lam's choice of categories, or is it a natural fit?
3. How does the device of *comparison and contrast* heighten the power of paragraph 9?
4. Why does Lam wait almost till the end to describe his own decision to become lieutenant-governor of British Columbia?

Style:

1. How easy or hard is the vocabulary of "Pulling Together"? How short or long are its sentences? Its paragraphs? Who do you see as its intended AUDIENCE?

Ideas for Discussion and Writing:

1. While stating "I believe in multiculturalism because it adds to our strength" (par. 16), Lam also advises New Canadians not to live "in either a physical or psychological ghetto" (par. 5). What is your view? Do you prefer the traditional American "melting pot" which is supposed to assimilate immigrants, or the Canadian "mosaic," in which New Canadians are encouraged, even funded, to retain their first language and culture? Which path is better for the individual? For the nation?

2. David Lam's adopted home of British Columbia is part of the Asia Pacific rim, and is itself one of the most multicultural spots on earth. If you live there, describe the ways in which the cosmopolitan mix of its population has influenced your own life. Or if you live in Toronto or Montreal, apply this topic to your own cosmopolitan city.

3. Lam says "The day is quickly coming when people with only one culture will find it difficult to compete, let alone to prosper" (par. 14). Do you think this is true for your own intended profession? Why or why not? If so, what have you done to prepare? If your family has immigrated, what are you doing to keep your first language and culture? If your family has earlier roots in Canada, what other languages, if any, have you learned to speak? What experiences have you had to make yourself feel at home with other cultures?

4. **PROCESS IN WRITING:** *Whether you have immigrated, yourself, or only know others who have, think about the main challenges that face immigrants to Canada. Fill a page with brainstorming on this topic, then look it over. Circle or highlight the main points, choose your THESIS STATEMENT, then rearrange these thoughts into a short conventional outline that* classifies *the challenges. Are there at least three categories in your* classification? *Are any main ones missing? Are all* classified *by the same principle? Do any seem to overlap? Now write a rapid version of your essay of* classification. *The next day look it over. Does it have enough* examples? *If not, add. Do TRANSITIONS move the argument from one point to the next? If not, add. Finally, check the punctuation and spelling before printing out your best version.*

Note: See also the Topics for Writing at the end of this chapter.

Erika Ritter

Bicycles

Playwright, humorist and radio personality, Erika Ritter is well known to Canadians for her satirical views on urban life, and especially on what drama critic Martin Knelman called "her favourite subject — the dilemma of the modern woman whose twentieth-century political programmes and mastery of power dressing keep bumping against her nineteenth-century psyche." Born in Regina, Ritter studied literature at McGill, then drama at the University of Toronto. Though she declines the label of "feminist," her major plays, The Splits *(1978),* Automatic Pilot *(1980),* The Passing Scene *(1982), and* Murder at McQueen *(1986) all examine the modern urban woman and her difficulty in maintaining relationships with men. In 1985 Ritter became the highly successful host of CBC Radio's* Dayshift, *a talk show, but in 1987 quit and turned her attention to writing.* Urban Scrawl *(1984) and* Ritter in Residence *(1987), her books of light satirical essays, indulge in slapstick humour, puns and fantasy, yet still develop Ritter's investigation of the modern woman and of urban life in general. Ritter's newest departure is a novel,* The Hidden Life of Humans *(1997), one of whose narrators is a dog. Our selection comes from* Urban Scrawl, *which Ritter dedicates to her mother — "who made the mistake of encouraging this kind of thing."*

1   It wasn't always like this. There was a time in the life of the world when adults were adults, having firmly put away childish things and thrown away the key.

2   Not any more. The change must have come about innocently enough, I imagine. Modern Man learning to play nicely in the sandbox with the other grown-ups. Very low-tension stuff.

3   Now, in every direction you look, your gaze is met by the risible spectacle of adults postponing adolescence well into senility by means of adult toys: running shoes, baseball bats, roller skates, and — bicycles!

4   But the attitude is no longer the fun-loving approach of a bunch of superannuated kids, and I'm sure you can envision how the evolution occurred. Jogging progressed from a casual encounter with the fresh air to an intensive relationship, attended by sixty-dollar jogging shoes and a designer sweatband. Playing baseball stopped being fun unless you had a Lacoste (as opposed to low-cost) tee-shirt in which to impress

your teammates. And where was the thrill in running around a squash court unless it was with a potentially important client?

As for bicycles — well, let's not even talk about bicycles. On the other hand, maybe we *should* talk about them, because there's something particularly poignant about how it all went wrong for the bicycle, by what declension this once proud and carefree vehicle sank into the role of beast of burden, to bear the weight of sobersided grown-ups at their supposed sport.

First, there was the earliest domestication of the North American bicycle *(cyclus pedalis americanus)* in the late Hippie Scene Era of the 1960s. This was the age of the no-nuke whole-grain cyclist, who saw in the bicycle the possibility of Making a Statement while he rode. A statement about pollution, about materialism, about imperialism, about militarism, about — enough already. You get the picture: two wheels good, four wheels bad.

Thus it was that the basic bicycle gradually evolved into a chunky three-speed number from China, bowed down under a plastic kiddie carrier, army surplus knapsacks, and a faded fender-sticker advising Make Tofu, Not War. And a rider clad in a red plaid lumber-jacket, Birkenstock sandals, and an expression of urgent concern for all living things.

Once the very act of bicycle riding had become an act of high moral purpose, it was an easy step to the next phase of the bicycle's journey along the path of post-Meanderthal seriousness.

I'm speaking of the era of the high-strung thoroughbred bicycle, whose rider had also made advances, from pedalling peacenik to a hunched and humorless habitué of the velodrome, clad in leather-seated shorts, white crash helmet, and fingerless gloves, whizzing sound-lessly, and with no hint of joy, down city streets and along the shoulders of super-highways, aboard a vehicle sculpted in wisps of silver chrome. A vehicle so overbred, in its final evolutionary stages, that it began to resemble the mere exoskeleton of a conventional cycle, its flesh picked away by birds of carrion.

Having been stripped of any connection with its innocent and lei-surely origins, the bicycle now no longer bore the slightest resemblance to the happy creature it once had been. And in the mid-Plastic Scene Era, another crippling blow was struck by the upscale name-brand cyclist, who came along to finish what the fanatical velodromist had refined. Namely, the complete transformation of an ambling and un-hurried mode of transit into a fast, nerve-wracking, expensive, and utterly competitive display of high speed, high technology, and high status.

The Upscale Cyclist was looking for a twelve-speed Bottecchia that matches his eyes, something that he'd look trendy upon the seat of, when riding to the office (the office!), and he was ready to pay in four figures for it.

12   Not only that, he was also prepared to shell out some heavy bread for those status accessories to complete the picture: the backpack designed by the engineers at NASA, the insulated water-bottle to keep his Perrier chilled just right, the sixteen-track Walkman that would virtually assure him the envy of all his friends.

13   So much for the cyclist. What of his poor debased mount?

14   Not surprisingly, amongst the breed of bicycle, morale is currently low, and personal pride all but a thing of the past. And yet . . . and yet, there are those who say that *cyclus pedalis americanus* is an indomitable creature, and that it is the bicycle, not its rider, who will make the last evolution of the wheel.

15   In fact, some theorize that the present high incidence of bicycle thievery, far from being evidence of crime, is actually an indication that the modern bicycle has had enough of oppressive exploitation and man's joyless ways, and is in the process of reverting to the wild in greater and greater numbers.

16   There have always remained a few aboriginal undomesticated bicycles — or so the theory goes — and now it is these free-spirited mavericks, down from the hills at night, who visit urban bikeracks, garages, and back porches to lure tame bicycles away with them.

17   Costly Kryptonite locks are wrenched asunder, expensive accoutrements are shrugged off, intricate gear systems are torn away, and lo — look what is revealed! Unadorned, undefiled *cyclus* in all his pristine glory, unfettered and unencumbered once more, and free to roam.

18   A wistful fantasy, you might say? The maundering illusions of someone who's been riding her bicycle too long without a crash helmet? I wonder.

19   Just the other day, there was that piece in the paper about a bicycle that went berserk in a shopping centre, smashing two display windows before it was subdued. And did you hear about the recent sighting of a whole herd of riderless bicycles, all rolling soundlessly across a park in the night?

20   It all kind of gets you to thinking. I mean, do *you* know where your ten-speed is tonight?

△ △

Explorations:

Erika Ritter,
> *Automatic Pilot*
> *Urban Scrawl*
> *Ritter in Residence*
> *The Hidden Life of Humans* (novel)

http://www.puc.ca/whoswho/e_ritter.html
http://faculty.babson.edu/petty/btopten.htm
http://members.aol.com/Jakajk/bikeweb2.html

Structure:

1. Are the words "It wasn't always like this" a good opening? Why or why not?

2. Ritter divides the evolution of *cyclus pedalis americanus* into three stages. Identify each category of her *classification* and show where it begins and ends.

3. Have any categories of this *classification* overlapped? Have any obvious ones been left out?

4. Ritter marks each major change of subject with a transitional passage. Point out three of these.

5. Ritter closes with the device examined in our previous chapter, *analogy*. As the bicycle starts "reverting to the wild," to what is it compared? Find at least ten terms that develop the analogy.

6. At the end Ritter asks, "do *you* know where your ten-speed is tonight?" To what does she allude? Is this ALLUSION a good closing?

Style:

1. Where did you first sense the light TONE of this selection? Describe Ritter's brand of humour.

2. In paragraph 4 what device of humour has baseball players wearing "Lacoste (as opposed to low-cost)" T-shirts?

3. Explain the word play of "the late Hippie Scene Era" (par. 6), "post-Meanderthal seriousness" (par. 8), and "the mid-Plastic Scene Era" (par. 10).

4. Is Ritter's informal style right for this selection? Point out her most COLLOQUIAL expressions.

5. Paragraph 9 shows the "thoroughbred" bicycle as so overbred "that it began to resemble the mere exoskeleton of a conventional cycle, its flesh picked away by birds of carrion." What FIGURES OF SPEECH do you see here?

Ideas for Discussion and Writing:

1. Erika Ritter has been well known in Canada as playwright and radio host; how does her approach to "Bicycles" reflect these other roles?
2. In paragraphs 13–20 humour turns to fantasy. Has Ritter gone too far, or is fantasy right for some essay subjects?
3. Is it true that we go too far in "improving" products such as the bicycle? Has this happened to the car, the house, the computer, food, the running shoe? If so, in what ways?
4. Do you have a bicycle? Tell how it does or does not fit into one of Ritter's categories.
5. **PROCESS IN WRITING:** *Ritter classifies evolutionary stages of the bicycle. In an essay, either funny or serious, do the same for one of these: cars, TV sets, cell phones, sound systems or computers. First generate a page of notes, to find the stages of this "evolution." Now write the discovery draft, and look it over. Do categories overlap? Is a main category missing? Is your TONE consistent? Do IMAGES help readers "see" the point? Improve these areas, then read aloud to check for style.*

Note: See also the Topics for Writing at the end of this chapter.

David Foot *with* Daniel Stoffman

Boomers and Other Cohorts

David Foot, an academic, and Daniel Stoffman, a journalist, combined forces to produce a book that in 1996 got the whole country thinking about its topic, and that dominated the Canadian bestseller list for over a year. Boom, Bust & Echo: How to Profit from the Coming Demographic Shift, *is an examination of demography (the study of population groups), that shows how people's collective behaviour at different ages determines major trends in society. In fact "Demographics," say the authors, "explain about two-thirds of everything."*

David Foot did an undergraduate degree in Australia and a doctorate in economics at Harvard. Now a professor of economics at the University of Toronto, he has published a vast number of articles, both scholarly and popular, on population-related topics as varied as school enrolment rates, youth unemployment, aging of the workforce, immigration, outdoor recreation, deforestation, and federalism. He writes often for The Globe and Mail, *advises governmental commissions, and has published several other books, among them* Provincial Public Finance in Ontario *(1977) and* The Growth of Public Employment in Canada *(1979). Foot is a popular teacher, twice having won the University of Toronto's undergraduate teaching award, and is in high demand as a public speaker, riveting his audiences with explanations of trends, and challenging the priorities of their status quo.*

Daniel Stoffman is a graduate of the University of British Columbia and the London School of Economics. An award-winning journalist, he writes on social issues for periodicals such as Report on Business, Canadian Business, Saturday Night, Toronto Life *and* Canadian Living. *His research in Canadian immigration policy led in 1993 to an influential book,* Toward a More Realistic Immigration Policy for Canada. *Stoffman provided much of the writing to put David Foot's research into* Boom, Bust & Echo. *Our selection is the first chapter of their book.*

E ach of us is a member of a "cohort." The baby boom is a cohort that includes everyone born during a 20-year span of sustained high numbers of births in Canada. It also includes those born elsewhere during those same years but now living in Canada. The other cohorts in Canada span shorter periods of time.

1

2   Most of think of ourselves as individuals and underestimate how much we have in common with fellow members of our cohort. And of course each of us *is* an individual. The 70-year-old who continues a lifelong pursuit of rock climbing while most in her age group have switched to more sedate recreations is a unique individual. So is the 12-year-old who prefers opera to rock music. But the chances are good that the young opera lover will rent his first apartment, buy his first car, and get married at about the same age as his peers. The timing of those events in his life will be determined largely by demographics. Before we can understand what demographics have in store for him and for all of us, we need to know the various cohorts that make up the Canadian population. Let's take a look at them now.

PRE-WORLD WAR I (BORN 1914 AND EARLIER)

3   Forget about the outmoded notion of "senior citizens" as one unified group sharing many characteristics in common. It's no longer true, if it ever was. An 85-year-old has no more in common with a 65-year-old than a 45-year-old has with a 25-year-old. They are different people, from different generations, with different interests, different financial circumstances, and different preoccupations and needs.

4   The most senior of seniors — the over-80-year-olds — constitute the one segment of the over-65 population that is currently growing rapidly because they were born in the first decade and a half of this century, when a high birth rate accompanied a booming Canadian economy. During this period, Canada also welcomed the largest concentrated influx of immigration in its history as part of a policy to settle the prairie provinces. Although the over-80s have a higher death rate than people in younger age groups, they are a growing cohort in the sense that those turning 80 during the 1990s are more numerous than their predecessors in the over-80 category. In 1996, 627,000 members of this cohort, born both in Canada and elsewhere, are living in Canada.

5   Because women, on average, live six years longer than men, most of this group is female. In their productive years, few women had independent careers outside the household and so they had little income of their own. They were married to men who didn't have transferable pensions. Not surprisingly, therefore, most of them are poor. Their greatest needs are appropriate housing and good health care. And their tragedy is that not enough of us are paying attention to them. As a society, we should be searching for innovative ways to combine housing with health care and related support services so that these women can conclude their lives in dignity and comfort. But the public sector is too

preoccupied with deficit-cutting to think about imaginative solutions to social problems, and the senior seniors are too poor to interest the private sector.

The increase over the next decade in the number of elderly widows in our society is going to have a major impact on a younger group of people — people in their 50s and 60s who will be taking on the responsibility of caring for elderly, and increasingly ill, mothers. Traditionally, this is a task that falls to daughters more than to sons. Some women will be shouldering this new obligation on top of major responsibilities at work.

Imagine a vice-president of a large corporation in Toronto, preparing for a crucial meeting. She's an ambitious and talented woman who doesn't plan on making vice-president her final stop on the corporate ladder. She has her eye on the CEO's job, and this meeting is an important step in that direction. Then she gets an urgent call from Saskatoon, saying her mother has just broken her hip. Forget the big meeting: Mom needs her now more than ever, and she's on the next plane to Saskatoon. For the next few years, a great deal of her time and energy will be devoted to her mother. Because of real-life scenarios like this, many women who have the ability to make it to the top in business and government are not going to get there.

WORLD WAR I (1915 TO 1919)

It's always an advantage to be part of a small cohort. That's why even a small difference in one's date of birth can make a big difference in life. If you were born in 1910, you were part of a big cohort. If you were born in 1917, you were part of a smaller group. That in itself was no guarantee of success, but it was an important advantage. It meant you were in a smaller class at school and therefore had more attention from the teacher. And when it was time to go out to work, there were fewer competitors for what jobs were available.

During World War I, many Canadian men went off to battle and, as a result, many Canadian women stopped having babies. That's why people born in the last half of the teens of this century have enjoyed the lifelong advantage of having little peer-group competition. On the other hand, they entered the workforce while Canada was still in the grip of the Great Depression and jobs were few. After that, their careers were disrupted by World War II. Even so, they were better off than those born a few years earlier, who were part of a larger group and had to establish careers during the Depression. In 1996, 589,000 members of this cohort live in Canada. In general, people born in the second part of the teens have done better than those born just before.

THE ROARING TWENTIES (1920 TO 1929)

10   When the boys came home from the war, they quickly made up for lost time, with the result that lots of babies were produced during the 1920s. These offspring of the Roaring Twenties are young seniors in the mid-1990s and, despite the lifelong disadvantage of being part of a large cohort, they've had a pretty good run. Some of them went overseas to fight in World War II, which had the result of reducing competition for jobs for those who remained in Canada.

11   Moreover, because of the war effort the economy was growing, and so the 1920s kids had a better chance to get established than those born in the 1910s. The Roaring Twenties generation also helped to produce the baby boom that began in 1947. The boomers proceeded to drive up the price of the real estate and other assets that the kids of both the 1910s and 1920s owned. So, in general, these people have done well but, because they were members of a large flock, numbering almost 2 million in 1996, not as well as the favoured group that followed them.

THE DEPRESSION BABIES (1930 TO 1939)

12   In hard economic times, many Canadians couldn't afford children, and so fertility declined. The lucky ones who were born then became the golden group of Canadian society. Although they had a tough start, they have subsequently lived a life of incredible good fortune. These are the people entering senior citizenship during the mid-1990s, and yet again their timing is flawless: they are going to have free banking, reduced theatre ticket prices, and all the other breaks our society gives to seniors, because it will be several years yet before the dispensers of these perks wake up and realize that today's youngest seniors are the cohort least in need of such advantages.

13   The Depression kids haven't always had it easy. The 1930s were a time of hardship for everyone, including young children. They lived through World War II, hardly a carefree time to be alive. Because of their youth, they didn't have to serve in the war. But once the war ended, everything went their way. Entering the workforce during the postwar reconstruction of the 1950s, they never had to worry about finding a job. On the contrary, they had their choice of jobs. They never had to worry about being promoted; rather, they were promoted faster than they ever expected to be. Because they were doing so well, they went out and got more of everything, including kids. The Depression kids gave us the baby boom because they could afford a house full of children on only one salary.

Most of them had three or four children, and that was the best 14
investment they could have made. Their kids sent real estate prices into
the stratosphere in the 1980s, and subsequently they boosted the value
of their parents' stock market holdings. Recently, some Depression kids
have been cashing in these assets, using the proceeds to bolster their
retirement nest eggs as well as for travel.

In 1996, 2.5 million Depression kids are living in Canada and still 15
doing pretty well for themselves. They are holding down many of the
senior jobs in this country — in government, in business, in major
educational and other institutions. Some of them are smart and capable and some of them aren't. Few of them realize how much they
owe their success to being part of a small cohort that has always been in
the right place at the right time.

WORLD WAR II (1940 TO 1946)

For those who postponed having children because of the Depression, 16
the biological clock was running out by the end of the 1930s and the
early years of the 1940s. Then the war kick-started the economy — and
the fertility rate. Canada, away from the main arenas of war, was a
pretty good place to be. Canadians had plenty of food and jobs were
plentiful. And so maternity wards started to fill up again. These wartime babies, the pre-boomers, number 2.2 million in 1996. They aren't
as prosperous as the 1930s generation before them because more of
them were born during each year. (The total number of Depression
kids is larger because their cohort spans ten years, compared with only
seven for the children of World War II.) On the other hand, the war
babies haven't had nearly as much peer-group competition as those
born in the following decade; so by comparison with everyone except
the Depression kids, they've done extremely well.

Why did Canada experience a decline in births during World War I 17
and an increase in births during World War II? A larger percentage of
Canadian men went overseas during World War I than in World War II,
and many more lost their lives: 60,661 in World War I, compared with
42,042 in World War II. Moreover, in August 1918, almost as many
Canadians were killed by a worldwide influenza epidemic as fell victim
to enemy fire during the war. Both calamities reduced the numbers of
Canadians in the child-producing age groups. Another reason for the
difference was that while World War I followed a period of prosperity
and high fertility, World War II followed the Depression. People had
been postponing having families in the 1930s, and those in a position
to start having children during World War II were eager to do so. Yet
another reason was that Canada's economy got a bigger boost from
World War II than from World War I. During World War II Canada

became a major producer of ships, cargo carriers, aircraft, tanks, and other military vehicles. As a result, Canadian incomes rose, and rising incomes always mean increased demand for everything, including children.

THE BABY BOOM (1947 TO 1966)

18   Even people with no knowledge of demographics have heard of the group born from 1947 to 1966. These are the baby-boomers. Some members of this particular cohort seem to think they are pretty special. To hear them talk, you'd think they were the most innovative and creative bunch of people Canada had ever seen, infusing all of society with new ways of thinking and new ways of doing things. This is nonsense. In fact, when they were 20, baby-boomers weren't much different from the 20-year-olds who had preceded them. And now that many of them are in their late 40s, they are behaving just as middle-aged people have always behaved.

19   The only thing special about the baby-boomers is that there are so many of them. It seems hard to imagine now, but at the height of the boom, Canadian women were averaging four offspring each. Canada produced more than 400,000 new Canadians in each year of the baby boom, peaking at 479,000 in 1959. But examining Canadian births alone isn't sufficient to define the baby boom. The largest single-year age group in Canada in the mid-1990s is those born in 1961, even though 3,600 fewer people were born here in that year than in 1959. That's because the 1961 group includes immigrants born in that year somewhere else. The most important demographic fact about 35-year-olds is how many of them there are in Canada in 1996, not how many people were born in Canada in 1961. The baby boom, both those born in Canada and those born elsewhere, totals 9.8 million people in 1996, almost 33% of the Canadian population.

20   Canada's was the loudest baby boom in the industrialized world. In fact, only three other Western countries — the United States, Australia, and New Zealand — had baby booms. Part of the reason was that these four countries were immigrant receivers, and immigrants tend to be in their 20s, the prime childbearing years. The U.S. boom started earlier, in 1946, and it also ended earlier, in 1964. That's why American periodicals in 1996 are full of articles about baby-boomers turning 50, an event that will be delayed until 1997 in Canada.

21   At its peak in 1957, the U.S. boom hit 3.7 children per family, nearly half a baby fewer than Canadian women were producing at the peak of the Canadian boom. The Americans started their boom earlier because more of their war effort was in the Pacific, and the Pacific war wound down sooner. The U.S. troops were brought home in 1945 and kids

started appearing in 1946. Canadian troops came home later, so Canadian births did not leap upwards until 1947. As for the Australians, they never got much higher than three babies per woman, but they compensated by continuing their boom ten years longer than Canada did. That happened because Australians were slower to adopt the birth-control pill and because Australian women were slower than their North American counterparts to enter the workforce in large numbers.

Because the Canadian baby boom was so big, Canadian boomers are a slightly more important factor in Canadian life than American boomers are in American life. Fully one-third of Canadians today are boomers, and for that reason alone, when they get interested in a particular product or idea, we all have to sit up and take notice. It's not that the product or idea is so great, it's just that everyone seems to be talking about it. The result is that phenomena such as the return to "family values" are often mistakenly identified as new social trends rather than the predictable demographic events they really are. (There is nothing new or remarkable about 35-year-olds raising families being interested in family values.) 22

Why did the baby boom happen? A likely explanation is that during those 20 years, Canadians knew they could afford large families. The postwar economy was robust, the future seemed full of promise, and young couples wanted to share that bright future with a big family. A second reason was the high immigration levels that prevailed during the 1950s; immigrants tend to be people of childbearing age, and they made an important contribution to the boom. The combination of two ingredients — lots of people in their high fertility years and high incomes — is a surefire recipe for filling up maternity wards. But you need both: immigration levels were raised in the early years of the 1990s but the fertility rate didn't respond because incomes were falling, and Canadians, immigrants and non-immigrants alike, didn't think they could afford extra mouths to feed. 23

Why did the boom end? Towards the end of the 1960s, an increasing number of women were pursuing higher education or entering the workforce. As a result, they were postponing childbirth and deciding to have fewer children. The introduction of the birth-control pill made this easier than ever to achieve. The more rapid acceptance of the pill in the United States may explain why the American boom ended before Canada's. 24

Like the seniors, the boomers break down into separate sub-groups. The front-end boomer, pushing 50, with a bulging waistline and equally bulging Registered Retirement Savings Plan, doesn't share much in the way of cultural attitudes or life experiences with the Generation-Xer, in his early 30s, whose career hasn't yet got off the ground and who has 25 trouble scraping up rent money every month. But as boomers, they have one very important thing in common: they are part of a huge cohort. For the front-end boomers, this was an advantage they could exploit. For the back-end boomers of Generation X, it is the cause of most of their problems.

26   It's important to grasp this point because the mass media have thoroughly confused it. Newspaper articles often mix up Generation X with the baby-bust generation that followed it. Well into the 1990s, the media are still calling Gen-Xers "twenty-somethings" even though most of them have already celebrated their 30th birthdays. Some writers are so confused they seem to think Generation X is the children of the boomers. But it isn't. Most boomers weren't yet old enough to have children when Generation X came along. To clarify matters, we'll look at the characteristics of each subgroup of boomers in turn.

27   The front-end boomers have done pretty well for themselves. There are a lot of them, so they had to compete for jobs when they entered the workforce over the 1960s. But the entry of vast numbers of younger baby-boomers into the marketplace through the 1970s and 1980s created wonderful opportunities for the front-enders already entrenched in business and government. New products, new services, new government programs, new universities — it was a period of seemingly endless expansion. The front-end boomers got there first, so they are the ones in good jobs now in both the public and private sectors. They understand the needs of the baby boom because they are the leading edge of it.

28   Those born towards the end of the 1950s also understand the baby boom but, unlike the front-enders, they are less well positioned to profit from that knowledge. Generally, most members of this boomer subgroup have just managed to get a house. But that house is in the suburbs, and during the first part of the 1990s, its value crashed as the peak of the boom passed through its prime purchasing years. Most of these people are in a career, but that career seems to be going nowhere because the rungs ahead of them are clogged with older boomers who are still 15 to 20 years from retirement.

29   Things are tough for the late-1950s group, but not nearly as bad as for the back end that arrived just after them. These are the 2.6 million people born from 1960 to 1966. They are the same age as the characters in Douglas Coupland's novel *Generation X*, which gave the early-1960s group its name. Many of them are still living at home with their parents because, faced with horrendous obstacles in the labour market, they haven't been able to get their careers on track. That is why, while front-end boomers were earning 30% more than their fathers by age 30, back-enders were making 10% less than their fathers at the same age.

Gen-Xers' life experience has led them to distrust any sort of large ₃₀
institution, whether in the public or private sector. It didn't take them
long to learn that, in an overcrowded world, they had no choice but to
"look out for number one." On their first day in kindergarten, the Gen-
Xers discovered there weren't enough seats for them. In elementary
school, many of them were squeezed into portables. They have been
part of a crowd every since. Whether it was trying to enrol in a ballet
class, get into a summer camp, or find a part-time job, waiting lists have
been a way of life for Generation X.

The millions of baby-boomers who preceded them drove up rents, ₃₁
drove up house prices, and claimed all the best jobs and opportunities.
As if that weren't enough, the Gen-Xers entered the labour market in
the late 1970s and early 1980s, just when a brutal recession gripped the
Canadian economy. In the best of circumstances, there would have
been few jobs; in the recession there were virtually none. And when
economic recovery finally began to create new demand for labour, the
Gen-Xers were told they were too old for entry-level jobs and too short
of experience for more senior ones. Is it any wonder we have 30-year-
olds living at home in the mid-1990s?

One of the worst things the Gen-Xers have to cope with is their ₃₂
parents — the Depression generation. These are the 55-to-60-year-olds
sitting at the top of the corporate ladder, approaching the end of very
successful careers, and unable to fathom why their 30-year-old offspring
are living at home. Tension is tremendous in these families. Often the
father is certain that his own success is based solely on his own merit
while he sees his son's failure as a result of lack of drive and ambition.

THE BABY BUST (1967 TO 1979)

The commercial introduction of the birth-control pill in 1961 and the ₃₃
rising participation of women in the labour market led to declining
fertility over the 1960s. The result was a decline in births and a smaller
cohort, often called the baby bust. In 1996, 5.4 million Canadians are
in this cohort. The baby-busters have done pretty well so far, especially
the younger ones. They have been able to get into just about any school
or summer camp they wanted. They had no difficulty finding babysitting,
lawn-mowing, and other part-time jobs in high school, unlike their
older brothers and sisters, who had less opportunity to earn money
while in high school because they had so many competitors. During the
1990s, university entry standards have been falling, making it easier for
busters to get into the school of their choice.

There is good reason for the twenty-something of the mid-1990s to ₃₄
be both more realistic and more idealistic than the thirty-something of

Generation X. In fact, the baby-busters resemble the front-end boomers, who could espouse idealistic causes during the 1960s safe in the knowledge that a good job and a prosperous lifestyle would be there for the taking once they were ready for those bourgeois things. But the back-end boomers, as we have seen, had no choice but to look out for their own best interests. They were less idealistic than their elders, not because they were worse people but because they couldn't afford to be idealistic. In contrast, the baby-busters have had a pretty good life so far, and when the world has treated you well, you have the luxury of being able to pay attention to social issues, such as peace, the environment, and AIDS, and therefore are more inclined to do so.

35   That's not to say there are no similarities between the Gen-Xers and the baby-busters. Both groups started their working careers in tough economic times when corporations were more interested in trimming payrolls than in hiring new staff. As a result, the older baby-busters face the same problems and frustrations that Generation X knows so well. But when the economy turns around, the 20-year-old with minimal experience will have better prospects than the 30-year-old with minimal experience. That's partly because employers usually prefer younger people for entry-level positions, because they are cheaper and more adaptable; partly because there are fewer busters than Gen-Xers; and partly because the busters are better equipped than the Gen-Xers with the computer skills that today's job market demands.

THE BABY-BOOM ECHO (1980 TO 1995)

36   These are the children of the boomers. The boomers were already having children in the 1970s, but by 1980 enough of them were reproducing to produce a mini-boom of their own. The boomers, however, never matched the reproductive prowess of their parents. At its peak, in 1990, the echo produced 406,000 babies from a population of 27.7 million, compared with 479,000 from a population of only 17.5 million in 1959. This generation is most noticeable in Ontario and western Canada. Quebec and the Atlantic provinces (except for Halifax) haven't had much of a baby-boom echo because so many of their boomers moved to Ontario and the western provinces and had their children there. So the echo won't have as much impact on society in eastern Canada as it will in Ontario and the west.

37   As of 1996, there are 6.9 million members of the echo generation. The boomers haven't finished having children, but over the remaining years of the decade the echo will dwindle to an end. This is predictable because most boomer women are past their prime childbearing years. Even if these women now decide they want big families, they won't be able to have them because they are too old.

What is the outlook for the echo kids? It won't be quite as smooth sailing as the baby-busters have had, but it won't be as disastrous as for Generation X either. These echo kids are part of a large cohort and that's always bad news. They crowded nurseries in the 1980s, pushed elementary school enrolments up in the late 1980s, and are about to do the same for high school enrolments in the mid-1990s. Like the baby boom, the echo has a front end, born in the 1980s, that will have an easier ride than its back end, born in the first half of the 1990s. The latter group, Generation X-II, will experience the familiar disadvantages of arriving at the rear of a large cohort. Think of a cohort as a group of people all wanting to get into the same theatre to see the same show. There is no reserved seating. So who claims the best seats? The ones who get there first. The back end of the echo generation, Gen X-II, will have a life experience similar to that of its parents, the first Generation X. Just as the first Gen-Xers have done, Gen X-II will have to scramble. ₃₈

However, Gen X-II should be better prepared than its parents were to cope with high youth unemployment and other difficulties associated with a large cohort. That's because these kids have their Gen-X parents to teach them. By contrast, the original Generation X was the offspring of a small cohort that wasn't equipped to prepare them for the difficult world they encountered when they left home in the early 1980s. ₃₉

THE FUTURE (1995 TO 2010)

These are the millennium kids, the generation that is following the baby-boom echo. The women producing them are the baby-busters, a cohort 19% smaller in each year than the baby-boomers and 45% smaller in total. Because of immigration, the millennium kids won't necessarily be 45% fewer than the echo kids, but they will definitely be a smaller group. As a result, as this book goes to press, we see another small, and therefore favoured, cohort emerging from Canada's maternity wards. ₄₀

△ △

Explorations:

David Foot with Daniel Stoffman, *Boom, Bust & Echo: How to Profit from the Coming Demographic Shift*
Douglas Coupland, *Generation X* (novel)
Jeremy Rifkin, *The End of Work: The Decline of the Global Labor Force and the Dawn of the Post-Market Era*
http://www.footwork.com

Structure:

1. David Foot divides the Canadian population by age group. Does each *category* follow this criterion? Has any category been left out? Do any of the "cohorts" overlap? Is nine "cohorts" too many to manage in this *classification*? Are the categories presented in a logical order?
2. Why are some of the categories larger than others?
3. Examine the *chronological order* that underlies Foot's *classification*. Can you think of any other way to clearly organize the nine parts?
4. What is Foot's THESIS STATEMENT?
5. Foot *classifies* by age group. Look around you. Think of ten other criteria for *class*ifying the population group of your own *class*. Which ways are relevant? Which, though they may be logical, are insignificant or even undesirable?
6. In paragraph 2, before discussing the average traits of each "cohort," Foot and Stoffman point out "the 70-year-old who continues a lifelong pursuit of rock climbing" and "the 12-year-old who prefers opera to rock music." Why? Do these exceptions help the authors avoid STEREOTYPING by age? Now do the same: describe one older person you know who enjoys a "younger" activity, and one younger person who enjoys an "older" activity.
7. In his analysis how much does Foot use *cause and effect*? See especially paragraphs 5–6, 8–9, 15, 17 and 21.

Style:

1. Does this selection seem like the writing of an economist and professor? How long are its sentences? How scholarly or technical is its vocabulary? What AUDIENCE do you conclude Foot and Stoffman were aiming for?
2. Identify the *analogy* in paragraph 38. How does it help explain?

Ideas for Discussion and Writing:

1. Look up "demography" in a desk-size dictionary. From what root words does it come?
2. Does "Boomers and Other Cohorts" make your future seem predetermined? Does the weight of its causality depress you? (For example, reread paragraphs 6–7 about the female vice-president whose caring for her aging mother may prevent her own promotion to CEO.) Or do you sense opportunity? Tell the class of any changes in life strategy you are likely to make after reading this selection about demographics.
3. *Generation X*, a novel by Canadian Douglas Coupland, first defined that term. Have you read it? How are the "Gen-Xers" you know

doing by now? To which "cohort" do you belong, yourself? How is it doing so far?

4. Should the generations bear more responsibility for each other? For example if seniors of a certain age have had an easy time and are now high rollers, should they be more heavily taxed, as Foot has suggested elsewhere, to help their children and grandchildren who have grown up in tougher times?

5. Around the world, business and investment analysts seize on analysis such as that of David Foot, or of futurists like Faith Popcorn and Jeremy Rifkin, to exploit trends and grow rich. Is their strategy cynical and corrupt, or just good common sense? Do ideas for their own sake excite you, or do you need practical applications before getting interested? Defend your view with reasons.

6. **PROCESS IN WRITING:** *Using a simple chronological framework, like Foot's,* classify *the student body of your school by year (one "cohort" for each year). Now that the easy part is done, focus further: by what criterion will these "cohorts" be examined: Academic achievement? Success in sports? Richness of social life? Economic status achieved by part-time jobs? Or what else? You decide, do a page of brainstorming, then, looking it over, choose a THESIS STATEMENT. Now do a fast discovery draft. Later look it over: Does every part support the main idea? Is there a TRANSITION between the discussion of each year? Is your paper long enough to be helped by subtitles, like the ones Foot has used? Have you, like Foot, crammed your analysis with* examples*? Most importantly, does each section analyze the students by the same criterion, so your paper is logical? Finally, check for spelling and punctuation before printing out your best version.*

Note: See also the Topics for Writing at the end of this chapter.

Topics for Writing
Chapter 7: Classification

Develop one of the following topics into an essay of classification. (See also the guidelines that follow.)

1. Internet Users
2. Salespersons
3. Martial Arts
4. Street People
5. Concerts
6. Television Commercials
7. Gamblers
8. Coaches
9. Drinkers
10. Bullies
11. Dancers
12. Teachers
13. Jazz
14. Drivers
15. Neighbours
16. Parties
17. Board Games
18. Bosses
19. Roommates
20. Mutual Funds
21. Hair Styles
22. Sports Fans
23. Parents
24. Music Lovers
25. Enemies
26. Sexism
27. Television Watchers
28. Dates
29. Chat Rooms
30. Interviews

Note also the Process in Writing topic after each selection in this chapter.

Process in Writing: Guidelines

Follow at least some of these steps in writing your essay of classification (your teacher may suggest which ones).

1. *Write a short outline, since the logic of classifying is difficult. Once you have chosen the principle on which to classify your topic, decide on the categories. Then ask: Do all relate to the same principle? If not, revise. Do any categories overlap? If so, revise. Is an obvious category missing? Add it.*

2. *Write your* THESIS STATEMENT. *Make it a significant point worth discussion.*

3. *Now arrange the categories in some climactic order that supports your thesis statement: smallest to largest, least important to most important, worst to best, etc.*

4. *Write a rapid first draft, not stopping now to revise or edit.*

5. *When this draft has "cooled off," look it over. Does it follow the outline? If not, do the changes make sense? Does every part support the thesis statement? If not, revise the parts, the thesis, or both.*

6. *In your second draft sharpen word choice. Add missing* IMAGES *or examples. Heighten* TRANSITIONS. *Cut deadwood.*

7. *Finally, check for things like spelling and punctuation before you print out your best version. Save it on disk in case your teacher suggests further revision.*

Alex Waterhouse-Hayward

"She was different from some of the other agents we encountered, who drove gold Mercedes and who staggered about in high heels and silk scarves. . . . Laura held my hand when I made the first offer — and my second, third and fourth. . . ."

—*Evelyn Lau, "I Sing the Song of My Condo"*

CHAPTER

8

PROCESS ANALYSIS

Here's how it's done. . .

T hink of the last time you bought something in kit form and tried to assemble it. Maybe you were lucky and everything fit together. More likely, though, you were sweating to make out diagrams that were too small, terminology you did not know, and vague directions that left out steps or got them in the wrong order. With your new exercise machine or computer desk or amplifier lying in parts on the floor, you wondered if you would *ever* get it together. And if you did, there were mysterious parts left over.

In today's world of mega-stores that sell everything from bookcases to bicycles in boxes, we buy things unassembled no matter how poor the directions may be. We also make things from scratch, following how-to-do-it books and magazines that give directions on everything from growing vegetables to building a house. In an age of mass production, we may crave the satisfaction of doing something ourselves. Or, surviving on a budget, we may need to save every cent. But whatever our motivation, do we still have the skills to do all these things our grandparents knew how to do?

Writing that tells us *how* can be called *process analysis*. Sometimes we write an essay that gives what could be called a *directional* process analysis. It is a sort of *narrative*, taking our readers from the beginning to the end of a task, usually in the strict time order required to grow tomatoes, tune up a car or paint a room, not to mention the many other things people do. It includes every step, for each is vital to the success of the project. And if it is written for the amateur, it includes all the details right down to the spacing and depth of seeds in the soil, the choice of motor oil, or the size of paint brush.

Have you ever eaten something so good that you asked for the recipe? An experienced cook has a hard time explaining. Instead of giving quantities, temperatures and measurements of time that we can actually apply, this old pro will say things like "add some yeast" or "now put in a little salt" or "take it out of the oven when it's done." The writer of recipes in a book, though, puts his or her own experience in the background and thinks instead about what the *audience* needs to know. The result is a set of directions so exact that, even if we know little about cooking, the product may actually turn out.

When you are writing directions, on whatever topic, this is the main challenge: keeping your audience in mind. If the subject is your area of expertise, you'll try to take short cuts, skipping details you assume anyone would know. But remember your own encounter with the kit in the middle of the floor. Explain! And when you write from expertise you'll tend to fill your essay with technical terms. But think of the last time you tried to interpret Revenue Canada's directions on your income tax return. If you estimate your readers' level of knowledge and write accordingly, your directions will succeed.

Another kind of process analysis could be called *informational*, for it satisfies not our practical needs but our curiosity. We may enjoy learning how airliners are hijacked, how stockholders are swindled, how El Niño causes tornadoes and floods, how the Second World War was won or how a heart is transplanted — knowing we will never do these things ourselves. Of course not every detail is given in this kind of armchair reading: only as many as it takes to inform and interest the reader. In this chapter Judy Stoffman tells all about aging, a process we do not try to perform, and which in fact most of us resist. Though we need no *directions*, Stoffman knows this is a topic of vital interest to all, so she explains in clear detail how it happens.

Sometimes a writer will use process analysis not to instruct or inform, but as a means to other ends. When Stephen Leacock tells us "How to Live to Be 200," he advises us to eat cement — a strange way to reach the goal — until we see that his goal is not longevity but laughs.

Whether you aim to help the reader accomplish a task, to satisfy the reader's curiosity, or even just to entertain, your process analysis will work only if you realize *why* you are writing it: Are you giving directions? Then follow all the advice above, so your readers' efforts will be successful. Are you just explaining something that occurs, like Stoffman's topic of aging? Or like Dan Strickland's subject of how species in nature prey on each other? Then above all, interest the reader with a multitude of examples, as they do. Are you even just going for laughs, like Leacock? Then do anything that is fun. But even then, you may find yourself making a serious point — like Leacock, who advises us to enjoy life.

Note: For more examples of process analysis, see these essays in other chapters:

Stuart McLean, "The Shocking Truth About Household Dust," p. 153
Mordecai Richler, "1944: The Year I Learned to Love a German,"
    p. 172
Brian Maracle, "Out of Touch and Loving It," p. 200
The Hon. David Lam, "Pulling Together," p. 246

Evelyn Lau

I Sing the Song of My Condo

At age 18 Evelyn Lau caused a sensation with her memoir Runaway: Diary of a Street Kid. *She had grown up in Vancouver, in a middle-class conservative home where her parents had urged her to study hard and become a doctor. From age six, though, Lau knew she wanted to be a writer. When her parents ordered her to stop writing, the honour student left at age 14 for the street, where she spent several years in prostitution, drug addiction and depression. Then one day she entered the office of a literary agent with a 900 page diary of her life as a runaway. It was edited down, published in 1989, became a bestseller, and was made into a two-hour CBC television movie entitled* The Diary of Evelyn Lau. *Today Lau has left the street, makes a living from writing, and has built a reputation as one of the nation's finest crafters of both poetry and prose. Among her subsequent publications are* You Are Not Who You Claim *(poems, 1990),* Oedipal Dreams *(poems, 1992),* In the House of Slaves *(poems, 1994) and* Other Women *(novel, 1995). Though Lau's schooling ended at grade 9, she has educated herself through serious reading, paying close attention to the style, even the sound, of the words on the page. This fine ear for style, and her success in putting it on her own page, shines through the prose of our selection, which appeared in the June 17, 1995,* Globe and Mail.

1   Late in the spring of last year, my fancy turned to thoughts of real estate and I joined the growing ranks of Canadians in their 20s who were looking for their first homes.

2   I had been a renter since I was 16 and I never wanted to deal with a landlord again. Instead, I wanted to know what it was like to worry if I spilled wine on my carpet, to agonize over the exact placement of a picture before pounding a nail in my wall, to open a closet door or rest my forehead against a kitchen cabinet and think, "I own this."

3   I went to the bank with a bundle of tax returns under my arm to prequalify for a first mortgage. After a long meeting during which the bank manager and I peered morosely at a computer screen and juggled numbers for savings, RRSPs and a writer's erratic income into a yearly figure, I walked out with a brochure titled Information for First Homebuyers in my hand.

The people depicted in the brochures were not like anyone I knew. The women were blond, with sunny smiles, and their husbands looked both chiselled and paternal. They were engaged in chummy family activities, like washing the dog or puttering in the garden, with the help of their model children. A white picket fence stood in soft focus in the background.

I knew then I wanted to live in the world of the mortgage brochures, which never showed these middle-class people lying awake among twisted sheets in their new master bedrooms or throwing up into their ceramic sinks from panic at hefty mortgages and rising interest rates. I wanted to sing the love song of the middle class. I wanted this to be the song of myself — a litany of mortgage payments and car payments, the weeping and gnashing at tax time, maximum RRSP payments and mutual funds, credit cards and credit's twin, debt.

Laura Cavanagh, the real-estate agent I acquired through a friend's connections, was an outgoing woman with tanned skin, long hair and hips so slim it seemed impossible she had two teenaged children. The male realtors we met in front of apartment buildings always held her hand for a beat too long and fastened their eyes upon hers with much intent and private meaning.

Together we toured a depressing number of 500-square-foot one-bedrooms listed by young married couples who had just had their first baby. Their apartments smelled of sour milk and spoiled food, and in the bedrooms a crib took up whatever space the double bed did not already occupy. The vendor's agent would gamely point out that new carpets weren't that expensive, really, and if I enlisted the help of friends I could easily strip away the velvet-textured and dung-coloured wallpaper. He would flick on all the light switches and then exclaim, "And look at how bright this unit is!"

I became increasingly dejected at what my savings could afford in Vancouver, when I knew the same amount could buy a house, with acreage attached, in Saskatoon. Laura, however, remained true to her business card's slogan — "The realtor with a positive attitude" — and came to my apartment several times a week to show me yet another suite.

Over the months I grew fond of her. She was different from some of the other agents we encountered, who drove gold Mercedes and who staggered about in high heels and silk scarves, arrived late for appointments and then whipped us through the apartment while their pagers and cell phones incessantly beeped and rang. Laura held my hand when I made my first offer — and my second, third and fourth, all unsuccessfully — and comforted me after I had spent another sleepless night over interest-rate calculations.

10   As summer passed into fall, I discovered that acquiring a real-estate agent was like acquiring a stray kitten or a runaway child — it was a lifetime commitment. She reminded me of little Gertrude in John Cheever's *The Country Husband*, with her uncanny knack of showing up in places I did not expect. I would open my front door on a Saturday morning to pick up the paper and there she would be, showered and perfumed, standing in the hallway and proffering the latest figures on a suite in which I had expressed a moment's interest. See, here's its sales history, its current assessment. Would I like to see it in 15 minutes? She would be wearing such a brave smile that I could only admire her and never find it in my heart to turn her away.

11   Meanwhile, my friends, who were older and therefore wealthier, were actually buying places. I went to a friend's housewarming party with a smile of congratulations on my face and envy in my heart. My former foster parent bought a penthouse with 12-foot ceilings in a new building; another friend purchased an actual house with the help of his well-off parents. I went to a cocktail party at his parents' home, where a hundred guests fit neatly into the kitchen. I was surrounded by half-a-dozen empty bedrooms, Jacuzzis and soaker tubs and murderous chandeliers in the marble foyer. Resentment blazed in me.

12   Now when I walked the streets of Vancouver, I glared up at the high windows of the condominiums and felt the owners were not as special as me, nor as deserving. When I gave poetry readings, I looked out at the audience and wondered how many of them owned their own homes. It came to me that I had rarely wanted anything this much before.

13   One afternoon Laura took me to the opening of a converted building where she said the suites were priced below market value. Balloons were tied to the gates and hedges, and dozens of would-be buyers stood about the grounds, gazing up at the suites with their brochures shielding their eyes.

14   The display suite was bustling with activity — realtors wearing suits and flustered smiles, the women with green eye shadow and trailing a scent of White Shoulders. They paced back and forth with their clients, pulling out calculators to demonstrate price per square foot and the amount of monthly payments. Even as I sat there, someone called out that suite 312 had just been sold and 105 down the hall and they were expecting an offer on 210.

15   The cell phones rang and rang and the anxiety of the buyers became a frenzy of panic. It was a fever that sparked smiles on the faces of the realtors. Offers were recklessly written, and a slim-waisted woman in a floral dress who represented the financing company stepped forward to give or withhold her approval.

16   I was tempted by the display suite, which was small but fully renovated, boasting a marble fireplace and slate tiles. Loden wallpaper in

the bathroom was printed with female Greek statues clutching scraps of fabric to their breasts. I realized that the suite was a good bargain, but as I sat on the rented leather couch I found I could not pull out my chequebook and write an offer, not without at least a night's reflection.

"In all good conscience, I can say you aren't going to lose money on this one," Laura said, but I was immobilized with terror. An hour later she drove me home. I spent the evening drinking heavily and calculating my finances. 17

The suite was priced within my range and by the light of morning I had decided I would make my move. I went back to the suite where I had sat on the couch and looked around my new home — this was where I would put my desk, my bed. I approached the sales agent — a beefy, blond man with a distracted air and an incessantly warbling pager — and said I would buy the display suite. 18

"Oh. That was sold yesterday," the man said, already turning away. 19

I surprised myself with my own reaction — it was grief. I very nearly heard the crack of my heart breaking. This was not the relief I felt when one of my previous offers had fallen through; this was my *home* being taken away. 20

I stumbled out in a daze and walked the three kilometres home, wiping away tears with the back of my hand the whole way. It seemed my song would be a different one after all, it would be the song of Rainer Maria Rilke's *Autumn Day:* "Whoever has no house now will never have one." It was all very well for Rilke — he had owned houses. He had written his famous elegies while staying in Princess Marie von Thurn und Taxis-Hohenloe's castle. I wished bankruptcy, illness and death upon whoever had bought my suite. 21

What surprised me for weeks afterward was how entirely alike this feeling of bereftness was to losing the person you love. Somehow, the real, intelligent, sensible desire to buy a first home and stop paying rent had mutated over the months into an obsession that was like a woman's obsession for a man who had deserted her, whom she could love only at a distance. 22

When I slept I was tortured by dreams in which I walked through beautiful apartments that were within my price range, then just as I pulled out my chequebook I would wake up. Several times I dreamed I bought an apartment with three balcony doors but no balconies, and I knew that one day I would open the doors, step out and fall to my death. In another, I had just moved into a new condominium and discovered that with the removal of the previous owner's furniture and pictures, I could see that the walls were pocked with holes the size of my fist. 23

Over the course of a year, my realtor and I saw 50 suites, I sat on 50 strangers' sofas, looked into their cupboards, sniffed inside their refrig- 24 erators, inspected their drapes and light switches. I checked the drains in their balconies and flushed their toilets. I looked for my own books on their bookshelves and was dismayed by the rows of American bestsellers or educational texts I found there. I peered into their closets and discovered if the owners were people who shopped in vintage stores or Sears or Holt Renfrew.

25   Once I saw the apartment of a little old lady whose obsession was turtles — troops of ceramic, glass and jade turtles filed across every available counter and desktop. She owned an aquarium of turtles, posters of turtles, a bedspread with a turtle stitched on it.

26   After 12 months of searching, I no longer believed I would purchase anything soon. I had visions of my realtor and me setting out at the turn of the millennium to look at our 300th suite.

27   When at last I found the right place, it happened so suddenly that the frustrations of the year vanished overnight. I went to an open house on Sunday and on the Monday Laura presented my offer. It was accepted that afternoon. She stopped by to give me the news and when she came down the hallway her eyes were shining.

28   "You have a home now," she said.

29   The rest of the week flashed by in a blur of telephone calls and meetings with the bank manager. I signed contracts, read bylaws and city council meeting minutes and certified deposit cheques. It was so stressful that I felt disconnected from reality. I vacillated between happiness, numb panic and a great, swelling pride. I had never been in debt for anything before, had never even owned a car or a computer, and now here I was committing myself to a $100,000 mortgage for 650 square feet. I had made a decision that was going to affect the rest of my life.

30   I take possession of the suite at the end of June, just days before my 24th birthday. I may never sleep again. But at last I am a homeowner.

△ △

Explorations:

Evelyn Lau,
    Runaway: Diary of a Street Kid
    Other Women (novel)
    You Are Not Who You Claim (poems)
    In the House of Slaves (poems)
http://www.nt.sympatico.ca/Features/Books/lau.html

Structure:

1. Lau presents her process analysis as a *narrative*, in almost pure chronological order. Identify at least ten words or phrases of TRANSITION (often at the beginnings of paragraphs) that speed us along. Is Lau's organizational choice a good one for her topic of buying real estate?
2. You've just read how Evelyn Lau found and bought her new home. Is her *process analysis* detailed enough that you could now do the same? Or is there more story and entertainment than actual directions? Are there both?
3. In paragraph 22 does Lau go too far in equating a deserted lover with a renter yearning for property? Or has the emotion of her essay risen to the point where this *comparison* works?

Style:

1. Has Lau reached the recommended 50% or higher level of *example* content? In which paragraphs does she offer especially vivid ANECDOTES and SENSE IMAGES? If you didn't know, might you guess from this essay that she also writes poetry and fiction?
2. In paragraph 23 Lau uses the device of dreams to portray her own state of mind. How effective is this passage?
3. Read paragraph 24 aloud in class. Where do you hear repetition? Does it come across as an error of style, or as a deliberate technique? What effect does it have?

Ideas for Discussion and Writing:

1. In paragraphs 3, 12 and 24, Lau hints at the economic perils of her own career as writer. And if you have read her autobiography *Runaway: Diary of a Street Kid*, you know the insecurities of the life she had escaped not long before writing this essay. Do these facts explain the strength of her desire to own a home? Or does everyone want to be an owner? Do you? What are your own future plans for shelter?
2. In the eighties Canadian real estate prices shot up, then in the early nineties fell by about a third. As of this writing, houses and apartments are rising in value but not by much, while lately stocks and bonds have risen faster. Is buying a house or apartment still a good investment? Or is it now more of a lifestyle decision?
3. Lau vividly portrays her real estate agent Laura Cavanagh at work. Now using this example, summarize to the class, in a verbal *process analysis*, how a good agent helps her client find and purchase a property.
4. Are there advantages to renting? Name them. Are there disadvantages? Name them.

5. Lau states that she "had never even owned a car or a computer" (par. 29), yet was now signing a $100,000 mortgage. Is your attitude towards ownership more like that of Lau *before* or *after* her decision to buy real estate? What are your own economic goals as you look into your future?

6. **PROCESS IN WRITING:** *Think about the time you selected and bought one of the following: a computer, a motorcycle, a used car, or a new car. Fill a page with brainstorming. Now look over what you have produced, circle or highlight the best items, and arrange them in a short outline. Do you have all the steps of the* process *you performed? Are they in time order? Do plentiful and exact details — without intimidating jargon — make the* directions *useful to your AUDIENCE? Or if not, are there enough ANECDOTES and ex-*amples *to make your* informational process analysis *entertaining? Now write a quick first draft. The next day look it over. Has it reached the 50% level of* example *content? Have you, like Lau, sped your reader on with TRANSITIONS? Does the whole* process *rise at the end, like hers, to a CLIMAX? Edit for these things, then finally for spelling and punctuation, before you print out your best version.*

Note: See also the Topics for Writing at the end of this chapter.

Stephen Leacock

How to Live to Be 200

During his lifetime Stephen Leacock became the world's best-known humorist writing in English, a Canadian successor to the American writer Mark Twain. Reading in person, Leacock was so funny that once a member of his audience literally died laughing. Though he was for decades Canada's favourite author, Leacock has gradually slipped into neglect. Born in England in 1869, at age six he came with his family to Ontario. He studied at Upper Canada College, the University of Toronto and the University of Chicago, where in 1903 he received a Ph.D. That year McGill hired him to teach economics and political science, and from 1908 till his retirement in 1936, he served as head of his department. He died in 1944. Leacock wrote over 60 books, many on academic subjects, but of course it is for his books of humour that he is remembered. The best-loved have been Literary Lapses *(1910),* Nonsense Novels *(1911),* Sunshine Sketches of a Little Town *(1912),* Arcadian Adventures with the Idle Rich *(1914), and* My Remarkable Uncle and Other Sketches *(1942). Our selection, from a later version of* Literary Lapses, *is vintage Leacock: through exaggeration and incongruities, it reduces to absurdity a topic that many people today, as in Leacock's time, take seriously.*

Twenty years ago I knew a man called Jiggins, who had the Health Habit.

He used to take a cold plunge every morning. He said it opened his pores. After it he took a hot sponge. He said it closed the pores. He got so that he could open and shut his pores at will.

Jiggins used to stand and breathe at an open window for half an hour before dressing. He said it expanded his lungs. He might, of course, have had it done in a shoe-store with a boot stretcher, but after all it cost him nothing this way, and what is half an hour?

After he had got his undershirt on, Jiggins used to hitch himself up like a dog in harness and do Sandow exercises. He did them forwards, backwards, and hind-side up.

He could have got a job as a dog anywhere. He spent all his time at this kind of thing. In his spare time at the office, he used to lie on his stomach on the floor and see if he could lift himself up with his knuckles. If he could, then he tried some other way until he found one that he couldn't do. Then he would spend the rest of his lunch hour on his stomach, perfectly happy.

6   In the evenings in his room he used to lift iron bars, cannon-balls, heave dumb-bells, and haul himself up to the ceiling with his teeth. You could hear the thumps half a mile.

7   He liked it.

8   He spent half the night slinging himself around the room. He said it made his brain clear. When he got his brain perfectly clear, he went to bed and slept. As soon as he woke, he began clearing it again.

9   Jiggins is dead. He was, of course, a pioneer, but the fact that he dumb-belled himself to death at an early age does not prevent a whole generation of young men from following in his path.

10   They are ridden by the Health Mania.

11   They make themselves a nuisance.

12   They get up at impossible hours. They go out in silly little suits and run Marathon heats before breakfast. They chase around barefoot to get the dew on their feet. They hunt for ozone. They bother about pepsin. They won't eat meat because it has too much nitrogen. They won't eat fruit because it hasn't any. They prefer albumen and starch and nitrogen to huckleberry pie and doughnuts. They won't drink water out of a tap. They won't eat sardines out of a can. They won't use oysters out of a pail. They won't drink milk out of a glass. They are afraid of alcohol in any shape. Yes sir, afraid. "Cowards."

13   And after all their fuss they presently incur some simple old-fashioned illness and die like anybody else.

14   Now people of this sort have no chance to attain any great age. They are on the wrong track.

15   Listen. Do you want to live to be really old, to enjoy a grand, green, exhuberant, boastful old age and to make yourself a nuisance to your whole neighbourhood with your reminiscences?

16   Then cut out all this nonsense. Cut it out. Get up in the morning at a sensible hour. The time to get up is when you have to, not before. If your office opens at eleven, get up at ten-thirty. Take your chance on ozone. There isn't any such thing anyway. Or, if there is, you can buy a Thermos bottle full for five cents, and put it on a shelf in your cupboard. If your work begins at seven in the morning, get up at ten minutes to, but don't be liar enough to say that you like it. It isn't exhilarating, and you know it.

17   Also, drop all that cold-bath business. You never did it when you were a boy. Don't be a fool now. If you must take a bath (you don't really need to), take it warm. The pleasure of getting out of a cold bed and creeping into a hot bath beats a cold plunge to death. In any case, stop gassing about your tub and your "shower," as if you were the only man who ever washed.

18   So much for that point.

Next, take the question of germs and bacilli. Don't be scared of them. That's all. That's the whole thing, and if you once get on to that you never need to worry again.

If you see a bacilli, walk right up to it, and look it in the eye. If one flies into your room, strike at it with your hat or with a towel. Hit it as hard as you can between the neck and the thorax. It will soon get sick of that.

But as a matter of fact, a bacilli is perfectly quiet and harmless if you are not afraid of it. Speak to it. Call out to it to "lie down." It will understand. I had a bacilli once, called Fido, that would come and lie at my feet while I was working. I never knew a more affectionate companion, and when it was run over by an automobile, I buried it in the garden with genuine sorrow.

(I admit this is an exaggeration. I don't really remember its name; it may have been Robert.)

Understand that it is only a fad of modern medicine to say that cholera and typhoid and diphtheria are caused by bacilli and germs; nonsense. Cholera is caused by a frightful pain in the stomach, and diphtheria is caused by trying to cure a sore throat.

Now take the question of food.

Eat what you want. Eat lots of it. Yes, eat too much of it. Eat till you can just stagger across the room with it and prop it up against a sofa cushion. Eat everything that you like until you can't eat any more. The only test is, can you pay for it? If you can't pay for it, don't eat it. And listen — don't worry as to whether your food contains starch, or albumen, or gluten, or nitrogen. If you are a damn fool enough to want these things, go and buy them and eat all you want of them. Go to a laundry and get a bag of starch, and eat your fill of it. Eat it, and take a good long drink of glue after it, and a spoonful of Portland cement. That will gluten you, good and solid.

If you like nitrogen, go and get a druggist to give you a canful of it at the soda counter, and let you sip it with a straw. Only don't think that you can mix all these things up with your food. There isn't any nitrogen or phosphorus or albumen in ordinary things to eat. In any decent household all that sort of stuff is washed out in the kitchen sink before the food is put on the table.

And just one word about fresh air and exercise. Don't bother with either of them. Get your room full of good air, then shut up the windows and keep it. It will keep for years. Anyway, don't keep using your lungs all the time. Let them rest. As for exercise, if you have to take it, take it and put up with it. But as long as you have the price of a hack and can hire other people to play baseball for you and run races and do gymnastics when you sit in the shade and smoke and watch them — great heavens, what more do you want?

△△

Explorations:

Stephen Leacock,
> *Sunshine Sketches of a Little Town*
> *Literary Lapses*
> *My Remarkable Uncle and Other Sketches*

Robertson Davies, *Stephen Leacock*
David Staines, *Stephen Leacock: A Reappraisal*
http://www.fitnessonline.com/

Structure:

1. This essay has two main parts. Where do they join? How do they differ?
2. We begin with Jiggins. How is his story organized? Were you surprised at his death in paragraph 9? Why? What literary device lies behind this effect? How does the death of Jiggins lead into Leacock's main argument?
3. Are Leacock's health tips given in order of application?
4. What is our first clue that Leacock's *process analysis* is meant not to instruct but to entertain?

Style:

1. Leacock writes "eat" ten times in paragraph 25. Read the passage aloud in class, with feeling. Is the repetition accidental? What effect does it have? In which other paragraph does Leacock exploit this device?
2. Paragraph 25 states, "That will gluten you, good and solid." What effect does the word "gluten" have here?
3. Reduction to absurdity is a comic device Leacock often uses, as in the "bacilli" as insects to swat or as a favourite dog run over by a car. Where else in this essay has he reduced something to total absurdity?

Ideas for Discussion and Writing:

1. Do you have the "Health Habit," like Jiggins, or do you prefer comfort and luxury, like our narrator? Give reasons.
2. Update Leacock's argument for our times. Which kinds of "Health Mania" would you drop? Which would you keep? Which might you add?
3. To women in the class: why does Leacock refer only to men pursuing the "Health Mania"? Give a *process analysis* of your own actions to keep healthy and fit.

4. **PROCESS IN WRITING:** *Write a* process analysis *of how to reach old age in good health. First brainstorm or freewrite. Then do a rapid "discovery draft," double-spaced. When it has "cooled off," analyze it: Are the steps in order? Are the instructions clear? Have you supplied examples? Revise accordingly. Now sharpen word choice as well. Heighten* TRANSITIONS. *Cut deadwood. Finally, test the prose aloud before writing a good version.*

Note: See also the Topics for Writing at the end of this chapter.

Judy Stoffman

The Way of All Flesh

Currently Judy Stoffman is publishing reporter for the Toronto Star, *though she has also worked for a variety of Canadian magazines, as well as CBC radio and television. At age ten she came from Hungary to Canada, and grew up in Vancouver. Stoffman studied English literature at the University of British Columbia and at Sussex University, England; she studied also in France. Her future seemed decided as early as grade two: when a teacher read her composition on recess to the class, Stoffman knew she would be a writer. Yet she says, "I love the research and dread the writing. Before I start writing I have a kind of stage fright and from talking to other writers I know they have it too, but they persist because when the words finally start to flow there is an exhilaration nothing else can give." Our selection appeared in 1979 in* Weekend Magazine. *To prepare, Stoffman read ten books on aging and interviewed three gerontologists, a family doctor and a sex therapist. "Then," she says, "I tried to synthesize what I had learned, while exploring my own deepest fears." Looking back at her 1979 essay, Stoffman calls it "pretty accurate in terms of my own subsequent experience of aging." Though she looks aging "squarely in the eye," with no attempt to "prettify it," she sees no cause for gloom. Writing the piece gave her "a renewed commitment to enjoy each day to the fullest," and she recommends the same perspective to her readers.*

1   When a man of 25 is told that aging is inexorable, inevitable, universal, he will nod somewhat impatiently at being told something so obvious. In fact, he has little idea of the meaning of the words. It has nothing to do with him. Why should it? He has had no tangible evidence yet that his body, as the poet Rilke said, enfolds old age and death as the fruit enfolds a stone.

2   The earliest deposits of fat in the aorta, the trunk artery carrying blood away from the heart, occur in the eighth year of life, but who can peer into his own aorta at this first sign of approaching debility? The young man has seen old people but he secretly believes himself to be the exception on whom the curse will never fall. "Never will the skin of my neck hang loose. My grip will never weaken. I will stand tall and walk with long strides as long as I live." The young girl scarcely pays

attention to her clothes; she scorns makeup. Her confidence in her body is boundless; smooth skin and a flat stomach will compensate, she knows, for any lapses in fashion or grooming. She stays up all night, as careless of her energy as of her looks, believing both will last forever.

In our early 20s, the lung capacity, the rapidity of motor responses and physical endurance are at their peak. This is the athlete's finest hour. Cindy Nicholas of Toronto was 19 when she first swam the English Channel in both directions. The tennis star Bjorn Borg was 23 when he triumphed at Wimbledon for the fourth time.

It is not only *athletic* prowess that is at its height between 20 and 30. James Boswell, writing in his journal in 1763 after he had finally won the favors of the actress Louisa, has left us this happy description of the sexual prowess of a 23-year-old: "I was in full glow of health and my bounding blood beat quick in high alarms. Five times was I fairly lost in supreme rapture. Louisa was madly fond of me; she declared I was a prodigy, and asked me if this was extraordinary in human nature. I said twice as much might be, but this was not, although in my own mind I was somewhat proud of my performance."

In our early 30s we are dumbfounded to discover the first grey hair at the temples. We pull out the strange filament and look at it closely, trying to grasp its meaning. It means simply that the pigment has disappeared from the hair shaft, never to return. It means also — but this thought we push away — that in 20 years or so we'll relinquish our identity as a blonde or a redhead. By 57, one out of four people is completely grey. Of all the changes wrought by time this is the most harmless, except to our vanity.

In this decade one also begins to notice the loss of upper register hearing, that is, the responsiveness to high frequency tones, but not all the changes are for the worse, not yet. Women don't reach their sexual prime until about 38, because their sexual response is learned rather than innate. The hand grip of both sexes increases in strength until 35, and intellectual powers are never stronger than at that age. There is a sense in the 30s of hitting your stride, of coming into your own. When Sigmund Freud was 38 an older colleague, Josef Breuer, wrote: "Freud's intellect is soaring at its highest. I gaze after him as a hen at a hawk."

Gail Sheehy in her book *Passages* calls the interval between 35 and 45 the Deadline Decade. It is the time we begin to sense danger. The body continually flashes us signals that time is running out. We must perform our quaint deeds, keep our promises, get on with our allotted tasks.

Signal: The woman attempts to become pregnant at 40 and finds she cannot. Though she menstruates each month, menstruation being merely the shedding of the inner lining of the womb, she may not be ovulating regularly.

9   Signal: Both men and women discover that, although they have not changed their eating habits over the years, they are much heavier than formerly. The man is paunchy around the waist; the woman no longer has those slim thighs and slender arms. A 120-pound woman needs 2,000 calories daily to maintain her weight when she is 25, 1,700 to maintain the same weight at 45, and only 1,500 calories at 65. A 170-pound man needs 3,100 calories daily at 25, 300 fewer a day at 45 and 450 calories fewer still at 65. This decreasing calorie need signals that the body consumes its fuel ever more slowly; the cellular fires are damped and our sense of energy diminishes.

10   In his mid-40s the man notices he can no longer run up the stairs three at a time. He is more easily winded and his joints are not as flexible as they once were. The strength of his hands has declined somewhat. The man feels humiliated: "I will not let this happen to me. I will turn back the tide and master my body." He starts going to the gym, playing squash, lifting weights. He takes up jogging. Though he may find it neither easy nor pleasant, terror drives him past pain. A regular exercise program can retard some of the symptoms of aging by improving the circulation and increasing the lung capacity, thereby raising our stamina and energy level, but no amount of exercise will make a 48-year-old 26 again. Take John Keeley of Mystic, Connecticut. In 1957, when he was 26, he won the Boston marathon with a time of 2:20. In 1979, fit and 48, he was as fiercely competitive as ever, yet it took him almost 30 minutes longer to run the same marathon.

11   In the middle of the fourth decade, the man whose eyesight has always been good will pick up a book and notice that he is holding it farther from his face than usual. The condition is presbyopia, a loss of the flexibility of the lens which makes adjustment from distant to near vision increasingly difficult. It's harder now to zoom in for a closeup. It also takes longer for the eyes to recover from glare; between 16 and 90, recovery time from exposure to glare is doubled every 13 years.

12   In our 50s, we notice that food is less and less tasty; our taste buds are starting to lose their acuity. The aged Queen Victoria was wont to complain that strawberries were not as sweet as when she was a girl.

13   Little is known about the causes of aging. We do not know if we are born with a biochemical messenger programed to keep the cells and tissues alive, a messenger that eventually gets lost, or if there is a 'death hormone,' absent from birth but later secreted by the thymus or by the mysterious pineal gland, or if, perhaps, aging results from a fatal flaw in the body's immune system. The belief that the body is a machine whose parts wear out is erroneous, for the machine does not have the body's capacity for self-repair.

14   "A man is as old as his arteries," observed Sir William Osler. From the 50s on, there's a progressive hardening and narrowing of the arteries

due to the gradual lifelong accumulation of calcium and fats along the arterial walls. Arteriosclerosis eventually affects the majority of the population in the affluent countries of the West. Lucky the man or woman who, through a combination of good genes and good nutrition, can escape it, for it is the most evil change of all. As the flow of blood carrying oxygen and nutrients to the muscles, the brain, the kidneys and other organs diminishes, these organs begin to starve. Although all aging organs lose weight, there is less shrinkage of organs such as the liver and kidneys, the cells of which regenerate, than there is shrinkage of the brain and the muscles, the cells of which, once lost, are lost forever.

For the woman it is now an ordeal to be asked her age. There is a fine tracery of lines around her eyes, a furrow in her brow even when she smiles. The bloom is off her cheeks. Around the age of 50 she will buy her last box of sanitary pads. The body's production of estrogen and progesterone, which govern menstruation (and also help to protect her from heart attack and the effects of stress), will have ceased almost completely. She may suffer palpitations, suddenly break into a sweat; her moods may shift abruptly. She looks in the mirror and asks, "Am I still a woman?" Eventually she becomes reconciled to her new self and even acknowledges its advantages: no more fears about pregnancy. "In any case," she laughs, "I still have not bad legs." 15

The man, too, will undergo a change. One night in his early 50s he has some trouble achieving a complete erection, and his powers of recovery are not what they once were. Whereas at 20 he was ready to make love again less than half an hour after doing so, it may now take two hours or more; he was not previously aware that his level of testosterone, the male hormone, has been gradually declining since the age of 20. He may develop headaches, be unable to sleep, become anxious about his performance, anticipate failure and so bring on what is called secondary impotence — impotence of psychological rather than physical origin. According to Masters and Johnson, 25 percent of all men are impotent by 65 and 50 percent by 75, yet this cannot be called an inevitable feature of aging. A loving, undemanding partner and a sense of confidence can do wonders. "The susceptibility of the human male to the power of suggestion with regard to his sexual prowess," observe Masters and Johnson, "is almost unbelievable." 16

After the menopause, the woman ages more rapidly. Her bones start to lose calcium, becoming brittle and porous. The walls of the vagina become thinner and drier, sexual intercourse now may be painful unless her partner is slow and gentle. The sweat glands begin to atrophy and the sebaceous glands that lubricate the skin decline; the complexion becomes thinner and drier and wrinkles appear around the mouth. The skin, which in youth varies from about one-fiftieth of an inch on 17 the eyelids to about a third of an inch on the palms and the soles of the feet, loses 50 percent of its thickness between the ages of 20 and 80. The woman no longer buys sleeveless dresses and avoids shorts. The girl who once disdained cosmetics is now a woman whose dressing table is covered with lotions, night creams and makeup.

18   Perhaps no one has written about the sensation of nearing 60 with more brutal honesty than the French novelist Simone de Beauvoir: "While I was able to look at my face without displeasure, I gave it no thought. I loathe my appearance now: the eyebrows slipping down toward the eyes, the bags underneath, the excessive fullness of the cheeks and the air of sadness around the mouth that wrinkles always bring. . . . Death is no longer a brutal event in the far distance; it haunts my sleep."

19   In his early 60s the man's calves are shrunken, his muscles stringy looking. The legs of the woman, too, are no longer shapely. Both start to lose their sense of smell and both lose most of the hair in the pubic area and the underarms. Hair, however, may make its appearance in new places, such as the woman's chin. Liver spots appear on the hands, the arms, the face; they are made of coagulated melanin, the coloring matter of the skin. The acid secretions of the stomach decrease, making digestion slow and more difficult.

20   Halfway through the 60s comes compulsory retirement for most men and working women, forcing upon the superannuated worker the realization that society now views him as useless and unproductive. The man who formerly gave orders to a staff of 20 now finds himself underfoot as his wife attempts to clean the house or get the shopping done. The woman fares a little better since there is a continuity in her pattern of performing a myriad of essential household tasks. Now they must both set new goals or see themselves wither mentally. The unsinkable American journalist I. F. Stone, when he retired in 1971 from editing *I. F. Stone's Weekly*, began to teach himself Greek and is now reading Plato in the original. When Somerset Maugham read that the Roman senator Cato the Elder learned Greek when he was 80, he remarked: "Old age is ready to undertake tasks that youth shirked because they would take too long."

21   However active we are, the fact of old age can no longer be evaded from about 65 onward. Not everyone is as strong minded about this as de Beauvoir was. When she made public in her memoirs her horror at her own deterioration, her readers were scandalized. She received hundreds of letters telling her that there is no such thing as old age, that some are just younger than others. Repeatedly she heard the hollow reassurance, "You're as young as you feel." But she considered this a lie. Our subjective reality, our inner sense of self, is not the only reality. There is also an objective reality, how we are seen by society. We receive

our revelation of old age from others. The woman whose figure is still trim may sense that a man is following her in the street; drawing abreast, the man catches sight of her face — and hurries on. The man of 68 may be told by a younger woman to whom he is attracted: "You remind me of my father."

Madame de Sévigné, the 17th-century French writer, struggled to rid herself of the illusion of perpetual youth. At 63 she wrote: "I have been dragged to this inevitable point where old age must be undergone: I see it there before me; I have reached it; and I should at least like so to arrange matters that I do not move on, that I do not travel further along this path of the infirmities, pains, losses of memory and the disfigurement. But I hear a voice saying: 'You must go along, whatever you may say; or indeed if you will not then you must die, which is an extremity from which nature recoils.'" 22

Now the man and the woman have their 70th birthday party. It is a sad affair because so many of their friends are missing, felled by strokes, heart attacks or cancers. Now the hands of the clock begin to race. The skeleton continues to degenerate from loss of calcium. The spine becomes compressed and there is a slight stoop nothing can prevent. Inches are lost from one's height. The joints may become thickened and creaking; in the morning the woman can't seem to get moving until she's had a hot bath. She has osteoarthritis. This, like the other age-related diseases, arteriosclerosis and diabetes, can and should be treated, but it can never be cured. The nails, particularly the toenails, become thick and lifeless because the circulation in the lower limbs is now poor. The man has difficulty learning new things because of the progressive loss of neurons from the brain. The woman goes to the store and forgets what she has come to buy. The two old people are often constipated because the involuntary muscles are weaker now. To make it worse, their children are always saying, "Sit down, rest, take it easy." Their digestive tract would be toned up if they went for a long walk or even a swim, although they feel a little foolish in bathing suits. 23

In his late 70s, the man develops glaucoma, pressure in the eyeball caused by the failure of the aqueous humour to drain away; this can now be treated with a steroid related to cortisone. The lenses in the eyes of the woman may thicken and become fibrous, blurring her vision. She has cataracts, but artificial lenses can now be implanted using cryosurgery. There is no reason to lose one's sight just as there's no reason to lose one's teeth; regular, lifelong dental care can prevent tooth loss. What can't be prevented is the yellowing of teeth, brought about by the shrinking of the living chamber within the tooth which supplies the outer enamel with moisture. 24

Between 75 and 85 the body loses most of its subcutaneous fat. On her 80th birthday the woman's granddaughter embraces her and mar- 25 vels: "How thin and frail and shrunken she is! Could this narrow, bony chest be the same warm, firm bosom to which she clasped me as a child?" Her children urge her to eat but she has no enjoyment of food now. Her mouth secretes little saliva, so she has difficulty tasting and swallowing. The loss of fat and shrinking muscles in the 80s diminish the body's capacity for homeostasis, that is, righting any physiological imbalance. The old man, if he is cold, can barely shiver (shivering serves to restore body heat.) If he lives long enough, the man will have an enlarged prostate, which causes the urinary stream to slow to a trickle. The man and the woman probably both wear hearing aids now; without a hearing aid, they hear vowels clearly but not consonants; if someone says "fat," they think they've heard the word "that."

26   At 80, the speed of nerve impulses is 10 percent less than it was at 25, the kidney filtration rate is down by 30 percent, the pumping efficiency of the heart is only 60 percent of what it was, and the maximum breathing capacity, 40 percent.

27   The old couple is fortunate in still being able to express physically the love they've built up over a lifetime. The old man may be capable of an erection once or twice a week (Charlie Chaplin fathered the last of his many children when he was 81), but he rarely has the urge to climax. When he does, he sometimes has the sensation of seepage rather than a triumphant explosion. Old people who say they are relieved that they are now free of the torments of sexual desire are usually the ones who found sex a troublesome function all their lives; those who found joy and renewal in the act will cling to their libido. Many older writers and artists have expressed the conviction that continued sexuality is linked to continued creativity: "There was a time when I was cruelly tormented, indeed obsessed by desire," wrote the novelist André Gide at the age of 73, "and I prayed, 'Oh let the moment come when my subjugated flesh will allow me to give myself entirely to. . . .' But to what? To art? To pure thought? To God? How ignorant I was! How mad! It was the same as believing that the flame would burn brighter in a lamp with no oil left. Even today it is my carnal self that feeds the flame, and now I pray that I may retain carnal desire until I die."

28   Aging, says an American gerontologist, "is not a simple slope which everyone slides down at the same speed; it is a flight of irregular stairs down which some journey more quickly than others." Now we arrive at the bottom of the stairs. The old man and the old woman whose progress we have been tracing will die either of a cancer (usually of the lungs, bowel or intestines) or of a stroke, a heart attack or in consequence of a fall. The man slips in the bathroom and breaks his thigh bone. But worse than the fracture is the enforced bed rest in the hospital which will probably bring on bed sores, infections, further weakening of the

muscles and finally, what Osler called "an old man's best friend": pneumonia. At 25 we have so much vitality that if a little is sapped by illness, there is still plenty left over. At 85 a little is all we have.

And then the light goes out.   29

The sheet is pulled over the face.   30

In the last book of Marcel Proust's remarkable work *Remembrance of Things Past*, the narrator, returning after a long absence from Paris, attends a party of his friends throughout which he has the impression of being at a masked ball: "I did not understand why I could not immediately recognize the master of the house, and the guests, who seemed to have made themselves up, in a way that completely changed their appearance. The Prince had rigged himself up with a white beard and what looked like leaden soles which made his feet drag heavily. A name was mentioned to me and I was dumbfounded at the thought that it applied to the blonde waltzing girl I had once known and to the stout, white-haired lady now walking just in front of me. We did not see our own appearance, but each like a facing mirror, saw the other's." The narrator is overcome by a simple but powerful truth: the old are not a different species. "It is out of young men who last long enough," wrote Proust, "that life makes its old men."   31

The wrinkled old man who lies with the sheet over his face was once the young man who vowed, "My grip will never weaken. I will walk with long strides and stand tall as long as I live." The young man who believed himself to be the exception.   32

△ △

Explorations:

Carol Shields, *The Stone Diaries*
Margaret Laurence, *The Stone Angel*
Michel Tremblay, *Albertine, in Five Times* (theatre)
Ernest Hemingway, *The Old Man and the Sea* (novella)
William Shakespeare, *King Lear*
http://www.fitnessonline.com/
http://www.hwc.ca/datahpsb/seniors/index.htm

Structure:

1. "The Way of All Flesh" is a striking example of chronological order used to organize a mass of information. Point out at least ten words, phrases or sentences that signal the flow of time.

2. Does Stoffman's *process analysis* tell us how to do something, how something is done by others, or how something happens?

3. How long would this essay be if its *examples* were all removed? How interesting would it be? How convincing?
4. What means of logic underlies paragraphs 14 and 16?
5. What effect do we feel when the last paragraph refers to the first paragraph?

Style:

1. Why are paragraphs 29 and 30 so short?
2. How heavily does Stoffman rely on statistics? What do they do for her argument?
3. How heavily does Stoffman rely on quotations? In fact, is this selection a research essay? Why or why not?
4. In a desk-size dictionary, find the origins of the word "gerontologist" (par. 28). How is it related to the words "geriatrics," "Geritol," "gerontocracy," "astrology" and "zoology."

Ideas for Discussion and Writing:

1. Does Stoffman's essay frighten or depress you? If so, is this effect a failure or a success on her part?
2. Is Stoffman's essay one-sided? If she wrote another called "The Joy of Aging," recommend at least five points she could make. Consult your parents or grandparents for examples.
3. One senior athlete told this story: During a routine physical his doctor stated, "Now that you are 40 you will want to stop exercising, because you might strain yourself." The man lived into his late 80s, playing tennis three times a week. What is your response?
4. These days we hear of people in their 50s being given the "golden handshake" as employers downsize; yet many believe they will have to work longer, perhaps till 70, before retiring on the Canada Pension Plan. What do you see as the best retirement age? Under what conditions can early or late retirement hurt people? When can it benefit them? When would you choose to retire, and why?
5. **PROCESS IN WRITING:** *Write a* process analysis *on one of these topics:*
   – How to stay physically fit past 30
   – How to feel worthwhile in old age
   – How to help parents and grandparents be happy in old age
   First visit the Health and Welfare Canada Web site listed in "Explorations," printing out parts relevant to the topic you have selected, or taking notes. Then make more notes from your own thoughts and knowledge. Now scan and sort to choose your points and the order in which they will appear. Write a rapid first draft of your essay. Later, add more TRANSITIONS to speed the chronology of your process. Are there enough IMAGES? Enough concrete ex-

amples? *Do you state your sources? (Your teacher will inform you if formal documentation is required.) Now share a draft with a small group of class members; do they think they could actually follow your directions? If not, clarify weak points. Finally, as someone else reads your best version to the whole class, try to hear it with "new ears," estimating how effective it is for its AUDIENCE.*

Note: See also the Topics for Writing at the end of this chapter.

Dan Strickland

The Last Laugh at Dark-Eyed Susan's Roadside Café

Dan Strickland is Chief Naturalist of Algonquin Provincial Park, the much-loved wilderness of lakes, rocks and forest north of Toronto. Born in 1942, he began as an amateur naturalist, went on to a degree in biochemistry at the University of Toronto, studied at the Université de Strasbourg, then completed an M.Sc. at the Université de Montréal, doing research on the Gray Jay. (He has written further scientific papers on this species, and is the foremost authority on it.) After four summers on the interpretive staff of Quetico Provincial Park, Strickland came in 1965 to Algonquin. Today he could be called the voice of Algonquin Park, for his interpretations to park visitors of its species and its complex ecosystems. He has authored or co-authored many pamphlets, guides and books, such as Fishing in Algonquin Park *(1988),* Birds of Algonquin Park *(1990),* A Pictorial History of Algonquin Park *(1991),* Mammals of Algonquin Provincial Park *(1992),* Wildflowers of Algonquin Provincial Park *(1993), and* Barron Canyon Trail *(1994). Strickland also authors* The Raven, *a weekly park newsletter whose 135,000 copies per year interpret to park visitors a species, an ecosystem, a new discovery of park research and sometimes a tragedy. When a few years ago two German canoeists camping on an island were brutally killed by a bear, it was Strickland whose reasoned dialogue with nature attempted to make sense of the event, examining theories of why the bear stalked them, reviewing other bear attacks, and giving a statistical overview to weigh the dangers for other visitors. Our selection, about much smaller predators, appeared in* The Raven *of August 22, 1996.*

1 Especially at this time of year, we humans are often lulled by the beauty and apparent harmony of nature and we gloss over the fact that pure "selfishness" is a large and unavoidable part of the real world. We admire the family life of a moose and her calf and forget about all the shrubs and young trees that, without a thought, are killed or crippled for life by those very same animals. We chuckle at the antics of young foxes but "forget about" the mother and baby chipmunks ripped apart every day to fuel those shenanigans. And, whenever we actually do face up to the existence of conflicts in nature, we often make the further mistakes of imagining, either that they involve what we humans call

"cruelty", or that all is taking place according to some carefully pre-planned scheme.

We had an excellent reminder of all this not long ago when we stopped along the highway one morning to admire the beautiful stand of Dark-eyed Susans near the entrance to the Lookout Trail. With their large, golden-yellow, daisy-like petals surrounding dark centres (made up of hundreds of tiny separate true flowers), the dozens of flower-heads in the morning sun made a memorably beautiful sight against the lush green background.

Dark-eyed Susans are fairly recent arrivals here, being natives of the prairies out west. Apart from their alien origin, however, they would seem to be a perfect example of what people think of as peace, beauty, and harmony in nature. After all, flowers in general and Dark-eyed Susans in particular are undeniably beautiful to look at and are probably the classic example of "peaceful cooperation" in the natural world. As just about everyone knows, big showy flower heads like those of the Dark-eyed Susan serve to attract insects that then alight on the blossom to feed on the sweet nectar so "thoughtfully" provided by the flower. In return for this service, the insects then transport pollen from one flower head to the next, thereby assuring that the individual plants are cross-pollinated, (which makes for healthier offspring).

This is, indeed, an accepted picture of what we tend to think of as nature's "grand harmonious scheme". But, to the extent that we embrace this view, we are really missing the underlying reality of fundamental "selfishness" in all the actors involved. The fact is that nobody is really doing anybody any favours here. The insects perform their valuable service only because they are bribed with nectar to visit the flowers in the first place and because the details of flower structure and pollen stickiness then result in pollen being attached to the bodies of nectar-drinking bees, beetles and butterflies. As for the flowers, they don't do any more than they have to. They probably wouldn't produce any nectar at all if insects weren't so good at carrying pollen from one blossom to the next. The fact is, however, that nectar-feeding insects are highly efficient (much better than depending on wind, for example) and as long as this is the case the flowers that will do best at getting pollinated and leaving descendants are the ones that give insects some reason (like nectar) for paying them a visit. Even the exact amount of nectar produced is best seen as a compromise between the need to compete with other flowers for the attentions of nectar-transporting insects and the considerable cost of producing the bribe. The point is that it's "strictly business" for both flowers and insects. Although neither are capable of thinking about what they are doing, they each unconsciously act in their own best interests. Any individuals that don't do this will end up leaving fewer descendants than the ones we actually see and the "unbusiness-like" tendency will disappear after a few generations. The appearance of harmony is just the accidental by-product of each actor being unconsciously forced into the best course of action for itself with no regard or knowledge of how it might be affecting others.

5   While we were admiring the Dark-eyed Susans and their busy insect visitors, we saw an even better example of the total lack of consideration of living things for the so-called harmony of the natural world. By the purest of chance our eyes happened to fall on something sitting on the petals of one of the Dark-eyed Susans. Although its golden-yellow colour matched that of the petals almost exactly, we looked closely and saw that it was facing towards the flower head's dark centre and that its two, extremely long front legs were held outstretched and waiting . . .

6   We were looking at a female crab spider. The name comes from the ability of these spiders to scuttle sideways or backwards like a real crab but their most remarkable attribute is their colouration (pink, white, or yellow). This, and a limited capacity to actually change colours, allows them to achieve some amazingly close colour matches with the flowers where they wait in ambush for pollinating insects. We humans hardly ever get to see them precisely because their disguise is so good and, for insects, whose vision is considerably inferior to ours, crab spiders must be close to invisible.

7   If you think this is an ingredient for a devastatingly effective predator, you might also want to think about how a crab spider actually makes a kill. When an insect arrives at the flower and starts to drink the nectar, the crab spider slowly closes its long front legs until they ever so lightly touch the doomed insect. Then, with a sudden lunge, she stabs her fangs into the victim's head and injects venom directly into its brain. When the brain is dissolved and the struggling has stopped, the crab spider may or may not switch to the insect's neck and start to suck out its body fluids through the two tiny fang holes. Because the insect's stiff outer skeleton is still intact, the spider has to suck against an increasingly strong vacuum. After a few minutes the spider relaxes its powerful sucking muscles and lets most of the fluid it has extracted from the insect flow back into the partly emptied insect. This has the effect of letting more tissue-dissolving spider venom back into the insect where it can liquefy more of the insect's body tissues, even those quite far away from the puncture holes. After swishing the nutritious soup back and forth between the dead insect and its own stomach like this a few times, the spider sucks up all it can one last time, withdraws its fangs, and then moves to the insect's abdomen and repeats the whole process there as well.

8   Now, there is no doubt that this is the description of an almost unbelievably sophisticated killer but what else can we say about it? Well,

for one thing, we should resist the temptation to call it "cruel". However much it might seem that way to humans, there is simply no reason to think that crab spiders do or can think one way or the other about the pain (if any?) that they inflict on their victims. They simply act the way they do because they are programmed that way. If one of them ever did have a thinking brain and could tell us about her life it might be something along the lines of:

"I am a female crab spider. I wait here on my Dark-eyed Susan because many nutritious insects come here to drink nectar. I match the colour of my flower so as to be unnoticed by things that might eat me and by things I want to eat myself. By liquefying the insides of as many insects as I can catch and drinking them to the very last drop, I grow as big and fat as I possibly can. This means that I can lay the greatest possible number of eggs and leave the greatest possible number of sons and daughters in the next and succeeding generations. If I did anything less I would have fewer descendants than other crab spiders and my line would have died out long ago. Nothing else matters." 9

But quite apart from what the behaviour of crab spiders says about "cruelty" in nature, it also gives us a profound lesson about what we sometimes imagine to be nature's "pre-planned harmony". As we know, the mutually beneficial relationship between flowers and pollinating insects is often cited as a fine example of that supposed harmony. But crab spiders are no less a part of nature than flowers and insects and yet their chief effect is to wipe out the benefits of plant-insect "cooperation". Quite obviously, when a female crab spider sets up residence on a flower, the visiting insects get death, and the flower gets wasted nectar and no pollination. Not much harmony left (!) and, unless we are very selective and superficial about the evidence, we can hardly argue in favour of nature tending towards "peace, cooperation and mutual benefits". 10

Once again, the best interpretation of what we actually see in nature is that each player is (unconsciously) out for him or herself. There are certainly winners and losers in the real world but no evidence of a "plan". Nor is there any reason to think any species other than us ever gives — or is capable of giving — any thought to the feelings or welfare of its victims, neighbours, or "cooperators". 11

And yet nature is nothing if not complicated and we are nothing if not human. It is hard for us to imagine that Dark-eyed Susans would not be miffed at female crab spiders for using their showy petals as places to ambush and eat the pollinators which the flowers have gone to such great pains to attract. It is even harder for us to imagine that they would be happy with the tiny male crab spiders that steal nectar when they aren't using the flower petals as mating platforms with as many females as possible. 12

13   But, by the same token, Dark-eyed Susans would be pleased to know that male crab spiders while stealing nectar, and female crab spiders while subduing their victims, both frequently get pollen stuck to their bodies. Even better, the spiders often move afterwards from one flower head to another and thus achieve cross-pollination. This may not be the way flower fertilization is supposed to happen but why would a Dark-eyed Susan care? If anything there might be a delicious irony in having the killer of your intended bribe recipients unknowingly end up doing what you had intended to accomplish with your showy petals and energy rich nectar in the first place.

14   Life in the real natural world knows no care, no pity, no consciousness. Still, we couldn't help wondering on our visit to the Lookout Trail flower stand last week if Dark-eyed Susans would smile if they could understand what is happening in the great evolutionary shoot-out between them, their pollinators, and the crab spiders. They get the last laugh at their own roadside café.

△ △

Explorations:

Dan Strickland and John LeVay, *Wildflowers of Algonquin Provincial Park*
Dan Strickland and Russ Rutter, *The Best of the Raven: 150 Essays from Algonquin Park's Popular Newsletter*
Lawrence Newcomb, *Newcomb's Wildflower Guide*
Charles G. D. Roberts, "The Prisoners of the Pitcher-Plant" (short story, from *The Haunters of the Silences*)
Annie Dillard, *Pilgrim at Tinker Creek*
Pierre Morency, *The Eye Is an Eagle: Nature Stories from the New World*
http://www.algonquinpark.on.ca

Structure:

1. How do the opening *examples* of the moose and the fox help prepare us for this essay's subject? Tell how they exploit the device of *contrast.*
2. What effects does Strickland achieve by "framing" the argument at beginning and end with his visit to the roadside stand of Dark-eyed Susans?
3. Point out the THESIS STATEMENT.
4. This whole selection is a *process analysis* of how species in nature act out the "selfishness" of their instincts. Which paragraph, though, gives a more detailed *process analysis* of how a particular species goes about its work of feeding on another?

Style:

1. Do you like the title of this selection? What is "the last laugh"? What is "Dark-Eyed Susan's Roadside Café?" What FIGURES OF SPEECH are at work here?

2. As a biologist, Strickland might have said in paragraph 7 that the spider "inserts her proboscis into the insect's cephalic region," but instead tells how she "stabs her fangs into the victim's head." Find at least 5 other violent or even gross terms meant to excite our interest. Is this TONE appropriate for Strickland's AUDIENCE, the people who camp in Algonquin Provincial Park and pick up copies of *The Raven* at the park office?

3. Are the long paragraphs right for Strickland's AUDIENCE? Tell why you would either keep them as is, or would break some into shorter ones.

4. What device of style powers this sentence from paragraph 14: "Life in the real natural world knows no care, no pity, no consciousness." And why does Strickland place this device in his closing paragraph?

Ideas for Discussion and Writing:

1. As a child did you watch cartoons of animals that talked and acted like humans? Name them. Now do you find Strickland's mechanistic portrait of nature bleak or cruel? Or is it only scientific?

2. Has your own dog or cat shown evidence of higher thought and emotion? Or has it, like the species in this essay, acted out of blind self-interest? Tell *examples* to the class.

3. In paragraph 4, Strickland calls the interrelationships of flowers and insects "strictly business." Do companies in the human world behave like the Dark-eyed Susan, the insects and the crab spider? Do they undergo "survival of the fittest," as Darwin said of species in the natural world? Give examples to support this *analogy*.

4. Our author is Chief Naturalist of Algonquin Provincial Park, a vast area of lakes and forest north of Toronto. Have you camped, hiked, skied or canoed in places like this? Why do we drive hours from the city to do so? What are we seeking? If you have had an outdoor adventure like this, *narrate* it to the class. Also check "Margaret's Algonquin Park Page" on the Web for other adventures in canoeing and hiking: http://www.clo.com/~mkean/margpark.html.

5. **PROCESS IN WRITING:** *You have just read an essay of "informational" process analysis. Now write a "directional" one on the topic of how to enjoy nature in the city. First take a walk in your part of town, observing every plant and animal species you see (even if you live in a densely populated area*

of highrises, you will see some). Back at home, freewrite for a few minutes, never stopping the movement of your pen or keyboard. Looking over what you have produced, now write a rapid first draft. Let it sit, then revise. Do you see a THESIS STATEMENT? Examples? Transitions between parts? Meaningful conclusion? Share your final version with the class.

Note: See also the Topics for Writing at the end of this chapter.

Susanna Moodie

Dandelion Coffee*

Although Susanna Moodie (1803–1885) became our most celebrated pioneer, an almost legendary woman who could raise crops, chase bears and paddle a canoe, she began life in very different surroundings. Born in Suffolk, England, she spent her childhood in the gentility of her father's estate near Southwold. But when a poor investment took the family fortune, and when in 1831 she married a half-pay military officer, the only way to avoid poverty was to emigrate. In 1832 the couple joined Susanna's brother Samuel Strickland and her sister Catharine Parr Traill in the bush of Upper Canada. Moodie had published light fiction in England and continued to write for periodicals. But it was not till 1852, when the Moodies had left the wilds for town life in Belleville, that she told her whole story in the memoir that is now a Canadian classic: Roughing It in the Bush. *In this work she reveals ambiguous feelings: without the sunny optimism of her sister or brother, she detested her exile from polite society; yet her love for nature shines through her privations. Over a century later Margaret Atwood explored these ambiguities in her cycle of poems,* The Journals of Susanna Moodie *(1970), raising to almost mythic status this unwilling pioneer. Our own selection, which reveals Moodie's practical side, is from* Roughing It in the Bush.

The first year we came to this country, I met with an account of dandelion coffee, published in the *New York Albion*, given by a Dr. Harrison, of Edinburgh, who earnestly recommended it as an article of general use.

"It possesses," he says, "all the fine flavour and exhilarating properties of coffee, without any of its deleterious effects. The plant being of a soporific nature, the coffee made from it when drunk at night produces a tendency to sleep, instead of exciting wakefulness, and may be safely used as a cheap and wholesome substitute for the Arabian berry, being equal in substance and flavour to the best Mocha coffee."

I was much struck with this paragraph at the time, and for several years felt a great inclination to try the Doctor's coffee; but something or other always came in the way, and it was put off till another opportu-

* Editor's title.

nity. During the fall of '35, I was assisting my husband in taking up a crop of potatoes in the field, and observing a vast number of fine dandelion roots among the potatoes, it brought the dandelion coffee back to my memory, and I determined to try some for our supper. Without saying anything to my husband, I threw aside some of the roots, and when we left work, collecting a sufficient quantity for the experiment, I carefully washed the roots quite clean, without depriving them of the fine brown skin which covers them, and which contains the aromatic flavour which so nearly resembles coffee that it is difficult to distinguish it from it while roasting.

4   I cut my roots into small pieces, the size of a kidney-bean, and roasted them on an iron baking-pan in the stove-oven, until they were as brown and crisp as coffee. I then ground and transferred a small cupful of the powder to the coffee-pot, pouring upon it scalding water, and boiling it for a few minutes briskly over the fire. The result was beyond my expectations. The coffee proved excellent — far superior to the common coffee we procured at the stores.

5   To persons residing in the bush, and to whom tea and coffee are very expensive articles of luxury, the knowledge of this valuable property in a plant scattered so abundantly through their fields, would prove highly beneficial. For years we used no other article; and my Indian friends who frequented the house gladly adopted the root, and made me show them the whole process of manufacturing it into coffee.

6   Experience taught me that the root of the dandelion is not so good when applied to this purpose in the spring as it is in the fall. I tried it in the spring, but the juice of the plant, having contributed to the production of leaves and flowers, was weak, and destitute of the fine bitter flavour so peculiar to coffee. The time of gathering in the potato crop is the best suited for collecting and drying the roots of the dandelion; and as they always abound in the same hills, both may be accomplished at the same time. Those who want to keep a quantity for winter use may wash and cut up the roots, and dry them on boards in the sun. They will keep for years, and can be roasted when required.

△ △

Explorations

Susanna Moodie, *Roughing It in the Bush*
Margaret Atwood, *The Journals of Susanna Moodie* (poems)
Catharine Parr Traill, *The Backwoods of Canada*
Samuel Strickland, *Twenty-Seven Years in Canada West*
Marilyn Walker, *Harvesting the Northern Wild*
http://malvm1.mala.bc.ca/~mcneil/moodie.htm

Structure:

1. In which paragraphs of this selection does Susanna Moodie rely most fully on *narration* to develop her *process analysis?*
2. Point out three passages in which Moodie develops her subject of dandelion coffee through *comparison and contrast* with "common coffee."
3. Explain how *cause and effect* helps to develop paragraph 6.

Style:

1. How FORMAL is the STYLE of this selection, especially in vocabulary, sentence length, and paragraph length? Give examples. Choose any very recent selection in this anthology, and *contrast* its style, giving examples.
2. Point out at least three SENSE IMAGES that help to bring Moodie's prose alive.

Ideas for Discussion and Writing:

1. Is Moodie's *process analysis* meant as directions? Is her recipe clear and exact enough for you to follow?
2. Though from a background of privilege and luxury in England, Susanna Moodie soon learned the prime survival tactic of the North American pioneer: innovation. Do we still have this ability in the new millennium? Give examples.
3. With your present abilities, could you have made it as a pioneer in Upper Canada of the 1830s? Give a verbal *process analysis* of one of your skills that would help you "rough it in the bush."
4. In paragraph 2 Dr. Harrison praises dandelion coffee for putting us to sleep instead of "exciting wakefulness." Why do so many of us in our time "excite wakefulness" with coffee, tea, or caffeinated soft drinks? Name at least three alternative, drug-free ways of staying alert.
5. **PROCESS IN WRITING:** *Write a* process analysis *of something you do to avoid depending on a commercial product or service, as Moodie avoided commercial coffee. First take some notes, then use the best in a quick discovery draft. Looking it over later, add even more detail to help your reader follow the directions. Have you specified* measurements *of time or size or quantity? Have you* defined *terms* your reader may not know? Have you used *time* signals *to highlight the progression of steps? Now share your directions with a small group of classmates, then revise any step they didn't understand. Finally, test your prose aloud before writing the finished version.*

Note: See also the Topics for Writing at the end of this chapter.

Topics for Writing
Chapter 8: Process Analysis

Tell your reader how to perform one of these processes. (See also the guidelines that follow.)

1. Conduct an Internet Search
2. Break off a Romance
3. Choose Your Style in Clothing
4. Get Along in a Blended Family
5. Choose a Used Car
6. Survive as a Homeless Person
7. Make Friends in a New School
8. Portage a Canoe
9. Flirt
10. Borrow Money
11. Save Money
12. Win Back an Enemy
13. Stay Healthy in Winter
14. Crack a Good Joke
15. Study Better in Less Time
16. Move Back Home
17. Survive Driving in City Traffic
18. Get Along Without Owning a Car
19. Avoid Criminal Attack in the Big City
20. Update Your Wardrobe
21. Choose an Apartment
22. Find a Summer Job
23. Balance Work and Study
24. Gain Self-Confidence
25. Win At the Race Track
26. Get Along with Roommates
27. Enjoy Winter
28. Eat Better for Less
29. Succeed as a Single Parent
30. Choose an Internet Service Provider

Note also the Process in Writing topic after each selection in this chapter.

Process in Writing: Guidelines

Follow at least some of these steps in writing your essay of process analysis (your teacher may suggest which ones).

1. *Spend time deciding which topic you like best, so your motivation will increase your performance.*

2. *Visualize your audience (see step 6 below), and choose the level of terminology accordingly.*

3. *Fill a page with brief notes. Scan and sort them to choose the steps of your process analysis, and their order.*

4. *Write a rapid first draft, not stopping now to revise or edit. If you do notice a word that needs replacing or a passage that needs work, insert a signal such as a row of letters (like this: xxxxxxxxxx), so you will find and fix it later.*

5. *When this draft has "cooled off," look it over. Are all steps of the process given? Do TRANSITIONS introduce them? In technical topics like those on computers or e-mail, have you defined terms that may puzzle your audience? Revise accordingly.*

6. *Now share the second draft with a group of classmates. Do they believe they could actually follow your directions? If not, revise.*

7. *If you have consulted books or periodicals to write this paper, follow standard practice in quoting and in documenting your sources. Remember that plagiarism is a serious offence.*

8. *As you produce your good copy, edit for things like spelling and punctuation before printing out your best version. Save it on disk, in case your teacher suggests further revisions.*

Paul Chiasson/Canadian Press

"Fourteen of our bright and shining daughters won places in engineering schools, doing things we, their mothers, only dreamed of. That we lost them has broken our hearts; what is worse is that we are not surprised."

—*Stevie Cameron, "Our Daughters, Ourselves"*

CHAPTER

⟨9⟩

ARGUMENTATION AND PERSUASION

Therefore. . .

S o far the essays in this book have taken many paths in developing their subject. They have narrated events, they have described, they have explained, and some have entertained. But you have surely realized that in one way or another, whatever else they do, almost all the selections have tried to make a point. After all, an essay without a point is "pointless." The very use of a thesis statement implies a main idea or opinion. In this final chapter, we now focus more closely on how the writer makes that point. The process takes two complementary forms: *argumentation* and *persuasion*.

Argumentation

This word has a broad set of meanings, but here we will consider it the writer's attempt to convince the reader *through logic*. This stance implies respect: it considers the reader a mature individual capable of independent thought. It assumes the reader will also respect the thoughts of the writer, if those thoughts are presented in a logical way. In summary, the writer and reader are *partners*: since the writer does not play on the reader's emotions, the reader considers the argument with a more open mind. If the logic makes sense, the reader may be convinced. Argumentation through logic takes two opposite forms, *deduction* and *induction*. Let's look at each.

Deduction

Deduction accepts a general principle as true, then applies it to specific cases. For over two thousand years logicians have expressed this process in a formula called the *syllogism*. Here's a well-known example:

> **Major premise: All men are mortal.**
> **Minor premise: Socrates is a man.**
> **Conclusion: Socrates is mortal.**

This chain of reasoning is about as foolproof as any: since no human in the history of the world has yet lived much longer than a century, we feel safe in assuming that no one ever will; therefore "all men are mortal." And since all historical records about Socrates portray him as a man — not, say, as a rock or horse or tree — we accept the minor premise as well. Logic tells us that if both the major and minor premises are true, then the conclusion will inevitably be true as well.

But now let's look at a syllogism whose logic is not as clear:

> **Major premise: Progress is good.**
> **Minor premise: The automobile represents progress.**
> **Conclusion: The automobile is good.**

At first glance the argument may seem all right: it certainly reflects values common in our society. But let's examine the major premise, the foundation on which all the rest is built: is it true that "progress is good"? Well, how do we know until we define "progress"? Is it more jobs? More production? More cars? Higher sales? More consumption? A rising stock market? Or are all these the opposite of true "progress" because our natural resources are dwindling, our highways are choked with traffic, our lakes and forests are dying of acid rain, the greenhouse effect is already disrupting our climate, and around the world several species of life per hour are becoming extinct? Our values will determine our response.

If we cannot agree on what "progress" is, how can we say it is "good"? And how could we go on to our minor premise, saying that "the automobile represents progress"? How could we build even further on this shaky foundation, claiming in our conclusion that "the automobile is good"? Within its own framework the argument may be "valid" (or logical). But only those who accept the original premise will view the conclusion as true. Those who do not will reject it as false.

And that is the problem with deduction: not always can we agree on premises. Five hundred years ago society ran on deduction: the King or the Church or our parents told us what to believe, and we simply applied those principles to any case that came up. But in the 20th century many of us dislike being told what to think. Not only do many people now question systems of belief such as Marxism or codes of religion, but scientists even question previously accepted "laws" of nature. How is a person to know what is true? It is therefore no coincidence that most contemporary essays argue not through deduction but through induction.

Induction

We have discussed how deduction applies a general rule to explain particular cases. Induction is the opposite: it first observes particular cases, then from them formulates a general rule. This is the basis of the scientific way, the procedure that enables humans to conquer disease, communicate by computer and travel to the moon. It can produce faulty results, just like deduction, but the open mind required to use it appeals to our modern sensibilities. Let's take an example:

> **After a summer in the factory Joan thought she could afford a car, so the week before school began she bought a sporty red three-year-old Japanese model. Speeding around town with the stereo turned up was so much fun that she didn't mind the $350-a-month payments. But when the insurance company hit her for $2500 as a new driver, her savings took a dive. Each month she found herself paying $100 for gas and $150 for parking. A fall tuneup set her back $180, and new tires $450. Then came the repairs: $250 for brakes, $325 for a clutch, $225 for an exhaust system, then $480 for a timing belt. In desperation Joan took a part-time job selling shoes. That helped her bankbook but took her study time. Two weeks after exams, holding a sickly grade report in her hand, Joan decided to sell the car. Nobody could have told her to, since, like most people, she likes to make up her own mind. But the long string of evidence did the teaching: now Joan knows, through *induction*, that as a student she cannot afford a car.**

Induction is not infallible. Conceivably Joan's next car might never need a repair. Next year insurance might somehow drop from $2500 to, say, $75. Gas stations might sell premium for 10¢ a litre, and on Boxing Day a good tire might cost $1.99. Anything is possible. But Joan feels that the consistency of her results — the steady high cost of her car ownership — will *probably* not change. Likewise, the scientist believes that her or his years of research have yielded results that will not be disproved by the very next experiment. But in all humility both writer and scientist must consider the new principle not a fact, not an unchangeable law, but simply an idea with a very high probability of being true.

Finally, suppose that Joan analyzes her experience in an essay. If she sets up her paper as most essayists do, we will read her thesis statement near the beginning — even though the principle it states is the *result* of the evidence still to come. This positioning is not a flaw of logic: Joan simply *introduces* the main idea so we can see where we are going, then tells us how she arrived at it, letting her evidence lead inductively toward the main point which will be restated at the end. You will find this pattern at work, for example, in this chapter's inductive essay by Martin Hocking.

You will also find that, although deduction and induction represent opposite methods of logic, sometimes both are used in the same argument (when the writer's original opinion is confirmed by the evidence). This does not necessarily mean weakness in logic either. Another link between these opposites is that most principles which we accept as true, and upon which we base our own deductions, originated in someone else's induction. (Newton arrived inductively at his theory of gravity, through evidence such as the famous apple that fell on his head; almost all of us now believe Newton and his theory without waiting for an apple, or anything else, to fall on our own heads.) Similarly, a conclusion we derive from our own induction could become the premise of someone else's deduction — a link in an ongoing chain of logic. To keep this chain from breaking, the individual has a double task: to check over any links provided by others, then to make her or his own link as strong as possible.

Persuasion

We have just seen how *argumentation* seeks to convince through logic. But, whether deductive or inductive, is logic enough? Now let's look at the complementary approach of persuasion, which attempts to convince through emotion. A century of inductive research into psychology has shown that we humans are seldom rational. Even when we think we are "reasoning," we are often building arguments merely to justify what we thought or felt already. It is possible to write an argumentative essay with enough restraint to be almost purely logical. But to most people the effort is difficult and unnatural, requiring a great deal of revision, and the result may seem cold and uninviting to those who have not spent years reading the almost pure argumentation of scholarly journals. Most professional writers would say that a little feeling and a little colour can help an essay. But how do we take this approach without slipping into dishonesty? Let's look now at the major techniques of *persuasion* — both their uses and abuses.

Word choice: Is a person "slim," "thin" or "skinny"? Is a governmental expenditure an "investment," a "cost," a "waste" or a "boondoggle"? Is an oil spill an "incident," an "accident," a "mistake," a "crime" or an "environmental tragedy"? Essayists tend to choose the term that reflects their feeling and the feeling they hope to encourage in the readers. While deliberate choice of words is one of the central tasks of all writers, including essayists, let's not abuse the process. Bertrand Russell once quipped, "I am firm; you are stubborn; he is pig-headed." If too many of your word choices follow the model of "pig-headed," you will alarm an alert reader and unfairly overwhelm a careless one.

Example: Although examples form the basis of logical induction, they can also add colour and feeling to a persuasive essay. Choose vivid ones. An attempt to show old people as active may be helped by the example of your grandmother who skis. But avoid dubious cases like that of the man in Azerbaijan who is rumoured to have ridden a horse at age 155.

Repetition: Although we try to cut accidental repetition from our writing (as in the case of one student who used the word "tire" 55 times in an essay about, you guessed it, tires), intentional repetition can build feeling. Stephen Leacock builds emphasis by using the word "eat" over and over in paragraph 25 of his essay (see p. 283), and in paragraphs 14–17 of her selection (see p. 337) Joy Kogawa builds feeling by starting a whole string of sentences with the contraction "it's."

Hyperbole (exaggeration): A humorist can exaggerate and get away with it, as Stephen Leacock does when he tells us "How to Live to Be 200." By contrast, an essay that is objective in tone should stay strictly with the truth. In her factual investigation of child abuse, Michele Landsberg writes that in one country girls only 13 and 14 years old "work 17-hour days at their sewing machines." While these numbers are shocking, if she had claimed the children worked 24 hours a day we would refuse to believe her, because no one can go without sleep at all.

Analogy and figures of speech: You have seen in Chapter 6 how we can suggest a point by comparing one thing with another from a different category: a monster with the forestry industry, or a house with a ship at sea. Analogies, and their shorter cousins similes and metaphors, are powerful tools of persuasion; avoid abusing them through name-calling. Think twice before casting a political party as a dinosaur, entrepreneurs as piranhas, or police officers as gorillas. Remember, above all, that neither analogies nor figures of speech are logical proof of anything.

Irony: When in Chapter 4 Naheed Mustafa covers herself with the traditional *hijab* in order to be free, when in Chapter 8 Judy Stoffman describes the once-young athlete dying of old age, and when in this chapter Rita Schindler "thanks" her son's assailants for not killing him — we feel the power of irony. A writer can use this device for a lifetime without exhausting its emotional power; yet irony lends itself less easily to abuses than do many tools of persuasion, for both its use and its appreciation demand a certain exercise of intelligence.

Appeal to authority or prestige: Opponents of nuclear weapons love to quote Albert Einstein on their dangers; after all, since his discoveries made this hardware possible, he should know. We also invite our reader to believe what a famous economist says about money, what a judge says about law, or what an educator says about education. This approach appeals to our reader's ethical sense: he or she believes these people know the facts and tell the truth. But avoid the common abuse of quoting people on matters outside their competence — Wayne Gretzky on baseball, Madonna on communism, a disgraced politician on honesty, or a convicted murderer on religion.

Fright: You can be sure that a frightened reader is an interested reader, for fright is personal: what you say in your essay could be important! Avoid cheap effects, though. Frighten a reader only with facts that really are scary (such as the number of times computer error nearly launched World War III).

Climax: Whatever your argument, don't trail off from strong to weak. After a good introduction, drop to your least important or least dramatic point, then progress upward to your strongest. This very rise produces an emotion in the reader, like that of the concertgoer who thrills to the final chords of "The Hallelujah Chorus."

Playing Fair in Argumentation and Persuasion

We have looked at some abuses both of argumentation and of persuasion. Now read the following communication, an actual chain letter that arrived one day in the mail. (Versions of it are also circulating on the Internet; you may have seen one.) What attempts does it make at *deduction* or *induction*? Are they logical? What attempts does it make at *persuasion*? Are they fair? (For your information, the person who received this letter did not send it on. So far he has not died or been fired — but then, neither has he won a lottery!)

**Kiss Someone You Love When You Get This Letter
and Make Some Magic**

This paper has been sent to you for good luck. The original copy is in New England. It has been around the world nine times. The luck has sent it to you. You will receive good luck within four days of receiving this letter, provided you send it back out. THIS IS NO JOKE. You will receive it in the mail. Send copies to people that you think need good luck. Don't send money as fate has no price. Do not keep this letter. It must leave your hands within 96 hours. An R.A.F. officer became a hero. Joe Elliot received $40,000, and lost it because he broke the chain. While in the Philippines, Gene Welch lost his wife six days after receiving this letter. He failed to circulate the letter. However, before her death she had won $50,000.00 in a lottery. The money was transferred to him four days after he decided to mail out this letter. Please send twenty copies of this letter and see what happens in four days. The chain came from Venezuela and was written in South America. Since the copy must make a tour of the world you must make copies and send them to your friends and associates. After a few days you will get a surprise. This is true even if you are not superstitious. Do note the following: Constantine Dias received the chain in 1953. He asked his secretary to type twenty copies and send them out. A few days later he won a lottery of $2,000,000. Aria Daddit, an office employee, received the letter and forgot that it had to leave his hands within 96 hours. He lost his job. Later, finding the letter again, he mailed out twenty copies. A few days later he got a better job. Dalen Fairchild received the letter and not believing, threw it away. Nine days later he died. PLEASE SEND NO MONEY. PLEASE DON'T IGNORE THIS. IT WORKS!

Note: No essay in this chapter adopts a stance of pure logic to the exclusion of emotion, or of pure emotion to the exclusion of logic. The eight essays represent different proportions of both elements, and are arranged in approximate order from most argumentative to most persuasive.

For more examples of argumentation and persuasion, see these essays in other chapters:

Martin Hocking

Capping the Great Cup Debate

Few scientists could be better equipped to investigate the subject of our selection than Martin Hocking. With a Ph.D. in organic chemistry from the University of Southampton (1963), experience as research chemist in industry, then extensive research and publication as professor of chemistry at the University of Victoria, Hocking has become a prominent voice in his field. He has advised government on scientific issues; has taught industrial and environmental chemistry for many years; holds ten patents in the fields of monomers, process chemistry and medicine; has published two editions of a reference book which covers these areas; and has published over 70 scientific papers. It was his comparative analysis in the journal Science *which in 1991 sparked debate on the environmental effects of paper cups and foam cups. Hocking concluded that, contrary to public opinion, foam was better. Some scientists questioned his emission figures and his view of paper mill energy use; others commended his open revealing of data sources, a practice not all scientists follow, and the relevance of his "cradle-to-grave" scope: from logging the raw resources to discarding the old cups in landfills. Then Hocking adapted his article for a general audience; on February 16, 1991,* The Globe and Mail *published this selection.*

1   The polystyrene foam cup has long suffered contempt from an environmentally aware public that assumes paper cups are ecologically friendlier. It's easy to understand why: paper cups are made out of a wood product, a renewable resource, and therefore would seem to be the proper conservationist choice.

2   In fact, foam cups are proving to be the environmentally better choice.

3   For one thing, people overlook the fact that logging necessary for the paper industry has adverse effects on the landscape that range from the construction of roads to clear-cutting practices that typically increase the likelihood of flood and drought in immediate watershed areas.

4   In addition, a review of other factors does not support the use of paper. A comparative analysis of paper versus polystyrene conducted by us at the University of Victoria leads to the inevitable conclusion that foam cups are better from a range of standpoints.

5   Here are the principal findings of the analysis:

Hydrocarbons

The extraction and delivery of oil and gas hydrocarbons have a significant impact on sensitive ecosystems. A polyfoam cup is made entirely from hydrocarbons, but a similar amount of hydrocarbons are also used to produce a paper cup.

6

Paper cups are made from bleached pulp, which in turn is obtained from wood chips. Although bark, some wood waste, and organic residues from chemical pulping are burned to supply part of the energy required in papermaking, fuel oil or gas is used to provide much of the rest. Even more petroleum is needed if the paper cup has a plastic or wax coating.

7

Inorganic chemicals

In the making of paper cups, relatively small amounts of sodium hydroxide or sodium sulphate are needed for chemical pulping makeup requirements, since the recycling of these in the kraft pulping process is quite efficient. But larger amounts of chlorine, sodium hydroxide, sodium chlorate, sulphuric acid, sulphur dioxide and calcium hydroxide are normally used on a once-through basis to the extent of 160 to 200 kilograms per metric ton of pulp.

8

The total non-recycled chemical requirement works out to an average of about 1.8 grams per cup.

9

Polystyrene is far superior to wood pulp for cup construction; only about one-sixth as much material is needed to produce a foam cup. Chemical requirements for the polystyrene foam cup are small because several of the stages in its preparation use catalysts that nudge the process along without being consumed themselves.

10

Alkylation of benzene with ethene (ethylene) also uses aluminum chloride catalytically to the extent of about 10 kilograms per metric ton of ethylbenzene produced.

11

The spent aluminum chloride is later neutralized with roughly the same amount of sodium hydroxide. Further small amounts of sulphuric acid and sodium hydroxide are also consumed to give a total chemical requirement of about 33 kilograms per metric ton of polystyrene.

12

This works out to 0.05 grams per cup, or about 3 per cent of the chemical requirement of the paper cup.

13

Utility consumption

In terms of energy consumption, polystyrene cups also appear to come out ahead. One paper cup consumes about 12 times as much steam, 36 times as much electricity, and twice as much cooling water as one polystyrene foam cup, while producing 58 times the volume of waste water.

14

The contaminants present in the waste water from pulping and bleaching operations are removed to varying degrees, but the residuals (with

15

the exception of metal salts) still amount to 10 to 100 times those present in the waste-water streams from polystyrene processing.

Air pollution

16   The wholesale price of a paper cup is about 2.5 times that of polyfoam since it consumes more in terms of raw materials and energy. But their respective purchase prices are not so closely linked to the environmental costs of productions and recycling or final disposal. Air emissions total 22.7 kilograms per metric ton of bleached pulp compared to about 53 kilograms per metric ton of polystyrene.

17   On a per-cup basis, however, this comparison becomes 0.23 grams for paper versus 0.08 grams for polyfoam.

Emissions

18   In terms of mass, the 43 kilograms of pentane employed as the blowing agent for each metric ton of the foamable beads used to make polystyrene foam cups is the largest single emission to air from the two technologies.

19   Pentane's atmospheric lifetime is estimated to be seven years or less, about a tenth that of the chlorofluorocarbons formerly used in some foamable beads. Unlike the chlorofluorocarbons, pentane would tend to cause a net increase in ozone concentrations, both at ground level and in the stratosphere.

20   However, its contributions to atmospheric ozone and as a "greenhouse effect" gas are almost certainly less than those of the methane losses generated from disposal of paper cups in landfill sites.

21   If the six metric tons of paper equivalent to a metric ton of polystyrene completely biodegrade anaerobically in a landfill, theoretically the paper could generate 2,370 kilograms of methane along with 3,260 kilograms of carbon dioxide.

22   Both are "greenhouse gases" that contribute to global warming.

Recycling

23   The technical side of recycle capability with polystyrene foam is straightforward. All that is required is granulation and washing, followed by hot-air drying and re-extrusion of the resin for re-use. Though recycled resin may not be used in food applications, this only partially limits the many possible uses for recycled polystyrene products.

24   Such uses are in packaging materials, insulation, flotation billets, patio furniture and drainage tiles.

25   An improved collection infrastructure is all that is needed to make this option a more significant reality and convert this perceived negative aspect of polyfoam use to a positive one.

26   Paper cups use a non-water soluble hot melt or solvent-based adhesive to hold the parts together.

For this reason, cups are technically excluded from paper recycling 27
programs because the adhesive resin cannot be removed during
repulping.

If the paper is coated with a plastic film or wax, this too prevents 28
recycling, at least for renewed paper products.

Final disposal

Polystyrene is relatively inert to decomposition when discarded in land- 29
fill. However, there is also increasing evidence that disposal of paper to
landfill does not necessarily result in degradation or biodecomposition,
particularly in arid regions.

In wet landfills, where degradation occurs, the paper cup produces 30
methane, a gas which has five to 20 times greater global-warming effect
than carbon dioxide. Water-soluble fragments of cellulose from the
decomposition also contribute biochemical oxygen demand to leachate (any water that percolates through the land-filled waste) from the
landfill.

Leachate may be treated to remove contaminants to control environ- 31
mental impact on discharge, or may be lost to surface waters or underground aquifers (a porous rock layer that holds water) to exacerbate
the oxygen demand in these raw water sources.

Thus, as a result of our analysis, it would appear that polystyrene 32
foam cups are the ecologically better choice.

At the very least, they appear to be no worse than paper in one-use 33
applications, contrary to the instinctive consumer impression.

△ △

Explorations:

Peter Kruus, *Chemicals in the Environment*
Rachel Carson, *Silent Spring*
http://www.ec.gc.ca/ecocycle/

Structure:

1. How does the opening prepare us for Hocking's argument?
2. Identify the THESIS STATEMENT.
3. Hocking's argument is a model *comparison and contrast* of paper and
   foam cups, organized *point by point*. Identify each of these major
   points.
4. Find three passages where Hocking reasons through *cause and effect*.
5. Do the subtitles help? Have you tried subtitles yourself?

Style:

1. What AUDIENCE does Hocking write for in this condensation of a scientific journal article? Are the many technical terms a barrier to these readers? Are they to you? Why or why not?

Argumentation and Persuasion:

1. Written by a scientist, "Capping the Great Cup Debate" is the most *argumentative* essay of this chapter. Can you find any passage at all that appeals to *emotion* rather than *reason*? Does all the logic reduce your interest in this essay, or does the quality of thought increase it?
2. As the introduction to this chapter suggests, science is based on *induction*. In saying "A comparative analysis. . .leads to the inevitable conclusion that foam cups are better. . . ." (par. 4), scientist Martin Hocking in fact labels his argument as *inductive*. Is he right? How fully does he base his conclusion on evidence? Does he successfully avoid reasoning from prior values or assumptions?
3. How much of this argument consists of *examples*? How many are numeric (statistics)?
4. *Comparison and contrast, cause and effect*, massive *examples* and *process analysis* all help Hocking make his point. Do you think he planned to use these all, or did some just appear as he wrote? How fully *should* we organize before writing?

Ideas for Discussion and Writing:

1. Did you think paper cups were better for the environment? Do you still, or did Hocking change your mind? Tell why.
2. "Think globally, act locally," say environmentalists. Consider the pollution caused by disposable pens, lighters, razors, towels and tissues, plastic wrap, diapers, paper plates—and cups, whether paper or foam. What "acts" could you perform to help "globally"?
3. Name one act you already perform to reduce pollution.
4. Is science outside the realm of values? Or are scientists responsible for the good and bad effects of their discoveries? Defend your view with examples, including Hocking.
5. Which is more important to you right now, the economy or the environment? Which will seem more important by the time you have grandchildren? What implications can you *deduce* from your answer?
6. **PROCESS IN WRITING:** *At the library, read and take notes on how vitamin C affects humans, making sure your evidence comes from the work of scientists, not health faddists. Let this collected evidence lead to your THESIS STATEMENT: whether or not taking large doses of vitamin C improves our health. Now write your argument of induction, using any form(s) of orga-*

nization that work, but basing your argument very heavily on evidence. (Your teacher may advise whether to document informally or use full MLA style.) Proofread any quotations word for word against the originals, and be sure to enclose them, even short phrases of two or three words, in quotation marks. Now read your draft aloud. Does its STYLE promote thought or does it promote feeling? Replace any loaded or very INFORMAL words with more OBJECTIVE ones. State your conclusion *clearly. Finally, edit for things like spelling and punctuation as you produce the final version.*

Note: See also the Topics for Writing at the end of this chapter.

Kildare Dobbs

The Scar*

Kildare Dobbs was born in Meerut, Uttar Pradesh, India, in 1923, was educated in Ireland, then during World War II spent five years in the Royal Navy. After the war he worked in the British Colonial Service in Tanganyika and, after earning an M.A. at Cambridge, came in 1952 to Canada. Dobbs has been a teacher, editor for Macmillan, managing editor of Saturday Night, *and book editor of* The Toronto Star. *He was one of the founders, in 1956, of the* Tamarack Review. *He is also the author of several books, among them* Running to Paradise *(essays, 1962, winner of the Governor General's Literary Award);* Canada *(an illustrated travel book, 1964);* Reading the Time *(essays, 1968);* The Great Fur Opera *(a comic history of the Hudsons Bay Company, 1970);* Pride and Fall *(short fiction, 1981);* Anatolian Suite *(travel, 1989);* Ribbon of Highway *(travel, 1992), and* The Eleventh Hour: Poems for the Third Millennium *(1997). Our selection is from* Reading the Time. *It is about an event Dobbs did not witness, yet the vivid details with which he supports his argument recreate all too clearly what that event must have been like.*

1   This is the story I was told in 1963 by Emiko Okamoto, a young Japanese woman who had come to live in Toronto. She spoke through an interpreter, since at that time she knew no English. It is Emiko's story, although I have had to complete it from other sources.

2   But why am I telling it? Everyone knows how terrible this story is. Everyone knows the truth of what von Clausewitz said: "Force to meet force arms itself with the inventions of art and science." First the bow-and-arrow, then Greek fire, gunpowder, poison-gas — and so on up the lethal scale. These things, we're told, should be considered calmly. No sweat — we should think about the unthinkable, or so Herman Kahn suggests, dispassionately. And he writes: "We do not expect illustrations in a book of surgery to be captioned 'Good health is preferable to this kind of cancer.' Excessive comments such as 'And now there is a lot of blood' or 'This particular cut really hurts' are out of place. . . . To dwell on such things is morbid." Perhaps the answer to Herman Kahn is

---

* Editor's title.

that if surgeons hadn't dwelt on those things we wouldn't now have anaesthetics, or artery forceps either, for that matter.

To think about thermonuclear war in the abstract is obscene. To think about any kind of warfare with less than the whole of our mind and imagination is obscene. This is the worst treason.   3

Before that morning in 1945 only a few conventional bombs, none of which did any great damage, had fallen on the city. Fleets of U.S. bombers had, however, devastated many cities round about, and Hiroshima had begun a program of evacuation which had reduced its population from 380,000 to some 245,000. Among the evacuees were Emiko and her family.   4

"We were moved out to Otake, a town about an hour's train-ride out of the city," Emiko told me. She had been a fifteen-year-old student in 1945. Fragile and vivacious, versed in the gentle traditions of the tea ceremony and flower arrangement, Emiko still had an air of the frail school-child when I talked with her. Every day, she and her sister Hideko used to commute into Hiroshima to school. Hideko was thirteen. Their father was an antique-dealer and he owned a house in the city, although it was empty now. Tetsuro, Emiko's thirteen-year-old brother, was at the Manchurian front with the Imperial Army. Her mother was kept busy looking after the children, for her youngest daughter Eiko was sick with heart trouble, and rations were scarce. All of them were undernourished.   5

The night of August 5, 1945, little Eiko was dangerously ill. She was not expected to live. Everybody took turns watching by her bed, soothing her by massaging her arms and legs. Emiko retired at 8:30 (most Japanese people go to bed early) and at midnight was roused to take her turn with the sick girl. At 2 a.m. she went back to sleep.   6

While Emiko slept, the *Enola Gay,* a U.S. B-29 carrying the world's first operational atom bomb, was already in the air. She had taken off from the Pacific island of Iwo Jima at 1:45 a.m., and now Captain William Parsons, U.S.N. ordnance expert, was busy in her bomb-hold with the final assembly of Little Boy. Little Boy looked much like an outsize T.N.T. block-buster but the crew knew there was something different about him. Only Parsons and the pilot, Colonel Paul Tibbets, knew exactly in what manner Little Boy was different. Course was set for Hiroshima.   7

Emiko slept.   8

On board the *Enola Gay* co-pilot Captain Robert Lewis was writing up his personal log. "After leaving Iwo," he recorded, "we began to pick up some low stratus and before very long we were flying on top of an under-cast. Outside of a thin, high cirrus and the low stuff, it's a very beautiful day."   9

Emiko and Hideko were up at six in the morning. They dressed in the uniform of their women's college — white blouse, quilted hat, and   10 black skirt — breakfasted and packed their aluminum lunch-boxes with white rice and eggs. These they stuffed into their shoulder bags as they hurried for the seven-o'clock train to Hiroshima. Today there would be no classes. Along with many women's groups, high school students, and others, the sisters were going to work on demolition. The city had begun a project of clearance to make fire-breaks in its downtown huddle of wood and paper buildings.

11   It was a lovely morning.

12   While the two young girls were at breakfast, Captain Lewis, over the Pacific, had made an entry in his log. "We are loaded. The bomb is now alive, and it's a funny feeling knowing it's right in back of you. Knock wood!"

13   In the train Hideko suddenly said she was hungry. She wanted to eat her lunch. Emiko dissuaded her: she'd be much hungrier later on. The two sisters argued, but Hideko at last agreed to keep her lunch till later. They decided to meet at the main station that afternoon and catch the five-o'clock train home. By now they had arrived at the first of Hiroshima's three stations. This was where Hideko got off, for she was to work in a different area from her sister. "Sayonara!" she called. "Goodbye." Emiko never saw her again.

14   There had been an air-raid at 7 a.m., but before Emiko arrived at Hiroshima's main station, two stops farther on, the sirens had sounded the all-clear. Just after eight, Emiko stepped off the train, walked through the station, and waited in the morning sunshine for her streetcar.

15   At about the same moment Lewis was writing in his log. "There'll be a short intermission while we bomb our target."

16   It was hot in the sun. Emiko saw a class-mate and greeted her. Together they moved back into the shade of a high concrete wall to chat. Emiko looked up at the sky and saw, far up in the cloudless blue, a single B-29.

17   It was exactly 8:10 a.m. The other people waiting for the streetcar saw it too and began to discuss it anxiously. Emiko felt scared. She felt that at all costs she must go on talking to her friend. Just as she was thinking this, there was a tremendous greenish-white flash in the sky. It was far brighter than the sun. Emiko afterwards remembered vaguely that there was a roaring or a rushing sound as well, but she was not sure, for just at that moment she lost consciousness.

18   "About 15 seconds after the flash," noted Lewis, 30,000 feet high and several miles away, "there were two very distinct slaps on the ship from the blast and the shock wave. That was all the physical effect we felt. We turned the ship so that we could observe the results."

19   When Emiko came to, she was lying on her face about forty feet away from where she had been standing. She was not aware of any pain. Her first thought was: "I'm alive!" She lifted her head slowly and looked

about her. It was growing dark. The air was seething with dust and black smoke. There was a smell of burning. Emiko felt something trickle into her eyes, tasted it in her mouth. Gingerly she put a hand to her head, then looked at it. She saw with a shock that it was covered with blood.

She did not give a thought to Hideko. It did not occur to her that her sister who was in another part of the city could possibly have been in danger. Like most of the survivors, Emiko assumed she had been close to a direct hit by a conventional bomb. She thought it had fallen on the post-office next to the station. With a hurt child's panic, Emiko, streaming with blood from gashes in her scalp, ran blindly in search of her mother and father. [20]

The people standing in front of the station had been burned to death instantly (a shadow had saved Emiko from the flash). The people inside the station had been crushed by falling masonry. Emiko heard their faint cries, saw hands scrabbling weakly from under the collapsed platform. All around her the maimed survivors were running and stumbling away from the roaring furnace that had been a city. She ran with them toward the mountains that ring the landward side of Hiroshima. [21]

From the *Enola Gay,* the strangers from North America looked down at their handiwork. "There, in front of our eyes," wrote Lewis, "was without a doubt the greatest explosion man had ever witnessed. The city was nine-tenths covered with smoke of a boiling nature, which seemed to indicate buildings blowing up, and a large white cloud which in less than three minutes reached 30,000 feet, then went to at least 50,000 feet." [22]

Far below, on the edge of this cauldron of smoke, at a distance of some 2,500 yards from the blast's epicentre, Emiko ran with the rest of the living. Some who could not run limped or dragged themselves along. Others were carried. Many, hideously burned, were screaming with pain; when they tripped they lay where they had fallen. There was a man whose face had been ripped open from mouth to ear, another whose forehead was a gaping wound. A young soldier was running with a foot-long splinter of bamboo protruding from one eye. But these, like Emiko, were the lightly wounded. [23]

Some of the burned people had been literally roasted. Skin hung from their flesh like sodden tissue paper. They did not bleed but plasma dripped from their seared limbs. [24]

The *Enola Gay,* mission completed, was returning to base. Lewis sought words to express his feelings, the feelings of all the crew. "I might say," he wrote, "I might say 'My God! What have we done?'" [25]

Emiko ran. When she had reached the safety of the mountain she remembered that she still had her shoulder bag. There was a small first-aid kit in it and she applied ointment to her wounds and to a small cut in her left hand. She bandaged her head. [26]

27   Emiko looked back at the city. It was a lake of fire. All around her the burned fugitives cried out in pain. Some were scorched on one side only. Others, naked and flayed, were burned all over. They were too many to help and most of them were dying. Emiko followed the walking wounded along a back road, still delirious, expecting suddenly to meet her father and mother.

28   The thousands dying by the roadside called feebly for help or water. Some of the more lightly injured were already walking in the other direction, back towards the flames. Others, with hardly any visible wounds, stopped, turned ashy pale, and died within minutes. No one knew then that they were victims of radiation.

29   Emiko reached the suburb of Nakayama.

30   Far off in the *Enola Gay*, Lewis, who had seen none of this, had been writing, "If I live a hundred years, I'll never get those few minutes out of my mind. Looking at Captain Parsons, why he is as confounded as the rest, and he is supposed to have known everything and expected this to happen. . . ."

31   At Nakayama, Emiko stood in line at a depot where riceballs were being distributed. Though it distressed her that the badly maimed could hardly feed themselves, the child found she was hungry. It was about 6 p.m. now. A little farther on, at Gion, a farmer called her by name. She did not recognize him, but it seemed he came monthly to her home to collect manure. The farmer took Emiko by the hand, led her to his own house, where his wife bathed her and fed her a meal of white rice. Then the child continued on her way. She passed another town where there were hundreds of injured. The dead were being hauled away in trucks. Among the injured a woman of about forty-five was waving frantically and muttering to herself. Emiko brought this woman a little water in a pumpkin leaf. She felt guilty about it; the schoolgirls had been warned not to give water to the seriously wounded. Emiko comforted herself with the thought that the woman would die soon anyway.

32   At Koi, she found standing-room in a train. It was heading for Otake with a full load of wounded. Many were put off at Ono, where there was a hospital; and two hours later the train rolled into Otake station. It was around 10 p.m.

33   A great crowd had gathered to look for their relations. It was a nightmare, Emiko remembered years afterwards; people were calling their dear kinfolk by name, searching frantically. It was necessary to call them by name, since most were so disfigured as to be unrecognizable. Doctors in the town council offices stitched Emiko's head-wounds. The place was crowded with casualties lying on the floor. Many died as Emiko watched.

34   The town council authorities made a strange announcement. They said a new and mysterious kind of bomb had fallen in Hiroshima. People were advised to stay away from the ruins.

Home at midnight, Emiko found her parents so happy to see her that they could not even cry. They could only give thanks that she was safe. Then they asked, "Where is your sister?"

For ten long days, while Emiko walked daily one and a half miles to have her wounds dressed with fresh gauze, her father searched the rubble of Hiroshima for his lost child. He could not have hoped to find her alive. All, as far as the eye could see, was a desolation of charred ashes and wreckage, relieved only by a few jagged ruins and by the seven estuarial rivers that flowed through the waste delta. The banks of these rivers were covered with the dead and in the rising tidal waters floated thousands of corpses. On one broad street in the Hakushima district the crowds who had been thronging there were all naked and scorched cadavers. Of thousands of others there was no trace at all. A fire several times hotter than the surface of the sun had turned them instantly to vapour.

On August 11 came the news that Nagasaki had suffered the same fate as Hiroshima; it was whispered that Japan had attacked the United States mainland with similar mysterious weapons. With the lavish circumstantiality of rumour, it was said that two out of a fleet of six-engined trans-Pacific bombers had failed to return. But on August 15, speaking for the first time over the radio to his people, the Emperor Hirohito announced his country's surrender. Emiko heard him. No more bombs! she thought. No more fear! The family did not learn till June the following year that this very day young Tetsuro had been killed in action in Manchuria.

Emiko's wounds healed slowly. In mid-September they had closed with a thin layer of pinkish skin. There had been a shortage of antiseptics and Emiko was happy to be getting well. Her satisfaction was short-lived. Mysteriously she came down with diarrhoea and high fever. The fever continued for a month. Then one day she started to bleed from the gums, her mouth and throat become acutely inflamed, and her hair started to fall out. Through her delirium the child heard the doctors whisper by her pillow that she could not live. By now the doctors must have known that ionizing radiation caused such destruction of the blood's white cells that victims were left with little or no resistance against infection.

Yet Emiko recovered.

The wound on her hand, however, was particularly troublesome and did not heal for a long time.

As she got better, Emiko began to acquire some notion of the fearful scale of the disaster. Few of her friends and acquaintances were still alive. But no one knew precisely how many had died in Hiroshima. To this day the claims of various agencies conflict.

According to General Douglas MacArthur's headquarters, there were 78,150 dead and 13,083 missing. The United States Atomic Bomb Casualty Commission claims there were 79,000 dead. Both sets of figures are probably far too low. There's reason to believe that at the time of the surrender Japanese authorities lied about the number of survivors, exaggerating it to get extra medical supplies. The Japanese welfare ministry's figures of 260,000 dead and 163,263 missing may well be too high. But the very order of such discrepancies speaks volumes about the scale of the catastrophe. The dead were literally uncountable.

43   This appalling toll of human life had been exacted from a city that had been prepared for air attack in a state of full wartime readiness. All civil-defence services had been overwhelmed from the first moment and it was many hours before any sort of organized rescue and relief could be put into effect.

44   It's true that single raids using so-called conventional weapons on other cities such as Tokyo and Dresden inflicted far greater casualties. And that it could not matter much to a victim whether he was burnt alive by a fire-storm caused by phosphorus, or by napalm or by nuclear fission. Yet in the whole of human history so savage a massacre had never before been inflicted with a single blow. And modern thermo-nuclear weapons are upwards of 1,000 times more powerful and deadly than the Hiroshima bomb.

45   The white scar I saw on Emiko's small, fine-boned hand was a tiny metaphor, a faint but eloquent memento.

△ △

Explorations:

Kildare Dobbs, *Reading the Time*
John Hershey, *Hiroshima*
Jonathan Schell, *The Fate of the Earth*
Ernie Regehr and Simon Rosenblum, eds., *The Road to Peace*
Treat, John Whittier, *Writing Ground Zero: Japanese Literature and the Atomic Bomb*
http://base.mng.nias.ac.jp/NoMre/Ge1-e.html

Structure:

1. Identify Dobbs' THESIS STATEMENT, the principle from which his argument is *deduced*. In what very direct way does the rest of this selection teach us to apply that principle?
2. "The Scar" is mostly a *narrative*, in fact two parallel narratives. How do the stories of Emiko and of Captain Lewis complement each other? How does each focus differently on nuclear war?
3. Dobbs' argument is a short essay enclosing a long narrative. Where does each part join the next? And what is the strategy behind this plan?

Style:

1. In his log Captain Lewis writes "it's a very beautiful day" (par. 9), and in paragraph 11 Dobbs adds "It was a lovely morning." What effect do these pleasant words have in the context of the situation? What literary device underlies their power?

2. Captain Lewis writes in his log, "There'll be a short intermission while we bomb our target" (par. 15). Do these words seem peculiar? If so, why?

3. In referring to the first operational nuclear bomb as "Little Boy" (par. 7), what does Dobbs add to the force of his narrative?

4. Paragraphs 23, 24, 27 and 36 are filled with gruesome details that show the effects of "Little Boy." Does this help Dobbs' argument? Do these details spur the reader to oppose nuclear weapons? Or, in their dreadfulness, do they move the reader to drop the subject and think of other things?

5. What qualifies the SYMBOL of Emiko's scar to close the essay?

Argumentation and Persuasion:

1. Dobbs' argument is *deductive*, based on his opening premise that "To think about thermonuclear war in the abstract is obscene. To think about any kind of warfare with less than the whole of our mind and imagination is obscene. This is the worst treason" (par. 3). Identify five passages in which he shuns abstraction to dwell on the CONCRETE and personal experience of nuclear war. Does he apply his own thesis by using "the whole of [his] mind and imagination"?

2. Point out three passages in which Dobbs shows Captain Lewis' abstract view of nuclear war to be "obscene." Does the *contrast* between Lewis' bird's-eye view and Emiko's ground-level view develop Dobbs' premise?

3. Does Dobbs make his point mostly through *argumentation* or *persuasion*? To what extent does he *argue* through objective logic, fact, and example? To what extent does he *persuade* through IRONY, loaded words, fright or other appeals to emotion?

4. In the closing, why does Dobbs shift from specific examples to generalizations and statistics (pars. 42–44)?

Ideas for Discussion and Writing:

1. Albert Einstein, discoverer of the mathematics behind the atomic bomb, said that if he had foreseen the results of his work, he would have chosen to be a shoemaker. Do you hold Einstein and the scientists who worked on "Little Boy" responsible for the carnage in Hiroshima? Or should the scientist pursue abstract truth and leave the application to others?

2. The Cold War and the Arms Race between East and West are said to be over. Can we stop dreading nuclear weapons now? Or might new nations or terrorists obtain and use them? And what might we do to help prevent this?

3. According to Marcus Gee, "in the 50 years since Hiroshima — and Nagasaki three days later — the United States and the Soviet Union have spent roughly $6-trillion. . . on the tools of nuclear warfare — 15 times the sum the United Nations estimates would be needed to wipe severe poverty from the face of the Earth" (*The Globe and Mail,* August 5, 1995). What is your response to these figures?

4. In her 1993 book *A Matter of Survival: Canada in the 21st Century,* the Canadian economist Diane Francis states, "Already a global government has formed through the auspices of the United Nations and the G-7 process." Will a true global government prevent war? To what extent should Canada function as the "police" of a "global government" through its UN peacekeeping missions? Defend your view with examples.

5. **PROCESS IN WRITING:** *Politicians often state that one letter received from a citizen is worth a thousand votes. Decide whether you think Canada should spend more or less on the military. Now write to the minister of defence, arguing your point deductively. Apply your premise to a specific example or examples, such as tanks, fighter planes, destroyers, military bases, etc. As you look over your "discovery draft," see whether you have specialized in either argumentation or persuasion. If your treatment seems too extreme, modify it in your second draft with a dose of the other approach, to produce a combined treatment like that of Dobbs. In your final draft edit for conciseness (the best letters to politicians are short). Finally, you need no stamp to mail a letter to any member of Parliament.*

Note: See also the Topics for Writing at the end of this chapter.

Bonnie Laing

An Ode to the User-Friendly Pencil

"Anyone can write," says Bonnie Laing, "it's the rewrites that kill you." She gave her own essay three drafts on the very computer whose behaviour she describes below. When it "stops dead" she plans to acquire a faster model like the ones she uses at work. Laing is a freelance advertising copywriter, and has also written speeches and press releases for government. She regularly publishes essays and fiction as well; her humorous articles have appeared in The Globe and Mail, Toronto Life, The Toronto Star, Ottawa Citizen *and* TV Guide, *and her short fiction in* Fiddlehead, Quarry *and* Matrix. *In 1992 was published* Marble Season, *a collection of her short stories about French-English relations in the East End of Montreal where she grew up. She also writes plays; since 1990 summer theatres across Canada have produced her comedy* Peggy *and* Grace. *Laing says that after completing an Honours B.A. in English at Queen's, she spent two years as a hippie in England. But once arrived in Toronto, she quickly entered advertising. As a "social marketer" of food and other "lifestyle products," Laing needs a keener sense of audience than even the essayist; in producing "target-specific" text, she says, you have to keep asking yourself "Who is this person I'm writing for?" Although she did have publication in mind, the audience of "An Ode to the User-Friendly Pencil" was herself: she vented her frustrations, felt better, then found that others liked the piece too. On April 29, 1989,* The Globe and Mail *published it. Laing currently lives in Dunvegan, Ontario.*

Recently I acquired a computer. Or perhaps I should say it acquired me. My therapist claims that acknowledging the superior partner in a destructive relationship is the first step toward recovery. I should point out that prior to this acquisition, my idea of modern technology at its best was frozen waffles. My mastery of business machines had advanced only as far as the stapler.

I was persuaded to make this investment by well-meaning friends who said the word-processing capacity of a computer would (a) make me a better writer (b) make me a more productive writer and (c) make me a richer writer. I pointed out that Chaucer was a pretty good writer even though he used a quill, and Dickens managed to produce 15 novels and numerous collections of short stories without so much as a typewriter. But I have to admit that option C got to me, even if I couldn't figure out how spending $3,000 on a piece of molded plastic was going to make me wealthier.

3   To date, my association with the computer has not been too successful. It has proved to be very sensitive to everything but my needs. At the last breakdown (its, not mine) the service man commented that it should have been called an Edsel, not an Epson, and suggested an exorcist be consulted. Needless to say, I am not yet in a position to open a numbered Swiss bank account.

4   But they say hardship teaches you who your friends are. And so, my computer experience has forced me to spend a lot more time with an old friend, the pencil. Its directness and simplicity have proven to be refreshing. In fact, the more I wrestled with my microchips (whatever they are), the more convinced I became that the pencil is superior to the computer. Allow me to cite a few examples.

5   To start with the purchase decision, you don't have to ask for a bank loan to buy a pencil. Since most pencils are not manufactured in Japan, you don't feel you're upsetting the nation's balance of trade by buying one.

6   In fact, pencils are constructed in part from that most Canadian of natural resources — wood. By buying pencils you create employment and prosperity for dozens of people in British Columbia. Well, a few anyway.

7   Of course, like most people I rarely *buy* a pencil, preferring to pick them up free from various places of employment, in the mistaken belief that they are a legitimate fringe benefit. It's best not to make that assumption about office computers.

8   Operationally, the pencil wins over the computer hands down. You can learn to use a pencil in less than 10 seconds. Personally, at the age of 2, I mastered the technology in 3.2 seconds. To be fair, erasing did take a further 2.4 seconds. I've never had to boot a pencil, interface with it or program it. I just write with it.

9   Compared to a computer, a pencil takes up far less space on a desk and it can be utilized in a car, bathroom or a telephone booth without the aid of batteries. You can even use one during an electrical storm. Pencils don't cause eye strain and no one has ever screamed, after four hours of creative endeavor, "The - - - - pencil ate my story!"

10   Pencils are wonderfully singleminded. They aren't used to open car doors, make the morning coffee or remind you that your Visa payment is overdue. They're user-friendly. (For the uninitiated, see comments on vocabulary.)

11   Of course, the technologically addicted among you will argue that the options of a pencil are rather limited. But the software of a pencil is both cheap and simple, consisting of a small rubber tip located at one end of the unit. A pencil is capable of producing more fonts or typefaces than any word processor, depending on the operator's skill.

Its graphic capability is limited only by the operator's talent, an ele-   12
ment referred to as the Dürer or Da Vinci Factor. Backup to a pencil
can usually be found in your purse or pocket. Although a pencil has no
memory, many of us who write badly consider that to be an advantage.

But it's in the area of maintenance that the pencil really proves its   13
superiority. Should a pencil break down, all you have to do to render it
operational again, is buy a small plastic device enclosing a sharp metal
strip, a purchase that can be made for under a dollar. A paring knife, a
piece of broken glass or even your teeth can be used in an emergency.
For the more technically advanced, an electronic pencil sharpener can
be obtained, but I should point out that these devices don't run on
electrical power but by devouring one-third of the pencil.

You never have to take a pencil to a service department located on an   14
industrial site on the outskirts of Moose Factory. Neither do you have to
do without them for two weeks before discovering that the malfunction
is not covered by the warranty and that the replacement part is on a
boat from Korea.

What finally won me over to the pencil was its lack of social preten-   15
sion. For instance, very few people suffer the nagging doubt that their
intelligence is below that of a pencil. No one has ever claimed that a
pencil put them out of a job. And the pencil has not created a whole
new class of workers who consider themselves superior to, let's say,
crayon operators. At parties, you meet very few people who will discuss
pencils with a fervor normally found only at student rallies in Tehran.
Fewer people boast about being 'pencil literate.'

Of course, the pencil is not without its flaws. It has a nasty habit of   16
hiding when most needed. If located beside a telephone, it will break
spontaneously if a caller wishes to leave a message. Those aspiring to be
professional writers should note that editors are unreasonably preju-
diced against submissions in pencil.

But a pencil won't argue with you if you wish to write more than 50   17
lines to the page. It won't insist on correcting your whimsical use of
grammar, and it won't be obsolete 10 seconds after you mortgage your
first-born to buy one. Just in case you remain unconvinced, I ask you,
can you imagine chewing on a computer while balancing your cheque
book? And what do computer operators use to scratch that place in the
middle of the back where they can't reach? The defence rests.

△ △

Explorations:

Bonnie Laing, *The Marble Season*
Henry David Thoreau, *Walden*
http://www.puc.ca/whoswho/b_laing.html

Structure:

1. Laing begins her whole essay of *contrast* with a series of shorter contrasts. In paragraph 1 identify each, and tell how it prepares us for the argument that follows.
2. Identify Laing's THESIS STATEMENT.
3. Identify the sentence of TRANSITION that moves us from Laing's introduction to the body of her argument.
4. Laing's argument is an exceptionally clear *comparison and contrast*. Does she proceed "point by point" or by "halves"?
5. The body of Laing's argument has four parts (par. 5–7, 8–12, 13–14, and 15). To organize her first draft she gave each part a heading, then later removed it. Restore those headings, labelling each division of her argument.
6. What techniques of closing do the final two paragraphs apply?

Style:

1. In paragraph 2 Laing dismisses her computer as a $3000 "piece of molded plastic." Point out five more IMAGES chosen to further her point of view.
2. In paragraph 4 Laing spends "a lot more time with an old friend, the pencil." Point out three other examples of PERSONIFICATION in her essay.
3. In paragraph 11 the pencil's "software" is its eraser. What device of humour has Laing used here?
4. In paragraph 8 Laing states, "I've never had to boot a pencil, interface with it or program it. I just write with it." Point out all the elements of repetition in this passage, and their effects. Are these effects accidental or deliberate?

Argumentation and Persuasion:

1. Laing's essay is a *comparison and contrast* as clearly organized and developed as any in the "Comparison and Contrast" chapter of this book. How well does the pattern lend itself to her *argumentative* and *persuasive* purpose? May essayists use any pattern that supports their purpose?
2. Is Laing's argument *deductive* or *inductive?* If it is deductive, point out its major and minor premises. If it is inductive, point out five major pieces of evidence that lead to the conclusion.
3. To what extent is this essay based on *argumentation?* To what extent on *persuasion?* Defend your answer with examples.
4. Laing's TONE is rich in IRONY. Point out every example of it in paragraph 15. What is the overall effect?

Ideas for Discussion and Writing:

1. Are you a technophobe, like Laing, or do you rejoice in high technology? Defend your answer with examples.

2. Do you now write with a computer? If so, tell all the *contrasts* you have personally experienced between "high-tech" and "low-tech" writing. Give specific examples.

3. The American philosopher Henry David Thoreau, who left town life for a cabin by Walden Pond, wrote "Our life is frittered away by detail. . . . Simplify, simplify." Has high technology simplified or complicated your life? Defend your view with examples.

4. **PROCESS IN WRITING:** *Choose one high-tech invention that you have used, and write an* inductive *essay that praises or condemns it. First freewrite on your subject for at least five minutes — automatically, never letting your user-friendly pencil stop — then look over what you have produced in order to learn your point of view. Now take more notes, gathering examples. Arrange these in order from least to most important, and from this rough outline write a draft. In the second draft adjust your tone: Is the whole argument serious and objective? Is it* argumentative? *Or is it more like Laing's essay: humorous, subjective, and therefore* persuasive? *Whichever it is, be consistent. Now read your essay aloud to family members or classmates, revise any part that fails to work on your* AUDIENCE, *then write the final version.*

Note: See also the Topics for Writing at the end of this chapter.

Joy Kogawa

Grinning and Happy*

With three published books of poetry to her credit — The Splintered Moon
(1967), A Choice of Dreams *(1974) and* Jericho Road *(1977) —* Joy
Kogawa *had become a respected minor poet. But in 1981 she created a sensation
with her first novel.* Obasan *represented a new step for Kogawa as a writer and
as a person: in it she explored her own past and one of the most dubious events
of Canadian history. Born in Vancouver in 1935, Kogawa was a child during
World War II when the federal government classified Japanese-Canadians as
"enemy aliens." Her parents' house in Vancouver was seized, and the family was
moved first to a relocation camp in Slocan, B.C., then to the sugar-beet fields of
southern Alberta, which are the setting of our selection from the novel. Our
narrator is modelled after Kogawa herself, Stephen is the narrator's brother,
Obasan is the narrator's silent and suffering aunt, and "Aunt Emily" is modelled after Muriel Kitagawa, a Japanese-Canadian activist whose letters Kogawa
studied in the National Archives in Ottawa. These same characters returned in
Kogawa's 1992 sequel* Itsuka, *about the struggle of Japanese-Canadians to gain
redress for the wrongs described in* Obasan. *Her third novel,* The Rain Ascends *(1995), looks to new subject matter, the unmasking of a respected Protes-
tant minister as a sexual abuser of children. Yet its themes echo those of* Obasan
and Itsuka, *as the sins of the fathers are visited upon new generations. Though
her recent works are well regarded, it is* Obasan *that places Kogawa among our
major Canadian writers.*

1   There is a folder in Aunt Emily's package containing only one newspaper clipping and an index card with the words "Facts about
evacuees in Alberta." The newspaper clipping has a photograph of one
family, all smiles, standing around a pile of beets. The caption reads:
"Grinning and Happy."

2   **Find Jap Evacuees Best Beet Workers**
Lethbridge, Alberta, Jan. 22.

3   **Japanese evacuees from British Columbia supplied the labour**
for 65% of Alberta's sugar beet acreage last year, Phil Baker, of

---

* Editor's title.

Lethbridge, president of the Alberta Sugar Beet Growers Association, stated today.

"They played an important part in producing our all-time record crop of 363,000 tons of beets in 1945," he added.   4

Mr. Baker explained Japanese evacuees worked 19,500 acres of beets and German prisoners of war worked 5,000 acres. The labour for the remaining 5,500 acres of Alberta's 30,000 acres of sugar beets was provided by farmers and their families. Some of the heaviest beet yields last year came from farms employing Japanese evacuees.   5

Generally speaking, Japanese evacuees have developed into most efficient beet workers, many of them being better than the transient workers who cared for beets in southern Alberta before Pearl Harbor. . . .   6

Facts about evacuees in Alberta? The fact is I never got used to it and I cannot, I cannot bear the memory. There are some nightmares from which there is no waking, only deeper and deeper sleep.   7

There is a word for it. Hardship. The hardship is so pervasive, so inescapable, so thorough it's a noose around my chest and I cannot move any more. All the oil in my joints has drained out and I have been invaded by dust and grit from the fields and mud is in my bone marrow. I can't move any more. My fingernails are black from scratching the scorching day and there is no escape.   8

Aunt Emily, are you a surgeon cutting at my scalp with your folders and your filing cards and your insistence on knowing all? The memory drains down the sides of my face, but it isn't enough, is it? It's your hands in my abdomen, pulling the growth from the lining of my walls, but bring back the anaesthetist turn on the ether clamp down the gas mask bring on the chloroform when will this operation be over Aunt Em?   9

Is it so bad?   10

Yes.   11

Do I really mind?   12

Yes, I mind. I mind everything. Even the flies. The flies and flies and flies from the cows in the barn and the manure pile — all the black flies that curtain the windows, and Obasan with a wad of toilet paper, spish, then with her bare hands as well, grabbing them and their shocking white eggs and the mosquitoes mixed there with the other insect corpses around the base of the gas lamp.   13

It's the chicken coop "house" we live in that I mind. The uninsulated unbelievable thin-as-a-cotton-dress hovel never before inhabited in winter by human beings. In summer it's a heat trap, an incubator, a dry sauna from which there is no relief. In winter the icicles drip down the inside of the windows and the ice is thicker than bricks at the ledge.   14

The only place that is warm is by the coal stove where we rotate like chickens on a spit and the feet are so cold they stop registering. We eat cloves of roasted garlic on winter nights to warm up.

15   It's the bedbugs and my having to sleep on the table to escape the nightly attack, and the welts over our bodies. And all the swamp bugs and the dust. It's Obasan uselessly packing all the cracks with rags. And the muddy water from the irrigation ditch which we strain and settle and boil, and the tiny carcasses of water creatures at the bottom of the cup. It's walking in winter to the reservoir and keeping the hole open with the axe and dragging up the water in pails and lugging it back and sometimes the water spills down your boots and your feet are red and itchy for days. And it's everybody taking a bath in the round galvanized tub, then Obasan washing clothes in the water after and standing outside hanging the clothes in the freezing weather where everything instantly stiffens on the line.

16   Or it's standing in the beet field under the maddening sun, standing with my black head a sun-trap even though it's covered, and lying down in the ditch, faint, and the nausea in waves and the cold sweat, and getting up and tackling the next row. The whole field is an oven and there's not a tree within walking distance. We are tiny as insects crawling along the grill and there is no protection anywhere. The eyes are lidded against the dust and the air cracks the skin, the lips crack, Stephen's flutes crack and there is no energy to sing any more anyway.

17   It's standing in the field and staring out at the heat waves that waver and shimmer like see-through curtains over the brown clods and over the tiny distant bodies of Stephen and Uncle and Obasan miles away across the field day after day and not even wondering how this has come about.

18   There she is, Obasan, wearing Uncle's shirt over a pair of dark baggy trousers, her head covered by a straw hat that is held on by a white cloth tied under her chin. She is moving like a tiny earth cloud over the hard clay clods. Her hoe moves rhythmically up down up down, tiny as a toothpick. And over there, Uncle pauses to straighten his back, his hands on his hips. And Stephen farther behind, so tiny I can barely see him.

19   It's hard, Aunt Emily, with my hoe, the blade getting dull and mud-caked as I slash out the Canada thistle, dandelions, crab grass, and other nameless non-beet plants, then on my knees, pulling out the extra beets from the cluster, leaving just one to mature, then three hand spans to the next plant, whack whack, and down on my knees again, pull, flick flick, and on to the end of the long long row and the next and the next and it will never be done thinning and weeding and weeding and weeding. It's so hard and so hot that my tear glands burn out.

And then it's cold. The lumps of clay mud stick on my gumboots and   20
weight my legs and the skin under the boots beneath the knees at the
level of the calves grows red and hard and itchy from the flap flap of
the boots and the fine hairs on my legs grow coarse there and ugly.

I mind growing ugly.   21

I mind the harvest time and the hands and the wrists bound in rags   22
to keep the wrists from breaking open. I lift the heavy mud-clotted
beets out of the ground with the hook like an eagle's beak, thick and
heavy as a nail attached to the top of the sugar-beet knife. Thwack. Into
the beet and yank from the shoulder till it's out of the ground dragging
the surrounding mud with it. Then crack two beets together till most of
the mud drops off and splat, the knife slices into the beet scalp and the
green top is tossed into one pile, the beet heaved onto another, one
more one more one more down the icy line. I cannot tell about this
time, Aunt Emily. The body will not tell.

We are surrounded by a horizon of denim-blue sky with clouds clear   23
as spilled milk that turn pink at sunset. Pink I hear is the colour of
llama's milk. I wouldn't know. The clouds are the shape of our new
prison walls — untouchable, impersonal, random.

There are no other people in the entire world. We work together all   24
day. At night we eat and sleep. We hardly talk anymore. The boxes we
brought from Slocan are not unpacked. The King George/Queen Elizabeth mugs stay muffled in the *Vancouver Daily Province*. The camera
phone does not sing. Obasan wraps layers of cloth around her feet and
her torn sweater hangs unmended over her sagging dress.

Down the miles we are obedient as machines in this odd ballet with-   25
out accompaniment of flute or song.

"Grinning and happy" and all smiles standing around a pile of beets?   26
That is one telling. It's not how it was.

△△△

Explorations:

Joy Kogawa,
  Obasan
  Itsuka
  The Rain Ascends
Barry Broadfoot, *Years of Sorrow, Years of Shame: The Story of Japanese
  Canadians in World War II*
Ken Adachi, *The Enemy That Never Was: A History of the Japanese Canadians*
Ann Sunahara, *The Politics of Racism: The Uprooting of Japanese Canadians
  During the Second World War*
http://www.najc.ca

Structure:

1. Why does Kogawa "frame" her argument by citing the newspaper article in both her opening and closing?
2. How does the device of *contrast* help organize this selection?
3. What percentage of *examples* has Kogawa reached in the content of this selection? Is it enough? Do you use enough?
4. How important is *description* to the success of this passage?
5. Most THESIS STATEMENTS are placed early in an argument; why is Kogawa's put in the very last line?

Style:

1. Until *Obasan*, Kogawa was best known as a poet. What poetical qualities do you see in her PROSE?
2. To what extent does Kogawa communicate by SENSE IMAGES? Cite one case each of appeals to sight, hearing, touch, taste and smell.
3. The poet Kogawa fills her prose with FIGURES OF SPEECH. Point out three good SIMILES and three good METAPHORS.
4. In paragraphs 14 through 17, how many times does the contraction "it's" appear at or near the beginning of a sentence? Is the *repetition* accidental or deliberate? What is its effect?
5. How many words long is the first sentence of paragraph 19? How many times does it use the word "and"? Is this run-on sentence accidental or deliberate? What is its effect?

Argumentation and Persuasion:

1. As a member of a persecuted minority, Kogawa's narrator rejects a *deductive* stance; she shuns the official "telling" of the newspaper article, and instead produces her own eyewitness "telling." Point out at least ten pieces of evidence that lead *inductively* to her own conclusion that the newspaper's version of the truth is "not how it was."
2. Does Kogawa rely more on *argumentation* or on *persuasion*? To what extent does she communicate through reason, and to what extent through emotion?
3. Analyze Kogawa's tools of *persuasion*: point out at least five loaded words, five SENSE IMAGES and five FIGURES OF SPEECH that build emotion. Identify one case of deliberate repetition, and one of extreme sentence length, both of which build emotion. Does all this persuasion put you on guard? Or does it convince you?

Ideas for Discussion and Writing:

1. How often are you, like Kogawa's narrator, caught between two or more views of the truth? Cite a recent case. Did you act *deductively*, accepting a view already held by yourself or others, or did you move *inductively* to a new conclusion?

2. The narrator and her family are Canadian citizens of Japanese descent, removed by our federal government from the coast of British Columbia during World War II for fear they would betray Canada to enemy Japan. (Not a single case of such betrayal was ever found.) Many families were separated and their property taken. Attack or defend these official actions against citizens like Kogawa's fictional family. Have such acts occurred in Canada before? Since? Can you imagine them happening in future to any group you belong to?

3. During the war the Canadian government confiscated an island off British Columbia, compensating its Japanese-Canadian owner with $2000. Two generations later his granddaughter, a university student, estimated the worth of this property at 200 million dollars. In 1988 the Canadian government officially apologized to the Japanese-Canadians and offered each survivor of the epoch $21,000. Has the wrong been righted? Attack or defend our government's actions.

4. You are the student in question 3 above. Write to the prime minister, arguing either *deductively* or *inductively* that the island be restored to the heirs of its original owner. *Or* you are the present owner. Write to the prime minister, arguing either *deductively* or *inductively* that your island should not be seized and given to descendants of the man who once owned it.

5. **PROCESS IN WRITING:** *Name a group that you think has been badly treated by Canadian society (for example, disabled people, the elderly, Native peoples, farmers, immigrants, refugees, single parents, etc.). Take notes, then write an* inductive argument *giving the evidence that led to your belief. In a further draft fine-tune the balance of* argumentation and persuasion. *Now share this version with a small group of classmates, and apply their best advice. At home, read aloud to detect wordiness and awkwardness. Edit. Finally, read your good version aloud to the whole class, and be prepared to defend your view.*

Note: See also the Topics for Writing at the end of this chapter.

Rita Schindler

Thanks for Not Killing My Son

All we know about Rita Schindler is what she herself says in her letter. It was a student who noticed "Thanks for Not Killing My Son" in the "Have Your Say" feature of the December 30, 1990, Toronto Star. *He tore it out and brought it to his writing teacher, exclaiming what a fine argument it was. The teacher agreed. By the time the editor of this book tried to reach Ms. Schindler, though, the* Star *had discarded her address. None of the many Schindlers listed in the Toronto phone book knew her, and the hospital mentioned in her letter would not divulge information. The publisher even talked with a detective agency. Finally, though, the Copyright Board of Canada gave permission to reprint the letter, as it can do in such cases. We sincerely believe that Ms. Schindler would want her eloquent and highly principled argument made available to more persons of her son's generation. If you happen to know her, please show her this book and ask her to contact the publisher, who will direct her to the government office where her author's fee is waiting.*

1   I hope you will print my letter of gratitude to the strangers who have affected our lives.

2   Sometime between 1:30 p.m., Dec. 8, and 1 a.m., Dec. 9, a young man was viciously attacked — beaten and kicked unconscious for no apparent reason other than walking by you on a public sidewalk.

3   He was left lying in a pool of blood from an open head wound — in the Victoria Park-Terraview area. He was found around 1 a.m. and taken to Scarborough General Hospital where ironically his mother spent 48 hours in labor before giving him birth, 23 years earlier.

4   His mother is angry of course, but thankful for the following reasons.

5   First of all — his eye socket was shattered and hemorrhaging but his eyesight will not be affected. Thank you.

6   His ear canal was lacerated internally from a tremendous blow to the side of his head. The cut could not be stitched and the bleeding was difficult to stop. But his eardrum seems to be undamaged — thank you.

7   He required numerous stitches to his forehead, temple and face but your boots didn't knock one tooth out — thank you. His head was swollen almost twice its size — but Mom knew that his brain was intact — for he held her hand for six hours as he lay on a gurney, by the

nurses station, I.V. in his arm — his head covered and crusted with dried blood — waiting for x-ray results and the surgeon to stitch him up.

So, thank you for this eyesight, his hearing and his hands which you   8
could have easily crushed.

His hands — human hands — the most intricately beautiful and   9
complex instruments of incredible mechanism — the result of billions of years of evolution — and you people used yours to beat another human being. Five guys and two girls to beat one person. Who do I thank? Did you know he was a talented young musician with a budding career — and that playing his keyboards and piano mean more to him than my words can say.

And when his friends were talking about revenge, I heard him say,   10
"No, I don't want someone else's mother to go through what mine has." That's who you were kicking in the head. And so — I thank you for not causing the most horrible and devastating thing that can happen to any parent — that is — the untimely tragic loss of a child — at any age.

You could have kicked him to death but you only left him to die,   11
thank you. A person found him and called for help.

I am his mother — and I have been given a second chance — thanks   12
to you.

I hope that someday you'll have children and love them as much as I   13
love mine — but I wouldn't wish on your child what you did to mine.

Rita Schindler
Scarborough

ΔΔΔΔΔΔΔΔΔΔΔΔΔΔΔΔΔΔΔΔΔΔΔΔΔΔΔΔΔΔΔΔΔΔΔΔΔΔΔΔΔΔΔΔΔΔΔΔΔ

Explorations:

Anthony Burgess, *A Clockwork Orange*
Dan Korem, *Suburban Gangs: The Affluent Rebels*
http://www.sgc.gc.ca/EFact/egangs.htm
http://www.sgc.gc.ca/Quiz/youth/equizbp2.htm

Structure:

1. Schindler's argument is cast as a letter. For what *audience* is it meant? The youths who attacked her son? All the readers of *The Toronto Star*? How well does her "letter" work as an essay?
2. Schindler organizes her letter by examining in turn each injury inflicted on her son. Point out each. What proportion of the letter's content is given to these *examples*? Could the point have been made without them?

3. After all her ironic "thanking," Schindler ends more literally: "I wouldn't wish on your child what you did to mine." Is her closing weak because it drops the IRONY, or strong because it caps the point?

Style:

1. Six of Schindler's paragraphs have only one sentence. Give reasons. Is this style effective?
2. How CONCISE is this selection? Try to find one passage of deadwood that could have been cut.
3. How FORMAL or INFORMAL is Schindler's TONE? Give examples. Does the tone fit the content? Why or why not?

Argumentation and Persuasion:

1. "You could have kicked him to death, but you only left him to die, thank you," writes the victim's mother in paragraph 11. Her letter of "thanks" is *persuasion* as strong as any in this book. Explain the IRONY of Schindler's "thanking" her son's attackers.
2. Find and explain at least 10 more IRONIES in this selection.
3. The author might have called her son's attackers "thugs," "goons" or worse. Would this openly *persuasive* mode be more effective than the "thanks" she gives? Defend your answer with reasons.
4. In addition to *irony*, the introduction to this chapter lists *repetition*, *fright* and *climax* as techniques of persuasion. How does Schindler use each? Respond with examples.
5. Does Schindler make her point *deductively* (through an innate rejection of violence) or *inductively* (through the many examples she cites, leading to her point)? Can an argument go both ways at once? Would this be a failure of logic?

Ideas for Discussion and Writing:

1. Does Schindler attempt only to heap shame on her son's attackers, or do you also detect, for example in the closing, a desire for reconciliation?
2. When his friends desired revenge, the son said, "No, I don't want someone else's mother to go through what mine has" (par. 10). What would *you* have said? Defend your answer with reasons.
3. How much do techniques of nonviolent resisters such as Mahatma Gandhi and Martin Luther King have in common with the responses of Rita Schindler and her son? Is their way ultimately weaker or stronger than the way of those who defend themselves through violence? Give examples.

4. Is there violent crime at your school or campus? If so, give examples. Defend or attack the "zero tolerance" policy of some school boards that permanently expel students who commit violent offences. Are there other solutions that would work?

5. Are public forums such as the letters to the editor column or electronic bulletin boards good vehicles for promoting our own ideas? Do others actually read and heed what we say?

6. **PROCESS IN WRITING:** *Read the crime news in your newspaper or hear it on radio or TV. Choose one violent act that provokes your anger or concern. Consider how, like Rita Schindler, you can respond to it through* IRONY *to persuade your audience to take your side. Make notes, look them over, then write a rapid first draft of a letter to the perpetrator, to the public, or to both. The next day look it over. Will it startle and persuade the* AUDIENCE *by meaning the opposite of what it says? (Remember Schindler's "thanking" the attackers, or in Chapter 5 Russell Baker's "criticizing" Toronto, or in Chapter 8 Stephen Leacock's "advice" on how to live to be 200.) Is the ironic* TONE *consistent? Is the letter concise, like Schindler's? If not, revise. Finally, check the spelling and grammar. When you have produced your good draft, send it as a letter to the editor of the newspaper you read. Or, if you are online, send it from your computer to an appropriate "bulletin board" on the Internet. Check either for responses. Collect them, then show them, with the original letter, to the class.*

Note: See also the Topics for Writing at the end of this Chapter.

Dionne Brand

Job

Born in Trinidad in 1953, Dionne Brand came to Canada in 1970, and that year experienced the frustrating event described in "Job." Since then she has become a strong voice in the fight against racism and sexism in our society. After a B.A. in English and philosophy, an M.A. in education, and then more work in women's studies, all at the University of Toronto, Brand put her egalitarian values into action. She has worked at the Immigrant Women's Centre and the Black Youth Hotline; has been a community relations worker for the Board of Education; and helped found Our Lives, *a community newspaper, and the International Coalition of Black Trade Unionists. She has also worked with the Women's Committee of the Ontario Federation of Labour, and the Metro Labour Council Anti-Racism Conference, and has been on the board of a shelter for battered women. In 1983 while Brand was doing community development in Grenada, the United States invaded the little Caribbean country and she was evacuated. Brand has made several documentaries for the National Film Board of Canada, such as* Older, Stronger, Wiser *(1989), and* Sisters in the Struggle *(1991). Dozens of her socially conscious poems and stories have appeared in periodicals and anthologies, and Brand has also published over a dozen books of her own, among them* Sans Souci and Other Stories *(1988),* Bread Out of Stone *(essays, 1994),* In Another Place, Not Here *(novel, 1996), and* Land to Light On *(1997, winner of the Governor General's Award for Poetry). Our selection is from* Bread Out of Stone.*

1   It was that tiny office in the back of a building on Keele Street. I had called the morning before, looking for a job, and the man answering remarked on that strong Scottish name of my putative father and told me to come right in and the job would be mine. Yes, it was that tiny office in the back of a building on Keele when I was turning eighteen, and I dressed up in my best suit outfit with high heels and lipstick and ninety-seven pounds of trying hard desperate feminine heterosexuality, wanting to look like the man on the phone's imagination so I could get the job. When I went to that tiny office and saw the smile of the man on the phone fade and the job disappear because all of a sudden it needed experience or was just given to somebody else and, no, there would be no interview and if it were today I would have sued the pig for making

346

me walk away with my eighteen-year-old self trying not to cry and feeling laughter, that laughter that Black people get, derisive and self-derisive rising inside my chest. Yes, it was that man on the phone, that office on Keele Street, that man's imagination for a Scottish girl he could molest as she filed papers in the cabinets in the tiny office, it was that wanting to cry in my best suit and high heels I could barely walk in and the lipstick my sister helped me to put on straight and plucked my eyebrows and made me wear foundation cream in order, I suppose, to dull the impact of my blackness so that the man in the tiny office would give me that job. What propelled my legs back to the subway was shame. That I could ever think of getting such a job, even so small and mean a job, that some white man could forget himself and at least see me as someone he could exploit, and I was willing to be considered as someone to exploit. It was 1970. A kitchen then, maybe, but not an office. My sister worked the kitchens of hospitals, and that is where I did find a job the next week, and that is where we waited out the ebb and flow of favour and need in this white place.

△ △

Explorations:

Dionne Brand,
> *Bread Out of Stone*
> *Land to Light On*
> *In Another Place, Not Here*

Francis Henry, *The Caribbean Diaspora in Toronto*

http://utl2.library.utoronto.ca/disk1/www/documents/canpoetry/
brand/index.html

Structure:

1. Why does "Job" move from start to finish with no paragraph breaks? How would it be different if it had them? Would you have used them or not, for this subject?
2. What organizational technique does Brand employ when she closes on the words ". . . in this white place"?

Style:

1. Brand begins four key sentences and phrases with the words "It was . . . ."? Do you think this repetition is accidental or deliberate? What effects does it achieve?
2. Count the words in Brand's fourth sentence. Would you write one so long? Why does she? What are the effects?

Argumentation and Persuasion:

1. Review the list of *persuasive* devices on pp. 313-314 of this chapter's introduction. Which ones does Brand use here? Give an example for each of your answers.
2. Does "Job" also have an *argumentative* dimension? If so, is it *deductive* or *inductive*? Tell how.

Ideas for Discussion and Writing:

1. Dionne Brand had recently arrived in Canada when she lived the event she writes of here. How much have things changed since 1970, when she was 18? Would this scene be possible in Toronto today? In your own town or city? If it did happen, what legal recourse is now available?
2. Brand and her sister "waited out the ebb and flow of favour and need in this white place," working in kitchen hospitals, till things changed. Why, in our time, does she still remember the racist who refused her an interview some 30 years ago? Should she try to forget? Or will remembering serve her better in the present and future? How?
3. Our author calls the man who refused her interview a "pig." Do you consider this name-calling justified? Or, in labelling her enemy, does she begin to share his attitudes? What would you do?
4. Every group in Canadian society is now a minority. Has yours suffered unfairness? Illustrate, as Brand has done, with an incident.
5. **PROCESS IN WRITING:** *Use persuasion in the act of writing, as Brand has done, to expose an unfairness that happened to you. Close your eyes and recall the incident, then freewrite on it for several minutes. Look over what you have produced, then work the best of it into a fast discovery draft, adding images and details (remember Brand "showing" us her high heels and lipstick, the man's smile fading, the difficult walk back to the subway). Later look over the nine devices of persuasion listed on pp. 313-314 of our chapter introduction; what do you see that will strengthen your message? Use it. Now edit for style and mechanics, then read the piece aloud, with feeling, to the class. Finally, ask for reactions. Which passages communicated most strongly, and why?*

Note: See also the Topics for Writing at the end of this chapter.

Nathalie Petrowski

The Seven-Minute Life of
Marc Lépine*

Translated from the French by Ronald Conrad

Nathalie Petrowski, columnist for La Presse *and formerly for* Le Devoir, *is one of Quebec's favourite print journalists — quirky, personal and satirical. She has also published a novel,* Il Restera toujours le Nebraska *(1990), and a book on having children in middle age (*Maman, last call, *1995). In her* Devoir *column of December 16, 1989, Petrowski had a special challenge: ten days before, a 25-year-old man had walked into an engineering class at the University of Montreal's École Polytechnique, shouted at the women students "You're all a bunch of feminists, and I hate feminists," ordered the men to leave — then lifted his rifle and shot the women. Six died. During the next minutes of terror (seven according to Petrowski, twenty according to later reports) he roamed the building, shooting as he went. Altogether he gunned down 27 students, killing 14, all women. Then Marc Lépine turned the weapon on himself and died too. The nation felt a shock wave of anger and remorse, for not only was this the worst one-day mass murder in the country's history, but its selectivity seemed to express a general sexism in society. In the next days, as the flag over Parliament flew at half-mast, citizens learned that Lépine's father had beat him and mistreated the mother, that the parents had divorced, and that the boy, though intelligent, had problems in school both academically and socially. He loved war movies, and from a paratrooper uncle learned to handle firearms. Now on December 6 of every year, ceremonies across the nation honour the 14 young women, training for a profession still dominated by men, who were killed by a man whose suicide note blamed feminists for ruining his life. The essay that follows (originally entitled "Pitié pour les salauds") has a special poignancy, for Nathalie Petrowski wrote it in shock, as she and the nation first struggled to see meaning in the event. (Note: See also "Our Daughters, Ourselves," by Stevie Cameron, on the same subject.)*

Pardon if I insist, pardon if I don't just mourn and forget, but it's stronger than I am, for a week I can't stop thinking about Marc Lépine. A psychoanalyst would say I'm identifying with the aggressor.

1

---

* Editor's title.

But I'd say that inside every aggressor, every villain, there hides a victim.

2   I think of Marc Lépine to block out all the talk that just confuses things: Rambo, television, violence towards women, pornography, abortion, and firearms in display windows.

3   I think of Marc Lépine, still wondering what happened and exactly when the hellish countdown of his act was unleashed. Was it the morning of December 6, was it November 21 when he bought his rifle or September 4 when he applied for the firearm permit? Was it the day of his birth, the first time his father beat him, the day his parents divorced, the week when he suddenly quit all his courses, the night a girl didn't want to dance with him? What about all the hours, the days, the weeks, the years that passed before the bomb inside him went off?

4   Still, journalists have told us everything: where he lived, the schools he went to, the names of teachers and students he knew. We know how much he paid for his rifle and how he loved war movies. But once all this has been said, nothing has been said.

5   We know nothing of the ache that consumed him, of the torture inside him. We know nothing of the evil path he slipped into smiling the cruel smile of the angel of destruction, no longer himself, knowing only that he was put on earth to destroy.

6   I think of Marc Lépine but equally of Nadia, his sister who was beaten, too, for singing out loud in the morning, Nadia who came from the same family but didn't fall prey to the same madness. Why Marc and not Nadia, why Marc and not another? That's what I ask myself when facts only deepen the mystery, when social criticism only confuses things.

7   No one remembers him from grade school, or from Sainte-Justine Hospital where he spent a year in therapy with his mother and sister. Until last week Marc Lépine did not exist. He was an unknown quantity, a number, an anonymous face in the crowd, a nobody who no one would even look at or give the least warmth, the slightest affection. In a few moments he went from a nothing to one of a kind, a pathological case who the experts claim in no way represents the society where he was born and grew up.

8   For a week I've been talking with these experts, hoping to understand. For a week all I've seen is that there is no one answer, there are a thousand. For a week I've dealt with the official and professional voices who keep their files under key, who keep repeating that there's no use wanting to know more, that Marc Lépine is dead, that he can no longer be healed or saved, that it's too late to do anything at all. Sometimes their excuses and justifications sound like lies.

9   But I refuse to hear the silence of death that falls like snow, the shameful silence that freezes my blood. Somewhere deep in the ruins

of our private space we hide the truth, we try to protect ourselves saying that families — ours, his, the victims' — have been traumatized.

Forget about the past, say the authorities, let's move on and not let Marc Lépine's act dictate our choices. Yet the surest way to let this act dictate our choices is to hide it, to let it become a medical, psychological and criminal secret, to push it into the smallest hollow of our collective memory till it's erased and we can say it never existed at all.

In this province where memory is reduced to a slogan on a licence plate°, we want to forget Marc Lépine like we forget all events that can disturb us and make us think. Though I know nothing of Marc Lépine's story, I've met enough young people in the high schools and colleges to know that chance as well as reasons, randomness as well as all the wrong conditions in one person's life, caused this act. His tragic destiny looks more and more like a tangle of shattered hopes, of frustrated dreams, of hopeless waits on a long and cold road without a single hand extended to help, and no guardrail.

Marc Lépine died the evening of December 6, but unlike his victims, he had died long before. In the end his life lasted just seven minutes. Before and after, he was forgotten.

So pardon my pessimism, but I cannot help believing that somewhere, at this moment, there are other Marc Lépines who won't ask for anything because they don't even know what to ask for — other children turned into monsters by abusive fathers and impersonal school systems, by a society so intent on excellence that every day it hammers the nail of Defeat further in, and plants seeds of frustration and violence in the fragile spirits of its children.

Though nothing can be done now for Marc Lépine, something can still be done for the others, whose inner clock has already begun the terrible countdown. It would be a mistake to forget them.

△ △

Explorations:

Nathalie Petrowski, *Il Restera toujours le Nebraska* (novel; available only in French)
Louise Malette and Marie Chalouh, eds., *Polytechnique, 6 décembre* (writings on the Montreal Massacre; available only in French)
Elliott Leyton, *Hunting Humans* (book on multiple murders)
Camilo José Cela, *Pascal Duarte's family* (novel, Spain)
Gabriel García Márquez, *Chronicle of a Death Foretold* (novella, Colombia)
Anne Hébert, *The Torrent* (novella)

° Quebec licence plates bear the motto "Je me souviens" ("I remember"); Quebeckers consider this a reference to their history, and especially the Conquest.

http://dionysos.ulaval.ca/impact/ic/icart.951114.html (in French)
http://www.whiteribbon.ca

Structure:

1. Where is Petrowski's THESIS STATEMENT?
2. Tragic events leave people asking "why?" Point out all the reasons that Petrowski examines to explain this event. To what extent is her essay constructed through *cause and effect?*
3. How does paragraph 6 use *comparison and contrast?*
4. What often-used technique of conclusion gives force to the closing?

Style:

1. In paragraph 1 and elsewhere, Petrowski groups sentences together with commas. Do you view this as faulty punctuation, or is it a way for Petrowski to express feelings about this subject? Are we ever justified in breaking rules of punctuation and sentence structure?
2. Identify all the FIGURES OF SPEECH in paragraph 9. What do they contribute?
3. What feeling does paragraph 3 convey in its flurry of questions?

Argumentation and Persuasion:

1. It seems natural that, as a journalist, Petrowski select *induction* for her logic. What difficulties does she have, though, obtaining the evidence she needs to draw a conclusion?
2. Point out five techniques of *persuasion* that Petrowski uses (consult the list in our chapter introduction). Which one has the most impact? How *persuasive* is the essay as a whole? Does Petrowski's TONE fit her subject?

Ideas for Discussion and Writing:

1. After murdering 14 engineering students because they were women, Marc Lépine also killed himself. But in what sense had he "died long before" (par. 12)? In what sense did his life last only "seven minutes" (par. 12)?
2. In her essay "Our Daughters, Ourselves," Stevie Cameron mourns Lépine's victims. Petrowski opens her own essay with the belief that "inside every aggressor, every villain, there hides a victim." Can we and should we view Marc Lépine, the killer, as himself a victim? If so, a victim of who or what?
3. In its issue covering the Montreal Massacre, *Maclean's* reported that in Canada one of every four women is harrassed sexually at some

time in life, and that a million women are abused each year by their husbands or partners. It also quoted a study by Rosemary Gartner who found that "as women move into nontraditional roles, they run a significantly higher risk of being killed." Do you see any relationship between this information and the act of Marc Lépine? Explain.

4. On that day, Lépine carried one of the most popular rifles in Canada, a .223-calibre Sturm, Ruger semiautomatic, with two 30-clip magazines holding shells with expanding slugs. Are firearms such as this a danger in your city or town? Attack or defend the sale of arms, including handguns, over the counter. Are our strengthened gun laws an attack on civil liberties, as many hunters maintain, or are they still not strong enough to stop the next Marc Lépine?

5. What concrete steps might have been taken, and by whom, to help Marc Lépine before it was too late?

6. **PROCESS IN WRITING:** *Lépine used a rifle, but handguns are the weapon of choice for shootings. At the library, gather information on the role of handguns in crime in Canada. Research also our current regulations for their sale and use. Now decide your* THESIS: *whether Canada should end, more severely limit, or continue to permit the sale of handguns to civilians. List your reasons. From this short outline write a fast discovery draft of your essay, developed mainly through* argumentation, *not stopping now to fix things like spelling or punctuation. The next day look it over. Is every point backed by a reason or example? Does your* evidence *lead clearly to your* conclusion? *(Remember that many essayists will change a conclusion or even a thesis statement when writing gives them new ideas). Finally, edit for correctness as you produce your final version.*

Note: See also the Topics for Writing at the end of this chapter.

Stevie Cameron

Our Daughters, Ourselves

Every democracy has its muckrakers, journalists who probe the dark side of public life and bring it into the open. Stephanie "Stevie" Cameron is the best of ours. When her blockbuster exposé On the Take: Crime, Corruption and Greed in the Mulroney Years *was published in 1994, its massive documentation of alleged graft, backroom politics and even suspicious deaths prompted* Globe and Mail *reviewer Clark Davey to write, "Conservatives who read this book will weep for their party. Other Canadians must weep for their country." Some hated the book: Toronto* Sun *columnist Douglas Fisher called it "trash." Stevie Cameron has travelled a long path from her beginnings as food and lifestyle writer to a controversial investigative journalist whose wrath can shake political parties and governments. Daughter of a soldier of fortune who flew in the Spanish Civil War, who may have been a CIA agent, and who was then killed in a 1956 plane crash, Cameron grew up in Switzerland, Venezuela and Canada. It was her love of cooking that led her to the famous Cordon Bleu School in Paris, and from there to her beginnings in food journalism.*

Cameron now probes wider issues in society. It was on December 9, 1989, that her article "Our Daughters, Ourselves" appeared in The Globe and Mail. *Three days earlier had occurred one of the worst crimes in Canadian history: a 25-year-old man had murdered 14 engineering students in Montreal because they were women, and had left a suicide note blaming feminists for ruining his life. (See a fuller account of the Montreal Massacre in the introduction to Nathalie Petrowski's essay "The Seven-Minute Life of Marc Lépine," also in this chapter.) While Cameron's lyrical and devastating essay is directed at the 14 young women who had aimed at a profession dominated by men, it also examines the context of this crime — the problems of sexism routinely faced by all daughters of our society. Cameron's elegy aroused such public response that The Canadian Research Institute for the Advancement of Women later named it best feminist article of the year, and on the first anniversary of the murders the* Globe *printed it again.*

1   T hey are so precious to us, our daughters. When they are born we see their futures as unlimited, and as they grow and learn we try so hard to protect them: This is how we cross the street, hold my hand,

wear your boots, don't talk to strangers, run to the neighbors if a man tries to get you in his car.

We tell our bright, shining girls that they can be anything: firefighters, doctors, policewomen, lawyers, scientists, soldiers, athletes, artists. What we don't tell them, yet, is how hard it will be. Maybe, we say to ourselves, by the time they're older it will be easier for them than it was for us. 2

But as they grow and learn, with aching hearts we have to start dealing with their bewilderment about injustice. Why do the boys get the best gyms, the best equipment and the best times on the field? Most of the school sports budget? Why does football matter more than gymnastics? Why are most of the teachers women and most of the principals men? Why do the boys make more money at their part-time jobs than we do? 3

And as they grow and learn we have to go on trying to protect them: We'll pick you up at the subway, we'll fetch you from the movie, stay with the group, make sure the parents drive you home from babysitting, don't walk across the park alone, lock the house if we're not there. 4

It's not fair, they say. Boys can walk where they want, come in when they want, work where they want. Not really, we say; boys get attacked too. But boys are not targets for men the way girls are, so girls have to be more careful. 5

Sometimes our girls don't make it. Sometimes, despite our best efforts and all our love, they go on drugs, drop out, screw up. On the whole, however, our daughters turn into interesting, delightful people. They plan for college and university, and with wonder and pride we see them competing with the boys for spaces in engineering schools, medical schools, law schools, business schools. For them we dream of Rhodes scholarships, Harvard graduate school, gold medals; sometimes, we even dare to say these words out loud and our daughters reward us with indulgent hugs. Our message is that anything is possible. 6

We bite back the cautions that we feel we should give them; maybe by the time they've graduated, things will have changed, we say to ourselves. Probably by the time they're out, they will make partner when the men do, be asked to join the same clubs, run for political office. Perhaps they'll even be able to tee off at the same time men do at the golf club. 7

But we still warn them: park close to the movie, get a deadbolt for your apartment, check your windows, tell your roommates where you are. Call me. Call me. 8

And then with aching hearts we take our precious daughters to lunch and listen to them talk about their friends: the one who was beaten by her boy friend and then shunned by his friends when she asked for 9 help from the dean; the one who was attacked in the parking lot; the one who gets obscene and threatening calls from a boy in her residence; the one who gets raped on a date; the one who was mocked by the male students in the public meeting.

10   They tell us about the sexism they're discovering in the adult world at university. Women professors who can't get jobs, who can't get tenure. Male professors who cannot comprehend women's stony silence after sexist jokes. An administration that only pays lip service to women's issues and refuses to accept the reality of physical danger to women on campus.

11   They tell us they're talking among themselves about how men are demanding rights over unborn children; it's not old dinosaurs who go to court to prevent a woman's abortion, it's young men. It's young men, they say with disbelief, their own generation, their own buddies with good education, from "nice" families, who are abusive.

12   What can we say to our bright and shining daughters? How can we tell them how much we hurt to see them developing the same scars we've carried? How much we wanted it to be different for them? It's all about power, we say to them. Sharing power is not easy for anyone and men do not find it easy to share among themselves, much less with a group of equally talented, able women. So men make all those stupid cracks about needing a sex-change operation to get a job or a promotion and they wind up believing it.

13   Now our daughters have been shocked to the core, as we all have, by the violence in Montreal. They hear the women were separated from the men and meticulously slaughtered by a man who blamed feminists for his troubles. They ask themselves why nobody was able to help the terrified women, to somehow stop the hunter as he roamed the engineering building.

14   So now our daughters are truly frightened and it makes their mothers furious that they are frightened. They survived all the childhood dangers, they were careful as we trained them to be, they worked hard. Anything was possible and our daughters proved it. And now they are more scared than they were when they were little girls.

15   Fourteen of our bright and shining daughters won places in engineering schools, doing things we, their mothers, only dreamed of. That we lost them has broken our hearts; what is worse is that we are not surprised.

△ △

Explorations:

Doris Anderson, *The Unfinished Revolution*
Jane Gaskell, *Gender Matters from School to Work*
Jesse Vorst, ed., *Race, Class, Gender: Bonds and Barriers*
Margaret Atwood, *The Handmaid's Tale* (novel)
Manuel Puig, *Boquitas pintadas* (novel, Argentina; available only in
    Spanish)
http://www.whiteribbon.ca

Structure:

1. How well does Cameron's title reflect the essay that follows?
2. In opening with the word "They," what strategy does Cameron use?
3. Identify the THESIS STATEMENT.
4. Is Cameron's *chronological order* a good choice for showing what happens to the daughters of our society? Give reasons.
5. To what extent does *comparison and contrast* help organize the essay? Cite passages based on it.

Style:

1. Paragraph 3 asks five questions in a row. Why? What is their overall effect?
2. What FIGURE OF SPEECH is the term "dinosaurs" in paragraph 11?

Argumentation and Persuasion:

1. Cameron's many examples lead through *induction* to her conclusion. Cite those which best show why the mothers, at the end, are "not surprised."
2. Stevie Cameron wrote "Our Daughters, Ourselves" in the heat of reaction to the Montreal massacre — the murder of 14 women engineering students by a male who blamed feminists for his problems. Though her examples do argue through logic, her appeals to emotion are so deep that this selection is one of the most *persuasive* in the book. Point out examples of all these techniques of *persuasion*:
    A. Repetition
    B. Figures of speech
    C. Irony
    D. Fright
    E. Climax
3. In what ways does this elegy to a generation of daughters transcend PROSE to become POETRY?

Ideas for Discussion and Writing:

1. Do you feel safe on campus? Downtown at night? Home alone? If not, tell why. Is your feeling related at all to your gender? If so, give examples to show why.

2. If your family has both sisters and brothers, have the parents protected the sisters more, as Cameron suggests in paragraphs 4, 5 and 8? If so, give examples. Is such protection needed in today's society? Tell why or why not.

3. Rita Schindler's letter in this chapter describes a near-fatal attack on a male victim, her son. What *comparisons*, if any, would you make with the violence towards women discussed by Cameron? What *contrasts*?

4. Nathalie Petrowski's essay in this chapter reflects on the life of Marc Lépine who murdered the 14 women engineering students mourned by both Petrowski and Cameron. Do you view Lépine as a victim of our society, like those he himself killed? Tell why or why not. If so, what factors ultimately *caused* the violence?

5. Marc Lépine thought women should not be engineers. Are employees in the field you intend to enter mostly male or mostly female? Why? What pressures have you felt, if any, to choose according to your gender? Give examples.

6. Are you "surprised" or "not surprised" at the act of Marc Lépine? Tell why, giving examples.

7. **PROCESS IN WRITING:** *Either read today's newspaper or think about recent news you have read or heard. Choose a crime of violence, with a victim either female or male, and decide whether you are "surprised" or "not surprised." Now write either "surprised" or "not surprised" in the centre of a blank page, and around it add other words that explain why. Connect related items with lines, then from this cluster outline devise your THESIS STATEMENT. Now incorporate the material into a fast discovery draft which, like Stevie Cameron's essay, uses emotion to persuade. The next day look it over. Are there enough persuasive elements like deliberate repetition, FIGURES OF SPEECH, IRONY and fright to move the reader? Do examples help the reader "see" your point? Do they show "why"? Do TRANSITIONS such as "because," "therefore" and "since" highlight causes and effects? Do your points rise to a climax? If not, revise. Finally, check for things like spelling and punctuation as you produce your best version.*

Note: See also the Topics for Writing at the end of this chapter.

Topics for Writing

Chapter 9: Argumentation and Persuasion

Develop one of the following topics into an essay of argumentation and/or persuasion, choosing the side you wish to take. If you wish, modify the topic so it says more exactly what you think. (See also the guidelines that follow.)

1. Extreme Sports Are (Good Fun/Risky but Worth It/Too Dangerous).
2. Class Sizes at my School Are (Acceptable/Too Large).
3. There (Is/Is Not) Life in Outer Space.
4. Most Canadians Watch Far More Foreign TV Programming, Especially American, Than Canadian; Should Our Government Increase the Canadian Content Required on Television Channels?
5. Canada Post (Should/Should Not) Be Privatized.
6. Putting Money Into the Stock Market Is (A Dangerous Gamble/A Calculated Risk/A Good Way to Get Rich).
7. Knowing (French/Spanish/Cantonese) (Will/Will Not Be) Important in My Future Career.
8. Clearcutting of Old-Growth Forests Should Be (Permitted/Regulated/Outlawed).
9. Drunk Drivers (Should/Should Not) Lose their Licences Permanently.
10. Companies (Should/Should Not) Be Held Liable for Their Own Pollution.
11. Canada Should (Decrease/Maintain/Increase) Its Level of Immigration.
12. The School Computer Facilities Are (Terrible/Fair/Mediocre/Good/Excellent).
13. Food in the School Cafeteria Is (Terrible/Fair/Mediocre/Good/Excellent).
14. The School Library Is (Terrible/Fair/Mediocre/Good/Excellent).
15. Hockey in Canada Is (Better/As Good as/Worse Than) It Was a Generation Ago.
16. Pit Bulls (Should/Should Not) Be Outlawed.
17. It (Is/Is Not) Important for New Canadians to Pass Their First Language on to Their Children.
18. When the Federal Government or a Provincial Government Runs a Budget Surplus, the Extra Should Be Used to (Increase Services/Reduce the Public Debt).
19. Use of Cars in the Centre of Cities Should Be (Abolished/Reduced/Maintained).
20. The Great Majority of Films Shown in Canadian Theatres Are Foreign, Mostly American; Should Theatres Be Required to Show a Higher Percentage of Our Own Films?

21. Trapping for Furs Should Be (Encouraged/Permitted/Ended).
22. Adopted Children (Should/Should Not) Be Told Who Their Birth Parents Are.
23. The Minimum Driving Age Should Be (Lowered/Maintained/ Raised).
24. Canada's Healthcare System Is (Better than/As Good as/Worse than) It Was Ten Years Ago.
25. Television Has Been a (Good/Neutral/Bad) Influence on My Life.
26. Car Insurance (Should/Should not) Cost the Same for Males and Females.
27. Futurists Predict Increasing Droughts Around the World; Should Canada, Which Has a Great Many Lakes, Ever Export This Resource in Large Quantities?
28. Cloning of Mammals Should Be (Encouraged/Permitted/Outlawed).
29. With Computerization, Employees Are Now Working (Less/As Much/More).
30. Video Lottery Terminals (Are/Are Not) a Legitimate Means for Governments to Raise Money.

Note also the Process in Writing topics after each selection in this chapter.

Process in Writing: Guidelines

Follow at least some of these steps in writing your essay of argumentation and/or persuasion (your teacher may suggest which ones).

1. *Choose a good topic, if necessary customize it, then go to either 2 or 3 below.*

2. **DEDUCTION**: *Do you already know your point of view because of a moral or intellectual principle you hold? First examine that principle, the foundation of your argument: Is it extreme, or is it reasonable enough (and clear enough) that your* AUDIENCE *can accept it? If the latter, proceed. Make notes, then do a rapid first draft showing how the principle supports your point.*

OR

3. **INDUCTION**: *Did experience or observation teach you the point you wish to make? First generate a page of notes. Then put these experiences or observations into the order that led you to your conclusion. Now transfer this argument to a rapid first draft.*

4. *You have probably organized your draft through a pattern we studied in an earlier chapter.* Cause and effect *is a natural for either deduction or induction, and so is* comparison and contrast *(in this chapter see Nathalie Petrowski for the former and Bonnie Laing for the latter). You have surely* used examples, *perhaps* narrating *or* describing *them. You might also have* classified *your subject, or cast your logic in a* process analysis. *Apart from analogy, which appeals more to emotion than to logic, all the approaches we have studied so far can serve deduction or induction. Use whatever works. If your first draft makes partial use of a major pattern, consider revising to extend the pattern and strengthen its effect.*

5. *As you look over your first draft, add any missing examples, especially if your argument is inductive (the more evidence, the better). Heighten your logic with signals such as "however," "therefore," "as a result" and "in conclusion."*

6. *Now judge how* **argumentative** *or* **persuasive** *your approach has been so far. Does your cold logic need a little colour and life? If so, add it, consulting pages 313-314 on techniques of persuasion. Or do emotions dominate your argument? Do they even encourage the audience not to think? If so, revise towards a more blended stance in your second draft.*

7. *Now cut all deadwood. Check for spelling and punctuation before printing out your best version. Save it on disk in case your teacher suggests further revision.*

GLOSSARY

Abstract Theoretical, relying more on GENERALIZATION than on facts
and examples. Abstract writing may lack interest and force, because it is
hard to understand and hard to apply. *See also* the opposite of abstract,
CONCRETE.

Allegory In poetry or PROSE, a passage or an entire work that has two
levels of meaning: literal and symbolic (*see* SYMBOL). Like a parable, an
allegory draws such numerous or striking parallels between its literal
subject and its implied subject that, without ever stating "the moral of
the story," it leads us to perceive a moral or philosophical truth. An
allegory, however, is longer and more complex than a parable. It also
differs from an analogy in that it does not openly identify and compare
the two subjects.

Allusion An indirect reference to a passage in literature or scripture,
an event, a person, or anything else familiar to the reader. An allusion
is a device of compression in language, for in a few words it summons
up the meaning of the thing to which it refers, and applies that meaning to the subject at hand. Critics of big government, for example, will

often allude to Big Brother, the personification of governmental tyranny in George Orwell's novel *1984*.

Anecdote   A short account of an interesting incident. An anecdote can be a joke or a true story about others or oneself, and is often used as an example to introduce an essay, close an essay, or illustrate points within an essay.

Audience   The reader or readers. One of the essayist's crucial tasks is to match the level and strategy of an argument with the needs and qualities of the particular audience that will read it. *See* the section "Who is my audience?" in this book's introductory essay, "The Act of Writing," pp. 6-7.

Bias words   Terms which, either subtly or openly, encourage strong value judgements. SUBJECTIVE language is a vital ingredient of much good writing, especially in description and in persuasion; to avoid it completely is difficult and often undesirable. The important thing is to avoid blatantly loaded language in an essay: words like "jerk," "slob," "cretin," "Hogtown," "Newfie," "tree hugger" or "neo-con" will inflame an uncritical reader and offend a critical one. Note that many bias words are also SLANG.

Cliché   A worn-out expression that takes the place of original thought: "sadder but wiser," "bite the bullet," "hustle and bustle," "been there, done that," "the bottom line," and "no pain, no gain." All clichés were once fresh, but like last year's fad in clothing or music, have lost their appeal and may even annoy.

Climax   In an essay, the point where the argument reaches its culmination, its point of greatest intensity or importance. The closing of an essay is normally a climax; if it is not, it may give the impression of trailing feebly off into nothingness.

Colloquial   Speech-like. Colloquial expressions like "cop," "guy," "kid," "nitty gritty" and "okay" are often used in conversation but are usually avoided in essays, especially FORMAL essays. Though lively, colloquialisms can be inexact: "guy," for example, can refer to a rope as well as a person, and "kid" can refer to a goat as well as a child. *See also* SLANG.

Conciseness   The art of conveying the most meaning in the fewest words. A concise essay does not explain its topic less fully than a wordy one; it just uses words more efficiently. Concise writers get straight to the point and stay on topic. They are well enough organized to avoid repeating themselves. They give CONCRETE examples rather than pages of ABSTRACT argument. They use a short word unless a long one is more exact. And most concise writers, to achieve these goals, revise extensively.

Concrete   Factual and specific, relying more on examples than on abstract theory. Concrete language makes writing more forceful, interesting and convincing by recreating vividly for the reader what the writer has experienced or thought. SENSE IMAGES, ANECDOTES, FIGURES OF SPEECH and CONCISENESS all play a part in concrete language and are usually lacking in its opposite, ABSTRACT language.

Deduction   A kind of logic that accepts a general principle as true, then uses it to explain a specific case or cases. *See* "Deduction," p. 310, and its opposite, "Induction," p. 311.

Dialogue   The quoted conversation of two or more people. Normally a new paragraph begins with each change of speaker, to avoid confusion as to who says what. A bit of dialogue can lend colour to an essay, but heavy use of it is normally reserved for fiction and drama.

Economy   See CONCISENESS.

Epigram   A short, clever, and often wise saying. The best-known epigrams are proverbs, such as "What can't be cured must be endured" and "To know all is to forgive all."

Epigraph   A short introductory quotation prefixed to an essay or other piece of writing.

Essay   Derived from the French term *essai*, meaning a "try" or "attempt," the word "essay" refers to a short composition in which a point is made, usually through analysis and example. While most essays are alike in being limited to one topic, they may vary widely in other ways. The *formal essay*, for example, is objective and stylistically dignified, while the *familiar essay* is subjective, anecdotal and sometimes colloquial.

Euphemism   A polite expression that softens or even hides the truth: "pass away" for "die," "senior citizens" for "old people," "low-income neighbourhood" for "slum," "gosh darn" for "God damn," "perspire" for "sweat," "eliminate" for "kill," and "de-hire" or "select out" for "fire." Euphemisms have become more and more common in uses ranging from personal kindness to advertising to political repression.

Fable   A tale, usually about animals, that teaches a moral truth or lesson meant for humans. Examples range from the classical Greek fables of Aesop about animals such as the tortoise and the hare, to modern fables such as Basil Johnston's selection in this book, "Modern Cannibals of the Wilds."

Fiction   Imaginative literature written in PROSE. Consisting mainly of novels and short stories, fiction uses invented characters and plots to create a dramatic story; most ESSAYS, by contrast, rely on literal fact and analysis to create an argument. There is of course an area of overlap: some fiction is very factual and some essays are very imaginative.

Figures of speech   Descriptive and often poetic devices in which meaning is concentrated and heightened, usually through comparisons:
A.   **Simile**: A figure of speech in which one thing is said to be *like* another. ("With its high buildings on all sides, Bay Street is like a canyon.")
B.   **Metaphor:** A figure of speech, literally false but poetically true, in which one thing is said to *be* another. ("Bay Street is a canyon walled by cliffs of concrete.")
C.   **Hyperbole**: Exaggeration. ("The office buildings rise miles above the city.")
D.   **Personification**: A figure of speech in which a non-human object is described as human. ("At night the empty buildings stare from their windows at the street.")

Formal   Formal writing is deliberate and dignified. It avoids partial sentences, most contractions, colloquial expressions and slang. Instead its vocabulary is standard and its sentences are often long and qualified with dependent clauses. In general it follows the accepted rules of grammar and principles of style. *See also* INFORMAL.

Generalization   A broad statement of overall principle, as opposed to an explanation using specific examples. While an essay needs generalizations, especially in places such as the THESIS STATEMENT and the CONCLUSION, most arguments that lack concrete examples are dull and difficult to understand.

Hyperbole   *See* FIGURES OF SPEECH.

Image   In literature, a mental picture triggered by words. Because they strongly stimulate thought and feeling, yet take little space, well-chosen images are vital ingredients of writing that is CONCRETE and has CONCISENESS. *See also* SENSE IMAGES.

Induction A kind of logic that derives a general principle from the evidence of specific examples. *See* "Induction," p. 311, and its opposite, "Deduction," p. 310.

Informal Informal writing resembles speech and, in fact, is often a representation of speech in writing. It may contain partial sentences, many short sentences, contractions, COLLOQUIAL expressions and sometimes SLANG. *See also* its opposite, FORMAL.

Irony A manner of expression in which a statement that seems literally to mean one thing actually means another. "Wonderful!" is a literal remark when said by a dinner guest enjoying the pie, but an ironic complaint when said by a driver who has backed into a tree. In a larger sense, *irony of situation* is a contrast between what is expected to happen and what does happen. It is this that creates our interest in the national leader who is impeached, the orphan who becomes a millionaire, or the evangelist convicted of tax fraud. Irony is a powerful tool of argument and especially of SATIRE.

Jargon Technical language or language that seeks to impress by *appearing* difficult or technical. Specialized terms can hardly be avoided in technical explanations: How could two electricians discuss a radio without words like "capacitor," "diode" and "transistor"? But these same words may need defining when put in an essay for the general reader. Other jargon uses technical-sounding or otherwise difficult words to seem important. An honest essayist will try to avoid "input," "output," "feedback," "interface," "knowledgeable," "parameters" and other ugly words of this sort when writing for the general reader.

Juxtaposition The deliberate placing together of two or more thoughts, IMAGES or other elements that emphasize each other, usually by contrast. When in paragraph 17 of her essay in this book, Michele Landsberg tells of a man active in charity who runs a house of child prostitution, the juxtaposition of these two activities creates a shocking portrait of hypocrisy.

Metaphor *See* FIGURES OF SPEECH.

Neologism A newly invented word. Some new terms are accepted into our standard vocabulary. For example, the word "laser" quickly became standard because we needed it to label a new and important invention. Most newly minted words are nuisances, though, meaningless to the many readers who do not know them.

Objective The opposite of SUBJECTIVE. In objective writing the author relies more on hard evidence and logical proof than on intuitions, prejudices or interpretations.

Onomatopoeia A poetical device in which language sounds like what it means. Some onomatopoetic words, such as "boom," "bang" and "crash," are out-and-out sound effects; others, such as "slither," "ooze" and "clatter," are more subtle. Onomatopoeia can be achieved not only through word choice but also through larger aspects of style. A series of short sentences, for example, gives an impression of tenseness and rapidity.

Paradox A statement that seems illogical but that in some unexpected way may be true. The Bible is full of paradoxes, as in "Blessed are the meek, for they shall inherit the earth."

Personification *See* FIGURES OF SPEECH.

Prose Spoken or written language without the metrical structure that characterizes poetry. Conversations, letters, short stories, novels and essays are all prose.

Pun A play on words. A pun is based either on two meanings of one word or on two words that sound alike but have different meanings. Often called the lowest form of humour, the pun is the basis of many jokes. (Why did the fly fly? Because the spider spider.)

Quotation The words of one person reproduced exactly in the writing or speech of another person. A well-chosen quotation can add force to an argument by conveying the opinion of an authority or by presenting an idea in words so exact or memorable that they could hardly be improved upon. Quotations should be reproduced exactly, placed in quotation marks, and attributed to their source.

Reduction to absurdity A technique of SATIRE in which the subject is belittled through being portrayed as absurd. A favourite device of humorists, such as Stephen Leacock.

Sarcasm Scornful and contemptuous criticism, from the Greek word *sarkazein* ("to tear flesh").

Satire Humorous criticism meant to improve an individual or society by exposing abuses. In TONE, satire can range from light humour to bitter criticism. Its main tools are wit, IRONY, exaggeration, and sometimes SARCASM and ridicule.

Sense images Descriptive appeals to one or more of the reader's five senses: sight, hearing, touch, taste and smell. Sense images are vital in helping the reader to experience, at second hand, what the writer has lived in person. CONCRETE language has many sense images; ABSTRACT language does not.

Simile *See* FIGURES OF SPEECH.

Slang Racy, unconventional language often limited to a certain time, place or group. Slang is the extreme of colloquial language, terminology used in conversation but hardly ever in an ESSAY except for dialogue or special effects. One reason to avoid a slang term is that not everyone will know it: expressions like "swell," "square" and "far out" have gone out of use, while expressions like "bug juice," "croaker," "jointman" and "rounder" are known to only one group — in this case, prison inmates. *See also* COLLOQUIAL.

Stereotype An established mental image of something. Most stereotypes are of people and are based on their sex, race, colour, size or shape, economic or social class, or profession. Jokes about mothers-in-law, "Newfies," absent-minded professors, woman drivers or short people are all examples of stereotyping. While they may provoke humour, stereotypes are anything but harmless: they prevent recognition of people's individuality and they encourage prejudices which, at their extreme, can result in persecution like that of the Jews in Nazi Germany.

Style In general, the *way* something is written, as opposed to *what* it is written about. Style is to some extent a matter of TONE — light or serious, INFORMAL or FORMAL, ironic or literal. It is also a matter of technique. Word choice, FIGURES OF SPEECH, level of CONCISENESS, and characteristics of sentence structure and paragraphing are all ingredients of style. Although a writer should pay close attention to these matters, the idea that one deliberately seeks out "a style" is a mistake that only encourages imitation. An individual style emerges naturally as the sum of the writer's temperament, skills and experience.

Subjective The opposite of OBJECTIVE. In subjective writing the author relies more on intuitions, prejudices or interpretations than on hard evidence and logical proof.

Symbol One thing that stands for another, as in a flag representing a country, the cross representing Christianity, or a logo representing a company. Symbols appear frequently in poetry, drama, fiction and also essays.

Thesis statement   The sentence or sentences, usually in the introduction, which first state the main point and restrict the focus of an essay.

Tone   The manner of a writer toward the subject and reader. The tone of an essay can be light or serious, INFORMAL or FORMAL, ironic or literal. Tone is often determined by subject matter; for example an essay about cocktail parties is likely to be lighter and less formal than one about funerals. An innovative writer, though, could reverse these treatments to give each of the essays an ironic tone. The identity of the reader also influences tone. An essay for specialists to read in a technical journal will tend to be more OBJECTIVE and serious than one written for the general reader. The main point for the writer is to choose the tone most appropriate to a particular essay, then maintain it throughout.

Transition   A word, phrase, sentence or paragraph that moves the reader from one part of the essay to the next. Transitions even as short as "next," "then," "as a result," "on the other hand," "in conclusion" or "finally" are crucial not only to speeding the argument along, but also to pointing out its logic.